T0399049

LANDSCAPES OF THE LEARNED

Placing Gaelic Literati in Irish Lordships 1300–1600

Gaelic literati were an elite and influential group in Irish lordships and overlordships *c.* 1300–1600. Using theories of extra-social space and landscape as cultural practice and an instrument of power, this study develops a framework for interpreting the settings and built heritage of the estates of literati in lordship borderscapes. It shows that a more textured definition of what the learned class represented in Irish society can be achieved through an archaeology of the buildings and monuments they used and an appreciation of where their estates were situated in the political map.

More widely, this book contributes a landscape perspective to the study of autochthonous intellectual culture and the exercise of power by ruling families in late medieval and early modern northern European societies.

MEDIEVAL HISTORY
AND ARCHAEOLOGY

General Editors

John Blair   Helena Hamerow

The volumes in this series bring together archaeological, historical, and visual methods to offer new approaches to aspects of medieval society, economy, and material culture. The series seeks to present and interpret archaeological evidence in ways readily accessible to historians, while providing a historical perspective and context for the material culture of the period.

Landscapes of the Learned

Placing Gaelic Literati in Irish Lordships 1300–1600

ELIZABETH FITZPATRICK

OXFORD
UNIVERSITY PRESS

Great Clarendon Street, Oxford, OX2 6DP,
United Kingdom

Oxford University Press is a department of the University of Oxford.
It furthers the University's objective of excellence in research, scholarship,
and education by publishing worldwide. Oxford is a registered trade mark of
Oxford University Press in the UK and in certain other countries

Published in the United States of America by Oxford University Press
198 Madison Avenue, New York, NY 10016, United States of America

British Library Cataloguing in Publication Data

Data available

Library of Congress Control Number: 2022951017

ISBN 978–0–19–285574–9

DOI: 10.1093/oso/9780192855749.001.0001

Printed and bound by
CPI Group (UK) Ltd, Croydon, CR0 4YY

Links to third party websites are provided by Oxford in good faith and
for information only. Oxford disclaims any responsibility for the materials
contained in any third party website referenced in this work.

For my family, and in memory of my beloved parents,
and those we have lost.

PREFACE AND ACKNOWLEDGMENTS

"The places are what remain, are what you can possess, are what is immortal. They become the tangible landscape of memory, the places that made you, and in some way, you too become them."

(Rebecca Solnit 2005 *A field guide to getting lost*. New York. Random House).

Perceptions of historical landscape, place, and built heritage (common to all societies) have been generally under-utilized as a major source of understanding complexity in late medieval and early modern Irish society. In this book an approach to finding and placing Gaelic literati in the Irish lordships that they served has been developed through archaeological and topographic analyses of the landscapes and built heritages of their estates, imbricated where appropriate with historical and literary sources, lore, and place names.

Demonstrating how the estate landscapes of literati were integral to their intellectual and political cultures, and not simply a backdrop to their lives, is a core concern of the work. My hope in setting out this approach is that it will be useful to other scholars exploring material expressions of intellectual culture in autochthonous societies, understanding the role of the past in political cultures, and broadening views of historical settlement.

The research for this book had a long period of maturation because most of it was field-based and detailed work, which had to be continuously revised within the framework of understanding set out for it. The genesis of the project lies in the themes for future research proposed in *Gaelic Ireland 1200–1600: land, lordship and settlement*, ed. P. J. Duffy, D. Edwards, and E. FitzPatrick (2001; pb. ed. 2004), one of which was to identify, survey, and excavate a school of the learned class. I took up that challenge with my former students at NUI Galway (now the University of Galway) in the summer of 2005 with a walkover survey of the late medieval landholding of a family of brehon lawyers in Cahermacnaghten, Co. Clare, followed by three seasons of excavation in 2007, 2008, and 2010. In a series of subsequent field surveys in ten counties (2010–17), it became clear that investigating residences and schools of learned kindreds as self-contained monuments would provide some answers, but that a more comprehensive understanding would be generated by connecting them with the topography, archaeology, and associated place names and lore of the spatial domains in which the learned lived and performed their roles. The principal tool in animating the landscape context of their estates was mapping it in ArcGIS, which was expedited with great skill by the archaeological cartographer Noel McCarthy (University of Galway).

Foremost among those to be thanked are my former students, especially Eve Campbell, Richard Clutterbuck, Siobhán McDermot, Richard Long, and Paul Naessens, and all those students of Archaeology at NUI Galway who worked with me between 2007 and 2017 to record the sites that constitute the backbone of the book. Thanks to Noel McCarthy and Sara Nylund for maps; to Joe Fenwick (University of Galway) for geophysical surveys; Cormac Bruton and Liam Hickey for topographical surveys; Karl Karlinski (DPS) and Paul Naessens (Western Aerial Survey and Photography Services) for photogrammetry; Angela Gallagher for archaeological drawings; Nicholas Grundy and Cillian Irish for aerial photos; to Dan Tietzch-Tyler for his reconstruction drawings; and to Anthony Corns and Robert Shaw, the Discovery Programme, for LiDAR imaging at Cahermacnaghten.

My thanks to Cóilín Ó Drisceoil (Kilkenny Archaeology) for his professional collaboration in the investigation of Ballyorley law school; to Paul Walsh (Discovery Programme) and to Sinéad Ní Ghabhláin for sharing their respective knowledge of Dromnea (Co. Cork) and *Teach Breac* at Cahermacnaghten; to Mairín Ní Dhonnchadha (University of Galway) for her guidance on Irish language terminology and place names relating to Cahermacnaghten; and to Liam Breatnach (School of Celtic Studies, DIAS) for his comments on aspects of Gaelic literature referred to in Chapter 2.

There are people in cultural institutions to thank for their supportive services: Glenn Dunne, James Harte, Berni Metcalfe, and Chris Swift of the National Library of Ireland; Brenda O'Neill and Daniel O'Connell of Ordnance Survey Ireland; Jackie Dermody, Clare County Library; The Office of Public Works; Michael Stanley, Transport Infrastructure Ireland; Nessa O'Connor and Paul Mullarkey, National Museum of Ireland; Stephen Weir, the Picture Library, National Museums Northern Ireland; Joe Waterfield, Historic Environment Scotland Archives; and the British Library.

My sincere gratitude to John Blair (The Queen's College Oxford) and to Helena Hamerow (School of Archaeology, University of Oxford) for their generous encouragement and support of this book project; to Alicia McAuley (Publishing Services) for indexing, and gently pushing the project along; to Cathryn Steele, Acquisitions Editor at OUP, and Nivedha Vinayagamurthy and the production team, for their professionalism and patience. Any oversights, errors, or incapacities in thinking, are entirely mine.

The research for this study was generously funded by the Royal Irish Academy; the Irish Research Council; the Fulbright Commission; the Miltown Heritage Group; the committee of the O'Doran Law School Project; Clan Egan, and by private philanthropy.

Finally, I am forever grateful to my extended family and good friends, for moral and practical support in this journey to place Gaelic literati in the landscapes of Irish lordships.

CONTENTS

LIST OF FIGURES AND TABLES

FIGURES

TABLES

Appendix

CONVENTIONS

CHRONOLOGICAL FRAMEWORK

The following periodization is used in this work:
  Early medieval, *c.*400–1000
  High medieval, *c.*1000–1300
  Late medieval, *c.*1300–1550
  Early modern, *c.*1550–1800
  Modern, *c.*1800–

GEOGRAPHICAL TEMPLATE

The template for the map of the lordships of Ireland (Figs 1.1, 1.2) is based on K. W. Nicholls's "Lordships, *c.*1534" published in T. W. Moody, F. X. Martin, and F. J. Byrne (eds) 1976 *A new history of Ireland, iii: early modern Ireland 1534–1691*, 2–3. Oxford University Press; and on "Lordships of Ireland in the sixteenth century", published in E. Campbell, E. FitzPatrick, and A. Horning (eds) *Becoming and belonging in Ireland* AD *c.1200–1600: essays in identity and cultural practice*, xviii–xix. Cork University Press.

IRISH SPELLING

The Irish language names of Gaelic kindreds, lordships, and other territorial units are used in this book because the meanings they convey would otherwise be lost to the reader by using their Anglicized forms. These names are cited in early modern Irish throughout, and not italicized. Where pre-1200 historic persons, place names, terms, and texts are occasionally addressed, their Old Irish spelling forms are used. Terms for the professions and offices of Gaelic society, their cultural practices, settlement forms, and buildings are also given in Irish, where appropriate and relevant. They are italicized and provided in translation throughout. The names of learned kindred estates are cited in their Anglicized forms, in the first instance, to make their townland locations readily accessible to the reader in the modern landscape.

ABBREVIATIONS

AClon Murphy, D. (ed.) 1896 *The annals of Clonmacnoise: being the annals of Ireland from the earliest period to AD 1408. Translated into English AD 1627 by Conell Mageoghegan.* Dublin. Royal Society of Antiquaries of Ireland.

AClyn Williams, B. (ed. and tr.) 2007 *The annals of Ireland by Friar John Clyn.* Dublin. Four Courts Press.

AConn Freeman, A. M. (ed. and tr.) 1944 *Annála Connacht: the annals of Connacht (A.D. 1244–1544).* Dublin Institute for Advanced Studies.

ALC Hennessy, W. M. (ed. and tr.) 1871 *The annals of Loch Cé: a chronicle of Irish affairs from AD 1014 to AD 1590*, 2 vols. London. Longman.

AMacF O'Donovan, J. (ed.) 1846 The annals of Ireland, from the year 1443 to 1468, translated from the Irish by Dudley Firbisse or, as he is more usually called, Duald Mac Firbis, for Sir James Ware, in the year 1666. *The Miscellany of the Irish Archaeological Society*, i, 198–302. Dublin. Irish Archaeological Society.

ATF O'Donovan, J. (ed. and tr.) 1860 *Annals of Ireland: three fragments, copied from ancient sources by Dubhaltach MacFirbisigh.* Dublin. Irish Archaeological and Celtic Society.

HES *Historic Environment Scotland*

JRSAI *Journal of the Royal Society of Antiquaries of Ireland*

M O'Donovan, J. (ed. and tr.) 1856 *Annála ríoghachta Éireann: annals of the kingdom of Ireland by the Four Masters, from the earliest period to the year 1616*, 7 vols. Dublin. Hodges and Smith.

MI Middle Irish

MIA Ó hInnse, S. (ed. and tr.) 1947 *Miscellaneous Irish annals, AD 1114–1437.* Dublin Institute for Advanced Studies.

NFC National Folklore Collection

NLI National Library of Ireland

OD Ordnance Datum

OI Old Irish

PRONI Public Record Office of Northern Ireland

PRIA *Proceedings of the Royal Irish Academy*

RIA *Royal Irish Academy*

T Stokes, W. (ed.) 1895–7 (reprint 1993) *The Annals of Tigernach*, 2 vols. Felinfach. Llanerch.

U Hennessy, W. M. and McCarthy, B. (ed. and tr.) 1887–1901 *Annála Uladh: the annals of Ulster, otherwise Annála Senait: the annals of Senat: a chronicle of Irish affairs from AD 431 to AD 1540*, 4 vols. Dublin. HMSO.

1

Introduction

Place, Roles, and Lifeways

1.0 INTRODUCTION

Gaelic professional learned kindreds were an influential class in the social hierarchy of Irish lordships between *c.*1300 and 1600. The arts, which they practiced in a hereditary capacity, included law (*féneachas*),[1] medicine, music, poetry (*filidheacht*), and traditional history (*seanchas*),[2] as well as high-level crafts (*ceird*), especially those of the goldsmith and sculptor.[3] Some members of the learned class were attributed expertise in particular branches of the arts, such as topography, while others are known to have crossed over into fields of knowledge allied to their specific professions.[4]

In this study, the focus is primarily on historians, lawyers, physicians, and poets—literati who were involved in book-learning and composing poetry, for their professions and for patrons. They were an elite group within a broader tier of service providers to Gaelic chiefs and Old English lords.[5] However, in early Irish law, while physicians and lawyers were regarded as dependent professionals (*dóernemed*), poets were accorded the status of privileged professionals (*nemed*). They had considerable influence and were, for instance, permitted to use their powers of satire to impose law

---

[1] *Féneachas* was "Irish jurisprudence." It is more commonly referred to as "brehon law" (from the Irish *breitheamh*, meaning "judge"), because it was essentially "judge-made" law. See N. McLeod 2005 Brehon law. In S. Duffy (ed.), *Medieval Ireland: an encyclopedia*, 42–5. New York and London. Routledge.

[2] *Seanchas* was traditional historical lore, including genealogy. See K. Simms 2005 Bardic schools, learned families. In Duffy (ed.), *Medieval Ireland*, 36.

[3] Publications on *ceird* include: E. C. Rae 1971 Irish sepulchral monuments of the later Middle Ages: part II, the O'Tunney atelier. *JRSAI* 101 (1), 1–39; J. Hunt 1950 Rory O'Tunney and the Ossory tomb sculptures. *JRSAI* 80 (1), 22–8.

[4] Gréaghóir Ó Maoilchonaire was described in his obituary for 1400 as "skilled in the science of topography" (*saoí foirbhte*). See C. O'Conor 1818 *Bibliotheca MS. Stowensis. A descriptive catalogue of the manuscripts in the Stowe Library…*, i, 226. Buckingham. J. Seeley.

[5] E. FitzPatrick 2018 Gaelic service families and the landscape of *lucht tighe*. In E. Campbell, E. FitzPatrick, and A. Horning (eds), *Becoming and belonging in Ireland, AD c.1200–1600: essays in identity and cultural practice*, 169–72. Cork University Press.

Landscapes of the Learned: Placing Gaelic Literati in Irish Lordships 1300–1600. Elizabeth FitzPatrick, Oxford University Press.
© Elizabeth FitzPatrick 2023. DOI: 10.1093/oso/9780192855749.003.0001

"across boundaries."[6] Their special standing in Gaelic society endured into the early modern period.

The leading representatives of learned kindreds carried the title *ollamh* (professor, pl. *ollamhain*). It was common for an *ollamh* to hold a church office, either as a *comharba* (pl. *comharbai*) or as an *airchinneach* (pl. *airchinnigh*). A *comharba* was the head of a church, an administrative position often held in a lay capacity. He was regarded as the successor to the authority and revenues of the founder of an early monastery.[7] An *airchinneach* was a hereditary church tenant, usually an unordained layman but sometimes with quasi-clerical status.[8] He was responsible for the upkeep of church fabric, stewarding church land, and dispensing hospitality.

Alongside serving rulers in the arts, maintaining networks of learning, compiling manuscripts, and conducting schools, literati kept guest-houses and provided food from their farmed estates (3.3, 4.4).[9] Poets, traditional historians, and lawyers were also actors in the political assemblies of Gaelic chiefs, participating in inauguration ceremonies, open-air parliaments, and peace-making events in various capacities (2.2).

1.0.1 *The brief of* Landscapes of the Learned

This book presents an approach to finding and placing Gaelic literati in the lordships of Ireland 1300–1600. The thematic structure is largely mediated by detailed case studies. The objectives are to investigate the landscape contexts and built heritages of learned kindred estates, with the aim of showing that a more textured definition of what the learned class represented can be achieved through interpretation of the buildings and monuments they used and where their lands were positioned in the lordships. The approach is framed by theories of extra-social space and historical landscape as cultural practice and an instrument of power.[10] The methodology is predominantly field based, using archaeological investigation, topographic analyses, and mapping, but in referencing named people to places, connections are made to historical and literary texts and to place names. The principal argument is that the landscapes and built environments in which literati lived and worked were expressions of their intellectual and political cultures.

[6] F. Kelly 1988 *A guide to early Irish law*, 43, 49, 318. Dublin Institute for Advanced Studies.

[7] K. Simms 1987 *From kings to warlords: the changing political structure of Gaelic Ireland in the later Middle Ages*, 170, 173. Woodbridge. Boydell Press.

[8] K. W. Nicholls 2003 *Gaelic and gaelicized Ireland in the Middle Ages*, 224. Dublin. Lilliput Press; Simms, *From kings to warlords* 170; L. McInerney 2014 *Clerical and learned lineages of medieval Co. Clare: a survey of the fifteenth-century papal registers*, 295. Dublin. Four Courts Press.

[9] C. M. O'Sullivan 2003 *Hospitality in medieval Ireland 900–1500*, 158–63. Dublin. Four Courts Press.

[10] Ö. Harmanşah (ed.) 2014 *Of rocks and water: towards an archaeology of place*, 3, 11. Joukowsky Institute publication: 5. Oxford and Philadelphia. Oxbow Books; W. J. T. Mitchell (ed.) 2002 *Landscape and power*, 1–3. The University of Chicago Press.

The most enduring influence on perception of late medieval Gaelic society, its culture, and institutions are the large bodies of work of the historians Nicholls and Simms, among which Nicholls's *Gaelic and gaelicized Ireland* and Simms's *From kings to warlords* are perhaps best known.[11] The publication of *Gaelic Ireland 1250–1650: land, lordship and settlement* (2001, 2004), edited by Duffy, Edwards, and FitzPatrick, introduced a new dynamic by aspiring to create a dialogue between archaeologists, historians, and historical geographers working in this field. Since then, among a considerable volume of papers and edited books, there have been three book publications on major archaeological topics relating to late medieval Gaelic Ireland, namely, inauguration sites of ruling families, approaches to burial in Ulster, and a settlement study of a lordship in Munster.[12] One of the key statements of the editors of *Gaelic Ireland 1250–1650* in 2001 was a proposed agenda for future research in the archaeology, history, and historical geography of Gaelic Ireland. One of the collaborative research programs mooted in that agenda was an investigation of interfaces between Gaelic and colonial society, an aspiration which was endorsed by the publication in 2018 of *Becoming and belonging in Ireland*, AD c.*1200–1600: essays in identity and cultural practice*, edited by Campbell, FitzPatrick, and Horning.

Research on the late medieval and early modern Gaelic learned class in Ireland is a long and distinguished area of scholarship in both Celtic literature and history. The focus in Celtic literature is the works and manuscript traditions of the learned, and biographies of learned men. The literature is vast in those fields. Among the key book publications are Walsh's *Irish men of learning* (1947), Bergin's *Irish bardic poetry* (1984), Kelly's *A guide to early Irish law* (1988), Ó Muraíle's *Great book of Irish genealogies* (2003), Breatnach's *A companion to the Corpus iuris Hibernici* (2005), and the several edited collections of poems on Gaelic ruling families such as Hoyne's *Bardic poems on the Meic Dhiarmada* (2018).[13] The specialism of medical kindreds and their manuscripts has emerged as a leading area of enquiry pioneered by the work of Nic Dhonnchadha, Hayden and Sheehan.[14]

---

[11] Nicholls, *Gaelic and gaelicized Ireland*, and *passim*; Simms, *From kings to warlords*, and *passim*.

[12] E. FitzPatrick, 2004 *Royal inauguration in Gaelic Ireland c.1100–1600: a cultural landscape study*. Studies in Celtic history: 22. Woodbridge. Boydell Press; C. Breen 2005 *The Gaelic lordship of the O'Sullivan Beare: a landscape cultural history*. Dublin. Four Courts Press; C. J. McKenzie and E. M. Murphy 2018 *Life and death in medieval Gaelic Ireland: the skeletons from Ballyhanna, Co. Donegal*. Dublin. Four Courts Press.

[13] P. Walsh, 1947 *Irish men of learning: studies*. Dublin. Three Candles; O. Bergin (ed. and tr.) 1970 *Irish bardic poetry*. Dublin. Institute for Advanced Studies; Kelly, *A guide to early Irish law*; N. Ó Muraíle (ed.) 2003 *Leabhar mór na ngenealach: the great book of Irish genealogies, compiled (1645–66) by Dubhaltach Mac Fhirbhisigh*, 5 vols. Dublin. De Búrca; L. Breathnach 2005 *A companion to the Corpus iuris Hibernici*. Dublin Institute for Advanced Studies; M. Hoyne (ed.) 2018 *Fuidheall Áir: bardic poems on the Meic Dhiarmada of Magh Luirg c.1377–c.1637*. Dublin Institute for Advanced Studies.

[14] For material published in the last twenty years on Gaelic medical families see for example A. Nic Dhonnchadha 2006 The medical school of Aghmacart, Queen's County. *Ossory, Laois and Leinster* 2, 11–43; L. P. Ó Murchú (ed.) 2016 *Rosa Anglica: reassessments*. Irish Texts Society subsidiary series: 28. London. Irish Texts Society; D. Hayden 2019 Attribution and authority in an Irish medical manuscript. *Studia Hibernica* 45,

In history, Cunningham has contributed major works on the cultural and ideological worlds of early modern literati including *The annals of the Four Masters* (2009) and *The world of Geoffrey Keating* (2000). O'Sullivan's groundbreaking *Hospitality* (2003) included a detailed overview of learned men as guest-house keepers.[15] Learned activity is addressed in the more recent collection, *Gaelic Ireland c.600–c.1700* (2021), edited by McInerney and Simms.[16] Both of those historians have also published regional studies of members of the learned class, with Simms's *Gaelic Ulster in the Middle Ages* (2020) including material on learned kindreds in the province of Ulster, and McInerney focusing on Co. Clare in his study of church appointments among fifteenth-century *Clerical and learned lineages* (2014).[17]

There are three indispensable studies of Gaelic learned kindreds in Scotland, from the disciplines of history, Celtic literature, and archaeology. They are Bannerman's *The Beatons*, which investigates the genealogies and landholdings of the many branches of that medical kindred (1998), McLeod's *Divided Gaels* (2004), which explores Gaelic cultural identities in Scotland and Ireland through the lens of intellectual and literary culture, R. Barrowman's excavations on *Dùn Èistean* (2015) and C. Barrowman's survey of Habost in *The archaeology of Ness* (2015).[18] Both *Dùn Èistean* and Habost are associated with brehon lawyers of the Ó Muirgheasáin (Morison) family at Ness on the Isle of Lewis (4.2.3).

Unlike the considerable knowledge base for the physical environment of professional scholarship and schools in England and the Low Countries,[19] the focus in Ireland, Scotland, and Wales has, traditionally, been on the manuscripts rather than the landscapes and built heritage of literati.[20] In architectural history and archaeology,

19–51; A. Sheehan 2019 Locating the Gaelic medical families in Elizabethan Ireland. In J. Cunningham (ed.), *Early modern Ireland and the world of medicine: practitioners, collectors and contexts*, 29. Manchester University Press.

[15] B. Cunningham 2009 *The annals of the Four Masters: Irish history, kingship and society in the early seventeenth century*. Dublin. Four Courts Press; B. Cunningham 2000 *The world of Geoffrey Keating: history, myth and religion in seventeenth-century Ireland*. Dublin. Four Courts Press; O'Sullivan, *Hospitality*, See also K. Simms 1978 Guesting and feasting in Gaelic Ireland. *JRSAI* 108, 67–100.

[16] L. McInerney and K. Simms (eds) 2021 *Gaelic Ireland* (*c.600–c.1700*): *lordships, saints and learning: essays for the Irish chief's and clans' prize in history*, 39–40, 137–52, 153–73. Dublin. Wordwell.

[17] K. Simms 2020 *Gaelic Ulster in the Middle Ages: history, culture and* society, 335–403. Trinity Medieval Ireland Series: 4. Dublin. Four Courts Press; McInerney 2014 *Clerical and learned lineages*.

[18] J. Bannerman 1998 *The Beatons: a medical kindred in the classical Gaelic tradition*. Edinburgh. Birlinn; W. McLeod 2004 *Divided Gaels: Gaelic cultural identities in Scotland and Ireland c.1200–c.1650*. Oxford University Press; R. C. Barrowman 2015 *Dùn Èistean, Ness: the excavation of a clan stronghold*. Stornoway. Acair; C. S. Barrowman 2015 *The archaeology of Ness: results of the Ness Archaeological Landscape Survey*. Stornoway. Acair.

[19] N. Orme 2006 *Medieval schools from Roman Britain to Renaissance England*. New Haven and London. Yale University Press; A. Willemsen 2008 *Back to the schoolyard: the daily practice of medieval and Renaissance education*. Studies in Urban History 1100–1800: 15. Turnhout. Brepols.

[20] Some reference to school space is included in N. Orme 2015 Education in medieval Wales. *Welsh History Review/Cylchgrawn Hanes Cymru* 27 (4), 607–44; See the Bibliography for the author's contribution to redressing this imbalance in Ireland. FitzPatrick 2021, 2018, 2015b, 2013b, 2011, 2009, 2008.

buildings of literati have tended to be a subset of broader enquiries but nonetheless valuable sources for the topic. Among these are Tierney's commentary on the tower-houses of professional lineages, which he undertook as part of a study of late medieval tower-houses and power in east Co. Clare,[21] Moss's investigation of a parish church associated with a learned family of historians in Connacht, which she published as a wider investigation of Romanesque sculpture,[22] and Campbell's exploration of the settlement archaeology of Noughaval, Co. Clare, which provides important context for the physical environment of the clerical branch of the Ó Duibhdábhoireann brehon lawyers in the lordship of Boireann.[23]

Returning to *Gaelic Ireland 1250–1650* and the research agenda of 2001, among the topics proposed at that time was detailed archaeological survey and excavation of learned kindred schools and the development of a concept of studying Gaelic settlement within the appropriate historical matrices of lordship, estate, and smaller divisions of the landscape.[24] Both of those aspirations have been pursued in this book.

1.0.2 A note on sources used in this work

The Irish chronicles are cited throughout this study. Compiled by learned men, they are a major source of reference to literati and the sites with which they were associated. They have their idiosyncrasies, however. Simms has explained that the surviving manuscripts containing Irish annals largely date from between the fifteenth and the seventeenth centuries, the majority have a regional bias, and those compiled by the "Four Masters" in the seventeenth century are not contemporary with the events they describe, albeit that they drew on sources that are now lost.[25] To negotiate those difficulties, parallel entries have been provided from different sets of annals where available.

Land surveys of the seventeenth century are useful in associating landholdings with learned kindreds. They include the Strafford Survey of Connacht in the 1630s, the Civil Survey, which described all lands forfeited to the Commonwealth from the time of the Rebellion of 1641, the Down Survey (1656–8), which was the first detailed

---

[21] A. Tierney 2013 Tower houses and power: social and familial hierarchies in east County Clare *c.*1350–*c.*1600. *North Munster Antiquarian Journal* 53, 220–4; A. Tierney 2005 Pedigrees in stone? Castles, colonialism and Gaelic-Irish identity from the Middle Ages to the Celtic revival. PhD diss. University College Dublin.

[22] R. Moss 2010 Romanesque sculpture in north Roscommon. In T. Finan (ed.), *Medieval Lough Cé: history, archaeology and landscape*, 141–4. Dublin. Four Courts Press.

[23] E. Campbell 2013 Exploring the medieval and early modern settlement of Noughaval in the Burren. *The Other Clare* 37, 12–17.

[24] P. J. Duffy, D. Edwards and E. FitzPatrick 2001 Introduction. In Duffy, Edwards and FitzPatrick (eds) *Gaelic Ireland c.1250–c.1650: land, lordship and settlement*, 72. Dublin. Four Courts Press.

[25] K. Simms 2009 *Medieval Gaelic sources*, 1–38. Maynooth research guides for Irish local history: 14. Dublin. Four Courts Press.

land survey conducted on a national scale by Sir William Petty, and the Books of Survey and Distribution that contain details of the transfer of land, largely but not exclusively from Catholic to Protestant, in the second half of the century.[26]

Place names are an essential source of reference to the learned. Ireland is endowed with two major databases of place names that have supported this study. These are the Placenames Database of Ireland and the Northern Ireland Place-Name Project. All editions of the Ordnance Survey six-inch and twenty-five-inch maps for Ireland, the National Monuments Service Sites and Monuments database and supporting archive, the Geological Survey of Ireland spatial resources database, the Public Record Office of Northern Ireland historical maps viewer, and the Northern Ireland Department of Communities historic environment map viewer, were key aids to pinning down settlements of literati in the landscape.

There are historical studies that link learned kindreds with lands, which are useful sources for the archaeologist. They include O'Rahilly's account of poets, historians, and lawyers cited in English documents (1538–1615), in which he showed the potential of the Irish fiants to aid identification of the provenance of individual learned men cited in pardons issued by the Irish Chancery (a fiant was a warrant by the king's deputy or council to the Irish Chancery to publish orders that conveyed a pardon, a right, an office, or a title to property).[27] Others include Doan's study of the many branches of the Ó Dálaigh poets and their associated landholdings, Hughes's investigation of the lands of Ulster poets, and the aforementioned work of McInerney, which is extensively based on interpretations of late medieval and early modern primary historical documents.[28]

Finally, there are accounts by nineteenth- and early twentieth-century antiquaries of individual learned kindred settlements, such as Fennel's description of Inishmore Island on Lough Gill, Co. Sligo,[29] Lockwood's study of Kilbarron, Co. Donegal,[30] and the respective papers about Cahermacnaghten in the Burren, Co. Clare, by Macnamara and Westropp.[31] In the letters and memoranda that they wrote to head office from the

[26] W. J. Smyth 2006 *Map-making, landscapes and memory: a geography of colonial and early modern Ireland, c.1530–1750*, 166–221. Cork University Press.

[27] T. F. O'Rahilly 1922 Irish poets, historians, and judges in English documents, 1538–1615. *PRIA* 36C, 86–120; see K. W. Nicholls (ed.) 1994 *The Irish fiants of the Tudor sovereigns: during the reigns of Henry VIII, Edward VI, Philip and Mary, and Elizabeth I*, 4 vols. Dublin. Edmund Burke.

[28] J. E. Doan 1985 The Ó Dálaigh family of bardic poets, 1139–1691. *Éire–Ireland* 20 (2), 19–31; A. J. Hughes 1994–5 Land acquisitions by Gaelic bardic poets: insights from place-names and other sources. *Ainm: Bulletin of the Ulster Place-Name Society* 6, 74–102; McInerney, *Clerical and learned lineages*, and *passim*.

[29] W. J. Fennel 1904 Church Island or Inishmore, Lough Gill. *Ulster Journal of Archaeology* 10 (4), 166–9.

[30] F. W. Lockwood 1903 Kilbarron Castle and Church, Co. Donegal. *Ulster Journal of Archaeology* 9 (3), 111–16.

[31] G. U. Macnamara 1912–13 The O'Davorens of Cahermacnaughten, Burren, Co. Clare. *North Munster Archaeological Society Journal* 2, 63–212; T. J. Westropp 1897 Prehistoric stone forts of northern Clare (continued). *JRSAI* 7 (2), 116–27; T. J. Westropp 1906–7 Ancient remains near Lisdoonvarna. *Journal of the Limerick Field Club* 3, 52–159.

field, O'Donovan and the other antiquaries and surveyors who conducted the first Ordnance Survey of Ireland in the nineteenth century occasionally included details of sites associated with literati. Notable among those was Beirne's survey in 1845 of the remains of the "old college" building at Dromnea, associated with the estate of the Ó Dálaigh poets on the Sheepshead Peninsula, Co. Cork (6.3.1).[32]

1.1 DEFINING THE LEARNED

Learned kindreds developed and expanded as a major class in Gaelic society from the late twelfth century onward. The kin-based hereditary aspects of their professions, which they shared with autochthonous literati in medieval Scotland and Wales, made them unique functionaries in later medieval and early modern northern Europe.[33] Some of them were instantly recognizable by the fact that their surnames derived from their professions, such as Eogan Ruad Mac an Bhaird (d. 1510), "son of the poet," who was an *ollamh* in poetry to the Ó Domhnaill chief of Tír Conaill.[34]

But how did this class emerge? Both Flower and Mac Cana contended that late medieval hereditary literary kindreds arose from ecclesiastical families who had maintained possession of monastic land as *comharbai* and especially as *airchinnigh* when monastic schools broke up following the reform of the Irish Church in the twelfth century.[35] Some learned lineages certainly had churchmen as ancestors. A branch of the Mac an Bhaird poetic kindred, who had their origins as ecclesiastics in the midland monastery of Clonmacnoise, Co. Offaly, are found in the southern borderland of the lordship of Tír Conaill (Co. Donegal) in the northwest of Ireland by the later medieval period (2.1.1).[36] The Ó Dálaigh poets of Muinter Bháire, who had been associated with the midland monastery of Clonard in the kingdom of Teathbha (Co. Meath), were well established on the Sheepshead Peninsula of west Cork by *c*.1300 (2.2, 3.1).[37] For the reader unfamiliar with the ramifications of Gaelic families in Ireland, the multiplicity of learned kindred branches and their associated landholdings, situated in separate lordships, may seem puzzling. The proliferation into many branches of major learned kindreds, such as the Mac Aodhagáin and Mac Fhlannchadha lawyers and the Ó Dálaigh poets, was the result of successful migrations in search of patrons and estates.

---

[32] Ordnance Survey memoranda for Co. Cork, ii, 455–6. Dublin. Ordnance Survey Ireland.

[33] McLeod, *Divided Gaels*, 55–107; H. Pryce 2000 Lawbooks and literacy in medieval Wales. *Speculum* 75 (1), 44–5; D. S. Thomson 1968 Gaelic learned orders and literati in medieval Scotland. *Scottish Studies* 12, 60.

[34] AConn 1510.2, 615.

[35] P. Mac Cana 1974 The rise of the later schools of *filidheacht*. *Ériu* 25, 127–30; R. Flower 1947 *The Irish tradition*, 84. Oxford. Clarendon Press.

[36] Simms, *Gaelic Ulster in the Middle Ages*, 380.

[37] A. O'Sullivan 1971–2 Tadhg O'Daly and Sir George Carew. *Éigse* 14, 30.

Regional studies have revealed alternative circumstances for the emergence of learned people as a substantial class from the thirteenth century onward. Ó Scea has shown, in relation to south Ulster, that many of the *airchinnigh* who were learned were late arrivals to that clerical office and that their kindreds had no demonstrable long-standing links with pre-twelfth-century *airchinnigh*. For example, the Ó Breasláin lawyers and the Ó Cianáin chroniclers and historians, who were among the most important learned kindreds of the late medieval lordship of Fir Mhanach, did not become *airchinnigh* of the church lands of Derryvullan until after 1200, having migrated to Fir Mhanach from Donegal and Monaghan.[38] The respective roles of the *airchinneach* and of the *comharba* were redefined with the creation of a diocesan parish system throughout Ireland between the late twelfth and early fourteenth century, whereby they came within the jurisdiction of bishops and were therefore subject to episcopal dues and visitations.[39]

By the sixteenth century, there were approximately sixty Gaelic lordships in Ireland and an additional thirty Old English lordships that had adopted Gaelic cultural practices to varying degrees (Fig. 1.1).[40] With each ruling family patronizing at least one historian, lawyer, musician, physician, and poet (and many more in the larger lordships and overlordships), and taking into consideration that some served more than one chief or lord, the branches of learned kindreds directly serving rulers by that time were in their hundreds. Their prominence in Gaelic society was considered unusual. Commenting in 1606 on the character of the Gaelic people of the south Ulster lordship of Fir Mhanach, Sir John Davies (*c.*1569–1626), attorney general of Ireland, remarked that "the natives of this country are reputed the worst swordsmen of the north, being rather inclined to be scholars or husbandmen than to be kern or men of action."[41] His remark is supported by the historical presence of what has been described as "an unusually large number of poets and learned kindreds of all kinds settled within its borders."[42]

There were two periods when literati were particularly affected by political change. The first occurred in the thirteenth and fourteenth centuries, when the transition from kingship to lordship in Ireland led to the formation and consolidation of Gaelic lordships.[43] The second was the sixteenth and early seventeenth century, when the lordships came under sustained pressure from the Tudor government.[44] The first

[38] C. Ó Scea 2012 Erenachs, erenachships and church landholding in Gaelic Fermanagh, 1270–1609. *PRIA* 112C, 295–8.

[39] Ó Scea, Erenachs, erenachships, 273–4.

[40] S. G. Ellis and J. Murray (eds) 2017 *Calendar of state papers, Ireland, Tudor period 1509–1547*, 2–3. Dublin. Irish Manuscripts Commission.

[41] H. Morley (ed.) 1890 *Ireland under Elizabeth and James the First*, 370. London. Routledge.

[42] K. Simms 1977 The medieval kingdom of Lough Erne. *Clogher Record* 9 (2), 135.

[43] Simms, *From kings to warlords.*

[44] G. Kew (ed.) 1998 *The Irish sections of Fynes Moryson's unpublished itinerary*, 59. Dublin. Irish Manuscripts Commission; A. Keaveney and J. A. Madden (eds) 1992 *Sir William Herbert: croftus sive de Hibernia liber*, 107, 109. Dublin. Irish Manuscripts Commission.

change favored the learned, but the second was a period of profound transformation that very gradually but eventually erased their traditional roles in Irish society. New perspectives from the material record show how literati negotiated political and social change during the early modern period (4.5, 5.2.1, 6.4). Despite Tudor propaganda and prohibitions placed on their activities, the Gaelic schools were highly active and productive during the second half of the sixteenth century.[45]

Learned members of Gaelic society were attributed various scholarly titles in the chronicles, including *lechtóir* (lecturer),[46] *maighistir* (master),[47] *oide* (head of a school),[48] *saoí* (sage or learned one),[49] and *ollamh* which was the most preeminent, indicating a master of a learned or skilled profession. It was an academic title, but it also signified one who was appointed by a chief to the office of personal historian, lawyer, physician, or poet.[50] Breatnach's study of the personal or court poets of chiefs has revealed that the office was distinguished from the academic *ollamh filiodh* (master-poet) by the title *ollamh flatha* (chief's poet), the difference being that the former title was conferred by an *oide*, while the latter could only be bestowed by a chief.[51]

The role of *ollamh* in a learned art in late medieval Ireland appears to have been gendered. The term *banollamh* (woman professor) was documented posthumously (1666) in connection with Sadhbh Uí Mhaoilchonaire (d. 1447), in a chronicle reference to her death six years after that of her husband Maoilín (d. 1441), *ollamh* in *seanchas* to the chief of Síol Muiredaigh (Co. Roscommon).[52] It has been suggested that "a more proactive involvement in scholarship cannot be dismissed" for Sadhbh.[53] Her implied role, however, was in respect of dispensing hospitality, which suggests that guesting may have been the key function of the wife of an *ollamh* in late medieval Ireland. That a wife was ascribed her area of authority relative to her husband's role as *ollamh* is also implied in a chronicle description of Finnguala, wife of the historian Fearghal Ó Duibhgeannáin (d. 1344), as "the woman who was the best that was in Ireland in her own domain as the wife of a learned man."[54] Support roles to learned men are attributed to women in the sixteenth century. Sheehan has observed that the physician Risteard Ó Conchubhair of Aghmacart (6.2), who attended Mac Giolla Phadráig, chief of Osraighe, in the second half of the sixteenth century, was by his own testimony supported in his work by female relatives.[55] If precluded by their gender from becoming an *ollamh* in a learned art, Gaelic women c.1300–1600 may well have been involved in writing and making illuminated initials or head letters,

---

[45] C. Lennon 2007 Pedagogy as reform: the influence of Peter White on Irish education in the Renaissance. In T. Herron and M. Potterton (eds), *Ireland in the Renaissance, c.1540–1660*, 43–51. Dublin. Four Courts Press.

[46] U 1384.12.   [47] M 1384.1, iv, 692, 693.   [48] M 1575.6, v, 1682, 1683.

[49] M 1482.2, iv, 1118, 1119.   [50] P. A. Breatnach 1983 The chief's poet. *PRIA* 83C, 37.

[51] Breatnach, Chief's poet, 37–8, 67.   [52] AMacF, i, 218; AConn 1441.2, 484, 485.

[53] M. Ní Dhonnchadha 2002 Courts and coteries I, c.900–1600. In A. Bourke *et al.* (eds), *The Field Day anthology of Irish writing, iv: Irish women's writing and traditions*, 300, 301, 337. New York University Press.

[54] U 1344.7, ii, 486, 487.   [55] Sheehan, Locating the Gaelic medical families, 29.

na Glinnte
Clann Domhnaill

an Rúta
Mac Uidhilín

Inis Eoghain
Ó Dochartaigh

Ciannacht
Ó Catháin

Clann Aodha Buidhe
Ó Néill

Uí Eachach
Cobha
Mág Aonghusa

Cineál Dubhthrian Aird Uladh
Farghe

Iubhartaigh Mac
Artáin Leath
Cathail

Mughdhorna

Tír Conaill
Ó Domhnaill

Tír Eoghain
Ó Néill

na
Feadha

Oirthir
Ó h-Anluain

The Pale

Slape
Fleming

Fiond Mac
Suibhne

na d'Tuath
Mac Suibhne

Tuagh Mac Cionaodha

Oirghialla

Mac
Mathghamhna

Mac
Mathghamhna

Fearnaigh
Mac
Mathghamhna

Killen
Plunket

Cairbet
Tyrrell

Crioch
Bhaoigheallac
Ó Baoighill

Boghaineach
Mac Suibhne

Fir Mhanach
Mág Uidhir

Darraighe
Mac
Fhlannchadha

Mac
Samhradháin

Tuath
nEachach

Tealach Dhúnchadha
Mac Tighearnáin

Bréifne
Ó Raghallaigh

Dealbhna
Nugent

Magh V
Breacraighe
Delamer

Rathconnall
Dillon

Cineál
Fiacha
Tyrrell

Fir Tulach
Tyrrell

Caislenach
Dillon

Cairbre
Ó Conchobhair

Bréifne
Ó Ruairc

Tír Oilella & Corran
Mac Domhnchadha

Caol Ó bhFinn
Ó Gadhra Mac
Diarmada

Magh
Luirg
Mac
Diarmada

Muintir
Eolais
Mac
Raghnaill

Anghal
Ó Fearghail

Machaire Chonnacht
Ó Conchobhair Donn & Ruadh

Tír Fiachrach
Ó Dubhda

Luighne
Ó hEadhra

Clann Coisteabhaigh
Mac Coisteabhaigh

Clann Connmhaigh
MacDavid Burke

Uí Mhaine
Ó Ceallaigh

Gailenga
Mac
Siúrtáin

Clann Mhuiris
Mac Mhuiris

Comhaicne
Mac Fhiorraís

Tír Amhalghaidh
Barret

Clann Uilliam Íochtair
Burke

Umhaill
Ó Máille

Dúthaigh Sheoigheach
Seóigh

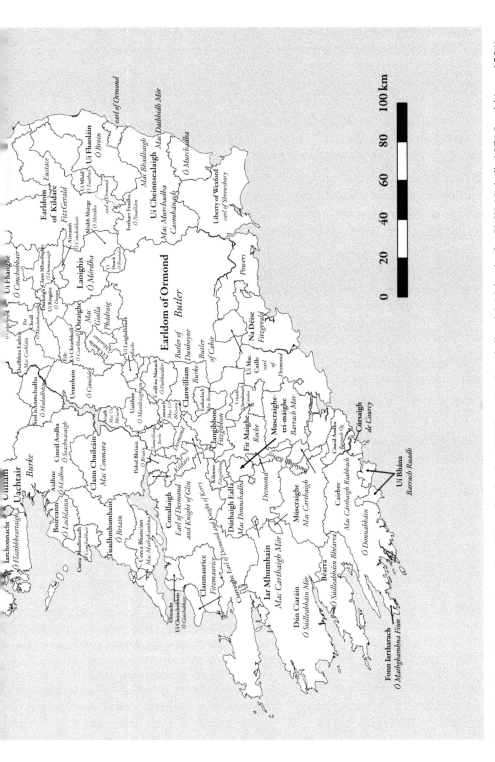

Fig. 1.1. Map of the approximated lordships of Ireland, c.1500 (map E. Campbell and S. Nylund, after K. W. Nicholls 1976 Lordships, c.1534). In T. W. Moody, F. X. Martin, and F. J. Byrne (eds), *A new history of Ireland, iii: early modern Ireland 1534–1691*. Oxford University Press (by permission of Oxford University Press).

as well as preparing parchment, inks, and pigments, and binding manuscripts, all of which was skilled work. In recognition that participation of Gaelic women in the arts is the invisible ink in an under-investigated area of research, the terms "literati" and "learned kindred" are used in this book except where the gender of a learned person is identified.

It was usual for an *ollamh* to serve a single lordship, but some of the more powerful learned kindreds, such as the many branches of the Mac Aodhagáin brehon lawyers, had multiple patrons.[56] In circumstances where a lordship achieved the status of an overlordship through the submission of a weaker territory, an *ollamh* normally served both the dominant and subordinate lordships (2.2).

Generally, *ollamhain* did not confine themselves to their primary hereditary professions but crossed over into other allied areas of the traditional arts. Simms has observed that the poetic art was studied in law schools and that there were poetic judges of brehon law among the learned.[57] Pryce has noted some limited evidence for hybrid learned practices among Welsh-speaking *ynaid*, legal experts in thirteenth-century Gwynedd, who had expertise in both law and religious poetry.[58] Polymathy was a feature of some of the fifteenth-century Welsh professional poets, such as Gutun Owain (fl. 1450–98) who had a notable ability as a genealogist while also knowledgeable in medicine and the related field of astrology.[59] Reflecting the cross-disciplinary interests of the Gaelic *ollamh*, manuscripts of their schools tended to contain a broad range of material, not just profession-specific texts. During the sixteenth century, the Ó Duibhdábhoireann law school at Cahermacnaghten (6.1.1) in the Burren uplands (Co. Clare) had the religious text known as the *Amrae Coluimb Chille* ("Miracles or wonders of Columcille") among its manuscript collections.[60]

It was not unknown for an *ollamh* to have acquired skills and training for one profession in a school largely dedicated to another. Gréaghóir, of the Ó Maoilchonaire kindred of traditional historians, who was destined to become an *ollamh* in *seanchas*, died in 1432 while being instructed in the law school of the Mac Aodhagáin *ollamh*,[61] at *Cluain Lethan* in the lordship of Urumhain (Co. Tipperary). The school was distinguished as "the capital of brehon law in Ireland" (6.1.3).[62] It was one of two

---

[56] See K. Simms 1990 The brehons of later medieval Ireland. In D. Hogan and W. N. Osborough (eds), *Brehons, serjeants and attorneys: studies in the history of the Irish legal profession*, 51. Dublin. Irish Academic Press; Kelly, *A guide to early Irish law*, 253–4.

[57] K. Simms 2007 The poetic brehon lawyers of early sixteenth-century Ireland. *Ériu* 57, 21–2.

[58] Pryce, Lawbooks and literacy, 44–5.

[59] A. O. H. Jarman and G. R. Hughes (eds.) 1991 *A guide to Welsh literature ii: 1282–c.1550*, revised by D. Johnston (2nd ed., 1998), 240–55. Cardiff. University of Wales Press.

[60] J. Bisagni (ed.) 2019 *Amrae Coluimb Chille: a critical edition*. Early Irish texts series: 1, 11–12. Dublin Institute for Advanced Studies.

[61] U 1432, iii, 122, 125.

[62] RIA MS 23 P 16, 1408–11, Leabhar breac: the Speckled book, 206. Dublin. Royal Irish Academy. J. Ó Longáin and J. J. Gilbert (eds) 1876, *Leabhar Breac, the Speckled Book...* ii, 38. Dublin. Royal Irish Academy.

locations where the *Leabhar breac* ("Speckled book"), which contained literature as well as religious and biblical material, was compiled between 1408 and 1411.[63] That text is likely to have formed part of Gréaghóir Ó Maoilchonaire's multidisciplinary instruction.

Hybridity in learned arts was also expressed in the names of some learned kindreds. Two distinguished branches of the Mac an Ghabhann kindred were respective traditional historians to the Ó Cinnéide, chief of Urumhain and to the Ó Lochlainn, chief of Boireann.[64] The name translates as "son of the smith," which suggests that its bearers had origins as high-level *ceird*. The Mac an Ghabhann historians of Urumhain are remembered in the townland name Ballygown, at Silvermines in Co. Tipperary.[65] The most famous of that learned lineage was Mac Raith Mac an Ghabhann na Sgéal, who wrote genealogies of Irish saints and kings in the mid-fourteenth century.[66] It is of interest that the condition of being many sided among learned kindreds is shared with the Gaelic legendary warrior-hunter and border hero Fionn mac Cumhaill, who exercised the *mentalité* of literati in late-medieval Ireland. Fionn (Finn) was the central figure of the literary genre known as *fianaigecht* (Finn cycle of tales). Stories of the hero and his *fian* or wild band were documented from perhaps as early as the eighth century, but may have been based on a preceding oral tradition.[67] They became the foremost literary form by the late medieval period—in ballads, lays, and prose—and continued in popularity into the seventeenth century and later, in Ireland and Scotland.[68] Fionn has been interpreted by Nagy as "a markedly rich and many-sided character with diverse functions," who, as an outsider, possessed the power and wisdom of a poet, while simultaneously having access to legal knowledge and the crafts of the leech and the smith.[69] In this study, Fionn is defined as epitomizing a particular borderland space in Gaelic polities, which was largely peculiar to poets (2.3).

The schools of *ollamhain* were dedicated to preserving and transmitting the Gaelic arts, but they were also adaptive to changing political circumstances as seen in the

---

[63] T. Ó Concheanainn 1973 The scribe of the "Leabhar breac." *Ériu* 24, 64–7.

[64] M 1425.12, iv, 866, 867.

[65] J. S. Brewer, and W. Bullen (eds) 1867 *Calendar of the Carew manuscripts, 1515–1574*, i, 165. London. Longmans, Green and Co. An entry for 1540 renders Ballygown "Bealathagoyn" from the Irish *Béal Átha Gabhann* ("mouth of the ford of the smith").

[66] MS Rawl. B. 486, part iv: miscellany, including historical narratives, genealogies of saints and others, lists of kings, etc. Oxford. Bodleian Library; F. J. Byrne 1979 *A thousand years of Irish script: an exhibition of Irish manuscripts in Oxford libraries*, 21. Oxford. Bodleian Library.

[67] K. Murray 2012 Interpreting the evidence: problems with dating the early *fianaigecht* corpus. In S. J. Arbuthnot and G. Parsons (eds), *The Gaelic Finn tradition*, i, 31–49. Dublin. Four Courts Press; J. F. Nagy 1985 *The wisdom of the outlaw: the boyhood deeds of Finn in Gaelic narrative tradition*, 1–3. Berkeley. University of California Press.

[68] K. Murray 2005 Fenian cycle. In Duffy (ed.), *Medieval Ireland*, 166–7. Among the most important collections of these are the seventeenth-century Irish *Duanaire Finn* and those in the Scottish *Book of the dean of Lismore* dated to the sixteenth century.

[69] Nagy, *Wisdom of the outlaw*, 17, 33.

sixteenth century (6.4). They served the interests of Gaelic chiefs and Old English lords, supporting them with genealogies and histories, legal and medical expertise, religious texts, poetry, and more. Latin and grammar were taught, in addition to specific arts.[70] The testimony of a fifteenth-century poet suggests that Gaelic schools of that period were seasonal, convening in early winter and breaking up at the end of spring, a cycle that would have facilitated the land-based activities of learned kindred estates (3.3).[71] Glimpses of schools at work in the sixteenth century suggest that a dozen or more might convene to compile a manuscript under the direction of an *ollamh* (6.1, 6.4).[72]

It was usual for an *ollamh* and attendant scribes to travel to copy texts kept at other schools. In that way, a book could be created for the use and prestige of the school. This peripatetic practice had a crucial role in generating networks of scholarly communities. It characterized much of the schools' work. There is especially good evidence in formal colophons and casual *marginalia* written on manuscript pages in the sixteenth century for such communities of practice. Scribes visiting or participating in other schools wrote revealing comments in the margins of manuscripts, sometimes referring to contemporary political events, to the company they were keeping, the date, and their place and conditions of writing. This common practice was in some sense epistolary, since personal inscriptions would be viewed and sometimes responded to by others working on the same manuscript. The operation of such a network is evident in *marginalia* penned by named learned men during the compilation of the book of the brehon lawyer Domhnall Ó Duibhdábhoireann (6.1.2).

Some learned networks extended to western Scotland—perhaps not surprisingly, because, as McLeod has observed, the principal poetic and medical kindreds, as well as sculptors and goldsmiths, of late medieval and early modern Gaelic Scotland, originated in Ireland.[73] One of the more remarkable exchanges in the late sixteenth century was between the hereditary physicians of Lorn and Islay in western Scotland and those of the province of Connacht and the lordship of Osraighe in Ireland (6.2).[74] Such networks must have led to exchange of ideas—not just about manuscripts, but also about the buildings in which they were produced and housed, and more generally about the physical environment of the landholdings in which learned kindreds lived, worked, and farmed.

---

[70] E. Campion 1571 (reprint 1809) *A historie of Irland, written in the yeare 1571*, 25–6. Dublin. Hibernia Press.

[71] O. Bergin (ed. and tr.) 1970 *Irish bardic poetry*, 147–8, 280. Dublin Institute for Advanced Studies.

[72] Campion, *Historie of Irland*, 26.

[73] McLeod, *Divided Gaels*, 106, notes a "close correspondence" between Gaelic Ireland and Gaelic Scotland in respect of the organization of the learned professions, but not to the extent of supporting an argument for a single "culture-province."

[74] Bannerman, *The Beatons*, 116–17.

1.2 A NEW APPROACH

It is possible to achieve a long-term perspective on the roles and lifeways of literati, beyond the usual functions attributed to them in written records, by investigating their lived experience in the landscapes of their estates and in the spaces where they were situated in the political map. A unique opportunity to explore the archaeology of social hierarchy, beneath the level of Gaelic chiefs and Old English lords, is presented by the large number of known estates, schools, and residences of learned kindreds. Ninety-four estates were consulted for this study, which is by no means exhaustive (Fig. 1.2; Appendix). The findings are supported by field-based case studies conducted on estates in ten counties, including excavations in law school settlements at Cahermacnaghten, Co. Clare and Ballyorley, Co. Wexford (6.1.1, 6.1.2).[75] The choice of individual sites for high-resolution study largely reflects the survival of built heritage on learned kindred estates and authoritative historical references linked with locations of specific families between the fourteenth and seventeenth centuries. Detailed survey and excavations on the Cahermacnaghten estate of the Ó Duibhdábhoireann brehon lawyers have yielded some significant findings for this study (Figs. 1.3; 4.2, 6.1.1).[76]

1.2.1 Theorizing relationships between territory and learned kindreds

The primary late medieval territorial unit of Ireland was the lordship (*oireacht/pobal*), variously ruled by Gaelic chiefs (*taoiseach*, pl. *taoisigh*) and by Old English lords of Anglo-Norman origin (Fig. 1.1).[77] The islandwide map of polities was a great jigsaw of mostly collective names, incorporating those of ancestors.[78] Chiefs claimed their titles through the male line and were commonly addressed by their surnames, such as the Ó Domhnaill and the Ó Lochlainn.[79] This form of title is also found among some Old English lords who had adopted Gaelic practices. For example, Richard Óg was

---

[75] Archaeological surveys were conducted at Ballymacegan and Redwood (Co. Tipperary), Ballyorley and Pallis (Co. Wexford), Cahermacnaghten, Toomullin and Lettermoylan/Formoyle (Co. Clare), Dromnea (Co. Cork), Dysart and Syonan (Co. Westmeath), Inishmore, Kilboglashy, Killerry and Kilglass-Lackan (Co. Sligo), Kilbarron and Ballymacaward (Co. Donegal), Kilronan (Co. Roscommon), Kilcloony and Park (Co. Galway), and Smarmore (Co. Louth); The excavation at Ballyorley (Co. Wexford) was directed by C. Ó Drisceoil (license E001065) for the O'Doran Law School Project.

[76] E. FitzPatrick and R. Clutterbuck 2013 Late medieval/early post-medieval Gaelic schoolhouse and post-medieval dwelling (10E0147). In I. Bennett (ed.), *Excavations 2010: summary accounts of excavations in Ireland*, 26–7. Dublin. Wordwell; E. FitzPatrick 2011 Cahermacnaghten: late medieval/early post-medieval building. In I. Bennett (ed.), *Excavations 2008: summary accounts of excavations in Ireland*, 41–3. Dublin. Wordwell; E. FitzPatrick 2008 Excavation of a building at Cahermacnaghten, Co. Clare. In I. Bennett (ed.), *Excavations 2008: summary accounts of excavations in Ireland*. Bray. Wordwell.

[77] Nicholls, *Gaelic and gaelicised Ireland*, 8–11, 21–5.

[78] F. J. Byrne 1973 *Irish kings and high-kings*, 93. London. Batsford; P. Woulfe 1923 (reprint 1993) *Sloinnte Gaedheal is Gall: Irish names and surnames*, 685–96. Baltimore. Genealogical Publishing.

[79] Simms, *From kings to warlords*, 34–5.

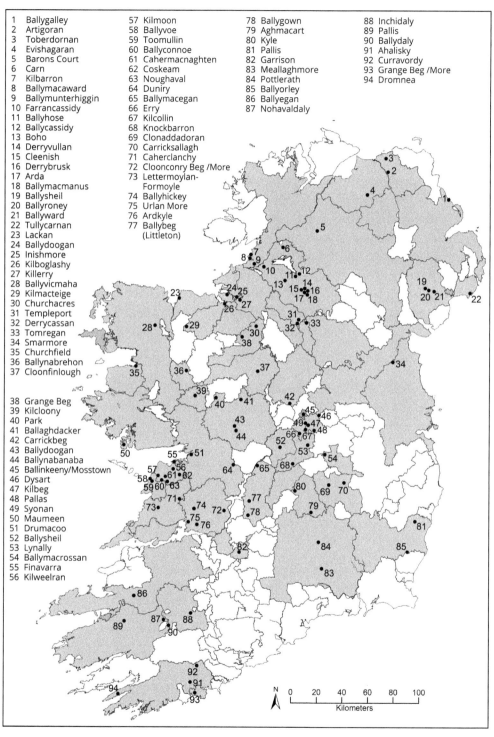

1 Ballygalley
2 Artigoran
3 Toberdornan
4 Evishagaran
5 Barons Court
6 Carn
7 Kilbarron
8 Ballymacaward
9 Ballymunterhiggin
10 Farrancassidy
11 Ballyhose
12 Ballycassidy
13 Boho
14 Derryvullan
15 Cleenish
16 Derrybrusk
17 Arda
18 Ballymacmanus
19 Ballysheil
20 Ballyroney
21 Ballyward
22 Tullycarnan
23 Lackan
24 Ballydoogan
25 Inishmore
26 Kilboglashy
27 Killerry
28 Ballyvicmaha
29 Kilmacteige
30 Churchacres
31 Templeport
32 Derrycassan
33 Tomregan
34 Smarmore
35 Churchfield
36 Ballynabrehon
37 Cloonfinlough

38 Grange Beg
39 Kilcloony
40 Park
41 Ballaghdacker
42 Carrickbeg
43 Ballydoogan
44 Ballynabanaba
45 Ballinkeeny/Mosstown
46 Dysart
47 Kilbeg
48 Pallas
49 Syonan
50 Maumeen
51 Drumacoo
52 Ballysheil
53 Lynally
54 Ballymacrossan
55 Finavarra
56 Kilweelran

57 Kilmoon
58 Ballyvoe
59 Toomullin
60 Ballyconnoe
61 Cahermacnaghten
62 Coskeam
63 Noughaval
64 Duniry
65 Ballymacegan
66 Erry
67 Kilcollin
68 Knockbarron
69 Clonaddadoran
70 Carricksallagh
71 Caherclanchy
72 Cloonconry Beg /More
73 Lettermoylan-
   Formoyle
74 Ballyhickey
75 Urlan More
76 Ardkyle
77 Ballybeg
   (Littleton)

78 Ballygown
79 Aghmacart
80 Kyle
81 Pallis
82 Garrison
83 Meallaghmore
84 Pottlerath
85 Ballyorley
86 Ballyegan
87 Nohavaldaly

88 Inchidaly
89 Pallis
90 Ballydaly
91 Ahalisky
92 Curravordy
93 Grange Beg /More
94 Dromnea

FIG. 1.2. Distribution of learned kindred estates and centers of learned activity in the lordships of Ireland consulted for this study. Use in conjunction with Appendix table (map N. McCarthy and S. Nylund).

FIG. 1.3. Excavation in *Teach Breac*, Cahermacnaghten (photo E. FitzPatrick).

the first of the Connacht branch of the Anglo-Norman family of de Burgo or Burke to carry the title "Mac Uilliam Uachtair", indicating that he was the leader of the "upper" or Co. Galway sept of the family.[80] Throughout the Gaelic lordships of Ireland, territory and landholding were framed by a concept of geography as lineage.[81] The bond between people and place is evident in the broad meaning of the words *oireacht* and *pobal*, an assembly of people together with their chief and territory.[82]

The map of the lordships of Ireland used in modern scholarship (Fig. 1.1) is based on early modern maps and surveys, mainly drawn up by English cartographers serving the Tudor administration in Ireland, with the intention of recording the strategic places of Gaelic lordships.[83] It is also founded on back-projecting boundaries from later English administrative units, such as the barony and county. The hard lines used to delineate the boundaries of a Gaelic lordship may be convenient spatial measures, but they do not reflect the reality of the *oireacht*. Gaelic chiefs, apparently, did not commission maps of their territories. There is no surviving evidence for or record of

<hr />

[80] See Nicholls, *Gaelic and gaelicised Ireland*, 146–8.

[81] J. Leerssen 1994 *The contention of the bards (Iomarbhágh na bhfileadh) and its place in Irish political and literary history*, 17. Irish Texts Society subsidiary series: 2. London. Irish Texts Society.

[82] Nicholls, *Gaelic and gaelicised Ireland*, 225.

[83] See, for instance, MPF 1/36, 1602–3, A map of the southern part of Ulster, Ireland, by Richard Bartlett. Kew. National Archives; M. Escolar 2003 Exploration, cartography and the modernisation of state power. In N. Brenner, B. Jessop, M. Jones, and G. MacLeod (eds), *State/space: a reader*, 33. Oxford. Blackwell.

a map ever having been authorized by a chief, nor is there any evidence for the art of conventional cartography among literati, despite their knowledge of topography and lore of notable places, and the obligation of poets, in particular, to have a complete knowledge of important territorial markers (*dinnshenchas* was a genre of early Irish literature and a distinguished area of Gaelic scholarship dealing with lore of famous places, especially their origin-legends).[84] Instead, the lordships of ruling families tended to be encoded in poems and prose and usually conveyed an idealized picture of their extents, recalling the pre-Norman overkingdoms that had preceded them.[85]

Lordships were not perceived or represented in the Gaelic *mentalité* as spaces that were fixed for all time. For ruling families this would have been tantamount to surrendering their claims to dynastic lands and limiting the possibilities of expansion. In Chapter 2, the tenacious claim of the Ó Ruairc chief of West Bréifne to a territory in the adjoining lordship of Cairbre, which had been part of the large pre-Norman overkingdom of Uí Briúin Bréifne, demonstrates the aspirational and dynamic nature of lordship boundaries (2.1.3). The Gaelic lordship could, therefore, be described as a mode rather than a defined form. This concept of lordship is sympathetic to Elden's idea of territory as a process, "made and remade, shaped and shaping, active and reactive."[86]

If lordship was a process, it can also be defined as a set of practices. Nicholls has remarked that the Irish lordship "must not be considered of as a closed and defined territory, but rather as a complex of rights, tributes and authority."[87] To that it may be added that it was also defined by iteration of claims to ancestral lands and by preserving the pedigrees of notable landmarks and monuments associated with predecessors and progenitors (2.2, 2.3).[88]

To find where learned kindred estates were situated in the territory of lordship and what constituted an estate, it is necessary to provide some understanding of the constituent territorial units and land denominations of late medieval lordships, which were based on pre-Norman territorial units.

The term used for a political community in early medieval Ireland was *túath* (pl. *túatha*). This was the prevailing concept of spatial organization applied to named spaces at different scales.[89] MacCotter's work has demonstrated that the idea of *túath*

---

[84] See N. Ó Muraíle 2005a Dinnshenchas. In Duffy (ed.), *Medieval Ireland*, 132–3; Simms (*Gaelic Ulster*, 361) notes that a fully trained poet was required to have "a thorough knowledge of sagas, genealogies, battle-lists and territorial boundaries."

[85] Smyth, *Map-making*, 83.

[86] S. Elden 2013 *The birth of territory*, 17. Chicago and London. University of Chicago Press.

[87] Nicholls, *Gaelic and gaelicised Ireland*, 22.

[88] J. Carney (ed.) 1943 *Topographical poems by Seaán Mór Ó Dubhagáin and Giolla-na-Naomh Ó hUidhrín.* Dublin Institute for Advanced Studies.

[89] P. MacCotter 2008 *Medieval Ireland: territorial, political, and economic divisions*, 22–5, Dublin. Four Courts Press; D. Ó Corráin 1993 Corcu Loígde: land and families. In P. O'Flanagan and C. Buttimer (eds), *Cork: history and society*, 63–81. Dublin. Geography Publications.

as a political community was used of three territorial denominations. The first was a small territory called a late-*túath*, ruled by a chieftain (OI *taísech túaithe*). The late-*túath* was equivalent to one or two medieval parishes, with origins perhaps in the tenth century. The second was a local kingdom called a *trícha cét* (pl. *céit*), ruled by a king (OI *rí*). This roughly correlated with the later Anglo-Norman cantred and the barony of the early modern period. The third was a *mórthúath*, ruled by an overking, which was a much larger regional territory that corresponded to the diocese and the high-medieval English county.[90] The structures linked with the *túath*, but not its meaning as a political community, carried through to the period of lordship.[91] The lordships that formed from 1200 onwards, during the long transition from kingship to lordship,[92] were essentially drawn from the matrix of late-*túath* and *trícha cét* territories, where they had not been occluded by Anglo-Norman administrative units.

Exemplary *túatha* structure survivals can be seen in various late medieval lordships of Ireland. The lordship of Fir Mhanach (Co. Fermanagh) was constituted by the "seven *túatha*" of the vassal chieftains of Mág Uidhir, chief of Fir Mhanach.[93] The *trícha cét* of Corcu Lóigde in west Co. Cork, which Ó Corráin proved had been divided into seven *túatha*, became the lordship of Corca Laoighdhe.[94] Nugent has shown the great extent of *trícha cét* and *túath* survival across the Gaelic lordships of Co. Clare.[95] The six constituent *túatha* of the lordship of Boireann, in the north of the county, were identified in a fourteenth-century rental and in the record of the Composition of Connacht in 1585, a taxation agreement made between the Crown, the Gaelic chiefs, and English lords and commons of the province of Connacht.[96] This picture of *túath* continuance is visible elsewhere in Ireland, on a 1563 Tudor map of the midland lordships of Laoighis and Uí Fhailge[97] and in the lordships of the northwest, especially in Cairbre, West Bréifne, and Tír Conaill.[98] As late as 1603, in a grant of the north Ulster lordship of An Rúta (Fig. 1.1) by James I to Sir Randall MacDonnell, 1st earl of Antrim, the lordship was described as comprising nine *túatha*, "which were all long in the tenure of his [MacDonnell's] predecessors, and were then in his own".[99]

[90] MacCotter, *Medieval Ireland*, 23, 45–8, 88–9; P. Nugent 2007 *The Gaelic clans of Co. Clare and their territories, 1100–1700 AD*, 13–23. Dublin. Geography Publications.

[91] Nugent (*Gaelic clans*, 13–23) demonstrates with great clarity the organization of structured political communities in the former Gaelic territories of County Clare.

[92] Simms, *From kings to warlords*.

[93] G. Mac Niocaill (ed.) 1964 *The Red Book of the earls of Kildare*, 32. Dublin. Irish Manuscripts Commission; K. Simms 2004 Medieval Fermanagh. In E. Murphy and W. J. Roulston (eds), *Fermanagh: history and society*, 84. Dublin. Geography Publications.

[94] Ó Corráin, Corcu Lóigde.   [95] Nugent, *Gaelic clans*, 138–74.

[96] Nugent, *Gaelic clans*, 138–42.

[97] BL Cotton MS Augustus I.ii.40, *c*.1565, A coloured map of Offalia, now forming King's and Queen's Counties. London. British Library.

[98] P. MacCotter 2019 The origins of the parish in Ireland. *PRIA* 119C, 58–9.

[99] M.C. Griffith (ed.) 1966 *Irish patent rolls of James I: facsimile of the Irish Record Commission's calendar*, 3. Dublin. Irish Manuscripts Commission.

Knowledge of *trícha cét* and *túath* territories is conveyed by literati in their late medieval and early modern writings. For example, the learned author of the sixteenth-century tract known as "*Criochairecht O Maine*" claimed with authority, in his description of the approximate extent of the territory of Uí Mhaine in east Connacht, that it had constituted "seven *trícha céit*, seven *tuatha*, seven *baile*, seven *leath-bhaile*."[100] In what could be construed as a mnemonic incantation, a remembrance of all that once belonged to Uí Mhaine, he articulated the approximate bounds, citing one notable topographical feature and legendary place of the territory after another, including fords, meadows, points, hills, and glacial moraines. Such evocation of erstwhile or aspirational territory is again expressed in a poem of the first half of the fifteenth century addressed to the chief of Cineál bhFiachach by the poet Maeleachlainn na nUirsgéal Ó hUiginn (2.2). In it he recalled key places of the predecessor of the lordship, the old *trícha cét* that had extended "From Killare of the pure streams to Birr on the border of Munster."[101] The pedigrees of those earlier polities were foundational and integral to the patrimonial claims of Gaelic chiefs and to their ambitions for overlordship.

The very titles that some *ollamhain* carried could be glossed as mnemonics of former territories of ruling families and of their claims to them. An *ollamh*'s title, or at least that attributed by the chroniclers, often alluded to an entire province, or more usually to a pre-Norman *mórthuath* or *trícha cét.*[102] Referring to pre-Norman polities was not just a literary or titular exercise. It was a political practice too, manifested in the location of learned kindred estates in the bounds of *trícha céit* and *túatha*, some of which were contiguous with lordship borderlands. For example, a map of the distribution of the core estates of some of the major learned kindreds of the lordship of Boireann, insofar as they can be accurately determined, shows that they reached into the approximated boundaries of the constituent *túatha* of the lordship (Fig. 1.4).[103] Three estates in that territory—those of Ó Dálaigh of Finavarra, *ollamh* in poetry,[104] Ó Beacháin, historian and learned *airchinneach* of Kilmoon,[105] and Ó Connmhaigh, *ollamh* in music[106]—were contiguous with the borderlands of the pre-Norman *trícha cét* and later lordship of Boireann. Likewise, the estates of literati in the lordship of Fir Mhanach were placed in boundary landscapes of the "seven *túatha*" (Fig. 1.5). The expressed belonging of learned kindreds was first and foremost to those earlier territorial structures, the essential building blocks of the lordships and overlordships.

[100] J. O'Donovan (ed. and tr.) 1843 *The tribes and customs of Hy-Many, commonly called O'Kelly's country*, 4–6. Dublin. Irish Archaeological Society.

[101] Cited in P. Walsh 1935 Cnoc Aiste. *Catholic Bulletin* 25, 393–7.

[102] M 1443.11, iv, 930, 931. Mac Aodhagáin, *ollamh* in brehon law of the lordship of Urumhain was addressed as "ollamh Mumhan i feineachus" ("professor of Munster in law").

[103] Nugent, *Gaelic clans*, 138–40.   [104] M 1415.2, iv, 820, 821.

[105] *Lateran regesta* 325: 1434–5. In J. A. Twemlow (ed.) 1909 *Calendar of papal registers, viii, 1427–1447*, 499–509. London. HMSO.

[106] M 1360.13, iii, 618, 619.

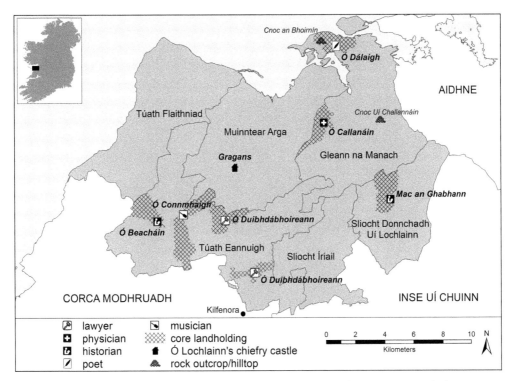

FIG. 1.4. Some learned-kindred estates in the lordship of Boireann and its constituent *túatha* (map N. McCarthy and S. Nylund).

A consequence of the exercise of territory as political practice by Gaelic chiefs was that learned kindreds were instrumentalized in different ways by the lordships they served. This perspective, presented in Chapter 2, is supported by the geopolitical setting and archaeological landscapes of the estates of literati.

Archaeology has traditionally tended to focus less on the physical composition and origins of boundaries and more on their military aspects, as well as interactions between different ethnic and social groups in that domain.[107] However, drawing on Naum's, Bhabha's, and Soja's respective conceptualizations of "third space" as both symbolic and material, and latent with the potential for hybridity, current archaeologies of borderlands envision them as ambiguous or extra-social space, charged with different cultural practices, identities, and political intentions.[108] For instance, investigation of church buildings and cemeteries (1300–1600) in the medieval Finnish

---

[107] See D. Mullin 2011 *Places in between: the archaeology of social, cultural and geographical borders and borderlands*, 1–12. Oxford. Oxbow Books; F. Curta (ed.) 2005 *Borders, barriers, and ethnogenesis: frontiers in late antiquity and the Middle Ages*, 1–9. Studies in the early Middle Age (SEM 12). Turnhout. Brepols; S. Rippon 2018 *Kingdom, civitas and county: the evolution of territorial identity in the English landscape*. Oxford University Press.

[108] M. Naum 2010 Re-emerging frontiers: postcolonial theory and historical archaeology of borderlands. *Journal of Archaeological Method and Theory* 17 (2), 101–2; H. K. Bhabha 1994 *The location of culture*. London. Routledge; E. W. Soja 1996 *Thirdspace: journeys to Los Angeles and other real-and-imagined places*. Malden. Blackwell.

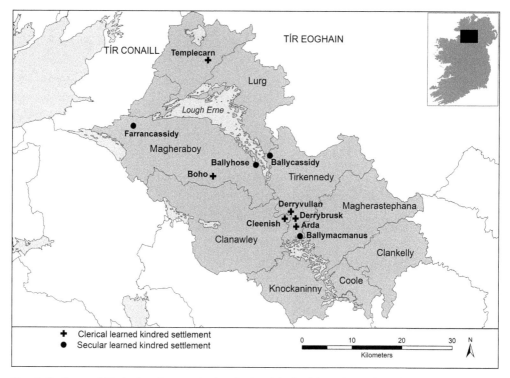

FIG. 1.5. Learned-kindred settlements in the *túatha* of the lordship of Fir Mhanach (map N. McCarthy and S. Nylund).

borderland territory of Northern Ostrobothnia has established that various agents negotiated their relations through complex material and spatial practices at those sites. The idea that unique archaeologies are a signature of borderlands, "spaces where people engage the material world under very specific geopolitical circumstances," and where contest and conflict can arise, has important applications in the Irish context.[109]

Drawing on those theoretical perspectives, the specialized borderland spaces given to the practices of elites and their agents in this work are defined as dynamic extrasocial space (Fig. 1.6).[110] The distribution of the ninety-four learned kindred estates of the period 1300–1600 consulted for this study (Fig. 1.2; Appendix), shows that the spaces in which they were situated had a high degree of correlation with points where *túath* and *trícha cét* boundaries corresponded to the bounds of lordships. These are, hereafter, referred to as premier borderlands (2.1). On the other hand, bounds of

[109] T. Ylimaunu *et al.* 2014 Borderlands as spaces: creating third spaces and fractured landscapes in medieval northern Finland. *Journal of Social Archaeology* 14 (2), 245.

[110] For interpretations of extra-social space see J. N. Bremmer 2012 Greek demons of the wilderness: the case of the centaurs. In L. Feldt (ed.), *Wilderness in mythology and religion: approaching religious spatialities, cosmologies, and ideas of wild nature*, 29. Boston and Berlin. De Gruyter.

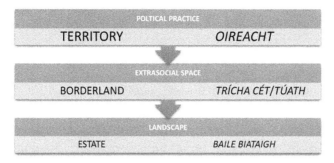

FIG. 1.6. Model of the belonging of learned kindreds.

túatha and *trícha céit* that were not contiguous with the marches of lordships are understood as subsidiary or relict borderland zones (see Figs 1.4, 1.5).

1.3 LAND AND THE LEARNED

In this study, estates of learned kindreds are conceptualized as discrete landscapes within the geopolitical space of borderland (Fig. 1.6). What constituted an *ollamh*'s estate and conditions of tenure are necessary background to the investigation of the scale and organization of estates, their land-use, farming practices, and natural resources discussed in Chapter 3.

The land of Gaelic lordships was managed in a sophisticated system that apportioned it to the chief and his family, his vassals, and his service providers. Lordships also contained church or termon land controlled by bishops and abbots of religious houses, most of whom were drawn from the chief's kin or favored by him. From the fifteenth century, bishoprics in Gaelic territories tended to be controlled by secularized "prince-bishops" who were members of Gaelic ruling families and behaved like lords.[111] Therefore, delineation of the ecclesiastical and the temporal could be quite indistinct. Although approaches varied within the lordships, Duffy's study of social and spatial order in the Ulster lordship of Oirghialla suggests that, in general, five different categories of landholding, four of which were inheritable, generally prevailed, but with some exceptions.[112] These included (1) The lands of the chief's family; (2) personal demesne land attached to the office of chief; (3) lands of the chief's householders—mensal land described as *lucht tighe* (literally, people of the house) apportioned to his service providers inclusive of members of the learned class;

---

[111] K. Simms 1974 The archbishops of Armagh and the O'Neills 1347–1471. *Irish Historical Studies* 19 (73), 53.

[112] P. J. Duffy 2001 Social and spatial order in the MacMahon lordship of Airghialla in the late sixteenth century. In Duffy, Edwards, and FitzPatrick (eds), *Gaelic Ireland*, 129; Nicholls, in *Gaelic and gaelicised Ireland*, has pointed out that not all chiefs had personal demesnes.

(4) lands of the vassal septs of a chief; (5) church lands controlled by bishops and abbots, where learned kindreds who held clerical offices had their estates.

Within this matrix of land categories there was an orderly mosaic of landholding units (3.1), descending in size from the *baile biataigh* (holding of a food provider) to the *ceathramadh* (quarter) and *baile* (holding, usually but not consistently equivalent to the townland in scale).[113] The intricacies of Gaelic landscape organization at this level have been comprehensively addressed by McErlean and more recently by Smyth.[114] A *baile biataigh* (ballybetagh) was the largest estate, which, theoretically, contained four *ceathramadha* or approximately sixteen *baile*, but sometimes included more. Units were, however, not always fixed in size and could increase or decrease while keeping their original denomination descriptors. Also, the names of *baile* were different in the Ulster lordships, where the terms "poll" and "tate" are recorded for them in seventeenth-century surveys.[115] This tenure system of named and quantified denominations was intended to provide a framework for taxation and to regulate the division of land resources among the people of the lordship according to social status.[116]

Lucht tighe and church land are the denominations in which most members of the learned class servicing the courts of Gaelic chiefs are found. Within them, the average learned kindred landholding was a *ceathramadh* or two, but high-ranking *ollamhain* could hold a *baile biataigh* (3.1), and even an entire *túath*, as was the case with the Mac Fhlannchadha lawyers of Túath Ghlae (3.4). There is a description of *lucht tighe* by Sir John Davies in his tract on the *Lawes of Irelande* (1609). It was perhaps because he was a lawyer and a poet that he noticed learned people among the service-providers who lived on *lucht tighe* land:

> The chief lord had certen landes in demesne which were called his loughty, or mensall landes wherein hee placed his principal officers, namely his Brehons, his marshall, his cupbearer, his Phisicion, his surgeon, his Chronicler, his Rimer, and others, which offices and possessions were hereditary and peculiar to certen septs and families.[117]

The principal means by which a member of the literati received land was through appointment as a chief's *ollamh* and by becoming a *comharba* or, more usually, an *airchinneach*. A chief's secular *ollamh* was granted *lucht tighe* land, while an *ollamh* who held the office of *comharba* or *airchinneach* received church land, usually in the form of episcopal mensal land or lands of a religious house linked with the ruling

---

[113] G. Toner 2004 *Baile*: settlement and landholding in medieval Ireland. *Éigse* 34, 26, 39, 40.

[114] T. McErlean 1983 The Irish townland system of landscape organisation. In T. Reeves-Smyth and F. Hamond (eds), *Landscape archaeology in Ireland*. BAR British series: 116, 315–38. Oxford: BAR; Smyth, *Map-making*, 66–86.

[115] E. Mac Neill and J. Hogan (eds) 1931 A booke of the kings lands founde upon the last generall survey within the province of Ulster, anno le: 1608. MS Rawlinson A. 237. The Bodleian Library, Oxford. *Analecta Hibernica* 3, 201.

[116] McErlean, Irish townland system, 334–6.

[117] H. Morgan 1993–5 "Lawes of Irelande": a tract by Sir John Davies. *Irish Jurist* 28–30, 311.

family. Both *lucht tighe* and church lands were automatically free of taxes, if not entirely without material obligations.[118] Clan chiefs in Scotland incentivized the transmission of secular learned professions by giving them hereditary possession of land so that they could retain a core of learned and other skilled people on their own estates.[119] Immunity for secular learned kindreds from *cíos* or tribute (an annual payment) is documented in Gaelic Ireland during the late medieval period.[120] As lawyers providing legal services to the overlords of Tuadhmhumhain, the Mac Fhlannchadha brehons held their estate at Túath Ghlae free of exemptions, from the fourteenth century (3.4, 5.2.1).[121] The immunity of a secular *ollamh* in poetry from *cíos* is revealed in a poem of complaint by Eochaidh Ó hEódhasa to his chief, Mág Uidhir of Fir Mhanach, in the late sixteenth century. The poet pointed out that "no payment in the world" was exacted from him for his estate, in return for his professional services to Mág Uidhir (3.3).[122]

However, it should be noted that literati did pay rent as tenants of aristocracy who eschewed Gaelic customs, such as the earls of Ormond in the sixteenth century (Fig. 1.1).[123] A pointed instance of this is the example of Domhnall Óg Ó Troightigh who was the physician of Thomas Butler, 10th earl of Ormond. He was granted tenancy of an estate at Ballybeg, west of Littleton village, in 1572 under the following terms:

> Indenture dated July 26, 1572, between Sir Thomas Butler, Earl of Ormond, and Donyll Oge O'Trehy [Ó Troightigh] of the Ballybeg *alias* Littletown, Co. Tipperary, physician, witnesses that said Earl grants said town of Ballybeg with the castle, meases, lands, etc., thereto belonging, reserving to himself all game, to have and to hold to said Donyll, his executors and assigns, for a term of 21 years at annual rent of 8l., a poundage hog, a summer sheep and 6 watch hens, with the moiety of all heriots, strays and profits of courts.[124]

In his seventeenth-century *Foras feasa ar Éirinn*, Keating ascribed the term "*fearann ollamhantachta*" (*ollamh*'s land) to the estate that an *ollamh* appointed by a Gaelic chief received as part of his service contract.[125] Some poets used the shorter term

---

[118] Simms, *Gaelic Ulster*, 380.

[119] R. A. Dodgshon 1998 *From chiefs to landlords: social and economic change in the western highlands and islands, c.1493–1820,* 89. Edinburgh University Press.

[120] Simms, *From kings to warlords*, 143–5, 172.

[121] J. Hardiman (ed.) 1828 Ancient Irish deeds and writings chiefly relating to landed property from the twelfth to seventeenth century: with translation, notes and a preliminary essay. *Transactions of the Royal Irish Academy* 15, 38, 42.

[122] O. Bergin (ed.) 1923 Unpublished Irish poems xxi: the poet insists on his rights. *Studies: An Irish Quarterly Review* 12 (45), 80, 82.

[123] The Butlers of the late medieval period, however, are known to have accepted limited use of Gaelic customs and law within their territory, as a peace-keeping strategy.

[124] E. Curtis (ed.) 1941 *Calendar of Ormond Deeds,* v, 1547–84, 232. Dublin. The Stationery Office.

[125] D. Comyn (ed.) 1902 *Foras feasa ar Éirinn: the history of Ireland by Geoffrey Keating,* i, 72. London. Irish Texts Society.

ollamhanacht (3.1) for their estates and exploited the opportunity that their art provided to emphasize long-standing agreements underpinning tenure of the land that accompanied the office of *ollamh*.[126] The estate of the Ó Dálaigh poets of Muinter Bháire, which was coterminous with the Sheepshead Peninsula, Co. Cork, was poetically claimed by Tadhg Ó Dálaigh to have been in his family for a long time (3.1). Addressing the kindred's patron, he stressed, "The head of our poetic family once got a promontory from the head of your family."[127]

Where literati were placed in the landscape of lordship was not an arbitrary decision. It was based on facilitating their roles in the service of chiefs and their families. As will be seen, the locus of literati varied as a response to key periods of change and political events. Thereby, the migrations of some branches of learned kindreds stretched the distribution of their estates beyond their original lands. A more common means by which learned professionals acquired estates in the later medieval period was through placement as tenants of abbots and bishops on church lands and assuming the role of *comharba* and more usually *airchinneach*.[128] The common phenomenon of an *ollamh* simultaneously holding clerical office implies that ruling families had control and influence over the practice of inserting learned men into church lands.

Holding church land was an attractive proposition for learned men because it came without taxes,[129] and for ruling families there was the additional benefit of having an *ollamh-airchinneach* or *ollamh-comharba* placed on a church estate in premier borderland (2.1.1). The clustering of learned kindreds as *airchinnigh* on church land, between 1200 and 1600, immediately north and south of Enniskillen in the lordship of Fir Mhanach is particularly strong evidence of the favorable circumstances of living on such land (3.1). It appears to have been a policy of successive Mág Uidhir chiefs to attract learned kindreds to settle in the lordship, filling church benefices with them and thereby promoting the development of a learned elite.[130]

The holding of land rent free by the learned professions in return for their services continued in Gaelic Scotland well into the seventeenth and eighteenth centuries. The late occurrence of this practice is documented in respect of early modern historians and harpers in rentals of the estates of clan chieftains. A hereditary harper living at Fanmore (*Fàn Mòr nan Clarsairean*, "large slope of the harper") in the northwest of the Isle of Mull, which was part of the estate of the Maclean of Duart, was recorded in a rental of 1674 as holding his lands rent free: "Phanmoir [Fanmore] possest be the harper and pretends kyndnes thereto for his services and pays nothing."[131] As late as 1748, one Neil Mac Mhuirich was recorded in a rental of that year as having "two

---

[126] Breatnach, The chief's poet, 61.   [127] O'Sullivan, Tadhg O'Daly, 27, 34, 37.
[128] Ó Scea, Erenachs, erenachships, 295–8.   [129] Simms, *Gaelic Ulster*, 379, 381.
[130] Ó Scea, Erenachs, erenachships, 296.
[131] J. R. N. Macphail (ed.) 1910–11 *Highland papers*, i, Scottish History Society, second series: 5, 279. Edinburgh. Constable.

pennyland" at Stilligarry (*Stadlaigearraidh*, "rock, fertile land"), on the South Uist estate lands of Clanranald, in return for his services as "Chronologer and Poet Laurent."[132]

Landscape has its own language, oral and aural, visual and tactile. Interpreting literati within the lands and borderland spaces that they occupied has considerable potential to convey a complex picture of their class as intellectuals and political actors and to make progress towards a more socially diverse understanding of historical landscape and built heritage in the lordships.

---

[132] Dodgshon, *From chiefs to landlords*, 89.

2

The Domain of Literati in the Landscape of Lordship

2.0 INTRODUCTION

A borderland context for the estates of literati was recognized as early as the 1970s,[1] but the implications of that norm and the physical manifestations of the bounds in which the learned were placed have not been addressed from a landscape perspective. In this chapter, an understanding of where prominent Ulster, Munster, and Connacht kindreds of historians, lawyers, and poets were situated in the lordships is presented in three case studies of the territorial settings of their estates. Subsequently, recurrent features of those settings, including places of political assembly, and hills and monuments associated with the legendary figure Fionn mac Cumhaill, are singled out for deeper analysis to enlighten the relationships that literati had with those expressions of borderland.

At first, it is necessary to tease out a definition of borderscape and the different manifestations of it to which literati belonged.

2.0.1 Literati and borderscapes

Investigation of relationships between settlement and medieval Irish territorial boundaries has focused mainly on early church sites.[2] One of two separate archaeological studies carried out on the relationship between early medieval churches and boundaries in the pre-twelfth-century kingdom of Corcu Modruad, in the north of the county of Clare,[3] established that about 60 percent of them were in the borderlands of that kingdom. Furthermore, it was found that high-status secular sites were situated close

---

[1] P. Ó Riain 1972 Boundary association in early Irish society. *Studia Celtica* 7, 19–21; D. Ó Corráin 1973 Aspects of early history. In B. G. Scott (ed.), *Perspectives in Irish archaeology*, 64–6. Belfast. Association of Young Irish Archaeologists.

[2] A. Connon 2016 Territoriality and the cult of Saint Ciarán of Saigir. In T. Ó Carragáin and S. Turner (eds), *Making Christian landscapes in Atlantic Europe*, 110–58. Cork University Press.

[3] H. Mytum 1982 The location of early churches in northern County Clare. In S. Pearce (ed.), *The early Church in western Britain and Ireland*, 351–61. British Archaeological Report. British Series 102. Oxford; J. Sheehan, 1982 The early historic church-sites of north Clare. *North Munster Antiquarian Journal* 24, 29–47.

TABLE 2.1 Key sites in the development of a borderland political center at Ballaghmore in the lordship of Osraighe

Feature	Name	Period of Origin
high road	Slige Dála	Iron Age?
monastic learned centre	Cluain Fearta Molua	Early Medieval
peace-mound (reused barrow)	Brehon's Chair	Early Medieval?
parish church	Kyleclonfertmolua	High Medieval
castle of chief & talismanic figure	Ballaghmore	Late Medieval
estate of physician	Ballyduff	Late Medieval

to some preeminent churches, suggesting that early churches ought to be studied in conjunction with "other, contemporaneous monument types and activities which feature prominently in these zones."[4] This insight is a starting point for understanding the development of areas of borderland that became strategically important as centers of power, and where literati fit within them.

Some early medieval boundary churches provided an impetus for the development of centers of power that involved the presence of learned men. The setting of the early church of Clonfert Molua at Kyle (Co. Laois; Fig. 1.2) is a particularly instructive case of a premise for the emergence of a strategically important late medieval borderland space between the Gaelic lordships of Osraighe, Éile Uí Chearbhaill, and Uí Chairín (Table 2.1). The Slieve Bloom Mountains and their foothills constituted a major landmark of the border between the three lordships, their pre-Norman ancestral polities, and the provinces of Leinster and Munster. In a boundary zone of an estimated 15 square kilometers, buildings were constructed, monuments were repurposed, and manors and estates were created, between the sixth and mid-seventeenth century. In that space, St Molua (d. 609) is attributed the foundation of the church of Clonfert Molua (*Cluain Fearta Molua*, "meadow of Molua's grave").[5] Sited on the route of the *Slige Dála*, the high road from west Munster to Tara, his church became a distinguished center of learning in the seventh century under St Laidcenn mac Baíth Bannaig (d. 661).[6] Described as "sapiens" in the chronicle record of his death, Laidcenn is credited with both an abridged version of Pope Gregory's *Egloga de moralibus Job*, and a *lorica*, a prayer meant to be apotropaic for those who recited it and which

---

[4] Sheehan, The early historic church-sites, 42; T. Ó Carragáin 2021 *Churches in the Irish landscape AD 400–1100*. Cork University Press.

[5] P. Ó Riain 2011 *A dictionary of Irish saints*, 490–2. Dublin. Four Courts Press.

[6] C. Ó Lochlainn 1940 Roadways in ancient Ireland. In J. Ryan (ed.), *Féil-sgríbhinn Eóin MacNeill: essays and studies presented to Professor Eoin MacNeill*, 471. Dublin. Three Candles; E. FitzPatrick 2003 On the trail of an ancient highway: rediscovering Dála's road. In J. Fenwick (ed.), *Lost and found: discovering Ireland's past*, 165–71. Bray. Wordwell; Ó Riain, *Dictionary*, 388.

enumerated body parts to be protected.[7] The *lorica* apparently shows such comprehensive knowledge of human anatomy that it could be taken for a medical tract.[8]

Clonfert Molua was elevated to parish status and became part of the Anglo-Norman manor of that name in the early thirteenth century.[9] The local family of Ó Duibhginn held the offices of *comharba* and rector of Clonfert Molua from at least 1401, and as late as 1622 the representative of the family was still addressed as "the Corbe [*comharba*]."[10] As holders of the office of *comharba*, they were hereditary keepers of the *mionn Molua* ("Molua's oath"), an early medieval bell and shrine attributed to the saint and used locally for swearing oaths, into the eighteenth century.[11]

Contributing to the deep layering of this borderland space, Mac Giolla Phádraig, chief of Osraighe, had a tower-house constructed in the fifteenth century at Ballaghmore, west of Molua's church (Table 2.1).[12] A female exhibitionist figure was carved on a quoin-stone high up on the west corner, as a talisman facing towards the lordships of Éile Uí Chearbhaill and Uí Chairín.[13]

Physicians, of necessity, needed to be near the residences of ruling families.[14] A member of the Mac Caisín medical kindred was recorded in 1566 as the holder of land at "Boulleduff".[15] This place name approximates to two townlands, both called Ballyduff, in the vicinity of Ballaghmore Castle. It is uncertain which of the two Mac Caisín held. One is on the boundary between counties Offaly and Laois, 1.5 km northwest of Ballaghmore. The other adjoins the east side of Clonfert Molua, 3.5 km from the castle. It belonged to the *comharba*, Ó Duibhginn, and had the alternative name "Kilballeduff".[16] The *comharba*'s land at Ballyduff was cited as the target of a cattle raid in the sixteenth century.[17] The Mac Caisín medical kindred were rivals to the ascendant Ó Conchubhair physicians in the sixteenth century (6.2). Their presence in this borderland space suggests that they may have first received their Ballyduff estate as personal physicians of the chief after Ballaghmore was built in the fifteenth century.

---

[7] U 661.1, i, 132, 133; Ó Riain, *Dictionary*, 388; M. W. Herren 1973 The authorship, date of composition and provenance of the so-called Lorica Gildae. *Ériu* 24, 35–51.

[8] M. W. Herren 1987 *The Hisperica famina*, ii, 25. Toronto. Pontifical Institute Mediaeval Studies.

[9] E. Curtis (ed. and tr.) 1932 *Calendar of Ormond Deeds*, i, 1172–1350, 9–10. Dublin. The Stationery Office.

[10] W. H. Bliss and J. A. Twemlow (eds) 1904 *Calendar of papal registers relating to Great Britain and Ireland, v, 1398–1404*, 364. London. HMSO; P. Dwyer 1878 *The diocese of Killaloe from the Reformation to the close of the eighteenth century, with an appendix*, 144. Dublin. Hodges, Foster, and Figgis.

[11] T. L. Cooke 1869 On ancient bells. *JRSAI* 1, 49–51.

[12] D. Sweetman, O. Alcock, and B. Moran 1995 *Archaeological inventory of County Laois*, 110. Dublin. The Stationery Office.

[13] Sweetman, Alcock, and Moran, *Archaeological inventory*, 122.

[14] E. FitzPatrick 2015b *Ollamh, biatach, comharba*: lifeways of Gaelic learned families in medieval and early modern Ireland. In L. Breathnach, R. Ó hUiginn, D. McManus and K. Simms (eds), *Proceedings of the XIV International Congress of Celtic Studies, Maynooth 2011*, 175. Dublin Institute for Advanced Studies.

[15] Nicholls, *Irish fiants*, ii, 101 [897].   [16] Nicholls, *Irish fiants*, iii, 491 [6551].

[17] S. Mac Airt (ed.) 1944 *Leabhar Branach: the book of the O'Byrnes*, 67, 360. Dublin Institute for Advanced Studies.

There is a monument on Kyle Hill, northwest of Ballaghmore, which has been known since the eighteenth century as the "Brehon's Chair." The antiquary, Ledwich, included a description of it in his *Antiquities of Ireland* (1790), referring to it as an "antient judgement-seat," which was locally regarded as a "Fairy-chair" where "the Brehon of the Fitz Patricks [Mac Giolla Phádraig] held his court."[18] The "chair" is usually identified as an outcrop of sandstone on the hill, but there is also a ring-barrow crowning the eastern half of the summit.[19] It has been argued that prehistoric mounds may have been appropriated for the exposition of law at Christian legal centers in the early medieval period.[20] Kyle Hill could have originated as a place of arbitration when Molua's church was founded, a view supported by the locus of the hill and its barrow, in a long-lived premier borderland. The use of barrows as "peace-mounds" for high-level arbitration and agreement has been recognized in other lordship borderlands (2.2).

Borderland narratives are rarely complete without an incidence of conflict (2.1.3). As a boundary space of long standing between three lordships, the center of power established by the chiefs of Osraighe was periodically disputed between them and the chiefs of Éile Uí Chearbhaill. The conflict was expressed, for instance, in several quarrels over the ownership of the castle of Ballaghmore which, as recorded by the Privy Council in 1543 and 1565–6, was at variance between the two lordships during the sixteenth century.[21]

There were a variety of circumstances and processes that rendered an area of borderland of strategic importance to a ruling family. Political conditions, which caused the contraction or expansion of a territory and required formation of new marches, made boundary visibility and consolidation a cause of concern. One such watershed for Gaelic rulers was the thirteenth and fourteenth centuries when their status changed from that of kings to lords.[22] It was a key period both for strengthening parts of lordship borderlands retained from pre-Norman polities and giving visibility to those newly formed (4.3). The fission of a lordship due to internecine conflict was also a catalyst for the formation of a new borderland between divided septs. In such circumstances, a *túath* territory containing an early medieval royal demesne with monuments of ancestral importance to both parties might be chosen as the demarcation between their lands (2.2; Fig. 2.17).

Declaration of overlordship, whereby a weak lordship was reduced to the status of a vassal territory, could also influence where literati, especially poets and lawyers, were granted estates (2.2, 2.3). Finally, there was a renewed concern by some Gaelic chiefs

---

[18] E. Ledwich 1790 *The antiquities of Ireland*, 278–9. Dublin.

[19] I referred to the monument on the summit of Kyle Hill as an "enclosure," in FitzPatrick, *Royal inauguration*, 135.

[20] C. Swift 1996 Pagan monuments and Christian legal centres in early Meath. *Ríocht na Midhe* 9 (2), 19.

[21] Historical Manuscripts Commission 1897 *The manuscripts of Charles Haliday: acts of the Privy Council in Ireland, 1556–1571*, 278, 149–50. London. HMSO.

[22] Simms, *From kings to warlords*.

to make their authority visible in key areas of their lordships during the sixteenth century, which led to the creation of new centers of power and the rejuvenation of old ones, typified by the construction of chiefry castles, around which estates of *lucht tighe* land were allocated to literati and servitors (4.3, 6.1.3).

Politically significant borderland centers of power of Gaelic chiefs do not have a homogeneous material identity, because they had different origins and served a variety of roles over time. Defining these politically important borderland spaces is a subject that requires a dynamic theoretical framework (1.2.1). New ways of framing topographies and archaeologies associated with extra-social space and in-between places suggest that they were not "epiphenomenal to the main structures of settlement in the landscape,"[23] but integral to the configuration of territory and created by interactions between the cultural practices of elites, their agents, topography, and monuments.

Gaelic centers of power that were created in premier borderlands tended to be accumulative, becoming deeply layered assemblages of settlement features, repurposed monuments, and storied topographies (Table 2.2). In what follows, three

TABLE 2.2 Indicators of a premier borderscape

Borderland Indicator	Manifestation
assembly place	court, execution, inauguration, *óenach*, *oireachtas*, peace-making sites
boundary marker	*fert*, ogham stone, holed stone
border castle	tower-house
center of learning	learned kindred estate, residence, guest-house, school-house
church	early church, parish church, sinecure chapel, cursing/curing stones
conflict site	bare-topped hill, battle site, hillfort, livestock raid, megalithic monuments
hunting ground	bare-topped hill, hilltop cairn/mound, megalithic monuments
myth & legend	place names/tales
natural resources	mineral/metal ores, quarriable stone
route	high road
royal & lordly retreat	feasting site, hospice, *pailís*
talisman	male/female exhibitionist figure

---

[23] Harmanşah, *Of rocks and water*, 3, 11.

different borderscapes are brought back into view using a landscape perspective that conceptualizes them as extra-social space instrumental to power.

2.1 PRESERVING THE PEDIGREE OF
PREMIER BORDERLANDS

Between the fourteenth and seventeenth centuries, estates of some of the leading Gaelic learned kindreds are found in premier borderlands that were important to the territories that they served. This is a phenomenon observable in the three borderscape studies presented here. The first is in Ulster, in the southern borderland of the lordship of Tír Conaill (Co. Donegal), where the estates of the Mac an Bhaird and Ó hUiginn poets and the Ó Cléirigh chroniclers and poet-historians clustered around the estuary of the River Erne (2.1.1). The second is in Munster, in the lordship of Cineál bhFearmaic (Co. Clare), where the leading branch of the Mac Bruaideadha kindred of poets served the Uí Bhriain overlords of Tuadhmhumhain from their estate in the historic borderscape of Slieve Callan (2.1.2), and the third is in north Connacht, in the conjoined *túatha* of Calraighe and Clann Fhearmhaíghe between the lordships of West Bréifne, Cairbre, and Tír Oilella-Corran, where the Ó Cuirnín poets and Mac an Óglaigh lawyers had their estates (2.1.3).

2.1.1 *Learned kindreds of the Erne estuary landscape of Tír Conaill*

The southern borderland of the lordship of Tír Conaill was an uneasy place, periodically marked by conflict, such as the battle fought in the Erne estuary in 1420 between the Ó Conchobhair-Sligo, chief of Cairbre, and the Ó Domhnaill, chief of Tír Conaill.[24] The estates of branches of the learned kindreds of Mac an Bhaird, Ó Cléirigh, and Ó hUiginn, who served the Ó Domhnaill, were concentrated on both sides of the Erne estuary, suggesting that they were placed there as a manifestation of the long-standing premier borderland between Tír Conaill and the neighboring lordships of Cairbre, Fir Mhanach, and Dartraighe (Fig. 2.1).

The bardic kindred of Mac an Bhaird ("son of the bard") lived at Ballymacaward on the Atlantic coast of the Erne estuary landscape (Fig. 2.2). From the early fifteenth century, the kindred were in the service of the Ó Domhnaill chiefs of Tír Conaill. By the sixteenth century they were well established in the lordship.[25] Their estate, which was bounded to the south by the broad estuary of the Erne and to the west by Donegal Bay, was recorded in the Ulster survey of 1608 as half a quarter of temporal land.[26] Outcropping rock on the southern coastline of their estate carries the name Carricknadanty (*Carraig na dánta*, "Rock of the poems"), alluding to the role of the

---

[24] M 1420.3, iv, 842, 845.   [25] Simms, *Gaelic Ulster*, 380.
[26] Mac Neill and Hogan, A booke of the kings lands, 183.

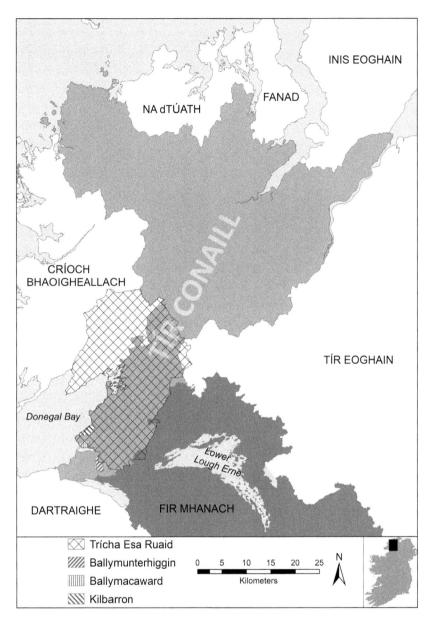

FIG. 2.1. Learned kindred estates in the southern borderland of the lordship of Tír Conaill (map N. McCarthy).

family as poets to the chief of Tír Conaill.[27] The late medieval residence of the Mac an Bhaird at Ballymacaward has not survived, but it was probably located in the area of Wardtown House, the residence of the Folliott family, who assumed ownership of Ballymacaward in the seventeenth century.[28]

[27] H. Allingham 1879 *Ballyshannon: its history and antiquities, with some account of the surrounding neighbourhood*, 103–4. Londonderry. James Montgomery.

[28] Allingham, *Ballyshannon*, 61–2.

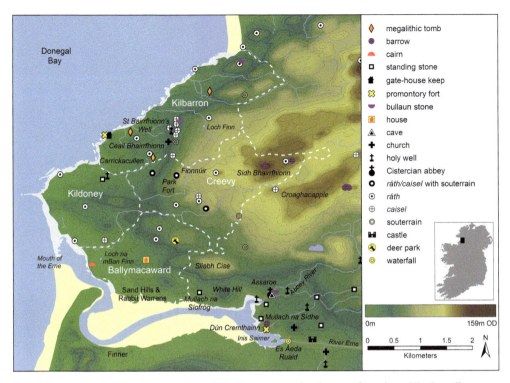

FIG. 2.2. Archaeology and topography of the Erne estuary landscape of southern Tír Conaill, showing the estate of the Mac an Bhaird poets of Ballymacaward, and the episcopal mensal land of Kilbarron and *lucht tighe lands* of Kildoney and Creevy (2.1), held by the Ó Cléirigh poet-historians (map N. McCarthy).

The near neighbors of the Mac an Bhaird poets were the Ó Cléirigh chroniclers and poet-historians of Kilbarron (Fig. 2.2). They too were late arrivals to the southern border of the lordship, having replaced their predecessors, the Ó Sgingín kindred, as court historians to the Ó Domhnaill around 1400.[29] They were *airchinnigh* of the bishop of Raphoe, and in that capacity the greater part of their estate was a quarter of episcopal mensal land in the parish of Kilbarron.[30] The residence of the kindred was a small gate-house keep, and a bawn containing buildings, inside a promontory fort overlooking Donegal Bay (4.5).

The Ó hUiginn poets were situated south of the Erne and southeast of the sandhills of Finner (Fig. 2.3). Their estate is remembered in the townland name Ballymunterhiggin (*Baile Mhuintir Ó hUiginn*, "the landholding of the O'Higgins"). It was recorded in the 1608 survey of Ulster as consisting of a quarter of land, suggesting that it was much larger than the area represented by the modern townland of Ballymunterhiggin.[31]

[29] Simms, Bardic schools, 36.

[30] M. A. Costello 1909 *De annatis Hiberniae: a calendar of the first fruits' fees levied on papal appointments to benefices in Ireland* AD *1400 to 1535*, i. 278. Dundalk. Tempest.

[31] Mac Neill and Hogan, A booke of the kings lands, 183.

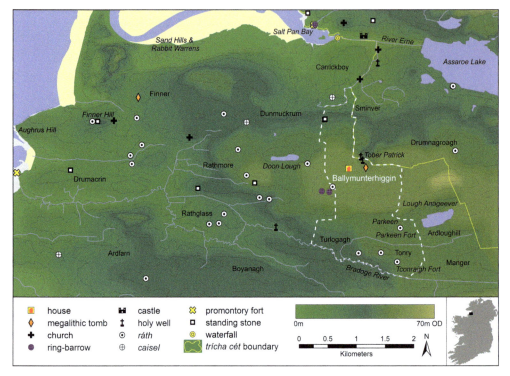

FIG. 2.3. The approximate estate of Ballymunterhiggin south of the Erne (map N. McCarthy).

All three learned kindred estates had belonged to the pre-Norman local kingdom of Trícha Esa Ruaid (Fig. 2.1). Most, but not all, of that land is represented by the later barony of Tirhugh. The estates had a history too as lands of the still earlier *túath* territories of Mag nÉne, Mag Sereth, and Túath Esa Áeda Ruaid that had originated at least as early as the seventh century and which were preserved as subdivisions of the *trícha cét*.[32]

Settlements of the learned class were an addition to the many other mnemonics of boundary consolidation that accumulated in this borderscape over time. Not least of those were the stories of *Es Áeda Ruaid* (Assaroe), the once-magnificent waterfall situated at the mouth of the Erne estuary at Ballyshannon (Fig. 2.2). Described in *The triads of Ireland* as one of the three waterfalls of the island,[33] it was very much the natural wonder of this borderland—"whose celebrated, well-known name is the...rapid, salmonful, seamonsterfull...furious-streamed, whirling in seal-abounding, royal and prosperous cataract."[34] It is portrayed as a place of

[32] B. Lacey 2006 *Cenél Conaill and the Donegal kingdoms* AD *500–800*, 62–3. Dublin. Four Courts Press; A. O'Kelleher and G. Schoepperle (eds and tr.) 1918 *Betha Colaim Chille: life of Columcille compiled by Manus O'Donnell in 1532*, 134, 135. Chicago. Irish Foundation Series of America.

[33] K. Meyer (ed. and tr.) 1906 *The triads of Ireland*, 55. Dublin. Hodges Figgis: "The three waterfalls of Ireland: Assaroe, Eas Danainne, Eas Maige."

[34] J. O'Donovan 1842 (ed. and tr.) *The banquet of Dun na n-Gedh and the battle of Magh Rath*, 104, 105. Dublin. Irish Archaeological Society; Gwynn, *Metrical Dindshenchas*, iv, 4, 5, 8, 9.

Christian miracles. After a blessing by Columcille, the saint reshaped it so that fish could be free to "go and come across the waterfall from the river to the great sea," thereby making the Erne the best place to fish in Ireland.[35] The thirteenth-century poet Giolla Brighde Mac Con Midhe referred to it as abundant in both salmon and trout, describing it as "a high column of the ancient, smooth slabs of rock, against which the pale, slender trout have leapt."[36]

The premier borderland represented by the Erne estuary hinterland was topograph-ically constituted by rivers, hills, sands, and bays (Fig. 2.2). By the late medieval period it incorporated a castle of the chief of Tír Conaill at Ballyshannon, the twelfth-century Cistercian abbey of Assaroe, a medieval Christian burial ground at Ballyhanna,[37] the early medieval Patrician landscape of *Dísert Pátraic*, and prehistoric funerary and ritual monuments. The poetically celebrated island *Inis Saimér* was situated in the estuary itself (4.4.2). It was a royal retreat for the early medieval Cenél Conaill kings and later chiefs of Tír Conaill, a hospitable chief's dwelling of plenty, "frequented by bands of poets" (Fig. 2.2).[38]

Reflecting medieval perception of boundaries as places "in-between," several of the place names of this premier borderland link former prehistoric funerary mounds with the Otherworld, a supernatural place inhabited by the *Tuatha Dé Danann*, the immortal beings of Irish myth (2.1.2).[39] The rich seam of myth associated with *Es Áeda Ruaid* includes *Síd Áeda* ("Áed's otherworld dwelling"), a former mound called *Mullach na Sídhe* ("summit of the otherworld dwelling/mound"), prominently situated on the north side of the Erne, and overlooking the renowned waterfall (Fig. 2.2).[40] *Mullach na Sídhe* was allegedly where St Patrick blessed Conall, son of Niall, and where Brigid and Patrick prophesized the birth of Columcille.[41] It was recorded as a place of execution during the sixteenth century, used by Aodh Ruadh Ó Domhnaill, chief of Tír Conaill.[42] Otherworld allusions are also ascribed to *Sliab Cise* (as named in *Bethu Phátraic*), a hill now known as Sheegys that lies to the northwest of *Mullach na Sídhe*.[43] It forms a discrete area of dark shale between gray limestone to the east and the sandstone that characterizes the landholding of the Mac an Bhaird

---

[35] O'Kelleher and Schoepperle, *Betha Colaim Chille*, 134, 135.

[36] N. J. A. Williams (ed. and tr.) 1980 *The poems of Giolla Brighde Mac Con Midhe*, 54, 55. Dublin. Irish Texts Society.

[37] McKenzie and Murphy, *Life and death*, 9–12, 389.

[38] M 1197.3, iii, 110; M 1333.11, iii, 552, 553; Williams, *The poems of Giolla Brighde*, 56, 57.

[39] This definition of the Irish otherworld is from J. Carey 1989 Otherworlds and verbal worlds in Middle Irish narrative. In W. Mahon (ed.), *Proceedings of the Harvard Celtic Colloquium* 9, 31–2, 38. Cambridge, Mass. Harvard University Press.

[40] Gwynn, *Metrical Dindshenchas*, iv, 2, 3; Allingham, *Ballyshannon*, 15. A star-shaped fort was built on the site of the mound in the 1590s.

[41] M. MacNeill 1962 *The festival of Lughnasa: a study of the survival of the Celtic festival of the beginning of harvest*, 601–2. Oxford University Press.

[42] M 1599.4, and 1599.5, vi, 2092, 2093; "Mullach-Sithe-Aedha," "summit of Áed's otherworld mound."

[43] K. Mulchrone 1939 (ed. and tr.) *Bethu Phátraic: the tripartite life of Patrick, i, text and sources*, 90. Dublin and London. Royal Irish Academy.

poets of Ballymacaward to the west (Fig. 2.2).[44] Local folklore relates that a hollow in "a little mound" on the hill was made by Fionn mac Cumhaill when he sat there to rest.[45] A third hill called *Mullach na Síofróg* ("otherworldy hilltop") sits on the southern boundary of *Sliab Cise* and, as its name suggests, it too may have once been crowned by a barrow.

The boundary aspect of the lands of the Ó Cléirigh chroniclers and historians is, arguably, articulated in the name of the saint after which their estate at Kilbarron was named. *Ceall Bhairrfhionn* refers to the church or cell of the Irish male saint Bairrfhionn, which is situated in the south of the townland of that name (5.2.2).[46] A holy well was dedicated to him north of the church, and a ring-barrow, *Sídh Bhairrfhionn* ("Bairrfhionn's otherworld dwelling/mound"), situated on a prominent hill in Creevy townland, was named after him (Fig. 2.2). Bairrfhionn translates as "white-topped" or "fair-headed," from *barr* (top) and *fionn* (white or fair). In reverse order, it forms the name Fionnbharr, as a result of which some saints are known by both names.[47] In the *Navigatio Sancti Brendani abbatis*, compiled between the early eighth and late ninth century, Bairrfhionn inspires St Brendan to find "*Terra repromissionis sanctorum*" ("Promised land of the saints"); in the mid-twelfth-century *Vita Merlini* he pilots Arthur's ship to Avalon; and in the late eleventh-century *Life of St David* he crosses the sea on horseback from Wales to Ireland, which has led to the suggestion that he was a sea deity in origin and possibly a manifestation of Manannán mac Lir.[48] While Bairrfhionn is personified as a guide in the texts, he may also be perceived as a saint of borderland. Church foundations associated with Bairrfhionn and Fionnbharr in Ireland were situated in premier borderlands and at crossings (5.2.2).

The borderland locus of the estate of the Mac an Bhaird poets at Ballymacaward is reflected in a *fert* (grave) situated among sand dunes and rabbit warrens on the western coast (Fig. 2.2). O'Brien's excavations of the Ballymacaward *fert* (1997–8) uncovered a cairn heaped onto outcropping rock in which two Bronze Age cists and an Iron Age pit containing the cremated remains of a female were found. In a small kerbed annexe at the northeastern edge of the cairn, deposits of cremated bone and charcoal, dating from between the first and fourth centuries, became the site of two episodes of insertion of female graves in the mid-fifth and early to mid-seventh century.[49] Charles-Edwards has

---

[44] C. B. Long *et al.* 1999 *Geology of south Donegal: a geological description of south Donegal, to accompany the bedrock geology 1:100,000 scale map series, sheet 3/4, south Donegal.* Dublin. Geological Survey of Ireland.

[45] NFC 1027, 75. National Folklore Collection, University College Dublin. A story collected from James Cassidy by Michael Cassidy, Ballyshannon, Co. Donegal, 1937–9.

[46] See "Cell Bhairrfhinn" in E. Hogan 1910 *Onomasticon Goedelicum*, 176. Dublin: Hodges, Figgis and Co.; Allingham, *Ballyshannon*, 16.

[47] A. C. L. Brown 1901 Barintus. *Revue Celtique* 22, 339–44; Ó Riain, *Dictionary*, 83.

[48] J. S. Mackley 2008 *The legend of St Brendan: a comparative study of the Latin and Anglo-Norman versions*, 81. Leiden and Boston. Brill; Brown, Barintus, 341.

[49] E. O'Brien 2020 *Mapping death: burial in late Iron Age and early medieval Ireland*, 13. Dublin. Four Courts Press; E. O'Brien 1999 Excavation of a multi-period burial site at Ballymacaward, Ballyshannon, Co. Donegal. *Donegal Annual* 51, 56–61.

interpreted Old Irish *fert* as an ancestral burial place used as a boundary marker, especially invoked in disputes over territorial claims.[50] The *fert* is normally distinguished by female burials inserted into a prehistoric sepulchral monument between AD 400 and 700. The purpose of this practice by ruling kindreds of early medieval kingdoms seems to have been to reinforce their claims to their territories. Burials may also have been introduced by an intrusive group to associate themselves with prehistoric "ancestors" and thereby legitimize their claim to new territory.[51]

The female presence in the Ballymacaward *fert* is intimated by the names attributed to a small lake on its northeast side (Fig. 2.2). Lough Namanfin, from the Irish *Loch na mBan Fionn*, which translates as "lake of the white, bright, or fair women," is also known as Lough Namansheefroge, a corruption of the Irish *Loch na mBan Síofróg*, "lake of the otherworldly women."[52] The women of the Ballymacaward *fert* and those referenced in the place name of the lake are perhaps a remarkable synchronism between the deposition of female burials in the cairn between the fifth and eight centuries and the naming of the lake.

Crossing to the south side of the Erne estuary, the most striking aspect of the land-scape are the gleaming sandhills of Finner (*Fionnúir*), overlooking Donegal Bay (Fig. 2.3),[53] which was the setting of Ballymunterhiggin, an estate of a branch of the Ó hUiginn poets. Finner had a strong prehistoric character, noted by Wakeman in the nineteenth century for its "array of primitive antiquities, sepulchral mounds, giants' graves, pillar stones and caves, and at least one cromleac, still most interesting, though recently denuded of its covering-stone."[54] Borlase recorded five megalithic antiquities in Finner in 1897, three of which have survived. They include a standing stone on Finner Hill and a cruciform passage tomb on the edge of the rabbit warren in the sands to the northeast of the hill.[55] Among the lost monuments of Finner are a former megalithic tomb and a monument attributed to Fionn mac Cumhaill, described in local tradition of 1898 as "the grave of the famous Irish Giant Fin Macoul" (1.3).[56] Over the rest of this landscape there are standing stones, ring-barrows, and a court tomb in Ballymunterhiggin itself (Fig. 2.3).[57]

---

[50] T. M. Charles-Edwards 1976 Boundaries in Irish law. In P. H. Sawyer (ed.), *Medieval settlement: continuity and change*, 83–7. London. Edward Arnold.

[51] E. O'Brien and E. Bhreathnach 2011 Irish boundary *ferta*, their physical manifestation and historical context. In F. Edmonds and P. Russell (eds), *Tome: studies in medieval Celtic history and law in honour of Thomas Charles-Edwards*, 55. Studies in Celtic history: 31. Woodbridge. Boydell Press.

[52] Allingham, *Ballyshannon*, 104; O'Brien and Bhreathnach, Irish boundary *ferta*, 60; In local lore, the daughters of Mac an Bhaird drowned in the lake. NFC 1029, 313. National Folklore Collection, University College Dublin. A story collected from Mary Regan, Ballyshannon, 1937–8.

[53] Allingham, *Ballyshannon*, 104.

[54] W. F. Wakeman 1896 Lough Erne and Ballyshannon excursion. *JRSAI* 26, 298; K. McDonald 2009 The lost tombs of Finner Camp, Co. Donegal. *Defence Forces Review*, 1–9.

[55] W. C. Borlase 1897 *The dolmens of Ireland*, i, 237–8. London. Chapman and Hall.

[56] McDonald, Lost tombs, 3.

[57] E. Cody 2002 *Survey of the megalithic tombs of Ireland, vi: County Donegal*, 17–20. Dublin. The Stationery Office.

The three estates discussed here have been conceptualized as late medieval mne-monics of the Erne estuary borderland, their learned occupants from *c*.1400 imbri-cated with the earlier manifestations of this in-between place. Their presence served to embolden the status of the estuary landscape as a pedigreed borderscape of long standing for the chiefs of Tír Conaill.

2.1.2 Poets in the landscape of Slieve Callan

The Mac Bruaideadha poets and chroniclers were among the most high-profile learned kindreds in Ireland, especially during the sixteenth and early seventeenth cen-turies. There were several branches of them, and their leading representatives served the family of Uí Bhriain, overlords of Tuadhmhumhain. The branch of particular interest to this chapter was settled at Slieve Callan, an extensive upland in south-central Co. Clare.

The Slieve Callan mountain landscape was a place of pedigree. It straddled the Gaelic lordships of Cineál bhFearmaic and Uí Bhreacáin (the modern baronies of Inchiquin and Ibrickan) and their pre-twelfth-century antecedent *trícha cét* territories (Fig. 2.4). The progenitors of the learned kindred of Mac Bruaideadha had been rul-ers of the pre-Norman *trícha cét* of Cenél Fermaic between *c*.1069 and 1114.[58] Both lordships were subject to the overlordship of the Uí Bhriain of Tuadhmhumhain. Furthermore, the landscape of Slieve Callan (*Collán*) is historically cited as the most westerly point of the pre-Norman overkingdom of the early medieval Dál Cais kings from whom the overlords of Tuadhmhumhain claimed their descent. A topographical poem of the late fourteenth or early fifteenth century cites the bounds of early medi-eval Dál Cais as "from Slieve Callan eastwards to the River Shannon" ("*ó Chollán soir go Sionainn*").[59] The designation of Slieve Callan (391 m OD) as a desirable bound-ary point of the former overkingdom reflected its status as a notable landmark.

The estate of the Mac Bruaideadha poets on that boundary is known from the six-teenth century. Situated within the old monastic termon of *Díseart* (Dysart), a place name that implies a desert or eremitic landscape,[60] it was mensal land of the bishop of Killaloe and incorporated about 5,000 acres of upland called Lettermoylan (*Leitir Maoláin*) and Formoyle (*Formaoil*).[61] The summit of Slieve Callan lay within the estate (Fig. 2.5).

---

[58] M.A. O'Brien (ed.) 1976 *Corpus genealogiarum Hiberniae*, i, 392. Dublin Institute for Advanced Studies; MacCotter, *Medieval Ireland*, 193.

[59] Carney (ed.), *Topographical poems*, 57, 125.

[60] McInerney, Lettermoylan, 85–7, 101; W. Davies 2014 Monastic landscapes and society. In J. H. Arnold (ed.), *The Oxford handbook of medieval Christianity*, 132–3. Oxford University Press.

[61] McInerney (Lettermoylan, 11, 221n.) estimates that Lettermoylan constituted 2,927 acres incorporating Ballynoe, Glennageer, Knockalassa, and Magherabaun. The combined townlands of Formoyle Eighteragh and Formoyle Oughteragh constitute 2,202 acres.

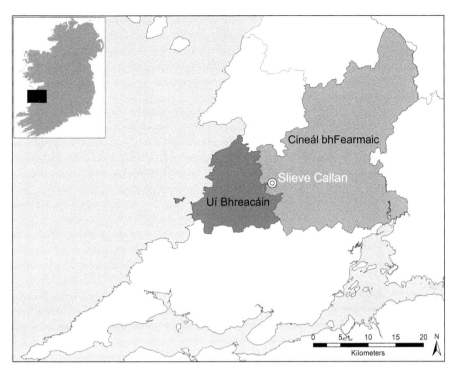

Cineál bhFearmaic

Slieve Callan

Uí Bhreacáin

FIG. 2.4. Slieve Callan in its territorial context (map N. McCarthy).

The saint, Mac Creiche of Díseart, is associated with a building held to have been a church, at Ballynoe, in the eastern extent of the estate (6.3; Fig. 2.5).[62] The relationship of the kindred with Mac Creiche suggests that they were *airchinnigh* of his church, but there is no corroborative evidence for members of the family in that office. Lettermoylan is obsolete as a place name. It is documented on the Down Survey barony map of Inchiquin, 1656–8, which shows that it extended from the River Inagh westwards to Slieve Callan incorporating several townlands including Knockalassa and the summit of Slieve Callan (Fig. 2.5).[63] Lettermoylan is cited in the chronicles in connection with the death there in 1595 of Mac Con Ó Cléirigh, *ollamh* in *seanchas* to the Ó Domhnaill of Tír Conaill.[64] His father, the *ollamh* Cú Coigcríche Ó Cléirigh, had been in exile for a time in Tuadhmhumhain from 1546. Since the families were intermarried, it is likely that the *ollamh* had sheltered with the Mac Bruaideadha kindred during part of his exile.[65]

[62] Ó Riain, *Dictionary*, 420–3.

[63] <http://downsurvey.tchpc.tcd.ie/down-survey-maps.php#bm=Inchiquin&c=Clare> (accessed February 16, 2022); McInerney, Lettermoylan, 81–2, 111–12.

[64] M 1595.6. vi, 1960, 1961.

[65] P. Walsh 1938 *The Ó Cléirigh family of Tír Conaill: an essay*, 12–16. Dublin. Three Candles.

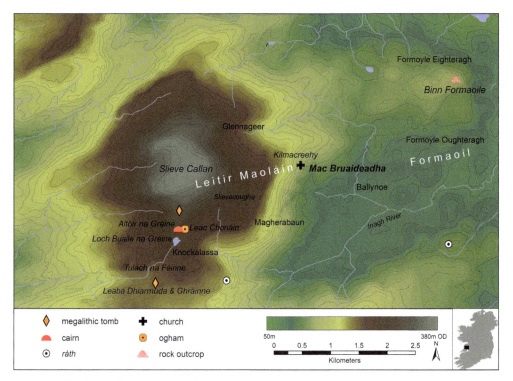

FIG. 2.5. The lands of the Mac Bruaideadha poets in the landscape of Slieve Callan, with *Binn Formaoile* top right (map N. McCarthy).

The presence of Ó Cléirigh learned men at Lettermoylan in the sixteenth century suggests that the Mac Bruaideadha poets had a building somewhere on their lands, perhaps a place to which they retreated to compose. They may have used the building dedicated to Mac Creiche in Ballynoe, the collapsed remains of which lie in commercial forestry west of Mount Callan House (Fig. 2.5). In common with several other late medieval "church" buildings on estates of learned families explored in Chapter 5, the building at Ballynoe has very low ecclesiastical visibility. Such buildings were, arguably, space for learned occupations rather than exclusively centers of spirituality, whether later adapted to that role or built for that purpose from the outset (5.1, 5.2, 6.3).

The identity of the lands of the Mac Bruaideadha poets as borderscape is compounded by the medieval place name *Binn Formaoile* ("peak of the bare-topped hill"), given to the highest point of the townland of Formoyle Eighteragh, a short distance northeast of Slieve Callan (Fig. 2.4). It has been established that hills described as *formaoil* (from OI *formáel*, meaning bare-topped) were symbolic components of borderlands of pre-twelfth-century territories and had continuity or re-use as pedigreed boundary landmarks of lordships (2.3).[66] *Binn Formaoile* is mentioned in the

[66] E. FitzPatrick 2013a *Formaoil na Fiann*: hunting preserves and assembly places in Gaelic Ireland. In D. Furchtgott, G. Henley and M. Holmberg (eds), *Proceedings of the Harvard Celtic Colloquium* 32, 2012,

chronicles as the place to which a faction of the Uí Bhriain and their allies retreated during a very violent conflict in a long internecine war in 1573.[67] A reading of the Irish forms of Formoyle and Lettermoylan in the Slieve Callan landscape, not just as a wet, bare upland environment, but a symbolically interstitial landscape, informs the domain of this poetic kindred.[68]

Other place names on their estate emphasize the bareness of the upland, a "stream-wasted mountain-height," as a Mac Bruaideadha poet described it in "A partition of Ireland," composed during the 1580s.[69] He complained that "from Inagh to Collán's slope—lands with most game are mostly alike—no one ever got poorer land and realm as share." He portrayed his Lettermoylan landholding as a harsh place that few coveted.[70] The hinterland of Slieve Callan was historically known as Bréntír Fearmacaigh or *Bréan Tír* ("the sour land") because, as described in the fourteenth-century *Caithréim Thoirdhealbhaigh* ("Triumphs of Turlough"), it was a wild, wooded, and lonely place, in the middle of which lay flat-topped Slieve Callan.[71] The vegetation cover of Slieve Callan and its historic place names point to rough grazing land. The mountain is a wetland consisting of blanket bog, grassland, and marsh, wet heath, scrub, rich fen, and flush.[72] Hazel, oak, and ash are its natural woodland cover, but plantations of conifers now dominate the mountain slopes and its lowland skirt. The keeping of cattle by the Mac Bruaideadha poets in this landscape is alluded to in the chronicles. In a raid into Tuadhmhumhain by the Ó Domhnaill chief of Tír Conaill in 1599, Mac Bruaideadha's cattle were taken but later returned to him at his request (3.3).[73]

Slieve Callan was a Lughnasa festive height.[74] Lughnasa (one of the quarterly feasts of the old Irish year) was a celebration of the harvest. In pre-Norman Ireland it assumed the form of an *óenach*, a periodic or seasonal gathering of a *túath* or larger territory presided over by a king.[75] Its central figure was the god Lugh, a master of many crafts (an *ollamh*, in effect) and the most brilliant of the immortals of Irish myth (2.1.1). The record of the celebration of the festival on Slieve Callan dates from the nineteenth century and later but, because it was held in a historic borderland, a typical

101–11. Cambridge, Mass. Harvard University Press; E. FitzPatrick 2019, Finn's wilderness and boundary landforms in medieval Ireland. In M. Egeler (ed.), *Landscape and myth in northwestern Europe*, 113–14, 124–9, 133, 136–8, 140–1. Borders, boundaries, landscapes: 2. Turnhout. Brepols.

[67] M 1573.10, iv, 1672, 1673. O'Donovan (6n., 1672) renders the place name "Binn-Formaoile."
[68] FitzPatrick, Finn's wilderness, 113–46.
[69] L. McKenna 1929b A partition of Ireland, part 2. *The Irish Monthly* 57 (673), 368.
[70] L. McKenna 1929a A partition of Ireland, part 1. *The Irish Monthly* 57 (672), 331.
[71] S. H. O'Grady (ed. and tr.) 1929 *Caithréim Thoirdhealbhaigh: the triumphs of Turlough*, 2 vols. London. Irish Texts Society, ii, 14. T. J. Westropp 1916 Notes on certain primitive remains (forts and dolmens) in Inagh and Killeimer, Co. Clare: part xiv (continued). *JRSAI* 6 (2), 101–2.
[72] P. J. Crushell and P. Foss 2008 *The County Clare wetland survey*, 140. Ennis. Clare County Council.
[73] M 1599.20, vi, 2104, 2105.   [74] MacNeill, *Festival of Lughnasa*, 193–201.
[75] C. Ó Danachair 1959 The quarter days in Irish tradition. *Arv: Journal of Scandinavian Folklore* 15, 47–55; MacNeill, *Festival of Lughnasa*, 1.

venue for an early medieval *óenach* and its intrinsic display of royal power, the annual Lughnasa celebration is likely to have had much earlier origins. The *óenach* was a political assembly with ritual associations, distinguished by horse and chariot races, trading, markets, and social festivities. Prehistoric funerary monuments and a boundary location were prerequisites of *óenach* venues.[76] In MacNeill's study of the festival of Lughnasa, she noted that the seasonal festivities at Slieve Callan had certain features "familiar to us from other mountains where Lughnasa was celebrated."[77] These included practices associated with particular monuments and a tale of a monster associated with the mountain, in which the legendary hero Fionn mac Cumhaill banished the phantom of Slieve Callan to Doolough, a lake to the south of the mountain.[78] The layering of place names and stories onto antiquities and topography at Slieve Callan is typical of the perception of prominent landmarks in the borderland estates of leading poets (2.3) and hints at a former early medieval royal assembly place of the Dál Cais kings.

The focus of the festive site was a cluster of megalithic monuments situated on the southern downslope of the mountain (Fig. 2.5). There are recollections of a local scholar (O'Looney), from 1844 and 1859, of their association with the celebration of Lughnasa at harvest time. He recalled that the "milking place of the sun" ("*Buaile na Gréine*") was the focus of Lughnasa celebrations at Slieve Callan and the site of what he believed was an earlier *óenach*.[79] He had witnessed the local cultural practices relating to the survival of the festival on the first Sunday of August 1844.[80] The megalithic monuments associated with the *óenach* were, according to him, "Conán's bed" ("*Leaba Chonáin*"); "altar of the sun" ("*Altóir na Gréine*"), a cairn and an associated megalithic tomb; "bed of Diarmuid and Gráinne" ("*Leaba Dhiarmuda agus Ghráinne*"), a wedge tomb north of the road that skirts the southern foot of Slieve Callan. They also included an unclassified megalithic tomb north of *Leaba Chonáin* on the upper reaches of the mountain (Fig. 2.5). Of these, the "bed of Diarmuid and Gráinne" is the only one to have survived intact (Fig. 2.6).

The archaeological identities of *Altóir na Gréine* and *Leaba Chonáin* are difficult to pin down.[81] However, the former (destroyed in 1859) was apparently a substantial megalithic tomb with a partially surviving cairn, while *Leaba Chonáin* was a composite monument that incorporated "Conán's flagstone or quarried stone" ("*Leac Chonáin*"). It was situated on the north side of *Loch Buaile na Gréine* (Fig. 2.5), in

[76] MacNeill, *Festival of Lughnasa*, 3–11, 311–49; P. Gleeson 2015 Kingdoms, communities, and *óenaig. Journal of the North Atlantic, Special Volume 8: Debating the Thing in the North II: Selected Papers from Workshops Organized by the Assembly Project*, 33–51.

[77] MacNeill, *Festival of Lughnasa*, 201.　　[78] MacNeill, *Festival of Lughnasa*, 199–200.

[79] S. Ferguson 1879b On the evidences bearing on sun-worship at Mount Callan, Co. Clare. *PRIA* 1, 267.

[80] Ferguson, On the evidences, 266.　　[81] Ferguson, On the evidences, 266–70.

FIG. 2.6. The wedge tomb, *Leaba Dhiarmuda agus Ghráinne*, Slieve Callan (Macnamara Photographic Collection, courtesy of Clare County Library).

an area of the mountain that carried the name "hill or mound of the *fían*" ("*Tulach na Féinne*") after the warrior band of Fionn mac Cumhaill (2.4).[82]

Popular belief of the eighteenth and nineteenth centuries linked both the *leaba* and the *leac* to the grave of Conán Maol, who was associated in local folklore with the mythological Conán mac Morna, also known as "Conán Maol na Mallacht", a member of Fionn's *fían*, with a reputation as a troublemaker.[83] His epithet *maol* (bald, bare) arose from an encounter with the Otherworld, where he lost the skin of his buttocks.[84]

[82] Ferguson, On the evidences, 269.

[83] Recorded by Burchett, cited in S. Ferguson 1879c On the alleged literary forgery respecting sun-worship on Mount Callan. *PRIA* 1, 322.

[84] This episode occurs in the late medieval Gaelic prose romance *Bruidhean chaorthainn*, which tells how Fionn and his men were entrapped in a disquieting otherworld hostel. Nagy, *Wisdom of the outlaw*, 154–5; D. A. Miller 2000 *The epic hero*, 155. Baltimore and London. Johns Hopkins University Press; O. Bergin and J. MacNeill (eds) 1901 *Eachtra Lomnochtáin [an tsléibhe riffe]*. Dublin. Gaelic League.

Leaba Chonáin appears to have been a monument in the form of a low memorial cairn (*leacht*), on top of which the half-reclining *Leac Chonáin* was positioned. The *leac*, according to Ferguson's record, was over 3 m long, 1 m wide, and 0.3 m thick, inclining southeast and facing towards *Buaile na Gréine*.[85] It carried an ogham inscription. By 1859 *Leaba Chonáin* and the *leac* had been removed from the mountain, the cairn was destroyed and the *leac* broken, but the pieces were returned to its original site and rearranged on a small pile of stones.[86] It is this reconstructed monument that Ferguson sketched in 1868 (Fig. 2.7).[87] Whether it was restored to the exact location in 1859 is itself disputed, as the first Ordnance Survey of the 1840s marked "Conan's Monument" around 200 m further north.

The alleged association of *Leac Chonáin* with Conán Maol was the subject of a prolonged controversy among Irish antiquaries.[88] The *leac* and its ogham inscription

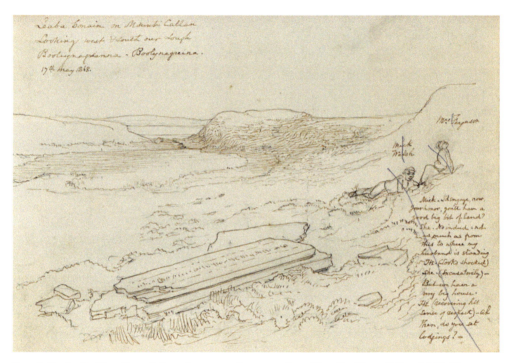

Fɪɢ. 2.7. *Leaba Chonáin* and the ogham stone known as *Leac Chonáin*, Slieve Callan, 1868. The struck-out text is by a later hand. From S. Ferguson's sketchbook of antiquities (NLI PD 2040 TX, 25, courtesy of the National Library of Ireland).

[85] S. Ferguson 1879a On the ogham-inscribed stone on Callan Mountain, Co. Clare. *PRIA* 1, 169–70.

[86] Ferguson, On the ogham-inscribed stone, 170–1.

[87] NLI PD 2040 TX, 25, 1868, Sketchbook of antiquities, mainly from Co. Clare by Sir Samuel Ferguson. Dublin. National Library of Ireland.

[88] T.J. Westropp 1904 Antiquities near Miltown Malbay, County Clare. *Journal of the Limerick Field Club* 2 (8), 250–54.

was first documented in 1780 by Lloyd.[89] In 1785, Vallancey claimed that he had identified it as Conán's burial place, based on a verse in the narrative *The battle of Gabhra*—"his grave was dug on the north-west side of the black mountain of Callán, and his name is inscribed in Ogham on a hewn stone."[90] Encouraged by Vallancey, the young student Theophilus O'Flanagan recorded the stone on Slieve Callan in 1785 and reported on it in 1787.[91] However, both the ogham and the verse were subsequently deemed forgeries by other scholars. Ledwich (1790) condemned O'Flanagan's "discovery" as "one of the boldest, most artless and groundless figments offered to the learned world."[92] Vallancey's citation was exposed as spurious by O'Kearney (1853), who noted that "the verses recording the death of Conán...cannot now be found in any copy extant."[93]

Leac Chonáin is identifiable today as a recumbent ogham stone (2.85 × 0.85 m) embedded in blanket bog on the northeast side of the lake called *Loch Buaile na Gréine*. The earliest ogham stones were placed in borderlands. Using a system of notches and horizontal or diagonal score-marks to represent the sounds of an early form of the Irish language, they date back at least as early as the fifth century and appear to relate to a practice of "placing the graves of dead kinsmen on the boundary of the kindred's land."[94] The now very eroded and just partially visible ogham inscription on *Leac Chonáin* is cut along a horizontal stem-line and not in the typically early ogham position along the edge of the stone. In modern scholarship it has been viewed as a forgery that was carved by O'Flanagan between 1785 and 1787 "to provide evidence of an Irish origin to Macpherson's Ossian."[95] However, Lloyd had already described the monument in 1780. Furthermore, local legend, collected in 1785, and in 1875 (from an old man who had lived in the mountain all his life and who had learned about *Leac Chonáin* from his father, who lived to be 103), related that it was the grave of Conán.[96] Therefore, there appears to have been an a priori tradition that linked Conán with the *leac*, before the ogham controversy began.

---

[89] J. Lloyd 1780 *A short tour and impartial and accurate description of the county of Clare*, 9. Ennis.

[90] C. Vallancey 1785 Observations on the alphabet of the pagan Irish and the age in which Finn and Ossian lived. *Archaeologia* 7, 276–85.

[91] T. O'Flanagan 1787 An account of an antient inscription in ogam character on the sepulchral monument of an Irish chief, discovered by Theophilus O'Flanagan, student of T.C.D. *Transactions of the Royal Irish Academy* 1, 3–16.

[92] E. Ledwich 1804 *Antiquities of Ireland: the second edition, with additions and corrections, to which is added, a collection of miscellaneous antiquities*, 341. Dublin. Grueber; D. A. Beaufort 1792 *Memoir of a map of Ireland*. Dublin and London.

[93] N. O'Kearney 1853 The battle of Gabhra: Garristown in the county of Dublin fought AD 283. *Transactions of the Ossianic Society* 1, 99. Dublin. John O'Daly.

[94] T. M. Charles-Edwards 2000 *Early Christian Ireland*, 175. Cambridge University Press.

[95] S. de hÓir 1983 The Mount Callan ogham stone and its context. *North Munster Antiquarian Journal* 25, 43.

[96] Recorded by Burton, cited in C. Vallancey 1786 *Collectanea de rebus Hibernicis*, 4, 528–9. Dublin. R. Marchbank; Ferguson, On the alleged literary forgery, 322.

Ferguson, who published three papers on the controversy in 1879, sensibly pointed out that the ogham inscription was unlikely to have been inscribed by O'Flanagan under instruction from Vallancey. He wrote, "in truth, the difficulty of such a fabrication would be so great, and the chances of detection so imminent, that, unless to serve the purpose of some contemplated literary fraud to be put in practice soon after its perpetration, the roguery cannot be conceived to be entertained by any reasonable being."[97] He also observed that the form of the ogham, drawn on a medial or horizontal line, was comparable to that found in medieval manuscripts, giving some credibility to the monument as late ogham.[98] It has been suggested that "scholastic ogham," reproduced in manuscripts and on bone, stone, and metal, over the long period from the eighth century to the nineteenth, was essentially a display of learning, with no more serious purpose than that.[99] For instance, an entire folio of the *Book of Ballymote* (*c.*1391) is dedicated to a key to the ogham alphabet, and ogham is twice displayed in the book (1564–70) of the brehon lawyer Domhnall Ó Duibhdábhoireann (6.1.2).[100] However, others eschew the use of the term "scholastic" and view such late ogham as essentially a continuum of the ogham tradition.[101] By the late medieval period the practice of using ogham was, in a sense, a learned conceit and an antiquarian practice.

In two drawings (Figs 2.8a, 2.8b) that Ferguson made of the Slieve Callan ogham stone in 1868, which he amended in 1870 and 1872, he noted that the inscription was "much abraided and uncertain" and that the letter strokes were smoothly incised while the stem-line and frame-lines were picked out. He read it as "FAN LIA DO LICA CONAF [N] COLGAC COSOBADA [C]" ("Under this stone is laid Conaf [n] the fierce [and] turbulent").[102] He expressed his uncertainty about Conán again in a letter dated 1887 in which he suggested it might also read "Collas" or "Cosas."[103]

The summit of Slieve Callan was integral to the estate of the Mac Bruaideadha poets. Moreover, as descendants of the dynasts of the pre-Norman *trícha cét* of Cenél Fermaic, they may have perceived the mountain heritage as personal to their own history.[104] Irrespective of whether Conán's name was inscribed on *Leac Chonáin* or not, Ferguson's interpretation of the whole inscription as late-tradition ogham, and not an eighteenth-century hoax, intimates that it may have originated with a Mac Bruaideadha poet during the sixteenth or the seventeenth century,[105] perhaps in

---

[97] Ferguson, On the ogham-inscribed stone, 168.   [98] Ferguson, On the ogham-inscribed stone, 168.
[99] De hÓir, The Mount Callan ogham stone, 43.
[100] RIA MS 23 P 12, The book of Ballymote, fo. 170r. Dublin. Royal Irish Academy; BL Egerton MS 88, 1564–70, Irish legal and grammatical miscellany compiled by Domhnall Ó Duibhdábhoirenn. London. British Library.
[101] I am grateful to Professor Katherine Forsyth for this perspective.
[102] NLI PD 2040 TX, 21–2, 23–4; Ferguson, On the ogham-inscribed stone, 171.
[103] S. Ferguson 1887 *Ogham inscriptions in Ireland, Wales, and Scotland*, 53–4. Edinburgh. David Douglas.
[104] MacCotter, *Medieval Ireland*, 193.   [105] Macnamara, O'Davorens, 153.

(a)

(b)

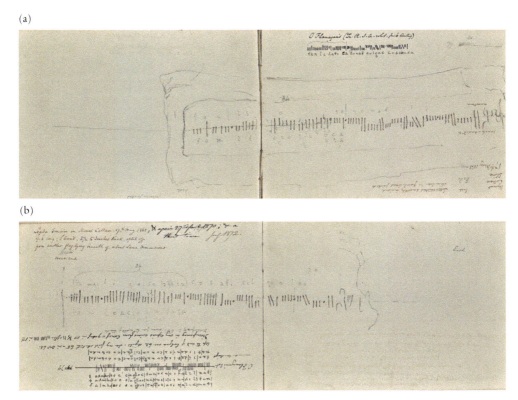

FIG. 2.8. Ferguson's first (a) and second (b) readings of the ogham inscription on *Leac Chonáin*, Slieve Callan (NLI PD 2040 TX, 21–4, courtesy of the National Library of Ireland).

commemoration of the historically important role of their mountain as a boundary place of the overkingdom of the Dál gCais kings. The location of Slieve Callan, combined with the connotations of *Formaoil* as the domain of the border hero Fionn mac Cumhaill, the setting of the ogham stone among prehistoric antiquities, and the traditions relating to a seasonal assembly on the mountain at Lughnasa, lend support to that view and imply a seminal role for the Mac Bruaideadha poets as keepers of the mountain landscape (2.3).

2.1.3 Literati in the landscape of Lough Gill

At different moments in time, members of learned kindreds are found in borderlands of lordships that were contested places. In north Connacht there were two pre-Norman *túatha*, Calraighe and Clann Fhearmhaíghe, that were coveted and a source of conflict between the three lordships of West Bréifne, Cairbre, and Tír Oilella-Corran (Fig. 2.9). They shared Lough Gill, a freshwater lake in the modern counties of Sligo and Leitrim, which contains about twenty islands, the largest of which is Inishmore or Church Island. Lough Gill is historically renowned for an

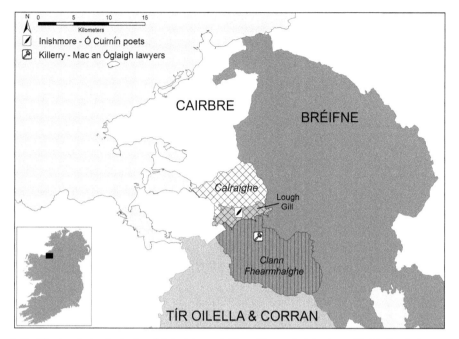

Fig. 2.9. The borderland *túatha* of Calraighe and Clann Fhearmhaíghe (map N. McCarthy).

abundance of spring salmon and brown trout, and the hinterland and islands are sylvan with oak, rowan, willow, and yew. It marks the meeting of sedimentary and metamorphic rocks, with hills and uplands of limestone and calcareous shale to the north, and mountains of paragneiss to the south. The topography of the north shore is characterized by rocky hillocks isolated from each other by a network of small valleys, with the bald summit of Formoyle (*Formaoil*) and the terraced Doons notable among them (Fig. 2.10). Precipitous cliffs and scars of limestone upland, including Slievemore, Cope's Mountain, the Crockauns, Keelogyboy, Leean Mountain, and Benbo, form a dramatic backdrop to the hills.[106] The south shore of Lough Gill is dominated by the domed forms of Killerry Mountain and Slieve Daeane, separated by Slishwood.

The *túath* of Calraighe was especially coveted and contested by the Ó Ruairc chief of West Bréifne and the Ó Conchobhair-Sligo chief of Cairbre from the fourteenth century to the end of the sixteenth. Some of those contests were recorded in the chronicles. A major battle was fought in the *túath* in 1346 between Ó Ruairc and Ó Conchobhair-Sligo, in which Ó Ruairc was defeated and killed by the Mac Donnchadha chief of Tír Oilella-Corran.[107] A small lake called Loughanelteen (*Loch Chinn Eiltín*, "lake of the head of the little doe"), situated on the north side of Lough Gill, is said

---

[106] J. R. Kilroe 1885 *Explanatory memoir to accompany sheet 55 of the maps of the Geological Survey of Ireland comprising portions of the counties of Sligo and Leitrim*, 8. Dublin. HMSO.

[107] AConn 1346.2, 298, 299.

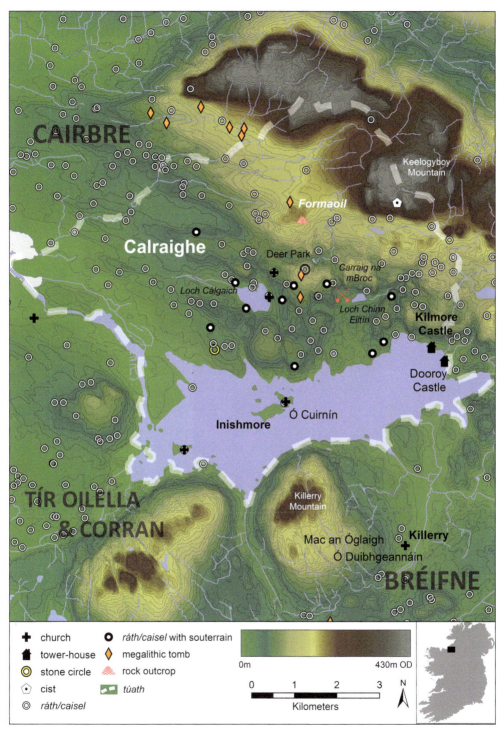

Fig. 2.10. Archaeology and topography, *túath* of Calraighe, and north Clann Fhearmhaíghe (map N. McCarthy).

to have been the setting of that battle (Figs 2.10, 2.14).[108] After 1346, Calraighe was considered part of the lordship of Cairbre, but it continued to be claimed by Ó Ruairc. Other recorded instances of conflict include a war in 1545 between Ó Ruairc and the son of Ó Conchobhair-Sligo.[109]

What was the historical relationship between Bréifne, Cairbre, and the *túath* of Calraighe? The *túath* was a possession of the powerful overkingdom of Uí Briúin Bréifne from at least 1029 until the late twelfth century.[110] The overkingdom extended from the River Sligo to the River Boyne in Meath during that period, and the *túath* of Calraighe lay on its northwestern edge (Fig. 2.11).[111] The expansion of the Bréifne overkingdom ceased after the defeat of Ó Ruairc by the Anglo-Norman magnate Hugh de Lacy in 1173.[112] Bréifne subsequently contracted to a modest lordship.

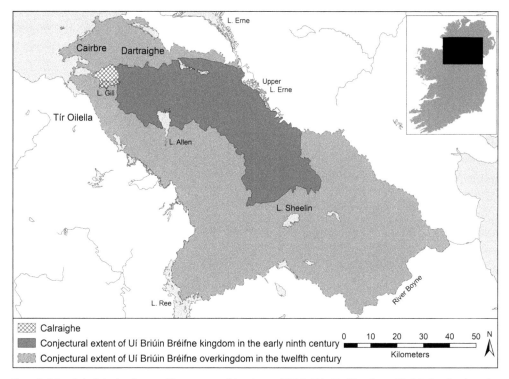

Fig. 2.11. Calraighe in the pre-Norman overkingdom of Uí Briúin Bréifne (map N. McCarthy, based on Ó Corráin 1972, 170).

[108] NFC 159, 212. National Folklore Collection, University College Dublin. A story collected from an "old man" by Annie Cullen, Calry, Co. Sligo, 1937–8.

[109] M 1545.10, v, 1492, 1493.

[110] T 1029.2, 369; By 1029, the expansionist overkingdom of Bréifne appears to have absorbed the kingdom of Cairbre, including the *túath* of Calraighe.

[111] D. Ó Corráin 1972 *Ireland before the Normans*, 10, 170. Dublin. Gill and Macmillan.

[112] F. J. Byrne 1987 The trembling sod: Ireland in 1169. In A. Cosgrove (ed.), *A new history of Ireland, ii: medieval Ireland 1169–1534*, 36–7. Oxford University Press.

When the boundaries between Cairbre and Bréifne were remade, possession of Calraighe became a source of conflict between the two lordships, with the Ó Ruairc chief claiming it as part of his patrimonial lands. What had once been royal marchland of a great overkingdom subsequently became disputed territory (Fig. 2.11).

Successive Ó Ruairc chiefs placed great importance on making their claim to Calraighe visible. Various strategies were used to achieve this, from inscribing entitlement to it in an encomiastic poem, to prosecuting livestock raids, maintaining a presence of literati, and positioning elite buildings in the *túath* landscape. In his inaugural ode for Brian Ó Ruairc, chief-elect of West Bréifne, the poet Fearghal Óg Mac an Bhaird (fl. 1560–1620) addressed him as "*Rí Calraighe na gcreach líonmhar*" ("king of Calraighe, of numerous cattle raids"), with the implication that Calraighe was Ó Ruairc's patrimony, from which he raided the livestock of rival territories.[113] Raiding by chiefs was a potent political practice.[114] Some raids were conducted in the borderland environs of learned kindred landholdings. They include the already noted (2.1.2) seizure of cattle in 1599 on the Slieve Callan estate of the Mac Bruaideadha poets, another in 1468 adjacent to Ballymackeagan (2.3.1), an estate of a branch of the Mac Aodhagáin lawyers in the lordship of southern Anghal (Co. Longford), and earlier, in 1392, on the lands of the poet Ó Cobhthaigh (2.3), in the lordship of Fir Tulach (Co. Westmeath).

One of the boldest statements of entitlement to Calraighe by Ó Ruairc was the tower-house that he built at Kilmore on the eastern shore of Lough Gill, referred to as Newtown or *Baile Nua* ("new settlement") in 1546 (Fig. 2.10).[115] The wall-footings of the tower-house and occupation material relating to it were recovered during excavations (1971–5) in the bawn of Parke's Castle, a fortified house built on the site of the tower-house in the seventeenth century. Newtown appears to have been built in the late fifteenth or early sixteenth century.[116] It was one of two Ó Ruairc castles on the eastern shore. The other, Dooroy (*Dubhráth*), stood 500 m to the south of Newtown, but when it originated has not yet been established. The Tudor governor of Connacht, Sir Richard Bingham, in his description of the lands of Ó Ruairc's country in 1591–2, remarked that "O Rourke's house, called the Newton [*recte* Newtown], is in none of these baronies [the five that constituted West Bréifne], but standeth upon the border of his country, near to Sligo."[117] Bingham was referring to the *túath* of Calraighe as the location of Ó Ruairc's castle and demesne.

---

[113] E. Knott 1957 (reprint 1981) *An introduction to Irish syllabic poetry of the period 1200–1600*, 23. Dublin Institute for Advanced Studies.

[114] U 1482, iii, 278, 281. Brian Ó Néill is attributed "most of raids of borderlands in his time."

[115] ALC 1546, ii, 348, 349.

[116] C. Foley and C. Donnelly 2012 *Parke's Castle, Co. Leitrim: archaeology, history and architecture*, 121–37. Archaeological monograph series: 7. Dublin. The Stationery Office.

[117] H. C. Hamilton 1885 *Calendar of the state papers relating to Ireland, of the reign of Elizabeth, 1588, August–1592, September*, iv, 464. London. HMSO.

The other highly visible and more enduring expression of the respective claims of the Ó Ruairc and Ó Conchobair-Sligo chiefs to Calraighe was the presence on the lake and the southeast shore of the poets, historians, lawyers, and musicians who served them between the fourteenth and sixteenth centuries (Fig. 2.10). The Ó Cuirnín *ollamh* in poetry, as recorded for the fifteenth century, resided on Inishmore at the center of the lake, where he was also *comharba* of the island church (5.2.1; Fig. 2.12).[118] The pedigree of the Ó Cuirnín poets suggests that they were among the early septs of Calraighe and that they had deep roots as a learned kindred in the landscape of Lough Gill.[119] Members of the kindred were court poets at least as early as 1347, when Sigraid Ó Cuirnín is cited as a learned poet and *ollamh* of Bréifne.[120] The deaths of several other members of the Ó Cuirnín family, who either held the position of *ollamh* or were in line for it, are chronicled for the fourteenth and fifteenth centuries. These include Domhnall, described as "prospective" *ollamh*, who died of plague in 1399, and Cathal, who passed away in 1411 before he succeeded to the office.[121] They were also historians and musicians, with Matthew (d. 1429), *ollamh* of Bréifne, described as universally learned in history and music, and Manus (d. 1459)

FIG. 2.12. Keelogyboy Mountain and Inishmore Island, Lough Gill (photo E. FitzPatrick).

[118] FitzPatrick, *Formaoil na Fiann*, 105–10, 117.
[119] Hogan, *Onomasticon Goedelicum*, 152.   [120] M 1347.13, iii, 589, 590.
[121] AConn 1399.16, 374, 375; AConn 1411.22, 411, 412.

cited as chief historian to Ó Ruairc.[122] They had additional roles as preceptors or teachers—Cormac Ó Cuirnín (d. 1475) was "a teacher [*oide eges*] of the learned of Ireland."[123] In the early fifteenth century, there was factionalism among them, with some of the kindred serving Ó Ruairc and others Ó Conchobhair-Sligo of Cairbre.[124]

Chronicle entries for 1416 confirm that the Ó Cuirnín *ollamh* to Ó Ruairc was, at that time, a churchman living on Inishmore.[125] There was a conflagration on the island in 1416, as a result of which he lost many of his valuables, including manuscripts, an ornamental cup, his timpe [*tiompán*], and his harp, but it is not stated whether it was accidental or the result of an attack (5.2.1).[126] In naming the belongings that he lost in the fire, the chroniclers emphasized his role as a learned person.

Mac an Óglaigh, *ollamh* in law to the Ó Ruairc chief of West Bréifne, had an ecclesiastical estate on the south side of the lake in the *túath* of Clann Fhearmhaíghe (Fig. 2.10). The chronicled death of Tómas Mac an Óglaigh in 1416 described him as chief professor of law in Connacht and *airchinneach* of the medieval parish church of Killerry.[127] From at least the first half of the fourteenth century into the first half of the fifteenth, members of the Mac an Óglaigh kindred simultaneously held the position of *ollamh* in law and *airchinneach*, and also archdeacon, of Killerry (*Cill Oiridh*).[128] The medieval parish of Killerry was part of the old *túath* landscape of Clann Fhearmhaíghe (Fig. 2.9). The termon lands of Killerry Church constituted *c.*1,975 acres, including Killerry Mountain. It was marginal, consisting of upland, underwood, and wet but very rich pastureland—especially so in the summer season (Fig. 2.13).

Clann Fhearmhaíghe was disputed between West Bréifne, Cairbre, and Tír Oilella-Corran and, like Calraighe, it was regarded as a territory apart (Fig. 2.9).[129] In the earliest acknowledgment of Ó Ruairc's claim to that *túath* in 1228, he was addressed in the chronicles as "king of Clann Fhearmhaighe."[130] The contest over the *túath* climaxed in the late fourteenth century between the three rival lordships. As late as 1585, when it had been held by Ó Ruairc for some time, Ó Conchobhair-Sligo tried to claim it.[131]

Members of the Ó Duibhgeannáin learned kindred lived in the lake landscape too. In 1561 Naoisse mac Cithruaidh Ó Duibhgeannáin, "the most eminent musician that was in Erinn," drowned in Lough Gill along with his unnamed wife, who

---

[122] M 1429.12, iv, 876, 877; M 1459.12, iv, 1004, 1005.   [123] AConn 1475.25, 574, 575.

[124] AConn 1409.8, 404, 405; M 1409.8, iv, 798, 799.   [125] AConn 1258.12, 128, 129.

[126] AConn 1416.23, 430, 431; M 1416.17, iv, 828, 829.

[127] M 1416.4, iv, 824, 825; AConn 1416.8, 428, 429.

[128] M 1333.1 iii, 550, 551; AConn 1362.15, 322, 323; Costello, *De annatis Hiberniae*, i, 57, 159; Twemlow, *Calendar of entries in the papal registers*, viii.

[129] M. J. Connellan 1951 Killery: an artificial adjunct of Tirerrill. *Journal of Ardagh and Clonmacnoise Antiquarian Society* 2 (12), 30.

[130] AConn 1228.12, 30, 31.   [131] Connellan, Killerry, 30–1.

FIG. 2.13. Cattle in a summer meadow, Killerry (photo E. FitzPatrick).

was the daughter of the Mac Donnchadha chief of Tír Oilella-Corran.[132] His son, Cithruadh mac Naoisse Ó Duibhgeannáin, was cited of Killerry in a pardon of 1590.[133]

The special relationship between the Ó Ruairc chiefs, their learned kindreds, and the *túatha* of Calraighe and Clann Fhearmhaíghe suggests that both *túatha* had an important role in the former early medieval overkingdom of Uí Briúin Bréifne (Fig. 2.11). The evident beauty and cultural resources of Calraighe, combined with the fact that it had been on the edge of a great overkingdom, intimates that together with Clann Fhearmhaíghe, it may have been a preserve of the kings of Uí Briúin Bréifne. An interpretation of Calraighe and Clann Fhearmhaíghe as early medieval royal marchland, perhaps even a royal forest,[134] of the Bréifne overkingdom, would also explain why both were viewed as extra-social space in the late medieval and early modern political geography of north Connacht, and so coveted.

Some support for this idea is found in an exceptional landscape with characteristics of a pre-Norman Gaelic royal center extending over the townlands of Formoyle and

---

[132] ALC 1561.12, ii, 380, 381.   [133] Nicholls, *Irish fiants*, iii, 108 [5439].

[134] E. FitzPatrick 2017 Finn's seat: topographies of power and royal marchlands of Gaelic polities in medieval Ireland. *Landscape History* 38:2, 29, 30, 45, 51, 59; FitzPatrick, Finn's wilderness, 114, 117, 136, 142; D. Rollason 2016 *The power of place: rulers and their palaces, landscapes, cities, and holy places*, 136–67. Princeton University Press.

Deerpark, opposite Inishmore, on the north side of Lough Gill (Fig. 2.14). There are traditions of an assembly place and a royal burial site of a king of Connacht associated with it.[135] From this place the great landmarks of north Connacht, including the Bricklieve Mountains and Knocknarea, are at once visible. Formoyle, from *formaoil* (already met in the context of the Slieve Callan borderland of the Mac Bruaideadha estate 2.1.2) is a distinctive hill consisting of a bald mass of limestone, rich in fossils and veined with calcite. It stands among a concentration of prehistoric funerary monuments (Figs 2.14, 2.15).

The rough pastureland where most of the monuments are found was enclosed as a deer park *c*.1722.[136] It contains one of the largest Neolithic court tombs in Ireland, recorded as both "*Leacht Con Mic Ruis*" and "*Leac Con Mic Ruis*" ("memorial cairn/stone of Con, son of Ros").[137] In local folklore of the last century, the tomb is pointed out as the burial place of Eogan Bél, a sixth-century king of Connacht (Fig. 2.16).[138] The heroic death and burial of Eogan are described in the Middle Irish tale *Caithréim Cellaigh* (also known as *Beatha Cheallaigh*), "The martial career of Cellach" (his son). According to that tale, following Eogan's death at the battle of Sligo, his remains were translated to a grave and buried face downward at "*Óenach Locha Gile*", the seasonal assembly place of Lough Gill (Fig. 2.14).[139] As noted (2.1.2), *óenach* settings included a range of sepulchral monuments, notably megalithic tombs, with and without their cairn coverings, as well as later Bronze Age and Iron Age burial and ritual monuments.[140] The intensely prehistoric, funerary aspect of the landscape of Formoyle and Deerpark is in keeping with the general profile of early medieval *óenach* venues (2.1.2, 2.4).

The *primh-druith* (chief poet) and *primh-ollamh* (chief learned one) of Connacht, Muireadhach Ua Cárthaigh, is recorded in this landscape for the year 1067. He was drowned in "*Loch Cálgaich*", a small lake just west of the court tomb (Fig. 2.14).[141] It would have been an event of significance that required the chief learned person of the province of Connacht to be at this location in 1067. It happened to be the year when Áed Ua Ruairc, king of Uí Briúin Bréifne, also became king of all Connacht

---

[135] FitzPatrick, Finn's wilderness, 125–6, 135–6; FitzPatrick, Formaoil na Fiann, 32, 105–8.

[136] *Registry of deeds*, vol. 34, 110 (Deed 20784) notes that it was a new deer park in 1722.

[137] T. J. Westropp 1887 The rude stone monuments of Ireland. *JRSAI* 8, 136; W. J. Hemp 1931 Leac Con Mic Ruis, Co. Sligo. *Antiquity* 5 (17), 98–101; S. Ó Nualláin 1989 *Survey of the megalithic tombs of Ireland, v, County Sligo*, 47. Dublin. The Stationery Office.

[138] NFC 159, 236–7. Brian Hargadon, an 82-year-old man from Colgagh, Co. Sligo, told the story that "The Giants Grave is situated in the Deerpark...some say that Giants were buried there and that it got its name from them. Others say that Owen Bell [Eogan Bél] was buried there and others say it was a Druids altar"; FitzPatrick, *Formaoil na Fiann*, 108.

[139] Byrne, *Irish kings*, 244; FitzPatrick, *Formaoil na Fiann*, 108.

[140] Gleeson, Kingdoms, communities, 40–3; E. FitzPatrick 2015a Assembly places and elite collective identities in medieval Ireland. *Journal of the North Atlantic, Special Volume 8: Debating the Thing in the North II: Selected Papers from Workshops Organized by the Assembly Project*, 55.

[141] T 1067.1, 405, 406; M 1067.6, ii, 892, 893; Hogan, *Onomasticon Goedelicum*, 496.

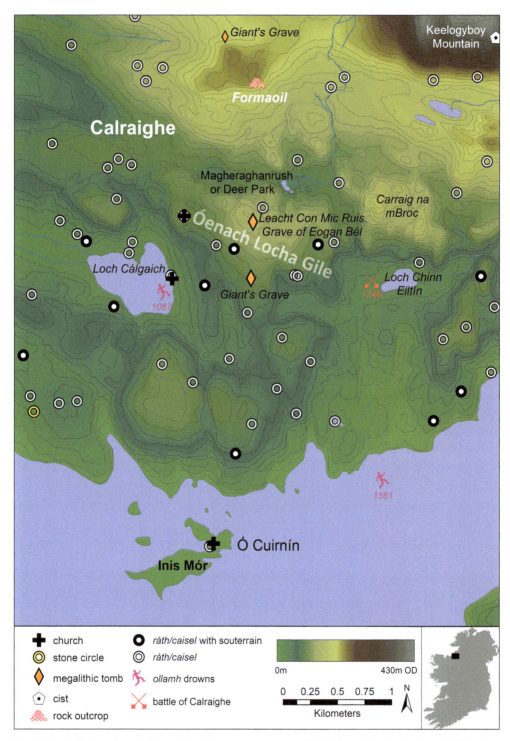

FIG. 2.14. The location of *Formaoil* and the proposed sites of *Loch Cálgaich* and the *óenach* of Lough Gill in Calraighe. The density of *ráth/caisel* sites suggests a populous landscape (map N. McCarthy).

FIG. 2.15. The distinct bare head of *Formaoil* in the *túath* of Calraighe (photo E. FitzPatrick).

FIG. 2.16. Deerpark court tomb, south of *Formaoil*, Lough Gill (photo E. FitzPatrick).

(1067–87).[142] It is conceivable that *Óenach Locha Gile* in the *túath* of Calraighe was a habitual assembly place of the pre-Norman overkingdom of Uí Briúin Bréifne, because it was situated on the northwestern edge of that extensive territory (Fig. 2.11). In his capacity as the new king of Connacht, Áed Ua Ruairc may have convened an *óenach* there in 1067, with his *ollamh* in attendance. Whether the landscape of *Óenach Locha Gile* had an after-life as a place of assembly for the Ó Conchobhair-Sligo chiefs of Cairbre in the late medieval period is unknown, but its territorial geography, extraordinary views, archaeological profile, and traditions as the alleged burial place of a historic king of Connacht and early medieval royal assembly, are attributes consistent with inauguration and *oireachtas* venues (2.2).[143]

The pedigree of the borderland *túath* of Calraighe was generated by its historicized monuments and landscape, and by the presence of learned people. It was both a prize and an enduring source of conflict for the lordships that laid claim to it.

2.2 PLACES OF POLITICAL ASSEMBLY

The estates of prominent kindreds of poets, lawyers, and physicians were situated in landscapes of political assembly that had various histories as venues for inauguration ceremonies, parliaments (*oireachtais*), peace-making events, and pre-Norman seasonal assemblies (*óenaigh*).[144] This juxtaposition is manifested by the presence of literati in borderscapes where there are notable prehistoric ritual and funerary monuments inferred as assembly venues in place names, literary allusions, or in more recent local lore. The locations of the *óenaigh* or seasonal assembly sites of *Óenach Buaile na Gréine* on the Slieve Callan lands of the Mac Bruaideadha poets (2.1.2) and *Óenach Locha Gile* in the *túath* of Calraighe (2.1.3) have been proposed using that premise. Whether they were active as sites of political assembly 1300–1600 in their respective lordships, or just valued as pedigreed places of the earlier overkingdoms of Dál Cais and Uí Briúin Bréifne, has not been proven, but continuity of *óenach* locations as inauguration venues and parley sites did happen in other lordships.

The estate of the Ó hÍceadha medical family was situated on the west side of Magh Adhair (Co. Clare), a political assembly place of long standing (Fig. 2.17).[145] It was frequented in the later medieval period and into the late sixteenth century by the Uí Bhriain overlords of Tuadhmhumhain and their principal vassals the Mac Conmara

---

[142] U 1067.4, i, 504, 505; <https://www.dib.ie/biography/ua-ruairc-aed-a8752> (accessed March 25, 2022).

[143] FitzPatrick, *Royal inauguration*, 40–97.

[144] Political assembly is defined here as an occasion when a group, often relatively large, convened for a specific purpose. It follows that set out in P. S. Barnwell and M. Mostert (eds) 2003 *Political assemblies in the earlier Middle Ages*, 3. Studies in the Early Middle Ages, 3. Turnhout. Brepols.

[145] FitzPatrick, *Ollamh, biatach, comharba*, 180.

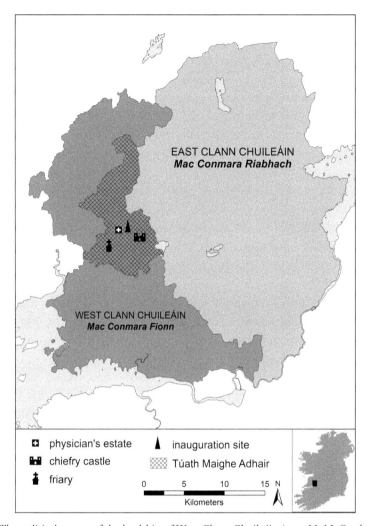

Fɪɢ. 2.17. The political center of the lordship of West Clann Chuileáin (map N. McCarthy).

chiefs of Clann Chuileáin.[146] The Ó hÍceadha kindred were hereditary physicians and
ollamhain in medicine to both the chief and the overlord. In 1586 the representative
of the family had an estate of one-and-a-half quarters of land at Ballyhickey.[147] Their
estate was named after them and was larger than the unit represented by the modern
townland of Ballyhickey (Fig. 3.18).[148]

---

[146] FitzPatrick, *Royal inauguration*, 52–9; O'Grady, *Caithréim Thoirdhealbhaigh*, i, 2, 5, 9, 31, 48–9, 50, 76, ii,
2, 6, 10, 32–3, 46–7, 48, 69.

[147] McInerney, West Clann Chuiléin lordship, 41.

[148] The estate included the townland of Drim. FitzPatrick, *Ollamh, biatach, comharba*, 175–6.

Ballyhickey was a parcel of *lucht tighe* (mensal land), of the Mac Conmara chief,[149] which had a much earlier and distinguished pedigree as part of the pre-Norman *túath* of Magh Adhair.[150] It was a place where the early medieval Dál Cais dynasty had held their royal assemblies, and where their kings had been inaugurated.[151] The place name of the *túath* translates as "Adar's plain" after the hero Adar, whose medieval genealogy attached him to the pre-Norman Dál Cais dynasty.[152] There were several reasons why the incoming Dál Cais appropriated the *túath* as royal land for their use between the eighth and tenth centuries (3.4). The remarkably well-preserved late prehistoric landscape of the *túath*, which incorporated hilltop and ceremonial enclosures, cairns, mounds, megalithic tombs, and standing stones, provided the essential antiquities for memorialization of the dynasty (Figs 2.18, 3.18). Within that landscape they adopted Magh Adhair, a complex of monuments at the junction of the Hell River and the Boolyree River, as their assembly place.[153] It later became the inauguration site and *oireachtais* venue of the overlords of Tuadhmhumhain, who claimed the Dál Cais as their "ancestors."[154]

The physician's estate at Ballyhickey was integral to the concentrated late prehistoric and early medieval landscape of the assembly site (Fig. 3.18). It incorporated medieval settlement enclosures, and a range of prehistoric monuments among which survive a large hilltop enclosure, a wedge tomb, a standing stone, and a burnt mound. The relatively good preservation of some of those monuments, especially the hilltop enclosure and wedge tomb, suggests that they may have been protected as mnemonics of the heroic past of Adar, and were perhaps even curated by the learned Ó hÍceadha physicians (Fig. 2.18). In the late medieval period, the *túath* landscape became an important borderland area and new political center when, following his death in 1366, the chief's sons divided Clann Chuiléain into east and west parts (Fig. 2.17).[155] Subsequently, Mac Conmara Riabhach held East Clann Chuileáin, while the more powerful Mac Conmara Fionn became chief of West Clann Chuileáin, assuming the *túath* of Magh Adhair as his center of power.

When the Ó hÍceadha physicians were first settled onto the *lucht tighe* of the Mac Conmara Fionn is not known, but it was probably from 1366 when the landscape of Magh Adhair became the head place of the West Clann Chuileáin lordship. Their addition to Adar's plain can be seen as part of the gradual evolution of a powerful geopolitical space for the Mac Conmara Fionn lordship and their overlords, which

[149] McInerney, West Clann Chuiléin lordship, 41.

[150] Nugent, *Gaelic clans*, 131, 132, 143, 144; FitzPatrick, *Royal inauguration*, 206.

[151] FitzPatrick, *Royal inauguration*, 57–9.   [152] O'Brien, *Corpus*, i, 243.

[153] E. Grogan 2005 *The North Munster Project, i: the later prehistoric landscape of south-east Clare*. Discovery Programme monograph: 6. Dublin. Wordwell; Magh Adhair is referred to as an "aenach" (*óenach*) in M 981.8, ii, 715; FitzPatrick, *Royal inauguration*, 52–9.

[154] FitzPatrick, *Royal inauguration*, 52–9; M. V. Ronan 1937 Some mediaeval documents. *JRSAI* 7 (2), 231.

[155] N. C. Macnamara 1896 *The story of an Irish sept*, 138. London. J. M. Dent; FitzPatrick, *Royal inauguration*, 206; Carney, *Topographical poems*, 58, "Mac Conmara of Magh Adhair".

FIG. 2.18. A wedge tomb on the physician's estate, Ballyhickey (photo E. FitzPatrick).

was based on and retained elements of the Dál Cais royal center and the legacy of prehistory.

There are indications in other lordships that it was not uncommon for estates of literati to be sited close to assembly places. A list of the granges of Boyle Abbey (Co. Roscommon) in the lordship of Magh Luirg, compiled between 1593 and 1603, included "Grange O'Mulchonry," which was grange land named after the poetic kindred of Ó Maoilchonaire.[156] The grange consisted of 70 acres of arable and 120 acres of mountain, situated south of the abbey and partly identifiable in the modern landscape with the townland of Grange Beg. On its immediate east side, in the townland of Knockadoobrusna, there is a drumlin ridge, the summit of which is distinguished by a large two-tiered mound—a bowl-barrow with what appears to be a small secondary mound on top. The monument is conjoined by an impressive henge and dominates a

---

[156] J. Hardiman (ed.) 1826 *Inquisitionum in officio rotulorum cancellariae Hiberniae*, i, 42. Dublin. Grierson and Keene.

complex of barrows that extend over the broad ridge. The prehistoric funerary character of this site and the historical circumstances of its setting within the lordship of Magh Luirg, support an identity for it as "Cruachan" (hill, mound), the recorded inauguration venue of the Mac Diarmada ruling family in 1315 and 1478.[157] The proximity of Ó Maoilchonaire's grange to this striking monumentalized ridge in the sixteenth century, and the setting of both within a premier borderland of the lordship (Fig. 1.2), suggests that his lineage may have held it from an earlier period. The main branch of the Ó Maoilchonaire kindred are best known as inaugurators and poets to the Ó Conchobhair chiefs of Machaire Chonnacht. However, by 1310, the Mac Diarmada chiefs, as principal vassals of their Ó Conchobhair overlords, assumed the role of inaugurator.[158] There is evidence to suggest that an Ó Maoilchonaire poet was writing praise poems for the Mac Diarmada family in the fifteenth century.[159] It is plausible, therefore, that a member of the kindred assumed the role of poet and inaugurator to the chiefs of Magh Luirg in the fourteenth or fifteenth century, at which time the grange land beside the numinous complex of prehistoric graves was allocated to him as his estate.

As earlier noted (2.1.1), the term *sídh* (OI *síd*) was applied to hills and mounds in the estuary landscape of Tír Conaill where its use contributed to making the medieval southern borderland. A connection with practices of lordly authority was noted in relation to *Mullach Sídhe*, where the chief of Tír Conaill presided over executions. *Sídh* is complex in its range of meanings, variously connoting the seat of a god, a fairy hill, and an otherworld dwelling, usually expressed as a prehistoric funerary mound.[160] But it also refers to "peace," which is of interest in the context of the use of the term "tulach síodh" by a sixteenth-century poet for the venue of his anticipated participation in future agreements between territories.[161] In one of two poems composed *c.*1589 for the chief of Fir Mhanach, the poet Eochaidh Ó hEódhasa complained to him, "If you think it is no loss to you that I am far away from you in time of assemblies, then can I endure the envy and harshness that I must bear living in an outlying border territory."[162] He stressed that he was entitled to be "chosen to go to the 'peace-mound' [*tulach síodh*]."[163] The context of his remarks is that he had been allocated a landholding in the vulnerable northern borderland of the lordship but he

---

[157] E. FitzPatrick 2001 The gathering place of Tír Fhiachrach? Archaeological and folkloric investigations at Aughris, Co. Sligo, *Proceedings of the Royal Irish Academy* 101C, 83–4; FitzPatrick, *Royal inauguration*, 82–4.

[158] FitzPatrick, *Royal inauguration*, 181.

[159] M. Hoyne (ed.) 2018 *Fuidheall Áir: bardic poems on the Meic Dhiarmada of Magh Luirg c.1377–c.1637*, 71. Dublin Institute for Advanced Studies.

[160] G. Bondarenko 2014 *Studies in Irish mythology, ix*, 30–4. Berlin. Curach Bhán.

[161] T. Ó Cathasaigh, 1977–8 The semantics of síd. *Éigse* 17, 146–50; P. Sims-Williams 1990 Some Celtic Otherworld terms, 61. In A. T. E. Matonis and D. F. Melia (eds), *Celtic language, Celtic literature*. Van Nuys. Ford and Bailie.

[162] J. Carney 1975 Eochaidh Ó hEoghusa, poet to the Maguires of Fermanagh. *Clogher Record* 3, 200.

[163] Carney, Eochaidh Ó hEoghusa, 200; Breatnach (Chief's poet, 56) translates "*tulach síodh*" as "peace-mound."

wished to be close to the chief's castle at Enniskillen and to the assembly place of the ruling family.

The gathering place of Fir Mhanach, for inauguration ceremonies and for *oireachtais* or parliaments, was Cornashee, southeast of Enniskillen. The written record of its use is for the sixteenth century, but it was probably a venue for lordly assemblies as early as the thirteenth century when the family of Mág Uidhir emerged as the most dominant within Fir Mhanach.[164] There are two sites within the assembly landscape of Cornashee that fit the descriptor "*tulach síodh.*" The first is an impressive prehistoric round cairn at Cornashee (*Ceathramhadh na Sídh*, "quarterland of the otherworld/ peace mound"),[165] upon which the chiefs-elect of Fir Mhanach were inaugurated. The second site is *Sídh Bheag* ("little otherworld mound"), a hengeiform enclosure and barrow situated south of the round cairn.[166]

Whether the mounds, barrows, and cairns that ruling families used for their inaugurations also functioned as "peace-mounds" for arbitration and making covenants has not been determined with certainty. However, the recorded circumstances and setting of a covenant made in 1566, between the chiefs of the midland lordships of Cineál bhFiachach and Muintir Thadhgáin, provides some clarity about the type of venue used, the status of the agreement, and the literati involved (Fig. 1.1). The covenant formally acknowledged the submission of the Ó Catharnaigh chief of Muintir Thadhgáin to the overlordship of Mac Eochagáin of Cineál bhFiachach.[167]

The venue for the covenant was *Suidhe Adhamhnáin* ("Adhamhnán's seat"),[168] later Anglicized as Syonan, Co. Westmeath. It has been identified as a former Bronze Age mound-barrow on the drift ridge of an esker, situated in the western borderland of the lordship of Cineál bhFiachach where it met the lordship of Muintir Thadhgáin (Fig. 2.19).[169] It was not the inauguration venue of the Mac Eochagáin chiefs; *Cnoc Buadha*, a bowl-barrow in the southern borderland of the lordship, facilitated that ritual.[170]

---

[164] FitzPatrick, *Royal inauguration*, 85.

[165] K. Muhr 2014 The place-names of County Fermanagh. In C. Foley and R. McHugh, *An archaeological survey of County Fermanagh i, part 1: the prehistoric period*, 40, 42. Newtownards. The Northern Ireland Environmental Agency.

[166] FitzPatrick, *Royal inauguration*, 84–7; E. FitzPatrick and E. Murphy *et al.*, 2011 Evoking the white mare: the cult landscape of Sgiath Gabhra and its medieval perception in Gaelic Fir Mhanach. In R. Schot, C. Newman, and E. Bhreathnach (eds), *Landscapes of cult and kingship*, 169–70, 181–3. Dublin. Four Courts Press.

[167] J. O'Donovan 1846a The covenant between Mageoghegan and the Fox, with brief historical notices of the two families. *The Miscellany of the Irish Archaeological Society*, i, 196, 197. Dublin. Irish Archaeological Society; According to P. Walsh (1932 Note on two Mageoghegans. *Irish Book Lover* 20, 75–81), O'Donovan incorrectly read the year of the making of the covenant as 1526. Walsh's reading suggests that it is 1566.

[168] O'Donovan, Covenant, 197; Ó Riain, *Dictionary*, 53–5.

[169] E. FitzPatrick 2022 Gaelic political assemblies and power-display in borderlands of Westmeath lordships. In S. O'Brien (ed.), *Westmeath: history and society*, 62–6. Dublin. Geography Publications.

[170] FitzPatrick, Gaelic political assemblies, 60–2.

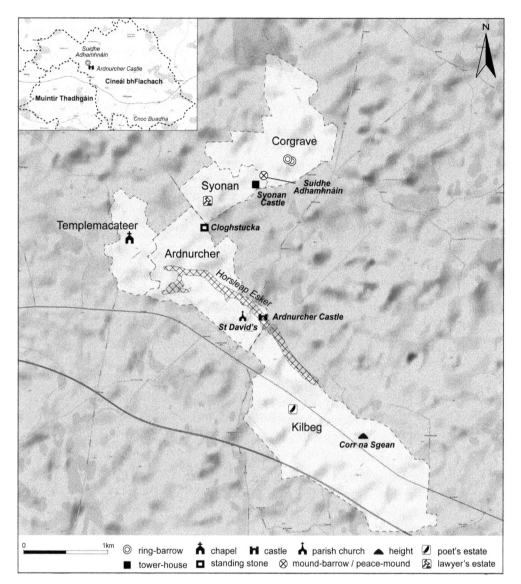

FIG. 2.19. Key sites of the borderland center of power of the overlordship of Cineál bhFiachach, *c.*1566, with inset showing its location in relation to the lordship of Muintir Thadhgáin (map S. Nylund).

That agreements were made at open-air venues in the sixteenth century, and presided over by brehon lawyers, was implied in 1577 by the scholar and diplomat Stanihurst. He observed that "the breighon sitteth on a banke, the lords and gentleman at variance round about him, and then they proceede."[171] By exploring the archaeology

---

[171] L. Miler and E. Power (eds) 1979 *Holinshed's Irish chronicle*, 114–15. Dublin. The Dolmen Press; N. Patterson 1989 Brehon law in late medieval Ireland: 'antiquarian and obsolete' or 'traditional and functional'? *Cambridge Medieval Celtic Studies* 17, 47.

and land occupancy of the borderscape in which *Suidhe Adhamháin* peace-mound was situated, it becomes clear that it was a center of power for the Mac Eochagáin rulers of Cineál bhFiachach between the fifteenth and seventeenth centuries, and that it was lived in and visited by poets and lawyers who served the lordships and the over-lordship.

The main residence of the Mac Eochagáin overlord, at least from the early fifteenth century, was Ardnurcher Castle, which was positioned on the line of Horseleap Esker, a long fluvio-glacial landform, 1.5 km south of the peace-mound (Fig. 2.19). The chiefry castle was symbolically important because it was on the site of an Anglo-Norman motte-and-bailey castle and medieval borough. The parish church of St David lay to the west of the castle, with Templemacateer, a chapel of ease, *c*.1.5 km to the northwest. Immediately around Ardnurcher, there is some evidence for the estates of literati who served the Mac Eochagáin overlord.

In 1600 the brehon lawyer Cairbre Mac Aodhagáin was living in Syonan, where there is a four-story tower-house just 200 m southwest of the peace-mound (Fig. 2.19).[172] Exactly when the Mac Aodhagáin brehons took up residence in that landscape is not known, but Cosnamach Óg Mac Aodhagáin, "law-*ollamh*" of Cineál bhFiachach was present in Mac Eochagáin's castle at Ardnurcher in 1422, which intimates that the family may have been resident at Syonan by that time.[173] South of Ardnurcher Castle, the large denomination of Kilbeg was occupied in the seventeenth century by a member of the Ó hUiginn poetic kindred.[174] The kindred are likely to have been established there in the fifteenth century, since one of their members served the Mac Eochagáin chief during that period. He was Maeleachlainn na nUirsgéal Ó hUiginn who composed a poem for Mac Eochagáin, which recalled the extent of the old *trícha cét* kingdom that had preceded the lordship (1.2.1).[175]

The covenant of 1566 designated both Ardnurcher and a place called "*Corr na Sgean*" as the venues for the overlord's biannual *oireachtas* or parliament.[176] The *oireachtas* was an institution of governance consisting mainly of a council of nobles.[177] It was convened as an open-air assembly at *Bealtaine* (May) and *Samhain* (November), two of the quarterly feasts of the old Irish year, when the Otherworld was traditionally deemed most accessible.[178] *Corr na Sgean* was identified in the seventeenth century as a subdivision of Kilbeg, which suggests that in the sixteenth century the *oireachtas* had been convened on or adjacent to the poet's estate (Fig. 2.19).[179]

Two of the most important figures in the making and witnessing of the agreement were not domiciled in the landscape where the declaration of overlordship had been

---

[172] O'Rahilly, Irish poets, 99.   [173] AConn 1422.9, 461.
[174] FitzPatrick, Gaelic political assemblies, 68.
[175] FitzPatrick, Gaelic political assemblies, 58.   [176] O'Donovan, Covenant, 192, 193.
[177] Simms, *From kings to warlords*, 64–5.   [178] Carey, Otherworlds, 32.
[179] P. Walsh 1957 *The place-names of Westmeath*, 256. Dublin Institute for Advanced Studies; In FitzPatrick, Gaelic political assemblies, 66, I was incorrect in suggesting that it might be found in the townland of Corgarve.

held in 1566. They were visitors to it. Their estates were situated around Kilcoursey Castle (Co. Offaly), the main residence and personal demesne of the Ó Catharnaigh chief, in the vassal lordship of Muintir Thadhgáin. Kilcoursey was a borderscape of Muintir Thadhgáin, touching the lordships of Cineál bhFiachach and Fir Cheall (Fig. 1.1). Muirchertach Ó Cionga, who was *ollamh* in poetry to the Mac Eochagáin overlord, was one of those figures. He witnessed the agreement at *Suidhe Adhamhnáin*, as *ollamh* of both lordships. Appropriately, he was described in the text of the agreement as "professor of both countries" ("*ollamh an da thir*").[180] He was also recorded in 1570 at Templemacateer where he wrote up an agreement on behalf of a member of Mac Eochagáin's family and her children (Fig. 2.19).[181] His estate at Kilcollin (Co. Offaly) was situated on the north side of Kilcoursey Castle (Fig. 1.2).[182] The other figure was the brehon lawyer Muirchertach Mac Aodhagáin. He is cited in the text of the covenant as the official to whom the Ó Catharnaigh vassal chief of Mac Eochagáin had recourse, if he were sued.[183] He held a large estate called Erry (from Irish *Aireamh* meaning cultivated land) immediately south of Kilcoursey Castle (Fig. 1.2).[184]

Recomposing this western borderscape of the overlordship of Cineál bhFiachach, from the starting point of the peace-mound used for the covenant of 1566, has enabled a view of the complexity of the relationships that literati had with centers of power in dominant and vassal territories during the sixteenth century.

2.3 POETS, STORIED TOPOGRAPHIES, AND MONUMENTS

Poets composing encomiastic poems for chiefs between the thirteenth and seventeenth centuries identified them with bare-topped hills which they referred to as *formaoil*, especially in relation to heroic deeds, or to evoke the site of a victory in battle.[185] A late example of this heroic association made between chiefs and bare-topped hills occurs in the late sixteenth-/early seventeenth-century poem "The tombs of friends are in the battle of Briain," composed by Fearghal Óg Mac an Bhaird. In it he described the chief of Ciannacht in north Ulster, as "king of the bare-topped hill" ("*rí Formaeile*").[186] An earlier instance of this interchange between poet, *formaoil*, and chief, can be found in Gofraidh Fionn Ó Dálaigh's fourteenth-century poem "Raised aloft is Murchadh's

---

[180] O'Donovan, The covenant, 196, 197.

[181] D. Harrel (ed.) 1897 The twenty-ninth report of the deputy keeper of the public records and keeper of state papers in Ireland, 44–5. Dublin. HMSO.

[182] K. W. Nicholls 1970 Some documents on Irish law and custom in the sixteenth century. *Analecta Hibernica* 26, 105–29.

[183] O'Donovan, Covenant, 192, 193.

[184] P. Walsh 1939 *The Mageoghegans*, 36. Mullingar. Westmeath Examiner.

[185] FitzPatrick, Finn's wilderness, 120.

[186] J. O'Donovan (ed.) 1849b *Miscellany of the Celtic Society*, i, 414–15. Dublin. The Celtic Society;

Banner," in which he referred to his patron as "the fair knight of Formaoil."[187] In his poem "Death of my Heart," the court poet of the chief of Tír Eoghain in the thirteenth century, Giolla Brighde Mac Con Midhe, recalled a significant battle for the chief's dynasty, "haughty were our men when we fought the battle of Formaoil." The battle fought in 967 CE saw the Cenél Conaill defeated by the Uí Néill ancestors of the chief.[188]

The bare-topped hill settings referenced by poets are the stuff of imagination in the Finn cycle of tales, where *Formaoil* is conceived as Fionn's quintessential domain, the landscape in which he and his warrior band hunt and fight.[189] The portrayal of his world in the tales, as a boundary zone "between and beyond tuatha,"[190] finds expression in real borderscapes distinguished by *formaoil* landforms.[191] As seen, just two instances of conflict are recorded in the securely identified context of *Formaoil* on the Mac Bruaideadha estate at Slieve Callan in the sixteenth century (2.1.2), and one major battle in Calraighe is chronicled for 1346 and referenced in folklore to the landscape of *Formaoil* by Lough Gill (2.1.3). But the fact that *formaoil* landforms are generally associated in historical and literary sources with medieval battles and violence suggests that those in Slieve Callan and Calraighe may have witnessed more and earlier conflicts.

There is some evidence that poets may have had a role as guardians of venerable bare-topped hills in borderscapes of lordships, or at least perceived themselves in that part. The close association made by poets between these timeless landmarks and chiefs, and the fact that they were invariably situated in borderlands, entails that they were regarded as validations of dynastic claims over territory.[192] The prehistoric profile of the archaeology of *formaoil* landscapes, with standing stones, stone circles, cairns, and megalithic tombs common to them, and hillforts on their summits in some instances, supports that interpretation.

The already mentioned fourteenth-century Munster poet Gofraidh Fionn Ó Dálaigh had a borderland estate called Ballydaly (*Baile Uí Dhálaigh*), which was at the foot of the hill of Claragh, a boundary landmark between the lordships of Dúthaigh Ealla and Iar Mhumhain (Fig. 1.2). He served both territories in the art of poetry.[193] Gofraidh dedicated an entire poem to the hill that overlooked his estate, lamenting its long association with conflict, battle, and death (Fig. 2.20).[194] Confirming that it was perceived as the *formaoil* of the lordship of Dúthaigh Ealla, he referred to the chief of

---

[187] L. McKenna (ed. and tr.) 1919 Historical poems of Gofraidh Fionn Ó Dálaigh. *Irish Monthly* 47 (549), 103.
[188] Williams, The Poems of Giolla Brighde, 148, 149; U 967.3, i, 405, 406.
[189] FitzPatrick, Finn's wilderness, 119-20, 129–41.   [190] Nagy, *Wisdom of the outlaw*, 36.
[191] FitzPatrick, *Formaoil na Fiann*, 103, 110, 117.
[192] FitzPatrick, *Formaoil na Fiann*, 103–4.
[193] McKenna, Historical poems of Gofraidh Fionn Ó Dálaigh, 166–70.
[194] McKenna, Historical poems, 166–70.

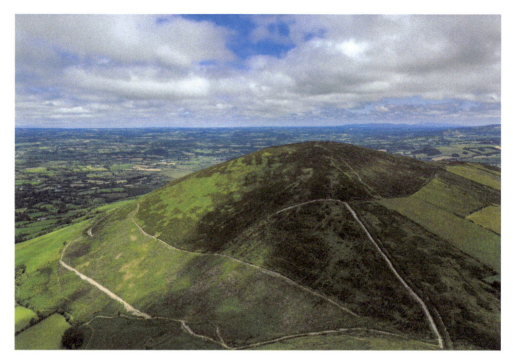

FIG. 2.20. The hill of Claragh and its summit hillfort in the western bounds of the lordship of Dúthaigh Ealla (photo Cillian Irish).

that lordship as "lord of the hill" ("*tighearna an chnuic*") and to Claragh itself as "the hill over Formhaoil's land" ("*an cnoc ós iath Fhormhaoile*").[195]

There is a hillfort on the summit of Claragh, a mnemonic of the violent past of a place of conflict in the poet's portrayal of "Formhaoil's land." It is a large drystone enclosure that incorporates a cairn and encompasses an area of over 1 hectare.[196] On the south side of the hill there are two stone circles and two standing stones. There is the scar of a second cairn on the southwest slope of the hill. Formerly conical and standing *c.* 1.5 m high and *c.* 2.5 m in diameter, the cairn had the name "Laghtnamna" ("monument of the woman")[197] suggesting possible origins as a *fert* or female boundary grave (2.1.1) The location and prehistory of the hill of Claragh, combined with the poetic allusions to it, communicate a quintessential role for it as a territorial landmark personal to the dynastic history of the chief of Dúthaigh Ealla.

A bare hill on a boundary, carrying the place name *formaoil*, can assist in corroborating the presence of a poet's estate. For instance, it has been suggested that *Baile Uí Ghéaráin*, the estate of Ó Géaráin, who was poet to the chief of Ciannacht in north

[195] McKenna, Historical poems, 169.

[196] W. O'Brien and J. O'Driscoll 2017 *Hillforts, warfare and society in Bronze Age Ireland*, 458. Oxford. Archaeopress.

[197] D. Power 1997 *Archaeological inventory of County Cork, volume 3: Mid Cork*, 148. Dublin. Government of Ireland.

Ulster, is synonymous with the townland of Evishagaran, Co. Derry (Fig. 1.2).[198] There is just the place name combining the family name to support this identification. However, the hilly grazingland of Evishagaran, bounded by the Gelvin River, is overlooked on the northeast side by the bare, bleak Formil Hill. Typical of the archaeology of the environs of *formaoil*, megalithic monuments including standing stones, a stone circle, and a cairn, are found on the south side of the hill.[199] The co-occurrence of this highly representative *formaoil*, with the family reference in the townland name, strengthens the case for Evishagaran as the poet's estate.

Hills and mountains carrying the place name *Suidhe Finn* ("Finn's seat", "white seat") are found again in the estate landscapes of poets. They are imagined in the Finn cycle of tales as the place from which Fionn observes the hunt.[200] The occurrence of the place name from the twelfth or thirteenth century onward is confirmed in Gaelic literature.[201] Several instances of the proximity of the estates of literati to hills and mountains named after Fionn mac Cumhaill have been observed. During the sixteenth century a branch of the Mac Craith kindred of poets of Munster had an estate at the foot of the volcanic hill of Knockseefin ("*Cnoc Suidhe Finn*", "hill of Finn's seat"), in Pallas Green (Co. Limerick).[202] In Ulster, the estates of the poetic kindreds of Mac an Bhaird of Ballyward and Ó Ruanadha of Ballyroney, as well as the Ó Siadhail physicians of Ballysheil, all of whom served the chiefs of Uí Eachach Coba (Co. Down), were massed around Seafin, a low hill with a castle, overlooking the River Bann (Fig. 1.2). During the progress of the Ordnance Survey of Co. Down in 1834, the legends of Seafin were recorded from an old woman "faithfully as she had heard them". She had been told that "Suidhe Finn signifies the Seat of Finn...the ruins of the castle at Seafin having been one of his military stations".[203] A variant of *Suidhe Finn*, Knockfin ("*Cnoc Finn*", "Finn's hill"), is also found in conjunction with learned kindred estates. In the sixteenth century and probably earlier, a branch of the renowned Connacht medical family of Ó Fearghusa were based at Oughaval (Co. Mayo), in the northeast boundary of the lordship of Umhaill (5.2; Fig. 1.2).[204] The landscape east of Oughaval is dominated by a long ridge rising to a bald summit (136 m OD) and at the foot of which, in the townland of Knockfin, there is an enclosure which has been known as "Finn Mac Cool's Grave" from at least as early as the first half of the nineteenth century.

An exemplary case of a mountain height, designated as *Suidhe Finn* on a poet's estate, occurs on Sheepshead Peninsula (Co. Cork) where it is found in conjunction with the local name *Formaoil*, given to the southern end of Dromnea Hill

---

[198] Hughes, Land acquisitions, 81–2.   [199] FitzPatrick, Finn's wilderness, 137–41.

[200] FitzPatrick Finn's seat, 29–62.   [201] See references in FitzPatrick, Finn's seat, 31–7.

[202] O'Rahilly, Irish poets, 93–4.

[203] RIA 14 C 13, Letters containing information relative to the antiquities of the county of Down, collected during the progress of the Ordnance Survey in 1834, by J. O'Donovan, 142–3. Dublin. Royal Irish Academy.

[204] R. Gillespie 2014 Scribes and manuscripts in Gaelic Ireland, 1400–1700. *Studia Hibernica* 40, 15–16.

(6.3.1; Fig. 6.27).[205] The Ó Dálaigh poets to the Ó Mathghamhna Fionn of the lordship of Fonn Iartharach ("western land"), and to the Anglo-Norman Carew family, lived on the peninsula (3.1; 6.3.1). They were well established there by *c*.1300, as attested by a plea roll dated 1299–1300, which records that the Anglo-Norman lord, Maurice Carew, sued them for lands there.[206] The lordship of Fonn Iartharach was the westernmost extent of the jurisdiction of Mac Cárthaigh Riabhach, chief of Cairbre in southwest Munster, who was overlord of Ó Mathghamhna Fionn (Fig. 2.21).[207]

The poets' peninsular estate was dominated by upland, extending westwards from Knockboolteenagh to Ballyroon Mountain at the tapering point of the peninsula. The main mountains of this range are Rosskerrig, Caher, and Seefin, which, at 352 m OD, is the highest point on the peninsula (Fig. 2.22). A locally preserved tale associates the bare mountain of Seefin with Fionn mac Cumhaill and his *fían*. It relates that Fionn sat on the mountain to wash his feet in Farranamanagh lake (Fig. 2.23). He kicked a piece of ground at the edge of the lake, which landed in the middle of Dunmanus Bay and became Carbery Island. Thereafter the mountain was called "Finn's seat".[208]

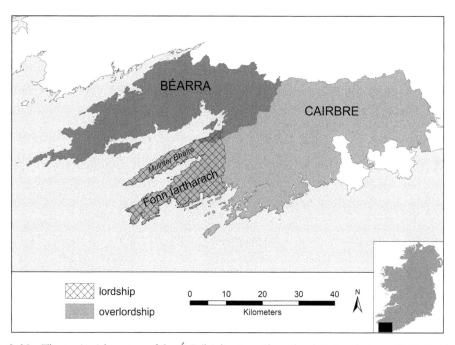

FIG. 2.21. The territorial context of the Ó Dálaigh estate, Sheepshead Peninsula (map N. McCarthy).

[205] FitzPatrick, *Ollamh, biatach, comharba*, 178-9; E. FitzPatrick 2013b The landscape and settlements of the Uí Dhálaigh poets of Muinter Bháire. In S. Duffy (ed.), *Princes, prelates, and poets in medieval Ireland: essays in honour of Katharine Simms*, 464. Dublin. Four Courts Press; J. Tierney 2016 Dromnea bardic school, Kilcrohane, Sheep's Head Peninsula, Co. Cork: conservation and tourism development, 9. Kinsale.

[206] Repertory of plea rolls 1815–25. In *Reports from the commissioners . . . respecting the public records of Ireland: with supplements and appendices*, ii. Report vi, 391, 573.

[207] C. O'Mahony 1913 *History of the O'Mahony septs of Kinelmeky and Ivagha*, 70. Cork. Guy and Co.

[208] A. McCarthy 2001 *Under the shadow of Suífinn: perspectives of Kilcrohane through the years*, 1. Kilcrohane.

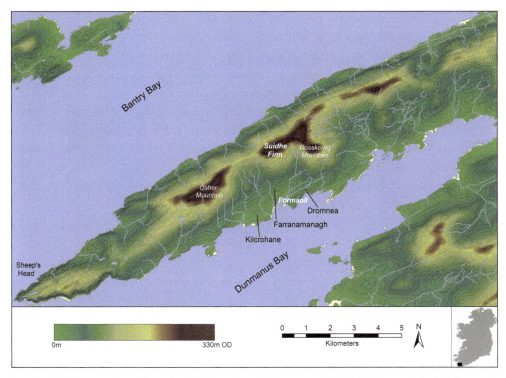

FIG. 2.22. Topography of Sheepshead Peninsula, with the mountain *Suidhe Finn* and the hill *Formaoil* (map N. McCarthy).

FIG. 2.23. Seefin Mountain (*Suidhe Finn*), Sheepshead Peninsula (photo E. FitzPatrick).

A study of the archaeology associated with instances of places named *Suidhe Finn* in Ireland has shown that over half of them are distinguished by hilltop cairns or mounds that may have had a role as signifiers of royal marchland.[209] On the narrow crest of the western declivity of Seefin Mountain, there is a cairn containing remains of a burial chamber. There are extensive views from the cairn across the peninsula, north to Bantry Bay and south to Dunmanus Bay. Seefin Mountain is such a dominant feature of the Ó Dálaigh estate, the poets may have been involved in naming it.

In view of the close relationship between bare-topped hills (with and without cairns), dynastic power, and the estates of poets, they need consideration as important landmarks of borderscapes and not just mnemonics of lore relating to Fionn mac Cumhaill.

2.4 CONCLUSIONS

The places in the lordships of Ireland where Gaelic kindreds of literati lived, were, in different ways, integral to the spatial politics of the ruling families they served. This study has identified a range of circumstances in which borderscapes involving the presence of literati emerged, with corresponding variation in how they were manifested. Borderlands were classified (1.2.1), in the first instance, as premier or subsidiary in status relative to whether they had been translated from pre-Norman polities to lordships. Subsequently, the circumstances in which borderscapes of power emerged at specific points within those borderlands were identified.

Literati mostly make an appearance in premier borderland spaces that had (a) chiefly residences newly built or repurposed from existing strongholds, from the fourteenth century to the late sixteenth, and around which *lucht tighe* lands were set aside for professionals and servitors; (b) church land where literati assumed roles as *comharbai* and *airchinnigh* from the thirteenth century to the seventeenth century; and (c) upland or marginal land distinguished by signature hills and mountains that were associated with the dynastic histories of chiefs by their poets.

The case studies of literati in the landscapes of the Erne estuary, Slieve Callan, and Calraighe have revealed contrasting borderscapes in premier borderlands. The Erne estuary landscape was a mature center of power of the ruling family of Tír Conaill by the time the Ó Cléirigh poet-historians and the Mac an Bhaird poets were allocated estates there, *c.*1400 (Fig. 2.2). As seen, the Ó Cléirigh kindred were incorporated into that important borderscape as tenants of church land, while the Mac an Bhaird kindred were established there as apparent occupants of *lucht tighe* land. The cultural profile of the lands that were allocated to them suggests that they were, to an extent, chosen to reflect responsibilities of the learned as curators of the borderland space. This is especially implied by the incorporation within the estate of the Mac an Bhaird

---

[209] FitzPatrick, Finn's seat, 42–4.

poets of the *fert* or boundary grave that overlooked Lough Namanfin in Ballymacaward (Fig. 2.2) and which signified legitimatization of past territorial claims to land. It is inferred too by named otherworld monuments linked with Fionn in that landscape. As argued (2.1.1), the connotations of the monuments associated with St Bairrfhionn, such as the church building (*Ceall Bhairrfhionn*) and the ring-barrow (*Sídh Bhairrfhionn*) named from him, articulate the border lands in which the Ó Cléirigh *ollamh* was placed. As the chronicled battle between the lordship of Tír Conaill and the lordship of Cairbre in 1420 indicates (2.1.3), instability was a feature of even the most long-lived border-scapes of power. The need for visible expressions of historical ownership of that space was an imperative of rulers, a strategy which involved the presence of literati, but perhaps also a role for them as keepers of the memory and pedigree of premier borderland.

In contrast, the estate of the Mac Bruaideadha poets (2.1.2), with its setting in the landscape of Slieve Callan (Fig. 2.5), was not integral to a borderscape of power that had the broad range of high-status indicators of borderland seen in the Erne estuary. It was wild upland in which the only medieval building appears to have been Ballynoe "church" dedicated to St Mac Creiche (6.3). The role of this western borderscape of the lordship of Cineál bhFearmaic is encapsulated in the name of lands that the Mac Bruaideadha poets occupied—*Formaoil* with its height *Binn Formaoile*, which was the scene of strife among factions of the Uí Bhriain in 1573. The literary associations of *formaoil* landforms with Fionn mac Cumhaill also connotes a possible role for it as a hunting ground of the late medieval chiefs of Cineál bhFearmaic. The designation *Formaoil* signals an eminence particular to the dynastic history of Cineál bhFearmaic and, as argued (2.1.2), a memorialized borderscape of the pre-Norman Dál Cais over-kingdom. The interpretation of the southern slope of Slieve Callan and its megalithic monuments, as a Lughnasa festive site and an earlier *óenach* venue, also implies previ-ous significance for this borderscape as a place of royal assembly. In that context, the late-tradition ogham stone (*Leac Chonáin*) may have been added to the *óenach* site by the Mac Bruaideadha poets. The possibility that the *óenach* venue had later use as a meeting site of Cineál bhFearmaic, for *oireachtais* and agreements, is encouraged by the attested repurposing of prehistoric graves, both as peace-mounds for sites of agreements and as venues for inaugurations of chiefs and overlords, and by the involvement of literati in those institutions as late as the sixteenth century (2.2).

The final case study, of the landscape of literati in the *túatha* of Calraighe and Clann Fhearmhaíghe, introduced the idea of a premier borderland contested between three late medieval lordships of north Connacht, from the fourteenth century to the late sixteenth (2.1.3). In that context, it has been argued that the archetypal *Formaoil* that stood among the venerable prehistoric funerary monu-ments at Deerpark, on the north shore of Lough Gill, was not consigned to memory as a pedigreed royal landscape of the pre-Norman overkingdom of Uí Briúin Bréifne. Rather, it was actively involved in the claims of both the Ó Ruairc chief of West Bréifne and the Ó Conchobhair chief of Cairbre to the *túath* landscape of

Calraighe, into the sixteenth century. As seen, hills termed *formaoil* had a specialized function for late medieval lordship, being particularized by poets to chiefs and the heroic deeds of their dynasties. What it symbolized for the rival lordships of Cairbre and West Bréifne is perhaps best reflected in the setting of the Battle of Calraighe, fought between them in 1346.

The formation of church-based estates of *ollamhain* who served successive Ó Ruairc chiefs have been traced from the first half of the fourteenth century, with the Mac an Óglaigh lawyers at Killerry on the south side of Lough Gill and the Ó Cuirnín poets on Inishmore (attested for the fifteenth century). The early modern poetic attribution of "king of Calraighe" to the Ó Ruairc chief, the new tower-house built on the eastern shore of the lake in 1546, and the record of musicians based at Killerry later in that century, underpin the continuity of the Ó Ruairc ruling family's claim to Calraighe and Clann Fhearmhaíghe as their patrimonial land, and the persistence of that borderscape as extra-social space in the political map.

Estate Landscapes of the Learned

3.0 INTRODUCTION

The estates of literati were farms that incorporated residences and spaces for their professional occupations. In this chapter, the size and organization of estates, their land use, and resources are investigated within the framework of estates as landscapes, which enables a view of the practices of literati at a human scale.

Defining farming on estates of the learned, between 1300 and 1600 is problematic. While there is considerable knowledge about early medieval farming,[1] a comprehensive overview of agrarian landscapes in late medieval and early modern Ireland has not yet been achieved. The most recent commentary on farming, between 1200 and 1600, observes that our knowledge of it remains "remarkably poor" and that the most efficacious means of making progress in this field may be to focus field-based enquiry on "the upland above the limit of later cultivation."[2] Considering this knowledge deficit, it is difficult to determine whether the evidence for agriculture from the estates of literati is peculiar to their needs, or broadly representative of the large tier of service providers of Gaelic ruling families who were tenants on *lucht tighe* land and church land. With those predicaments foregrounding this chapter, the intention is to draw together findings from walkover archaeological survey and from various historical and literary references, to begin to inform a picture of learned kindred estates.

A broad range of estates are referred to in respect of their scale, resources, evidence for herds, crops, and soil improvement practices. Autochthonous descriptions of estate lands are rare, but there is an extant account of the lands of the Ó Cuindlis historians at Ballaghdacker (Co. Galway) in Uí Mhaine, in the early fifteenth-century *Leabhar breac* ("Speckled book"), and of the estate of the Ó Duibhdábhoireann brehon lawyers at Cahermacnaghten, in an early seventeenth-century deed of land

---

[1] F. McCormick 2014 Agriculture, settlement and society in early medieval Ireland. *Quaternary International* 346, 119–30; M. McClatchie, F. McCormick, T. R. Kerr, and A. O'Sullivan 2015 Early medieval farming and food production: a review of the archaeobotanical evidence from archaeological excavations in Ireland. *Vegetation History and Archaeobotany* 24 (1), 179–86; F. Kelly 2000 *Early Irish farming*. Dublin Institute for Advanced Studies.

[2] M. Gardiner 2018 Landscape and farming in the north of Ireland in the late Middle Ages and early modern period: the evidence from the uplands. *The Journal of Irish Archaeology* 27, 117.

Landscapes of the Learned: Placing Gaelic Literati in Irish Lordships 1300–1600. Elizabeth FitzPatrick, Oxford University Press.
© Elizabeth FitzPatrick 2023. DOI: 10.1093/oso/9780192855749.003.0003

partition. Both texts provide insights to land utilization, fields and buildings, and the delineation of boundaries. The findings of a field-based survey on the Cahermacnaghten estate are favorably compared with named farming and boundary related features cited in the partition deed. References in the chronicles and bardic poetry to livestock and literati usefully point to cattle raided from them or received by them as spoils of raids, and riding horses gifted to them in exchange for services. There are rare vignettes of the types of foods produced on some estates, including Kilbarron of the Ó Cléirigh kindred in southern Tír Conaill, captured in the first decade of the seventeenth century in administrative records, and archaeological evidence for cereals recovered during excavations at Cahermacnaghten. The relationship of literati with parkland is highlighted, and what *páirc* signified in the context of Gaelic estates is raised in respect of the lands of the Mac Aodhagáin lawyers of Park in Corca Mogha and the Ó Maoilchonaire poet-historians at Ardkyle in West Clann Chuileáin.

Apart from food, learned kindreds had other requirements for their professional practices. Schools needed slate for making temporary and permanent records, hides for parchment, lime for processing hides, and pigments, inks, and pumice for manuscript production. In addition, physicians required plants and minerals for their medicines and access to chalybeate or spa wells. The availability of resources on estates is a major research project of itself. To begin to open the topic, potential sources of abrasive materials used in manuscript production, sandstone quarried for millstones, and the context of metal ores on the estates of literati are explored in this chapter. The case studies include Sheepshead Peninsula (Co. Cork), Ballysadare (Co. Sligo), and Túath Ghlae and Ballyhickey (Co. Clare).

3.1 THE SCALE AND ORGANIZATION OF ESTATES

Typically, the estate of a member of the learned class was configured as a *baile biataigh* (landholding of a food provider) and more usually as a *ceathramadh* (a quarter of a *baile biataigh*) and smaller divisions of it (1.4). The names of secular learned kindred estates commonly combine *baile* with the kindred name (Table 3.1) and sometimes with that of the profession practiced, such as Ballynabrehon (*Baile na mBreithiún*, "landholding of the brehons") in the lordship of Clann Mhuiris (Co. Mayo).[3] *Baile* implies habitation and was attached to farms and landholdings as early as the twelfth century. Its predominance in Irish townland names must therefore be understood as a habitation or settlement and not as a name for townland units.[4] The *baile biataigh* was primarily designed for tax evaluation and used by chiefs to distribute land during the late medieval period.[5] A landholding toponym that combined *baile* with a learned

---

[3] Nicholls, *Irish fiants*, iii, 114 [5451].   [4] Toner, *Baile*, 26, 39, 40.
[5] Toner, *Baile*, 43; Duffy, Social and spatial order, 107.

TABLE 3.1 Some *baile* place names linked with learned kindred personal names

Place name	Kindred	Profession	Lordship	County
Ballydoogan	Ó Dubhagáin	history	Uí Mhaine	Galway
Ballymacegan	Mac Aodhagáin	law	Urumhain	Tipperary
Ballyroney	Ó Ruanadha	poetry	Uí Eachach Cobha	Down
Ballysheil	Ó Siadhail	medicine	Dealbhna Eathra	Offaly

kindred name or profession (Table 3.1) can usually be interpreted as an estate of tax-free agricultural land of variable size.

There is some evidence from the later medieval period that the Gaelic place-naming process in Scotland included *baile* place names combined with the titles of learned professions. Bannerman proposed, for instance, that Balvaird (*Bail'* [*baile*] *an Bhaird*, "stead of the poet"), on the boundary between Fife and Perthshire, was the estate of the king's poet in the thirteenth century.[6]

The estate of the Mac Con Midhe poets, centered on Lough Catherine in Barons Court demesne (Fig. 1.2), south of the town of Ardstraw (Co. Tyrone),[7] was described in the late sixteenth century as "*Fearann an Reacaire*" ("reciter's land").[8] The term *fearann* was combined with some secular learned kindred names to designate their estates.[9] Farrancassidy (*Fearann Muintir Uí Chaiside* "land of the Ó Caiside people") in the northwest bounds of the *túath* of Magheraboy, lordship of Fir Mhanach, was an estate of the Ó Caiside medical family (Fig. 1.5).[10] Church land occupied by kindreds of learned *airchinnigh* during the late medieval period in the River Erne landscape of Fir Mhanach is also particularized to them in that way. *Fearann Muintire Cianáin* ("land of the people of Cianáin") was the estate name of the Ó Cianáin *ollamh* in *seanchas* and *airchinneach* of Cleenish Island.[11] The estate of the Ó Luinín hereditary historians was referred to as *Fearann na hArda Muintire Luinín* ("land of the heights of the people of Luinín").[12] No *airchinneach* of Arda is cited until the mid- to late fourteenth century and the office of *airchinneach* of Cleenish is mentioned for the first time in the fifteenth century. The Ó Cianáin kindred apparently migrated from Monaghan to Fir Mhanach *c*.1300 and the Ó Luinín kindred settled

---

[6] J. Bannerman 1996 The residence of the king's poet. *Scottish Gaelic Studies* 17, 25–6; for *baile* place names in Scotland see P. McNeill and R. Nicholson (eds) 1975 *An historical atlas of Scotland, c.400–c. 1600*, 4, 109. St Andrews. Atlas Committee of the Conference of Scottish Medievalists.

[7] S. Mac Airt and T. Ó Fiaich (eds) 1956 A thirteenth century poem on Armagh cathedral by Giolla Brighde Mac Con Midhe. *Seanchas Ardmhacha: Journal of the Armagh Diocesan Historical Society* 2 (1), 146.

[8] M. Dillon (ed. and tr.) 1966 Ceart Uí Néill. *Studia Celtica* 1, 8; Williams, *Poems of Giolla Brighde*, 2.

[9] Quin, *Dictionary*, 300:87. Old Irish *ferann* translates as a defined area of land, domain, or territory.

[10] Farrancassidy contains a spa or chalybeate well, and a Georgian farmhouse of *c*.1700.

[11] U 1400.8, iii, 44, 45.   [12] M 1396.2, iv, 742, 743; U 1512.11, iii, 504, 505.

in Fir Mhanach after 1200.[13] The integration of the kindred name with the place gave an impression of long-held hereditary status to lands that both kindreds had been allocated, for the first time, in the later medieval period.

Apart from the prefixes *baile* and *fearann*, topographical features were combined with learned kindred names in the designation of estates. A branch of the Ó Deóradháin brehon lawyers in the Leinster lordship of Laoighis lived at Clonadaddoran (*Cluain Fhada Ó nDeoráin*, "the long meadow of the O'Dorans") (Fig. 1.2).[14] It was recorded on a Tudor map of Laois and Offaly dated 1565.[15] Inchidaly in Co. Cork, from the Irish *Inse Uí Dhálaigh* ("the island or river meadow of the O'Dalys"), was the estate of the Ó Dálaigh poets who served Ó Ceallacháin, chief of the small Munster lordship of Pobul Uí Cheallacháin (Fig. 1.2). Inchidaly is bounded on its west side by the River Blackwater. It is a chain of midstream islands created by river bifurcation where the Blackwater and its tributary, the Glen River, meet. Clonmeen, the castle of Ó Ceallacháin,[16] and his lands at Pallas (*pailís*, 4.3),[17] lay immediately to the east, with the hill of Fermoyle (*formaoil*, 2.3) to the southwest.

Place names that link settlement features with learned kindreds are less common but, where they occur, there are well-founded historical names among them. In the fifteenth century, members of the Ó Fialáin kindred simultaneously held the office of *airchinneach* of the medieval parish church of Boho and *ollamh* in poetry to the Mág Uidhir chief of Fir Mhanach (Fig. 1.5).[18] Their clerical estate, as recorded in the fifteenth century, was *Botha Muintire Fialáin*, referring to the huts or cells (*botha*) of the Ó Fialáin kindred.[19] There is a high cross at Boho but no standing remains of medieval buildings.[20] The place name reference may be significant in view of late medieval poetic allusions to *botha* as the setting for the training of poets in bardic schools (6.3).[21]

There was considerable variation in the size of estates where their original denominations are known. The extent of an estate was commensurate with the prestige of a learned kindred and can be demonstrated in relation to leading Gaelic learned kindreds in Scotland as well as Ireland. Bannerman used Crown exchequer rolls and rentals of the first half of the sixteenth century to determine the former extent of the lands of the Mac Mhuirich kindred, who were "the most important exponents of

---

[13] Ó Scea, Erenachs, erenachships, 295–6.   [14] Nicholls, *Irish fiants*, ii, 361 [2722].

[15] It is found as "Chloenadodoran" on BL Cotton MS Augustus I.ii.40.

[16] E. Campbell 2017 Pobul Uí Cheallacháin: landscape and power in an early modern Gaelic lordship. *Landscapes* 18 (1), 19–36.

[17] Nicholls, *Irish fiants*, ii, 290 [2248], ii, 291 [2252], iii, 245 [5903]. Pallas is cited in 1573 and 1594 as land of the Ó Ceallacháin chief. Campbell, Pobul Uí Cheallacháin, 22–3, 31.

[18] U 1483.5, iii, 282, 283. Seán Ó Fialáin, *ollamh* in poetry to Mág Uidhir and *airchinneach* of Boho, died in 1483.

[19] U 1498, iii, 426, 427; Muhr, The place-names of County Fermanagh, 30–1.

[20] Foley and McHugh, *An archaeological survey of County Fermanagh i, part 2*, 809–13.

[21] Bergin, *Irish bardic poetry*, 118, 149, 150, 265, 281, 282.

classical Gaelic poetry in Scotland."[22] The kindred held about ten non-contiguous merklands in southern Kintyre, eight of which were noted in 1505 as the property of "John MacMhuirich *per poetam*."[23] However, confirming that the Kintyre lands constituted the *fearann ollamhanacht* of Mac Mhuirich, as the hereditary poet of the Clann Domhnaill lords of the Isles, is problematic because it has been noted that there is a distinct lack of poems by this kindred addressed to Clann Domhnaill chiefs.[24]

With some small exceptions, evidence for the quantities of land involved in learned kindred estates in Ireland comes from early seventeenth-century English land surveys and inquisitions in advance of the Ulster plantation, and from Sir William Petty's mid-seventeenth-century Down Survey of Ireland.[25] A closer estimation of the scale of estates can be made by combining evidence from disparate sources. In his poem "Heed, o George, my complaint" (*Gabh mo gherán a Sheóirse*), which he composed *c.*1618 for Sir George Carew (an Elizabethan military commander who had been lord president of Munster), the poet Tadhg Ó Dálaigh declared, "though every *ollamh* thinks that this grant of land we got was enormous, we gave your family renown that lasted long after." (1.3)[26] Tadhg was referring to the estate of his kindred, Muinter Bháire on the Sheepshead Peninsula (Fig. 3.1), which Sir George's ancestors, the Anglo-Norman Carew family, had granted to the Ó Dálaigh poets by 1300 (2.3).[27] The Carews appear to have adopted the Gaelic practice of placing their poets in a border-scape. Their power declined in the fourteenth century, but in the sixteenth century they renewed their claims to the peninsula, which Sir George pursued. This was the context in which Tadhg Ó Dálaigh's poem was written.[28]

Sheepshead Peninsula had been mapped in 1598 by the Tudor cartographer Francis Jobson as "Rymers" land, referencing the fact that the entire peninsula was the estate of the Ó Dálaigh kindred.[29] The amount of land involved was noted in 1599 as thirty-six ploughlands, three of which were church land.[30] In origin, the ploughland was the main unit of land evaluation in England, where it implied the amount of land required for a plough team. In the Anglo-Norman polities of Ireland, it was used as a unit of land assessment for taxation purposes.[31]

---

[22] McLeod, *Divided Gaels*, 74–5.

[23] Bannerman, Residence of the king's poet, 29; A merkland or markland was a unit of land assessment.

[24] McLeod, *Divided Gaels*, 74–5.

[25] See entries for Ballymacaward and Ballyhose in Fir Mhanach, in Mac Neill and Hogan, A booke of the kings lands, 183, 194.

[26] O'Sullivan, Tadhg O'Daly, 27, 34, 37; Hughes, Land acquisitions, 97.

[27] O'Sullivan, Tadhg O'Daly, 30.

[28] M. Caball 2012 Culture, continuity and change in early seventeenth-century southwest Munster. *Studia Hibernica* 37, 38.

[29] TCD MS 1209, 36, 1589, A map of the province of Munster, by Francis Jobson for Lord Burleigh. Trinity College Dublin.

[30] Brewer and Bullen, *Carew manuscripts*, iii, 352.   [31] McErlean, Irish townland system, 328.

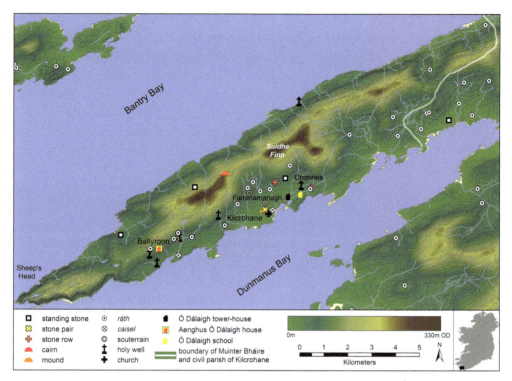

FIG. 3.1. Prehistoric and medieval monuments and buildings on the estate of the Ó Dálaigh poets, Sheepshead Peninsula (map N. McCarthy).

The substantial nature of their estate was documented again in 1633 by Sir George Carew's secretary, who noted that Tadhg Ó Dálaigh's ancestor had:

> the county of Moynterbary [Muinter Bháire] given unto him by the Lord President's ancestor, many hundred yeares past…; the service which odaly and his progenie were to doe, for so large a proportion of Lands unto Carew and his successors, was (according to the custome of that time) to bee their Rimers, or Chroniclers of their actions.[32]

While this might at first appear to be an unusually large estate for an *ollamh*, much of the spine of the peninsula is uninhabitable mountain, the lower slopes of which are given to grazing. It is a finger of upland, 24.5 km long and no more than 5 km wide, extending into the Atlantic between Bantry Bay and Dunmanus Bay (Fig. 3.1). Patches of ground nestling between the foot of the mountain ranges and the southern shore have been conducive to habitation and farming since the early medieval period. This is substantiated by the concentration of *ráth* and *caisel* enclosures and souterrains, and by occasional rudimentary remains of premodern field boundaries among nineteenth-century outfield and infield walls, on the south coastline (Figs 3.1, 3.2).

---

[32] T. Stafford 1633 (reprint 1810) *Pacata Hibernia or a history of the wars in Ireland during the reign of Queen Elizabeth: taken from the original chronicles*, i, 528–9. Dublin. Hibernia Press.

FIG. 3.2. A premodern field boundary at Dromnea, looking north to Rosskerrig Mountain, Sheepshead Peninsula (photo E. FitzPatrick).

The Ó Dálaigh poets conducted a school on that coastline at Dromnea, they lived in Farranamanagh tower-house west of Dromnea (6.3.1), and they were buried on the peninsula in the graveyard of the medieval parish church at Kilcrohane (Fig. 3.1).[33] Sheepshead was perceived as remote outland of the overlordship, its mountainous terrain prompting characterization of the peninsula in the seventeenth century as "a barbarous country."[34]

The extent of the Ó Cléirigh *ollamh*'s estate, which he held as *airchinneach* of Kilbarron in southern Tír Conaill, can be reckoned using both ecclesiastical and land-survey records. It consisted of a quarter of the mensal land of the bishop of Raphoe, incorporating the area now represented by the townlands of Kilbarron, Cloghbolie, Cool Beg, and Cool More (Fig. 1.1).[35] The quarter of Kildoney, adjoining the southwest side of Kilbarron, was listed as Ó Cléirigh's in 1609, which the family

[33] J. N. Healy 1988 *The castles of County Cork*, 200–1. Cork. Mercier Press; J. O'Donovan (ed. and tr.) 1852 *The tribes of Ireland: a satire by Aenghus O'Daly*, 13. Dublin. John O'Daly.

[34] FitzPatrick, The landscape and settlements, 462.

[35] Costello, *De annatis Hiberniae*, i, 278; G. Hill 1877 *An historical account of the plantation in Ulster at the commencement of the seventeenth century*. Belfast. McGaw, Stevenson and Orr.

held as *lucht tighe* land of the chief of Tír Conaill (Fig. 2.2).[36] Another parcel of *lucht tighe* at Creevy was apparently granted to Ó Cléirigh in the first three decades of the fifteenth century by the chief Niall Garbh Ó Domhnaill. Additional lands were attributed to the family arising from intermarriage with the learned kindred of Ó Sgingín.[37]

A learned *airchinneach* could hold different church lands simultaneously, including subdivisions of estates. This is seen among the many estates of *airchinnigh* along the stretch of the River Erne between the upper and lower lakes, in the lordship of Fir Mhanach. The historian and poet Piarais Cam Ó Luinín (d. 1441) was at once *airchinneach* of Arda and of the *trían* of Derryvullan, while Seán Ó Fiaich (d. 1506) was *airchinneach* of the *trían* of Derrybrusk.[38] The literal translation of Irish *trían* is "third part."[39] Subdivisions of church estates are to be expected in lordships where land set aside for *airchinnigh* was substantial. It has been estimated, for instance, that the *airchinneach* lands of Cleenish constituted 2,425 acres and those of Derryvullan 1,917 acres, entailing capacities to support several kindreds.[40]

Indications of learned kindred estates usually survive as townlands, but in many instances the original denominations will be found to have been larger than the townland units that now bear their names. The mid-seventeenth-century Down Survey parish maps contain records of the extents of some erstwhile learned kindred estates before they were broken up. The modern townland of Ardkyle (*Ard Choill*, "wood of the height") references the former estate of Ó Maoilchonaire, *ollamh* in *seanchas* to the overlord of Tuadhmhumhain and to the Mac Conmara chief of West Clann Chuileáin. Comparing the modern townland map and the Down Survey parish map of the area reveals that the Ardkyle estate was originally much larger, comprising the landmass represented by eight townlands.[41]

3.2 ESTATE PROFILES FROM TEXT TO LANDSCAPE

Contemporary Gaelic descriptions of learned kindred lands are rare, but there are two notable ones—from the fifteenth century and the early seventeenth century. These serve to bring some of the attributes of estates into sharper focus, bearing in mind that landholdings varied in size, in terrain, and in their settlement features.

---

[36] Allingham, *Ballyshannon*, 27, 39.   [37] Simms, *Gaelic Ulster*, 379–80.
[38] M 1441.10, iv, 924, 925; M 1506.1, vi, 1286, 1287.   [39] Quin, *Dictionary*, 607:306.
[40] Ó Scea, Erenachs, erenachships, 294.
[41] <http://downsurvey.tchpc.tcd.ie/down-survey-maps.php#bm=Bunratty&c=Clare> (accessed March 8, 2022). The townlands are Ardkyle, Seersha, Carrownalegaun, Donnybrook, Springfield, Cloghlea, Newpark, and Deerpark.

3.2.1 Ballaghdacker

The earlier of the two descriptions is found in the *Leabhar breac*, a largely religious work written by Murchadh Riabhach Ó Cuindlis between 1408 and 1411.[42] It contains a marginal note describing the boundaries and extent of the estate of Ó Cuindlis at Ballaghdacker (*Baile Locha Deacair*, "landholding of the lake of Deacair") in the lordship of Uí Mhaine (Figs 1.2, 3.3).[43] It refers to some of the topography, vegetation cover, and land-use on the estate and the means by which the bounds were demarcated. Several of the local place names cited by the scribe are obsolete:

> This is Ó Cuindlis's land and division of Bally-Lochdecar, viz. From the ditch of the Ceallabrath-Riabhach along the ditch of the Big Stone westwards, and to the old kiln on the western side of the Turner's field, and to Ó Cuindlis's Mire, and Inisfarannan in the lake and along Ó Cuindlis's field, and Ó Cuindlis's road eastwards, and along the ditch that runs from Ó Cuindlis's road eastwards to the ditch of the short field. And this is the land, which is known by the name of Corrbachalla, and Cluain Canann, with all its woods, bogs and arable land.[44]

The townlands of Ballaghdacker, Curraghbaghla, and Clooncannon constituted most of the former estate, its central feature being *Loch Deacair* after which it was named. The lake was shared between land denominations, with the southeast portion lying in Ballaghdacker. It has two islands, the larger of which, Stony Island, is cited as *Inisfarannain* in Ó Cuindlis's description. The smaller, Sally Island, lies 100 m north of it, in the separate townland of Easterfield. Both are *crannóg* sites. The *crannóg* of *Inisfarannain* (Fig. 3.3) may have been a residence and guest-house of the kindred, and the location within their estate where, in 1356, the son of the Ó Conchobhair, "king of Connacht," was murdered by members of the Ó Ceallaigh sept of Uí Mhaine and the local Mac an Bhaird kindred of poets, in revenge for his elopement with the wife of the Ó Ceallaigh chief.[45]

The terrain of the estate is characterized by wet grassland and bog influenced by the flood plain of the lake and the River Suck nearby to the east. The wetness is referenced in the field name *Lathach Uí Chuindlis* ("the miry or muddy place of Ó Cuindlis"), which is probably the area along the southeast shore of the lake. Woodland is also mentioned in terms of a natural resource, with one field on the estate noted as belonging to a wood turner (*Gort in Tornóra*). The four most common tree species in Irish wetland woods are alder, ash, birch, and hazel and, of those, alder and ash were

---

[42] M. Herbert 2009 Medieval collections of ecclesiastical and devotional materials: Leabhar breac, Liber Flavus Fergusiorum and the Book of Fenagh. In B. Cunningham, S. Fitzpatrick, and P. Schnabel (eds), *Treasures of the Royal Irish Academy Library*, 28. Dublin. Royal Irish Academy.

[43] Ó Concheanainn, Scribe, 66–7.

[44] Translation in Ó Concheanainn, Scribe, 66; RIA MS 23 P 16, 258.

[45] AConn 1356.2, 312, 313.

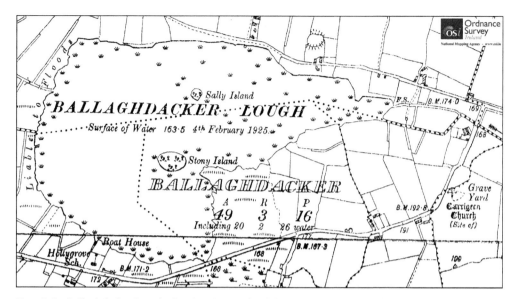

FIG. 3.3. Ballaghdacker Lough showing Stony Island (*Inisfarannain*) (© Ordnance Survey Ireland/ Government of Ireland Copyright Permit No. MP 002422).

favored by wood turners.[46] A kiln, described as old and perhaps disused, lay on the west side of the Turner's field. It is not stated whether it was for drying cereals or burning lime, but there are two limekilns shown on the nineteenth-century Ordnance Survey six-inch map, one at the north end of Ballaghdacker, close to the lake shore, and the other in Curraghbaghla, neither of which remains on the landscape. They were for burning lime to use as fertilizer and mortar. The application of lime as a soil nutritive was a common practice in Ireland between the twelfth and seventeenth centuries (3.3).[47] Since the estate in the fifteenth century included arable land, lime is likely to have been produced to fertilize it. The details of land-use and resource-related activities are what make this brief description of a Gaelic learned kindred landholding in the fifteenth century especially valuable.

3.2.2 Cahermacnaghten

The second documented estate is that of the Ó Duibhdábhoireann brehon lawyers of Cahermacnaghten in the lordship of Boireann (Fig. 1.4). The earliest citation of the Ó Duibhdábhoireann kindred name, which translates as "black of the two stony places,"

---

[46] S. F. Iremonger and D. L. Kelly 1988 The responses of four Irish wetland tree species to raised soil water levels. *New Phytologist* 109 (4), 491.

[47] M. Ó Súilleabháin, L. Downey and D. Downey 2017 *Antiquities of rural Ireland*, 68–9. Dublin. Wordwell.

is for 1023.[48] It is a name that expresses their inseparable bond with the Boireann, a distinctive region of exposed Upper Carboniferous limestone (karst) in north Co. Clare.[49] The Ó Duibhdábhoireann kindred were well established as lawyers of the Ó Lochlainn chiefs by the later fourteenth century.[50] Their earliest documented association with Cahermacnaghten dates from the second half of the sixteenth century.[51]

A land-partition deed, written in the Irish language by Aodh Ó Duibhdábhoireann, eldest son of the *ollamh* Giolla na Naomh Óg, and witnessed and signed at Cahermacnaghten in April 1606, provides detailed knowledge of the extent and some of the contents of the kindred's lands at that time (but also alluding to two previous generations), from an emic perspective.[52] The document, referred to as the Corofin manuscript, was kept and published by the Clare antiquary Macnamara and had been passed down to him by his father. It was a paper copy of three closely written pages in the Irish language, by an unknown writer, in "an affectedly archaic style of penmanship, being a mass of curious contractions."[53] The deed concerns the partition of certain lands and buildings between Aodh Ó Duibhdábhoireann and his brother Cosnamach. A second document dated 1675, known as the Ennistymon manuscript, which is an exact copy of the 1606 deed of partition signed by Aodh's son, was intended to assist him to regain his lands at Cahermacnaghten in the period after the Restoration (1660–6).[54]

Twelve members of the Ó Duibhdábhoireann kindred held approximately four quarters of land, amounting to *c*.1,500 Irish acres, at the time of the 1641 Rebellion and before the Cromwellian confiscations of the 1650s.[55] Their lands were for the most part non-contiguous, scattered throughout the parishes of Noughaval, Drumcreehy, and Rathbourney, in Túath Eannuigh, one of six *túatha* that constituted the earlier territorial matrix of the lordship of Boireann (Fig. 1.4).[56]

The 1606 partition deed concerning the inheritance of the two brothers singled out Cahermacnaghten as part of the "two quarters of the land of their father and grandfather."[57] In the deed, local Gaelic land-denomination units were cited: the term *seisreach* (land associated with a six-horse ploughing team) is used of the quarter,

---

[48] AI 1023.5, 191, 192.

[49] M. E. Mcnamara and R. W. Hennessy 2010 *The geology of the Burren region, Co. Clare, Ireland.* Ennistymon. The Burren Connect Project.

[50] AConn 1364.8, 324, 325.

[51] Bisagni, *Amrae Coluimb Chille*, 11–12.

[52] Macnamara, O'Davorens, 86–93.   [53] Macnamara, O'Davorens, 71–2, 75.

[54] RIA 14 B 23, 188–9; Macnamara, O'Davorens, 75–7.   [55] Nugent, *Gaelic clans*, 200.

[56] A. M. Freeman (ed.) 1936 *The compossicion booke of Conought*, 14, 21. Dublin. The Stationery Office; Nugent, *Gaelic clans*, 138–42, 164–5; Túath Eannuigh consisted of thirty-seven quarters of land.

[57] Macnamara, O'Davorens, 86, 89. The other lands listed as belonging to the two quarters were Kilcolmanbarry, Lismacteige, Lisgoogan, and the unidentified "Lios na Luachrainne," situated in other areas of the lordship.

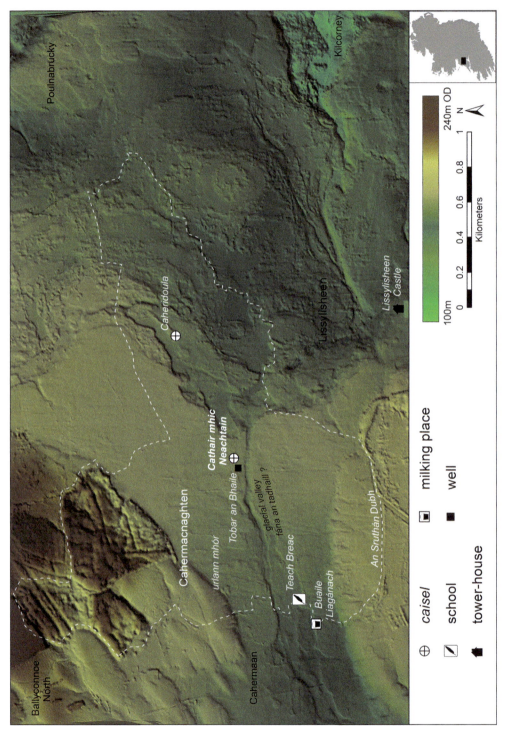

Fig. 3.4. Principal settlements and features of the half-quarter estate of Cahermacnaghten (map N. McCarthy).

leith sheisreach of the half-quarter, and *ceathú mír* of the cartron (a small unit, of which there were four to a quarter).[58] The description of the Ó Duibhdábhoireann estate focused on the half-quarter of Cahermacnaghten, which was subdivided between Aodh and Cosnamach into two cartrons.[59] The particular value of the 1606 deed for the archaeologist and historian lies in its description of the approximate extent, place names, and settlements of Cahermacnaghten and the insight it provides to partible inheritance, which was endemic among Gaelic kindreds in early modern Boireann (4.2.3, 4.5).[60]

Cahermacnaghten was situated in the northern bounds of Túath Eannuigh (Figs 1.4; 3.4). The *túath* is distinguished by a corridor of lowland, which contains a remarkably continuous and dense concentration of *caisel* complexes, houses, and enclosed fields, intermingled with surviving prehistoric monuments, extending west to east between Ballyinsheen Bog near Lisdoonvarna and Caheridoula in Cahermacnaghten townland. The density of settlement in the lowland corridor of Túath Eannuigh suggests that it had special status, perhaps mainly as *lucht tighe* estates occupied by service kindreds. In that regard, lands of both the Ó Duibhdábhoireann lawyers and the Ó Connmhaigh musicians can be identified within this corridor of settlement (Fig. 1.4).

The modern townland of Cahermacnaghten is not entirely representative of the extent of Ó Duibhdábhoireann's half-quarter estate (Fig. 3.4). The half-quarter of Cahermacnaghten included a subdenomination called Kilbrack (*Coill Breac*, "speckled wood"), which was used as an alias for Cahermacnaghten in the seventeenth century.[61] Kilbrack was coterminous with the southwestern area of the half-quarter. The northeastern extent of the modern townland was a separate denomination called Caheridoula, but it was not recorded as an Ó Duibhdábhoireann property before 1641.[62] There were three main settlement nodes relating to Cahermacnaghten and Caheridoula. Cahermacnaghten (*Cathair mhic Neachtain*) was distinguished by an early medieval *caisel* of that name, which was refurbished as a residence of members of the Ó Duibhdábhoireann kindred in the late medieval period (4.2). The subdenomination of Kilbrack in the southwest corner of the half-quarter had a settlement focused on *Teach Breac*, the building proposed in this study as the Ó Duibhdábhoireann law school-house (6.1.1).

Parts of the south and west of the modern townland of Cahermacnaghten preserve elements of the boundaries of the historical half-quarter, which were expressed as

---

[58] Macamara, O'Davorens, 86–93; McErlean, Irish townland system, 320.

[59] For cartron see K. Nicholls 1987 Gaelic society and economy in the high Middle Ages. In Cosgrove, *New history of Ireland*, ii, 408.

[60] Nugent, *Gaelic clans*, 255–8.

[61] R. C. Simington (ed.) 1967 *Books of survey and distribution, iv, County of Clare*, 465. Dublin. The Stationery Office for the Irish Manuscripts Commission.

[62] Simington, *Books of survey and distribution*, iv, 473.

TABLE 3.2 Topographical and settlement features of Cahermacnaghten in 1606

Place	Meaning
bóthar gharrdha Thaidhg Ruaidh	road of Tadhg Roe's garden
an bhuaile liagánach	stony milking place
faithche an bhuaile	green of the milking place
fána an tadhaill	slope, depression, or hollow of contact
mothar tortánach	enclosed thicket
sruthán dubh	black stream
urlann mhór	big tract of coarse pasture

landmarks and functional spaces of the estate in the 1606 partition deed. Some of these can still be identified on the ground (Table 3.2).[63]

The boundary of the southwestern extent of the half-quarter was described in 1606 as the black stream ("*sruthán dubh*").[64] It can be traced in the peaty upland of Binroe, at the south end of Cahermacnaghten. The course of the stream is recognizable as a fosse dug out of the peat, which is canopied with willow in high summer (Fig. 3.5).[65] The deed mentions a "*claidh*" (ditch, bank) extending from the black stream to a milking place ("*an bhuaile liagánach*").[66] The milking place is identifiable as an area of limestone pavement distinguished by remains of a drystone *clochán* and animal pens near the western boundary of the townland,[67] but the boundary itself is a relatively modern field wall and not an antiquity (Fig. 3.4). However, it runs along the top of a natural scarp, which may be what is intended by *claidh* in the deed.[68]

The identity of the northern boundary of the half-quarter is not quite so clear. The deed indicates that the *claidh* of the milking place ran northwards to meet the *claidh* of the "*urlann mhór*." The term *urlann* can mean a tract of coarse pasture but also an open area in front of a *ráth* or *caisel*.[69] However, since it led northwards from the milking place, it must refer to the open and relatively level tract of rough, rocky pasture that lies between the upland to the northwest and the flat-bottomed glacial depression that runs diagonally through most of the townland from northeast to

---

[63] E. FitzPatrick 2008 Antiquarian scholarship and the archaeology of Cahermacnaghten, Burren, Co. Clare. *The Other Clare* 32, 59–60.

[64] Macnamara, O'Davorens, 86, 90.

[65] T. J. Westropp 1911 Prehistoric remains (forts and dolmens) in the Burren, Co. Clare. *JRSAI* 1 (4), 366; FitzPatrick, Antiquarian scholarship, 59–60.

[66] Macnamara, O'Davorens, 86, 90.

[67] Westropp, Prehistoric remains, 366, noted that "Buaile liaganach is forgotten, but is probably some of the craggy pasture land at the west end of the townland full of the flat slabs, or *liags* [limestone pavement]."

[68] FitzPatrick, Antiquarian scholarship, 60.

[69] Macnamara, O'Davorens, 90n.; FitzPatrick, Antiquarian scholarship, 60; An Roinn Oideachais 1981 *Gearrfhoclóir Gaeilge–Béarla*, 804. Dublin. Oifig an tSoláthair.

FIG. 3.5. Willow trees indicate the "black stream" boundary, Cahermacnaghten (photo E. FitzPatrick).

southwest. The eastern limit of the half-quarter was defined by Westropp in 1911 as a "well-marked line of old walls [pre-modern slab-walls]" aligned north–south and lying between the *caisel* of Cahermacnaghten and the *caisel* of Caheridoula (Fig. 3.4).[70]

The half-quarter is described in the deed of 1606 as the "*ceann áit*" ("head place") of Cahermacnaghten, which defined the main residence and associated features of a family's landholding.[71] It included the *caisel* of Cahermacnaghten, the domestic well, the boggy stream that formed the southern boundary of the half-quarter, a series of gardens, a road, and the milking area or booley (Fig. 3.4).[72] In the legal subdivision of the half-quarter into two cartrons in 1606, Aodh Ó Duibhdábhoireann received the west half and Cosnamach the east. However, the core elements of the *ceann áit*, the *caisel* and its buildings, along with the domestic well, the road, and the milking place, were shared between them.

The dominant geographical landmarks on the skyline of Cahermacnaghten are Slieve Elva to the northwest, the foothills of Ailwee Mountain to the northeast, and distant Slieve Carran to the east. The microtopography of Cahermacnaghten is surprisingly varied. In the seventeenth-century *Books of survey and distribution*, it was described as "Boggie Mountain, rockie pasture and heathy pasture."[73] This description holds true of much of its cover today. Peaty upland (*c.*200 m OD) with good grass borders the northwest and southwest extremities, bare carboniferous limestone (karst) combined with marsh and sparse grass constitute most of the central area, while the eastern end is characterized by much higher ground, mostly clad with impenetrable hazel scrub. The karst, which typifies the Burren region of north Clare,

[70] Westropp, Prehistoric remains, 366; FitzPatrick, Antiquarian scholarship, 60.
[71] Nicholls, Gaelic society and economy, 405.   [72] Macnamara, O'Davorens, 86–7, 90–1.
[73] Simington, *Books of survey and distribution*, iv, 456.

but which is not unique to that region, occurs as pavements consisting of blocks of limestone (clints) isolated by deep fissures (grykes).[74] In the summer months the grykes host a rich supply of wild sorrel, rosemary, and mint. In 1681 Thomas Dineley, who kept a journal of his travels in Ireland, remarked that the Burren was "famous for Physical Herbs, the best in Ireland and equall to the best of England." He noted that "the sweet herbs intermixed and distributed every where" compensated for the lack of hay and made beef and mutton very palatable.[75]

A subtle but significant landform in the historical Ó Duibhdábhoireann half-quarter is the flat-bottomed glacial valley (*c.*30 m wide) that cuts a passageway through it, extending *c.*2.2 km from northeast to southwest (Figs 3.4, 3.6). This shallow valley affords covert passage on a journey from the *caisel* of Cahermacnaghten to *Teach Breac*, as a person walking along its floor cannot be seen except from much higher ground, such as the *caisel* that overlooks the valley. The hidden aspect of the valley suggests that it may be "*fána an tadhaill*," the slope, depression, or "hollow of contact" cited in the deed of 1606.[76] The section of the valley immediately south and southwest of the *caisel* contains deep, rich glacial drift that is very ploughable garden soil, making it an important site for cultivation in otherwise rocky pasture.[77] It could also have been used as a source of soil for less favorable areas of the landholding. Earth-moving and indeed earth-stealing was not unknown in historical Burren. In 1681 Dineley wrote, "Earth or mold is so precious here, that it is reported that Process has bin severall times made for one neighbours removing earth in baskets from anothers land."[78]

The glacial valley was the spine of the half-quarter. It was divided into small plots that are the best candidates for the "gardens," assigned in 1606 to Aodh Ó Duibhdábhoireann, as part of his share.[79] The boundaries of the fields or gardens of the depression are generally made of large stones, probably quarried from the rough edges of the valley, and rolled down onto its floor (Fig. 3.6). They survive as linear heaps, no more than two courses high, which conform to Plunkett-Dillon's definition of a "tumble wall" in her categorization of the field boundaries of the Burren. She found that tumble walls are especially associated with *caisel* settlements, suggesting that they were integral to the medieval creation of farming landscapes across the Burren.[80] Some of the garden divisions are of slab-wall type, but these are much less

---

[74] M. E. Mcnamara and R. W. Hennessy 2010 *The geology of the Burren region, Co. Clare, Ireland*, 22. Ennistymon. The Burren Connect Project.

[75] E. P. Shirley *et al.* 1867 Extracts from the journal of Thomas Dineley, Esquire, giving some account of his visit to Ireland in the reign of Charles II. *Journal of the Kilkenny and South-East of Ireland Archaeological Society* 6 (1), 191.

[76] Macnamara, O'Davorens, 87, 91.

[77] I am grateful to Ingelise Stuijts of the Discovery Programme for her opinion of the soil in the glacial valley.

[78] Shirley, Extracts from the journal, 191.   [79] Macnamara, O'Davorens, 87, 91.

[80] E. Plunkett-Dillon 1985 The field boundaries of the Burren, Co. Clare, 49, 83, 85. PhD diss. Trinity College Dublin.

FIG. 3.6. Garden divisions (foreground and background) in the glacial valley overlooked by the *caisel* of Cahermacnaghten (photo E. FitzPatrick).

common in the depression than they are elsewhere in the landscape of the half-quarter. Slab-walls, which consist of upended slabs of karst, leaning against each other in a single line and generally no more than two courses high, have been found to predate townland and medieval parish boundaries.[81] They were a common sight in the seventeenth-century Burren landscape. Dineley, writing in 1681, noted that the "particons of land are made by broad stones like slate turn'd up edgewise."[82] Some of the better-preserved boundaries are modern single-walls, which Plunkett-Dillon defined as one stone wide, often decreasing in size towards the top, and dating from between the seventeenth and twentieth century.[83]

Apart from the transverse walls that demarcate them, the valley gardens are also walled on their high north and south sides, which would have ensured that whatever was cultivated within them was well protected. There is some evidence to suggest that the gardens adjacent to the *caisel* were contained within a park.[84] The antiquaries Frost, Westropp, and Macnamara recorded the place name "*Páirc na Leacht*" ("park of the stone heaps/memorial cairns"), given to an enclosed area around the *caisel* of Cahermacnaghten (Fig. 3.7).[85] In Macnamara's opinion the "stone heaps" were

---

[81] Plunkett-Dillon, Field boundaries, 49–50, 190–1; Jones, Dating ancient field walls, 3.

[82] Shirley, Extracts from the journal, 193.   [83] Plunkett-Dillon, Field boundaries, 48, 198.

[84] FitzPatrick, Antiquarian scholarship, 62–3.

[85] Frost, *History and topography*, 17–21; Westropp, Prehistoric stone forts, 121, 122; Macnamara, O'Davorens, 64, 67–8.

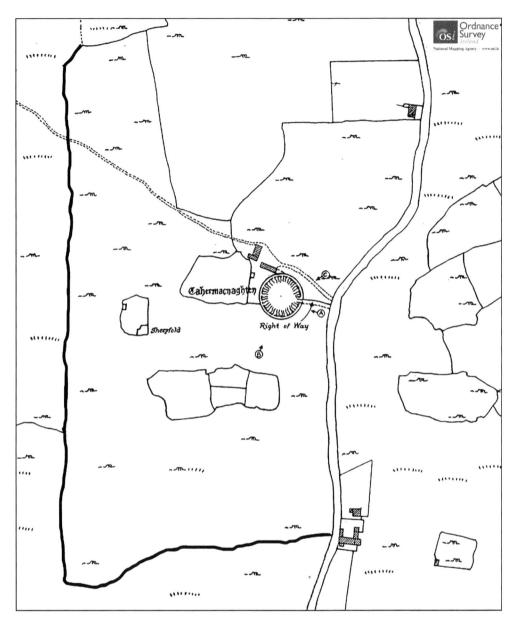

Fig. 3.7. *Páirc na Leacht*, Cahermacnaghten (scale 1:2500), with the west and south walls highlighted (© Ordnance Survey Ireland/Government of Ireland Copyright Permit No. MP 000323).

FIG. 3.8. The west wall of *Páirc na Leacht*, Cahermacnaghten (photo E. FitzPatrick).

not archaeological monuments but field-clearance cairns. He dismissed the place name as "a modern one of no archaeological interest whatever."[86]

The origin of the "park" (470 m north–south by 230 m east–west) is unknown, but it was a recognized feature of the Cahermacnaghten landscape in the late nineteenth century.[87] It is defined by tall drystone walls up to 3 m thick and 1.5 m high in places, especially along the western boundary (Fig. 3.8). A flimsy modern wall skirts the roadside to the east. The intention of the substantial walls can only have been to manage grazing herds and protect cultivated areas. The *caisel*, the domestic well, the gardens, and 26 acres of rocky pasture are contained within the park boundaries (Fig. 3.7). Notwithstanding that they have been augmented and altered over many years, the great thickness of the west and south walls, in comparison to the known categories of Burren field-walls, may represent a rare survival of part of a historic park occupied by a Gaelic learned kindred.

Parks are features of other learned kindred estates (3.3.1), some of which were documented in the sixteenth century and others of which were marked by the Ordnance Survey in association with *caisel* and *ráth* enclosures.[88]

3.3 FARMING ON ESTATES

Notwithstanding their immunity from taxation (1.3), Gaelic literati were obliged to provide food for particular occasions.[89] This obligation as church tenants and *lucht*

---

[86] Macnamara, O'Davorens, 69.   [87] FitzPatrick, Antiquarian scholarship, 62.
[88] FitzPatrick, Antiquarian scholarship, 63.   [89] Simms, *From kings to warlords*, 143–5, 172.

tighe land occupants, alongside feeding families, guests, and schools, predicates significant land-based activity.

There are glimpses of the agricultural world of learned kindreds in the landscapes of their estates, chronicle entries, poems, and prose texts, in church records and land surveys. It has been shown through the profile of the half-quarter landholding of Cahermacnaghten (3.2.2) how combinations of sources can bring a farming landscape of *c*.1600 back into view. The historically recorded varied vegetation cover, the upstanding archaeological evidence for gardens in the glacial valley, stout walls suggesting a possible former park, and the references to gardens and a milking place in 1606 imply that the half-quarter of Cahermacnaghten was, in Gaelic landholding terms, an economically viable unit.[90]

The cultivation of land allocated to an *ollamh* was considered an important task. Seán Mac Fhlannchadha, *ollamh* in law to the earl of Desmond (d.1578), was noted as having the best tillage of any brehon lawyer in Ireland in his time.[91] In a poem addressed to the chief of Fir Mhanach, the poet Ó hEódhasa decried "the wild mountain border-land" where he had been placed and instead requested "land beside a prince, with both grazing and tillage".[92] He was troubled by the rough land that he had been allocated in the northern bounds of the lordship, expressing that he was "not by any means the tiller of hills, which but yesterday were the habitation of wolves."[93]

A profile of learned men as farmers is glimpsed among some of the schools in the sixteenth century. Tending crops was viewed as important work, according to remarks made by scribes about harvesting between periods of compiling sections of manuscripts. While writing part of Domhnall Ó Duibhdábhoireann's book in the law school of the Mac Aodhagáin brehon lawyers at Park in 1569, Aodh Ó Duibhdábhoireann remarked, "You are well off, Domnall, to be getting in the harvest and I slaving for you" (6.1.2).[94] Consigned to writing when his fellow scribes were engaged in harvesting, he further declared that "Even now Domnall Óg [perhaps the son of Domhnall Ó Duibhdábhoireann] had come to fetch the scribe Giolla Pátraic to go ply the reaping hook."[95] Whether that harvest happened on the Park or Cahermacnaghten estate was not noted, but the occasion drew the learned community into the fields.

A cereal-drying kiln has been recorded at *Teach Breac* on the Cahermacnaghten estate of the Ó Duibhdábhoireann lawyers. Another was excavated in the vicinity of the parish church of Nohaval (Co. Kerry), which was established by 1302 on the

---

[90] McErlean, Irish townland system, 334.   [91] M 1578.18, v, 1710, 1711.

[92] Carney, Eochaidh Ó hEoghusa, 200.   [93] Bergin, Unpublished Irish poems, 81.

[94] S. H. O'Grady 1926 (reprint 1992) *Catalogue of Irish manuscripts in the British Library*, i, 128. Dublin Institute for Advanced Studies; BL Egerton MS 88, 1564–70, Irish legal and grammatical miscellany compiled by Domhnall Ó Duibhdábhoirenn, fo. 58. London. British Library.

[95] O'Grady, *Catalogue of Irish manuscripts*, i, 128; BL Egerton MS 88, 60r.

landholding of a branch of the Mac Aodhagáin lawyers at Ballyegan (5.2).[96] Both kilns are of keyhole type, which generally consists of a curvilinear drystone-built bowl, a flue, a stoke-hole, and a drying platform. Thirteenth- and fourteenth-century dates have been suggested for two kilns of this type at Rathbeg, Co. Antrim and Kilferagh, Co. Kilkenny.[97] However, the keyhole-plan kiln enjoyed a long period of use from about the fifth century to the seventeenth, suggesting that typology alone cannot be used to unequivocally date a cereal-drying kiln.[98] The kiln in the *Teach Breac* settlement (Fig. 6.2) is quite large at *c*.8.8 m in length and retains its bowl and linteled flue. The walls of the bowl are constructed of flat-bedded karst; the uppermost courses were corbelled to form the roof. Its presence in the settlement, so close to the glacial valley, and the recovery of quantities of oats during the *Teach Breac* excavations (6.1.1), suggests that cereals were historically produced in Cahermacnaghten.

The second kiln, at Ballyegan, was excavated in tandem with a nearby *caisel*.[99] Dating evidence supported a tenth-century construction period for the *caisel*. Archaeobotanical study of cereal samples recovered from it showed that oats dominated in individual samples.[100] No scientific date was established for the construction or use of the kiln, but it appears to have postdated the construction of the *caisel*. It may be the case that the Ballyegan kiln relates to the establishment of the parish church of Nohaval during the high medieval period and the implied role of the Mac Aodhagáin lawyers as *airchinnigh* of the church land.

The interest of learned kindreds in improving the quality of their land is demonstrated by the acquisition in 1548 of a "Marl-hole field" ("*Gort puill in mharla*") by Seán Ó Maoilchonaire of the Ardkyle branch of the Ó Maoilchonaire historians, in the lordship of Clann Chuiléain (3.1).[101] Both marling and liming were practiced to fertilize land at a localized level during the medieval period and became more widespread in the sixteenth and seventeenth centuries.[102] Marl is a soft, white to grey mud-like sediment found in the shallow waters of small lakes or ponds in limestone bedrock. It is a calcareous deposit formed through the combined action of aquatic plants and animals that inhabit water rich in dissolved calcium carbonate. It was valued

[96] The place name Ballyegan is an anglicization of *Baile Uí Aodhagáin*. See https://www.logainm.ie/en/24325?s=Ballyegan> (accessed October 3, 2020); J. O'Connell and M. A. Costello 1958 Obligationes pro annatis diocesis Ardfertensis. *Archivium Hibernicum* 21, 29–30.

[97] Ó Súilleabháin, Downey, and Downey, *Antiquities*, 98.

[98] F. McCormick, T.R. Kerr, M. McClatchie and A. O'Sullivan 2014 *Early medieval agriculture, livestock and cereal production in Ireland, AD 400–1100*, 27. BAR International Series 2647. Oxford. BAR Publishing.

[99] M. Byrne 1991 A report on the excavation of a cashel at Ballyegan, near Castleisland, Co. Kerry. *Journal of the Kerry Archaeological and Historical Society* 24, 5–31.

[100] M.A. Monk, J. Tierney, and M. Hannon 1998 Archaeobotanical studies and early medieval Munster. In M.A. Monk and J. Sheehan (eds), *Early medieval Munster: archaeology, history and society*, 68, 72. Cork University Press.

[101] O'Grady, *Catalogue of Irish manuscripts*, i, 156.

[102] R. A. Dodgshon 1978 Land improvement in Scottish farming: marl and lime in Roxburghshire and Berwickshire in the eighteenth century. *The Agricultural History Review* 26, 1–2.

for its positive effects on soil structure. There has been no study of the medieval use of marl in Ireland, but it has been scientifically established that turloughs or seasonal lakes in limestone bedrock are a significant source of the substance. Of ninety turloughs surveyed on the western limestone lowlands of Ireland, forty-six contained marl.[103] The northeast area of Ardkyle is dominated by a turlough, a promising location for Seán Ó Maoilchonaire's "Marl-hole field."

Documented obligations of some learned kindreds living on episcopal mensal land reveal the type of foods produced on their estates. The Ó Cléirigh *ollamh* was a tenant of the bishop of Raphoe (2.1.1, 5.2.2). The lands on which he lived and conducted his school constituted "one quarter lyeinge neere the chaple of Kilbarren [Kilbarron]," according to a survey conducted in 1608.[104] An enumeration of his estate lands at Kilbarron included a statement of his obligation to provide the bishop with dairy produce and cereal grain annually:

> …paying thereout yerelie to the lord bishop of Raphoe thirteene shillings foure pence Irish, per annum, six meathers [*meadracha*] of butter and thirtie-foure meathers of meale.[105]

The implication is that in the early seventeenth century dairy cattle were grazed on the Kilbarron estate and butter made from the milk. The "meather" (*meadar*, a measure) that contained the butter was normally a well-seasoned quadrangular wooden vessel. That dairy herds were significant on the estate of the Ó Cléirigh *ollamh* is also implied by the place name Cloghbolie (*Cloch Bhuaile*) given to the townland in which Kilbarron Castle was situated (4.5). It translates as "stony milking place, cattle fold, summer pasture," inferring that cows were taken to that coastal tract of land for summer grazing.

The type of cereal grain harvested on Kilbarron estate, and out of which the bishop received a portion, is not specified, but in this marginal land oats are likely to have been the staple. Apart from the quarter of land that Ó Cléirigh held as *airchinneach*, an inquisition of 1609 noted that Lughaidh Ó Cléirigh had tenure of three additional quarters in the parish of Kilbarron.[106] Since the kindred's lands had been mortgaged to them by the Ó Domhnaill chief for £40 during the second half of the sixteenth century, the three additional quarters including the denomination of Creevy appear to have been *lucht tighe* of the Ó Domhnaill chief (2.1.1). After Ó Domhnaill's death in 1609, the Ó Cléirigh kindred had to pay £4, two muttons, and a pair of gloves to the

---

[103] C. E. Coxon and P. Coxon 1994 Carbonate deposition in turloughs (seasonal lakes) on the western limestone lowlands of Ireland. *Irish Geography* 27, 28–35.

[104] Mac Neill and Hogan, A booke of the kings lands, 185.

[105] Costello, *De annatis Hiberniae*, i, 278; Mac Neill and Hogan, A booke of the kings lands, 185.

[106] Costello, *De annatis Hiberniae*, i, 276.

FIG. 3.9. Looking north across Lough Meelagh to the parish church of Kilronan with the bare head of Kilronan Mountain right of picture (photo E. FitzPatrick).

Crown annually, implying that sheep were reared on their lands, and that a leather-worker provided finished leather goods to them when required.[107]

The chronicles attribute large herds to some learned men. The obituary of Dubthach Ó Duibhgeannáin, *ollamh* in *seanchas* to Mac Diarmada, chief of Magh Luirg, notes his death in 1495 at his house in Kilronan (Fig. 3.9) and refers to him as "the richest of the literati of Ireland in flocks and herds."[108] Learned kindreds were not spared the cattle-raiding (*creach*) commonplace in borderlands of Gaelic lordships, which intimates the considerable land-based wealth of some of them. As earlier seen, the Mac Bruaideadha *ollamh* in poetry to the overlord of Tuadhmhumhain, had his cattle seized and returned to him during a raid in 1599 (2.1.2).[109] In 1392 the poet Ó Cobhthaigh, "candle of poetry and science of Western Europe," suffered a big raid (*creach mór*), but afterwards he received 800 cows, "the fullest restitution that a poet got in his time."[110] The chronicler notes that Ó Cobhthaigh was raided in revenge for an incursion of his own into north Leinster "seeking booty," which implies that learned men were as much perpetrators as victims of raiding.[111] The potential of literati to develop substantial herds of livestock was facilitated by gift-giving, which Gaelic chiefs indulged from the spoils of cattle that they seized from rivals. An encomiastic poem for Briain Mág Shamhradháin, chief of Tellach nEachach (d. 1298), praised his

---

[107] Costello, *De annatis Hiberniae*, i, 276. [108] M 1495.16, iv, 1218, 1219.

[109] M 1599.20, vi, 2104, 2105. [110] MIA fragment III 1392.5, 142, 143.

[111] See discussion of the period of fragment III in MIA, xiv–xix.

generosity in gifting livestock to poets. The unknown poet remarked how the chief often sent a cow from the wealth of his raids to his own house.[112]

The importance of gift-giving to acquiring a riding-horse (*each*)[113] was the subject of two late thirteenth-century poems by Giolla Pádraig Mac Naimhin. The poet complained to his patron, Briain Mág Shamhradháin, chief of Tellach nEachach in south Ulster, that he had a "small slow-paced horse" and would prefer a swifter one "when I ride after you, as I used to be covered with mud cast up from your steed's hooves, and filth is thrown up on my face."[114] In a second poem, he quarreled with his son, "Go and get a horse for yourself; put on your [poet's] dress and go thy round [*cuairt*] with thy poets; if thou takest a poem with thee thou shalt get a horse in return."[115]

3.3.1 The Park

Between the seventeenth and late nineteenth century, approximately 70 per cent of the former learned kindred estates consulted for this work (Fig. 1.2; Appendix) were incorporated into large and small landed estates or found on the fringes of them.[116] Park-related toponyms are a common occurrence in those contexts. What this might mean in respect of determining the nature of land utilization on the Gaelic estates that preceded the landed estates is explored in what follows.

The Irish *páirc* (park) is a Romance-language word borrowed into Irish during the period of Anglo-Norman settlement.[117] In Britain and Ireland, the fashion for parks as enclosures for semi-wild animals, especially deer, was advanced by Anglo-Norman society from the thirteenth century.[118] It was followed later, by the seventeenth-century park of symmetrical design, the naturalized parks of the late eighteenth century, and new parks demonstrating advances in agriculture and horticulture between 1840 and 1914.[119]

Reeves-Smyth has shown that "historical continuity is characteristic of Irish demesnes, with many of them retaining a medieval nucleus." Medieval buildings, specifically tower-houses and churches, have been cited as the obvious marks of that continuity.[120] A case can now also be made for the incorporation of Gaelic learned

---

[112] L. McKenna (ed.) 1947a *The Book of Magauran: Leabhar Méig Shamhradháin*, 21, 297, 403. Dublin Institute for Advanced Studies.

[113] Kelly, *Early Irish farming*, 89–90.   [114] McKenna, *Book of Magauran*, 54, 310.

[115] McKenna, *Book of Magauran*, 59, 311.   [116] FitzPatrick, *Ollamh, biatach, comharba*, 169–77.

[117] Quin, *Dictionary*, 494:172; F. Beglane 2015 *Anglo-Norman parks in medieval Ireland*. Dublin. Four Courts Press.

[118] Beglane, *Anglo-Norman parks*, 38–40.

[119] T. Reeves-Smyth 2011 Demesnes. In F. H. A. Aalen, K. Whelan, and M. Stout (eds), *Atlas of the Irish rural landscape*, 278–86. Cork University Press.

[120] Reeves-Smyth, Demesnes, 278.

kindred lands and buildings within early modern and modern demesnes. Furthermore, there is some evidence to support the creation of park landscapes by Gaelic chiefs in the late medieval period, within which learned kindreds were allocated estates.[121]

Medieval parks had multiple uses, enclosing livestock, pasture, crops, and trees.[122] Park-related place names survive as the names of townlands, fields, and monuments in Ireland.[123] The principal source of evidence for them is the first-edition six-inch Ordnance Survey, which notes a wide range of park-related townland names, such as "Deer Park," "Stone Park," "White Park," "Wood Park," but park place names are also mentioned in seventeenth-century rolls and surveys and occasionally cited in sixteenth-century Gaelic sources. The estate of a Connacht branch of the Mac Aodhagáin brehon lawyers was cited as "*an páirc*" ("the park") in 1567 by a scribe contributing to the book of Domhnall Ó Duibhdábhoireann.[124] It was listed as the property of John Mac Aodhagáin in an English inquisition of castles and their owners in Co. Galway, dated 1574.[125] Park was a quarter of land, 686 unprofitable and 207 profitable acres prone to flooding, dominated by bog in part, but containing good grazing for cattle and horses (Fig. 3.11). In the modern landscape, the townlands of Park East and Park West refer to the former Mac Aodhagáin estate. The half-quarters of Timard, adjoining Park on its south side, and Timadooaun to the west, were also lands of the Mac Aodhagáin lawyers.[126]

Park was situated in Corca Mogha, a vassal territory of the overlordship of Uí Mhaine, next to the Mac David Burke lordship of Clann Conmhaigh (Fig. 3.10). The dominant topography of this borderscape were large stretches of bog, and the lake of Kiltullagh (Fig. 3.11). Symptomatic of the fluid nature of Gaelic territorial boundaries, Park was described in the 1570s as being situated in the western extent of Uí Mhaine,[127] but by 1585 it was considered part of Clann Conmhaigh.[128]

A park was integral to Lackan (*Lecan*, Co. Sligo), the Atlantic seaboard estate of Mac Fhirbhisigh, *ollamh* in *seanchas* to the chief of Tír Fiachrach (Fig. 1.2). A small townland of 124 acres recorded as "Parke" in 1617 lay between Lackan and Kilglass (Fig. 3.12).[129] The Mac Fhirbhisigh hereditary historians were based at Lackan from at least as early as the fourteenth century. It was from there that Giolla Íosa Mac

---

[121] FitzPatrick, Antiquarian scholarship, 62-3; FitzPatrick, *Ollamh, biatach, comharba*, 169–76.

[122] O. Rackham 1976 *Trees and woodland in the British landscape*, 151–3. London. J. M. Dent.

[123] For park place-name evidence, see Beglane, *Anglo-Norman parks*, 20–2.

[124] O'Grady, *Catalogue of Irish manuscripts*, i, 111; BL Egerton MS 88, fo. 12b, col. 2; O'Sullivan, Book of Domhnall, 276–98.

[125] J. P. Nolan 1901 Galway castles and owners in 1574. *Journal of the Galway Archaeological and Historical Society* 1 (2), 122.

[126] Freeman, *Compossicion booke*, 80, 83; Griffith, *Patent rolls of James I*, 414; T. B. Costello 1940 The ancient law school of Park, Co. Galway. *Journal of the Galway Archaeological and Historical Society* 19 (1–2), 97.

[127] The western extent of Uí Mhaine is the barony of Tiaquin; Nolan, Galway castles, 122.

[128] Freeman, *Compossicion booke*, 80.   [129] Griffith, *Patent rolls of James I*, 332.

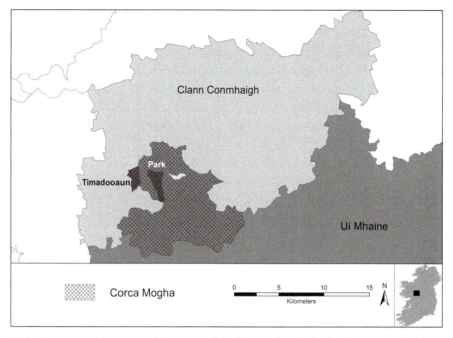

FIG. 3.10. The territorial context of the estate of the Mac Aodhagáin brehon lawyers at Park (map N. McCarthy).

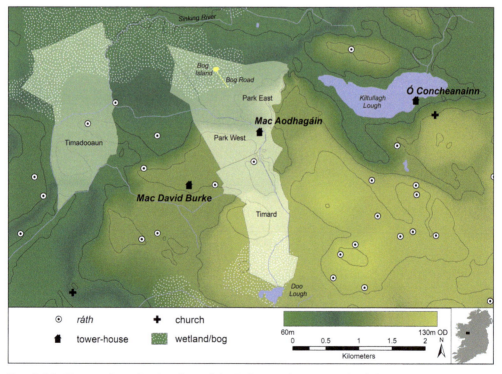

FIG. 3.11. Topography and archaeology of the Park estate (map N. McCarthy).

Fhirbhisigh wrote the *Book of Lecan* between 1397 and 1418, assisted by Murchadh Riabhach Ó Cuindlis and Adam Ó Cuirnín.[130] The writing may have taken place in the parish church of Kilglass, which adjoined the east side of Park. Various officials of that church in the fifteenth and sixteenth centuries were learned men, which suggests a community of knowledge focused on the learned occupations of the Mac Fhirbhisigh *ollamhain* in *seanchas* and their estate at Lackan (5.0).[131] Since Anglo-Norman manorial settlements were established in Tír Fiachrach in the thirteenth century, there is a possibility that the Lackan park had its origins, alongside two moated sites, in an Anglo-Norman occupation of this coastal landscape. However, the adoption and indeed construction of moated sites by Gaelic chiefs in the fourteenth century has been confirmed as a feature of some Gaelic lordships in north Connacht,[132] and it is therefore possible that the Lackan moated sites and the park represent a former fourteenth-century *pailís*-centered settlement of the chief of Tír Fiachrach that was later allocated to his *ollamh* (4.3).[133]

Park place names occur as field names, especially relating to horses and deer enclosed on the outlying lands of demesnes. For example, a branch of the Ó Cobhthaigh poets had an estate at Ballinkeeny (Co. Westmeath) in the lordship of Rathconrath, which became part of the demesne of Mosstown House.[134] The emparked landscape, containing a horse park and race park, incorporated a late medieval tower-house and two contiguous medieval settlement enclosures with wall-footings of three buildings, which may have been integral to the Ó Cobhthaigh phase of occupation of this land in the sixteenth and seventeenth centuries.[135]

Early modern and modern emparkment of former learned kindred estates and their immediate environs is especially defined by country-house deer parks.[136] Among them is the "Deer Parke" created, before it was mapped in 1734, on the demesne of the Dillon family of Clonbrock (Co. Galway). It adjoined Ballydoogan, the former estate of the Ó Dubhagáin historians to the Ó Ceallaigh chiefs (4.3).[137] Likewise, there was an "Old Deer Park" recorded in the nineteenth century adjoining the south side of

[130] N. Ó Muraíle 2005b Book of Lecan. In S. Duffy (ed.), *Medieval Ireland: an encyclopedia*, 269–70. New York and London. Routledge.

[131] O'Rahilly, Irish poets, 108.

[132] K. D. O'Conor 2000 The ethnicity of Irish moated sites. *Ruralia* 3, 101.

[133] E. FitzPatrick 2016 The last kings of Ireland: material expressions of Gaelic lordship *c.* 1300–1400 AD. In K. Buchanan and L. H. S. Dean, with M. Penman (eds), *Medieval and early modern representations of authority in Scotland and the British Isles*, 201–4. London and New York. Taylor and Francis.

[134] Nicholls, *Irish fiants*, iii, 353 [6378], 526 [6574]; D. O'Brien 2014 *The houses and landed families of Westmeath*, 152. Athlone.

[135] The medieval settlement enclosures and buildings were surveyed in 1979 by the Archaeological Survey of Ireland, before they were quarried out.

[136] FitzPatrick, *Ollamh, biatach, comharba*, 168–70.

[137] NLI Map 34 M; FitzPatrick, The last kings, 204; FitzPatrick, *Ollamh, biatach, comharba*, 168, 188.

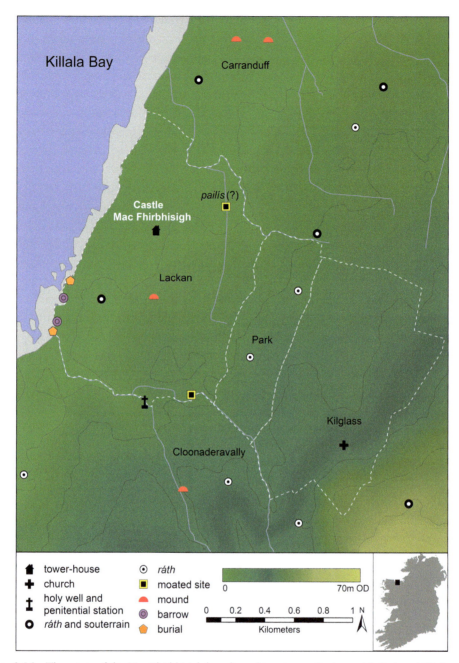

Killala Bay

Carranduff

pailís (?)

Castle
Mac Fhirbhisigh

Lackan

Park

Kilglass

Cloonaderavally

▲ tower-house	⊙ *ráth*
✚ church	☐ moated site
⚷ holy well and penitential station	⬤ mound
◉ *ráth* and souterrain	⦾ barrow
	⬠ burial

0   70m OD

0   0.2   0.4   0.6   0.8   1 N
Kilometers

FIG. 3.12. The estate of the Mac Fhirbhisigh hereditary historians at Lackan, with Park and Kilglass (map N. McCarthy).

Mount Pleasant Demesne and its Georgian house, at Curravordy (Co. Cork), which was the erstwhile estate of the Ó Cáinte poets who served the Mac Cárthaigh chiefs of Cairbre in Munster (Fig. 1.2).[138]

Ballymacaward, the former estate of the Mac an Bhaird poets (2.1.1) overlooking the Erne estuary in southern Tír Conaill, incorporates a deer park. Their estate was acquired by Trinity College Dublin as part of a grant of 4,000 acres of the barony of Tirhugh during the plantation of Ulster, and leased in 1616 to Henry Folliott, baron of Ballyshannon. The Folliott family transformed Ballymacaward into Wardtown Demesne. A substantial deer park enclosed by high stone walls was laid out on the northeast side of Wardtown House, the residence the family built in 1739–40 on the site of an earlier dwelling of the second half of the seventeenth century.[139]

Such co-occurrences of deer parks and former learned kindred lands might be reductively explained by the fact that their estates were absorbed within the demesnes and tenanted estates of modern country houses that created deer parks, but as suggested by the historical profiles of some deer parks, the relationship could also be attributed to deer environments that were already an established feature of some Gaelic learned kindred lands before modern emparkment.

The fosse and bank of a large deer park can be traced south of Redwood Castle (Co. Tipperary) on the former estate of the Mac Aodhagáin brehon lawyers of Ballymacegan and Redwood (6.1.3; Fig. 6.21), in the northern borderland of the Munster lordship of Urumhain. The deer park is overlooked by Carrigeen Hill, which is frequented by wild fallow deer (Fig. 3.13). Redwood Castle was recorded in 1543 as a residence of

FIG. 3.13. Carrigeen Hill, Redwood (photo E. FitzPatrick).

---

[138] O'Rahilly, *Irish poets*, 109. Various members of the Ó Cáinte learned kindred are provenanced to Curravordy in 1601.

[139] Allingham, *Ballyshannon*, 61–2.

Ó Cinnéide, chief of Urumhain, which, by *c*.1600, he had ceded to the Mac Aodhagáin lawyers as their residence.[140] As late as the seventeenth century, Ó Cinnéide held Carrigeen Hill and Ducappa in Redwood townland between which the deer park lies. It is possible that the park was created out of an existing deer covert that was a hunting preserve of the chief when in residence at Redwood.[141]

Research on historical deer parks in Britain has shown that they were created mainly through emparkment of woods already containing deer coverts.[142] There is no reason to believe that this process was any different in Ireland. Such a case can be made for the estate landscape of the Ó Maoilchonaire historians and poets at Ardkyle west of the Bunratty River and north of Bunratty Castle, which was the principal seat of the overlord of Tuadhmhumhain from *c*.1583. Ardkyle was a heavily emparked area associated with several demesnes by the nineteenth century. The English royal forest of Cratloe, documented in the thirteenth century, lay *c*.6 km to the southeast of it and is represented in the modern landscape by Cratloe Woods.[143] The extent of that royal forest is not known, but the concentration of later recorded parkland and deer parks, further north and west, suggests that it was more extensive in the medieval past than the bounds of its modern counterpart.

As noted (3.1), Ardkyle was originally larger than the townland that bears its name. It included Newpark and Deerpark in the parish of Drumline and possibly Woodpark and Deerpark in the adjoining parish of Bunratty. There is an insight to the parkland context of Ardkyle in a pardon issued to "Shane Parke O Mulchonile" [Ó Maoilchonaire] of Ardkyle in 1602–3.[144] His epithet "Parke" distinguished him by the place where he lived and suggests that long before the townlands of Deerpark and Woodpark were recorded by the first Ordnance Survey in the nineteenth century, there was a park within the Ardkyle landholding of the Ó Maoilchonaire kindred, or that their entire estate was parkland carved out of the fringes of the old royal forest of Cratloe.

In the same lordship of West Clann Chuileáin, a hunting scene was painted on a wall of the first floor of Urlan tower-house (Co. Clare), the residence of a branch of the Mac Fhlannchadha learned kindred of lawyers. It was destroyed when the

---

[140] E. Curtis (ed. and tr.) 1937 *Calendar of Ormond deeds 1509–1547*, 244. Dublin. Irish Manuscripts Commission.

[141] R. C. Simington 1934 *The civil survey* AD *1654–56, County of Tipperary, ii: western and northern baronies*, 238, 241. Dublin. The Stationery Office; Curtis, *Calendar of Ormond deeds*, 244.

[142] G. J. Cooper and W. D. Shannon 2017 The control of salters (deer-leaps) in private deer-parks associated with forests: a case study using a 1608 map of Leagram Park in the Forest of Bowland, Lancashire. *Landscape History* 38 (1), 43.

[143] H. S. Sweetman and G. F. Handcock (eds) 1886 *Calendar of documents relating to Ireland 1302–1307*, ii, no. 51. London. Longman; Beglane, Forests and chases, 92, 93.

[144] Nicholls, *Irish fiants*, iii, 617 [6765].

FIG. 3.14. Keel deer park, Ballymackeagan (photo E. FitzPatrick).

tower-house collapsed in 1999, but an earlier record of it shows a stag being attacked by two hunting hounds.[145]

The suitability of learned kindred lands for the keeping of deer and other livestock is sometimes indicated in chronicle entries and premodern place names during the lifetimes of those denominations. Ballymackeagan was the landholding of the branch of the Mac Aodhagáin brehon lawyers who served the Ó Fearghail Buidhe of Pallas, in the lordship of Southern Anghal (west and south Co. Longford). Within the estate landscape there are two deer parks, large tracts of rocky pasture enclosed by high stone walls (Fig. 3.14), which are indicated as areas of tree-cover on the mid seventeenth-century Down Survey parish map of Noughaval.[146] Historical tree cover is reflected too in the local place name Creevagh (*An Chraobhach*, "bushy/branchy place") by the River Inny, pointing to former underwood appropriate to deer and other livestock. Creevagh was the setting of a livestock raid in 1468 during which some forty riding-horses were taken, along with cattle.[147]

A notable woodland on the estate of a distinguished branch of the Ó Ceandamháin medical family, in the north Connacht lordship of Tír Amhalgaidh, is twice cited as "Neill's Wood" (*Coill Néill*) in medical texts compiled by a member of the family in 1563.[148] The wood features in a comment by Cairbre Ó Ceandamháin on a manuscript page he was preparing for the *ollamh* of Islay, John Mac Bethadh, while taking

[145] K. Morton and C. Oldenbourg 2005 Catalogue of the wall paintings. In C. Manning, P. Gosling, and J. Waddell (eds), *New survey of Clare Island, v: the abbey*, 4, 106–7. Dublin. Royal Irish Academy; D. F. Gleeson 1936 Drawing of a hunting scene, Urlan Castle, Co. Clare. *JRSAI* 6, 193.

[146] <https://downsurvey.tchpc.tcd.ie/down-survey-maps.php#bm=Abbeyshrule&c=Longford> (accessed December 9, 2020); FitzPatrick, *Ollamh, biatach, comharba*, 169–70.

[147] AConn 1468.38, 547.   [148] Gillespie, Scribes and manuscripts, 15.

refuge during Tudor military action in Connacht. In a note of apology to the *ollamh* for his work, he remarked "…no wonder; for I am ever on the move, flying before certain English, up and down Neill's Wood [*Coill Néill*], and it is in the very wood I have written a part of it, and prepared the skin [*an croicinn*]."[149] The name of the Ó Ceandamháin estate was Ballyvicmaha (*Baile Mhic Mhatha*, "holding/settlement of the son of Mathew"), which endures as the townland of Ballyvicmaha (Co. Mayo).[150] The place name *Coill Néill* is obsolete, but its extent is indicated by the historical denominations of Creevy ("bushy/branchy place") and Dervin (*Dairbhín*, "little oak grove") that adjoin the west and east sides of Ballyvicmaha. Creevy was part of the Ó Ceandamháin estate in 1592.[151] Its landscape is predominantly bog and wet grassland, with scatters of medieval settlement enclosures, and several lakes, the largest of which, Lough Agawna and Lough Naithim, each contain a *crannóg*.

Co-occurrences of park place names with medieval settlement enclosures aid identification of parks in Gaelic contexts. The *caisel* and the *ráth* occur with regularity in several of the park locations identified on Gaelic learned kindred landholdings. There are two *caisel* enclosures in an area of rocky pasture designated "Parknararra" in the southeast corner of Caherclanchy, the estate of a branch of the Mac Fhlannchadha brehon lawyers in Tuadhmhumhain (Fig. 4.2). Park Fort is a small enclosure in Creevy townland on the Kilbarron estate of the Ó Cléirigh historians (Fig.2.2). It has been levelled, but Lockwood's record of the monument indicates that it was a *caisel*, a "very perfect rampart of stone about fifteen feet thick [4.5 m], and at five or six feet in height [1.5 m] with an inside diameter of forty-three feet [14 m]." He described the small garth as "a perfect paradise of wild flowers—primrose and anemone, bluebells and white starwort—to be followed a little later on by wild rose and woodbine, amidst masses of tall bracken."[152]

The park-related names of these monuments were recorded by the nineteenth-century Ordnance Survey. It is not known when they were first conferred on them. Even if their names relate to early modern or modern periods of emparkment, the enclosures must have been selected for that distinction because of a preexisting role on learned kindred estates. The most obvious function for the large and small enclosures that have no trace of buildings within them is as holding-pens for cattle, sheep, and horses, milking-folds for cows, and perhaps areas for corralling and butchering deer.[153] Small *caisel* enclosures such as Park Fort in Creevy, with its masterfully constructed walls, may have had an alternative use for growing and protecting plants in the intensively pastoral farming landscapes of late medieval Gaelic estates.

---

[149] O'Grady, *Catalogue of Irish manuscripts*, 267; Bannerman, *The Beatons*, 117.

[150] Gillespie, Scribes and manuscripts, 15.

[151] Nicholls, *Irish fiants*, iii, 208 [5798]. Richard "O Cannovane, of Cryvagh" was pardoned in 1592.

[152] Lockwood, Some notes, 91.

[153] Beglane (*Anglo-Norman parks*, 191) suggested that early medieval ring-forts may have been reused as parkers' lodges in Anglo-Norman parks.

3.4 NATURAL RESOURCES ON ESTATES

The estates of certain high-profile learned kindreds were situated in landscapes endowed with earth materials, in respect of which two initial points need to be made. Little is known about the locations and workings of mines in the lordships of late medieval and early modern Ireland, and the evidence for the exploitation of metal ores and building stone in the environs of learned kindred estates is predominantly modern.

The presence of natural resources on the *lucht tighe* lands of some Gaelic chiefs, which included estates allocated to members of the learned class, poses important research questions. Were Gaelic chiefs aware of minerals, metal ores, and quarriable stone within their *lucht tighe* lands, and was the availability of earth materials a consideration in allocating an estate to an *ollamh*?

Literati who were engaged in manuscript production had immediate need of particular earth materials, such as chalk and pumice. Ciothruadh Mág Fhionngaill of Tory Island, who contributed to the compilation of a book (*Leabhar Chlainne Suibhne*) for the ruling family of the lordship of Fanad (Fig. 1.1), between 1513 and 1514, remarked that he "wrote this down to here, without chalk or pumice, with a bad implement."[154] The historian Tadhg Mac Fithil of Tír Conaill also found himself without adequate writing equipment when working on his contribution to the same book between 1532 and 1544. He explained that he wrote it, "in haste and with a bad implement [*le drochaidhme*], without chalk [*can chailc*], or pumice-stone [*can chubhar*]."[155]

Pumice is a volcanic rock that was valued by both parchment-makers and scribes for its abrasive quality. It has been found around the coasts of north Atlantic Europe, where it is distributed on contemporary and raised beaches in Iceland, Scandinavia, Germany, Russia, Britain (with concentrations in the Western Isles, Orkney, and Shetland).[156] It occurs to a lesser extent in Ireland, at the mouth of the River Bann, Co. Derry, and at Dundrum Bay, Co. Down, on a raised shoreline at Fortstewart west of the Inishowen Peninsula, Co. Donegal, and on Inis Mór, Co. Galway where brown pumice pieces were recovered from late Bronze Age deposits during excavations at *Dún Aonghasa*. The *Dún Aonghasa* pumice is believed to have been sourced from a local deposit.[157] Exchange of more specialist writing materials, such as pumice stone, may have happened because of scholarly networks within Ireland and between Ireland and western Scotland. However, other abrasive minerals, such as sandstone, would have been good substitutes.

---

[154] Walsh, P. 1920 *Leabhar Chlainne Suibhne: an account of the MacSweeney families in Ireland, with pedigrees*, xlv, fo. 25, xlv, fo. 68, xlv, fo. 86, xlvi, fo. 105. Dublin. Dollard.

[155] Walsh, *Leabhar Chlainne Suibhne*, 74–5.

[156] A. Newton 2000 Ocean-transported pumice in the north Atlantic, 71. PhD diss., University of Edinburgh.

[157] C. Cotter 2012 *The western stone forts project*, ii, 86–91. Dublin. Wordwell.

Chalk is evidently rare in Ireland. It is found on the Co. Antrim coast and at Ballydeenlea, Co. Kerry.[158] A deposit of chalk is known from the south and west slopes of Ballgalley Hill, north of Larne on the east coast of Antrim. The hill is distinguished by part of a volcanic plug of dolerite and by archaeological evidence for a Neolithic flint-mining settlement and a Bronze Age burial.[159] Both the hill and a late medieval building known as Carn Castle, situated at the northern tip of Ballygalley Head, are associated with the Ó Gnímh kindred of poets who served the lordship of Clann Aodha Buidhe and the later MacDonnells of the Glens of Antrim (Fig. 1.2).[160] Ballgalley Hill was a coastal boundary landmark of both the *túath* of Larne and the lordship of Clann Aodha Buidhe. Its physical profile, archaeology, territorial setting and associations with a poetic kindred suggest that it was a *formaoil* of the *túath* and the lordship. Whether the Ó Gnímh kindred extracted chalk on the hill for their own purposes is not known, but such a useful resource is unlikely to have been overlooked. Chalk was by no means an essential material for scribes. There were substitutes. Limestone, when burned, becomes calcium oxide or quicklime, small lumps of which could be handily used to whiten areas of a manuscript page where writing errors had been abraded.

The leading branch of the Mac Fhlannchadha brehon lawyers served the overlord of Tuadhmhumhain from their estate at Túath Ghlae on the Atlantic coast of the lordship of Corca Modhruadh (Co. Clare). Their substantial estate was coextensive with the parish of Killilagh, which is endowed with silver, lead and quarriable stone.[161] The seat of the family, as recorded in the sixteenth century, was Knockfin (Fig. 3.15), a sufficiently noteworthy place to have been marked by Robert Lythe on his map of Munster (1572) and recorded several times in the chronicles.[162] It is a long ridge where the limestone and shale bedrock of the estate meet and to which the antiquary O'Donovan ascribed the alternative name *Tulach Finn* ("Fionn's Hill"; 2.3).[163] In 1622 the estate of Túath Ghlae was regranted as the manor of Knockfin to Boetius Óg Mac Fhlannchadha by James I, "with liberty to enjoy free warren and chase," which suggests that the lands of the manor contained an established hunting ground.[164]

[158] G. L. Herries Davies 2011 The chalk outlier at Ballydeenlea, Co. Kerry: a story of discovery. *Irish Journal of Earth Sciences* 29, 27–38.

[159] A. E. P. Collins 1978 Excavations on Ballygalley Hill, County Antrim. *Ulster Journal of Archaeology* 41 (Third Series), 15–32.

[160] B. Ó Cuiv 1984 The family of Ó Gnímh in Ireland and Scotland: a look at the sources. *Nomina* 8, 68.

[161] D. F. Gleeson 1962 *A history of the diocese of Killaloe*, 508. Dublin. M. H. Gill.

[162] NA MPF/1/73, 1572, "A single draght of Mounster" by Robert Lythe. Kew. National Archives; M 1598.8, vi, 2050, 2051.

[163] J. O'Donovan (ed. and tr.) 1844 *The genealogies, tribes and customs of Hy-Fiachrach, commonly called O'Dowda's country*, 433. Dublin. Irish Archaeological Society.

[164] Griffith, *Irish patent rolls*, 526.

Within the bounds of Túath Ghlae, there were at least two areas that contained natural resources—Doolin, on the Atlantic coast, where there were deposits of lead and silver, and Ballyvara, in the southern bounds of the estate, which was marked by Knocknalarabana, a hill of millstone grit (Fig. 3.15). Boetius Mac Fhlannchadha of Knockfin was the proprietor of Doolin until 1641, and he shared the proprietorship of Ballyvara with a member of the Uí Bhriain ruling family until that time.[165]

The Ordnance Survey of 1839 noted a lead and silver mine at Doolin, south of Knockfin. When it was first opened has not yet been established, but it was obsolete by 1845.[166] The field evidence for the mine suggests that it was a small-scale operation. There are two enclosures close to it. They are integral to an extensive concentration of *caisel* enclosures, distributed along a terrace of cherty limestone on the western coastline of the Mac Fhlannchadha estate (Fig. 3.15). Electrical resistivity and magnetometry surveys around the disused modern mine and within the two medieval settlement enclosures adjacent to it would be useful methods of ascertaining whether smelting furnaces and slags can be identified in relatively datable contexts.

Quarrying has been conducted on the ridge of Knocknalarabana since at least the 1830s, but historically its coarse sandstone must have been an important source for millstone and quernstone production long before then.[167] Baug's investigations of the quarries at Hyllestad in western Norway has shown the potential of archaeological approaches to reveal quarry landscapes exploited to produce querns and millstones between the ninth and sixteenth centuries.[168] Potential production sites of grinding stones have not yet been the subject of archaeological research in Ireland, but looking on the bounds of learned kindred estates may prove to be a fruitful first step in that search.[169] Knocknalarabana was a landmark of the southern boundary of the medieval parish of Killilagh and Mac Fhlannchadha's estate of Túath Ghlae. A measure of the importance attached to it, and a clue to potentially earlier exploitation of its resource, is found in the mid-seventeenth-century Down Survey map of the barony of Corcomroe (the former lordship of Corca Modhruadh), which noted that even at that time it was a subject of controversy between the adjoining parishes.[170] There is a record too of an actively exploited source of grinding stones on the bounds of Ballymacaward, the former estate of the Mac Bhaird poets in southern Tír Conaill (2.1.1). In the nineteenth century a coastal rock formation of coarse-grained sandstone called "*Carraig na mbróinte*" ("rock of the millstones"), which marked the

---

[165] Simington, *Books of survey and distribution*, iv, 252, 254.

[166] K. M. Griffin, K. A. Griffin, and B. J. Griffin 2020 *Doolin: history and memories*, 91. Technological University Dublin.

[167] Nugent, *Gaelic clans*, 95.

[168] I. Baug 2006 The quarries in Hyllestad: production of quern stones and millstones in western Norway. In A. Belmont and F. Mangartz (eds), *Millstone quarries: research, protection and valorization of an European industrial heritage*, 55–9. Mainz. Verlag des Römisch-Germanisches Zentralmuseum.

[169] FitzPatrick, Finn's seat, 54–5.

[170] <http://downsurvey.tchpc.tcd.ie/down-survey-maps.php#bm=Corcumroe&c=Clare> (accessed March 8, 2022).

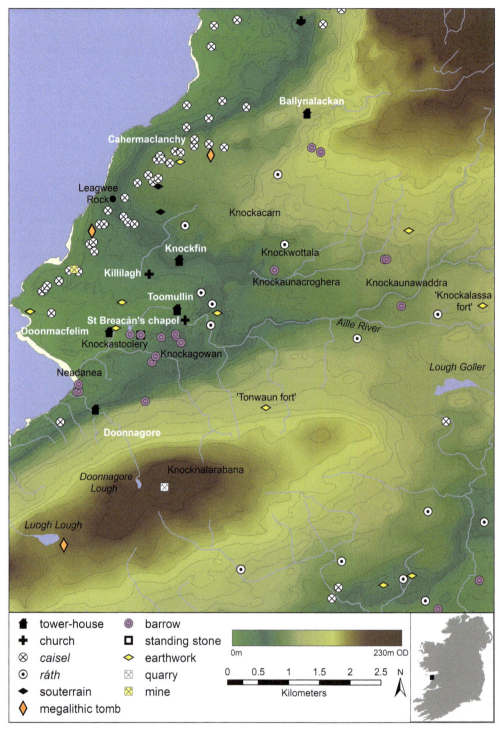

FIG. 3.15. Mac Fhlannchadha's estate of Túath Ghlae, prehistory, natural resources, and medieval settlement (map N. McCarthy).

southwesterly point of Ballymacaward, was quarried for querns. Writing in 1879, Allingham noted that a partially formed and abandoned upper stone of a quern had been found there, cut where it was quarried.[171]

As earlier established, the estate of the Ó Dálaigh poets of Muinter Bháire in the lordship of Fonn Iartharach was the entire Sheepshead Peninsula (3.1). It was considered remarkable only for its uncivilized landscape, dominated by Seefin Mountain (2.3), with a precipitous northern coastline mostly unsuited to settlement. However, the peninsula was well endowed with metal ores and slate along its north side, with concentrations of copper deposits between Seefin and Caher Mountain and further west on the coast. Copper was mined and blue slate quarried along the northern coastline in the nineteenth century (Fig. 3.16).[172] Slate was also worked on the south coast at Rosskerrig, a short distance southeast of the location of the Ó Dálaigh school

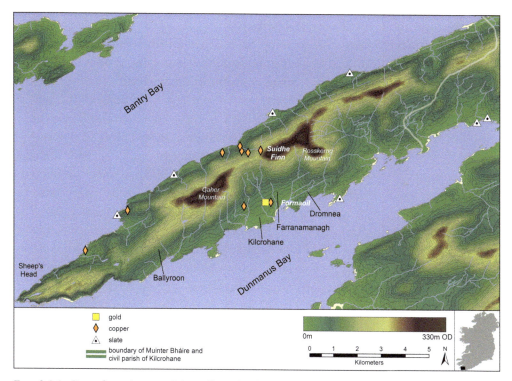

FIG. 3.16. Sites of metal ores and slate, Sheepshead Peninsula (map N. McCarthy).

[171] Allingham, *Ballyshannon*, 87.

[172] Copper was mined at Gortavallig and Killeen North, Glanalin, and Carravilleen; G. A. J. Cole 1922 *Memoir and map of localities of minerals of economic importance and metalliferous mines in Ireland*, 53, 56, 58. Dublin. The Stationery Office.

at Dromnea (6.3.1).[173] Over the 300 years or more that the Ó Dálaigh poets lived and worked on Sheepshead Peninsula, they are likely to have acquired some knowledge of the earth materials on their estate. The slate of the peninsula, for instance, would have been a useful resource for the work of their school (Fig. 3.16).

The brevity of a list of active mines in Ireland, compiled *c*.1600, implies that very little mining happened in Gaelic lordships.[174] Yet, law texts of early medieval origin, such as the *Senchas Már* ("Great Tradition"), indicate that laws of distraint were required in respect of mining, which suggests that it was commonplace activity. Extracting copper or iron ore from a cliff or excavating in a silver mine on the property of another person were considered crimes.[175] It is hardly conceivable that knowledge of the locations of resources was somehow lost between the early and late medieval period, and that mineral extraction was rare in Gaelic polities. The three Gaelic lordships listed as involved in mining *c*.1600 reflect those officially recorded by the English administration in Ireland.[176] There are likely to have been many more small-scale operations that were not detected.

No pre-seventeenth-century archaeological evidence for silver mining has yet been identified in a Gaelic lordship. English administrative documents confirm that mining for silver took place in the county of Tipperary in the late thirteenth century and at a few other centers controlled or influenced by the English Crown between the late fifteenth century and the early seventeenth.[177] One of those centers was the silver mine attributed to Ó Lochlainn, chief of Boireann, in the list of mines *c*.1600. It appears to have been in Ailwee Mountain, where the first Ordnance Survey later marked a lead and silver mine in 1842. It was described in the list of *c*.1600 as being "by his castell,"[178] which was Castle Mael (*Caisleán Maoil*, "bare castle"), *c*.700 m northeast of the Ailwee mine. Furthermore, the estate of the Ó Callanáin medical kindred of Kilweelran adjoined the north side of Ailwee. It was land of the Cistercian Abbey of Corcomroe on which the kindred had lived at least as early as the fifteenth century (Fig. 1.4).[179] The proximity to Ailwee of both a castle of the ruling family and the Cistercian-based estate of their hereditary medical kindred makes a strong case for it as the silver mine of the lordship cited in the list of *c*.1600. Just how early the resource

---

[173] Slate was quarried at Gortnakilly and Gouladoo; M. Pracht and A. G. Sleeman 2002 *Geology of west Cork: a geological description of west Cork and adjacent parts of Kerry to accompany the bedrock geology 1:100, 000 scale map series, sheet 24, west Cork*, 5, 12, 13, 15, 76–7. Dublin. Geological Survey of Ireland.

[174] J. Hardiman 1825 A catalogue of maps, charts, and plans, relating to Ireland preserved amongst the manuscripts in the library of Trinity College, Dublin. *Transactions of the Royal Irish Academy* 14, 63.

[175] Kelly, *Guide to early Irish law*, 105.

[176] The lordships are Béarra, Cairbre, and Boireann in Munster.

[177] P. Claughton and P. Rondelez 2013 Early silver mining in western Europe: an Irish perspective. *Journal of the Mining Heritage Trust of Ireland* 13, 1–8.

[178] Claughton and Rondelez, Early silver mining, 5; Hardiman, Catalogue of maps, 63.

[179] McInerney, *Clerical and learned lineages*, 162–4.

was exploited is unknown, but it is conceivable that it was integral to the grant of lands to the Cistercian community of Corcomroe.[180] From the late twelfth and early thirteenth century, Cistercian foundations in Europe were widely involved in mining, often leading regional initiatives to exploit metal ores. Lead was especially important to them because it was needed for water pipes, glazing, and covering roofs.[181]

The conjunction of a learned kindred estate, a medieval religious house, and a mine is found again on the coastline of the lordship of Luighne in north Connacht. The later medieval church of St Feichin (5.2.1) is situated in the townland of Kilboglashy, on the west bank of the Ballysadare River, facing north to Ballysadare Bay (Fig. 3.17). It overlooks *Eas Dara*, the waterfall from which the estate derived its name. The *airchinneach* of the church in the mid-twelfth century was Ua Dúilendáin, a brehon and *ollam* of *fénechas*, who also happened to be the *taísech* (leader) of the *túath* in which his church was situated.[182] Continuity of brehon lawyers as *airchinnigh* of the church was maintained in the late medieval period by the Mac an Bhreitheamhan ("son of the brehon") kindred of Ballysadare who, it has been suggested, were descendants of Ua Dúilendáin.[183] About 250 m west of St Feichin's Church, the ruins of the Augustinian Abbey of St Mary lie close to the coastline in Abbeytown, in the ignominious surroundings of a limestone quarry and concrete factory. The foundation date is not recorded, but St Mary's appears to have been pre-Norman, established on monastic termonland of St Feichin's Church and retaining the traditional Gaelic title of *comharba* for its abbots.[184] The last recorded abbot in the sixteenth century was a member of the Ó Siadhail kindred of hereditary physicians. He was appointed bishop of Elphin in 1545 by Henry VIII.[185] The profile of Ballysadare is therefore very much one of continuous association with learned people.

A disused lead, silver, and zinc mine (within the modern quarry) is situated 400 m west of Ballysadare Abbey (Fig. 3.17). It has been surmised that the mine was active during the sixteenth century and possibly earlier, but there is no authoritative testimony of mineral extraction at Abbeytown until 1747.[186] Nonetheless, the visibility of the natural resources of the tract of land on which the abbey was founded merits

---

[180] Frost, *History and topography*, 23.

[181] J. Burton and J. Kerr 2011 *The Cistercians in the Middle Ages*, 181–2. Woodbridge. Boydell Press.

[182] M 1158.2, ii, 1128, 1129.

[183] D. Ó Corráin 1978 Nationality and kingship in pre-Norman Ireland. In T. W. Moody, *Nationality and the pursuit of national independence: papers read before the conference held at Trinity College, Dublin, 26–31 May 1975*, 62n. Belfast. Appletree Press.

[184] A. Gwynn and R. N. Hadcock 1970 *Medieval religious houses: Ireland: with an appendix to early sites*, 160. London. Longmans.

[185] W. Harris (ed.) 1739 *The whole works of Sir James Ware concerning Ireland, revised and improved*, i, 633. Dublin. E. Jones.

[186] J. Kelly 2007 A history of Zn-Pb-Ag mining at Abbeytown, Co. Sligo. *Journal of the Mining Heritage Trust of Ireland* 7, 9–18.

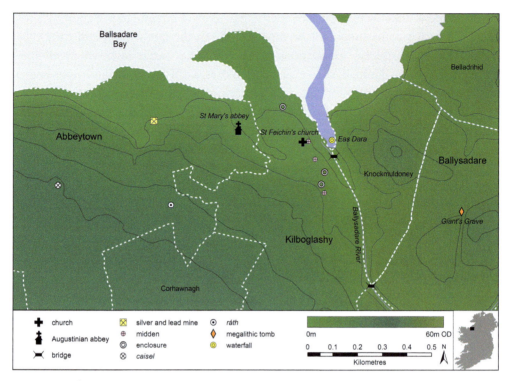

FIG. 3.17. The landscape of the church of St Feichin and the Augustinian priory, Ballysadare, showing the site of the silver mine on the lands of the religious house (map N. McCarthy).

consideration. The Abbeytown mineralization would have outcropped along the shore of the bay, close to where the abbey was built.[187] Moreover, the land of the abbey and church of St Feichin is a highly mineralized environment, producing, apart from ores, good-quality limestone, travertine, quartz and calcite crystals, and a wide range of other minerals.[188]

The estate of the physician, Ó hÍceadha, at Ballyhickey in the lordship of West Clann Chuileáin (Fig. 3.18) has been earlier explored (2.2) as an integral part of a power borderscape of the Mac Conmara Fionn chiefs. It was seen that the late medieval borderland center of West Clann Chuileáin emerged from an early medieval royal demesne of the Dál Cais kings that had been coextensive with the *túath* of Magh Adhair. Apart from its deeply layered cultural landscape, the natural resources of the *túath*, its rivers and abundant seasonal lakes, underwood, and rocky pasture, and mineral-rich environment of metal ores, may also have influenced the decision to

[187] Kelly, *History of Zn-Pb-Ag mining*, 9.

[188] S. Moreton, J. Lawson, and R. Lawson 2009 Abbeytown mine and quarry, Ballysadare, Co. Sligo. *UK Journal of Mines and Minerals* 30, 34–42.

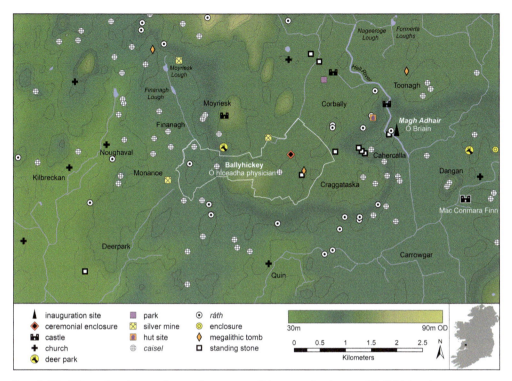

FIG. 3.18. The archaeology and natural resources of the estate landscape of Ballyhickey (map N. McCarthy).

appropriate it as a royal landscape, and subsequently to maintain a chiefry center there into the seventeenth century.

The physician's estate, in that long-standing place of elite power, was minerally rich in at least three locations (Fig. 3.18). Just within its northern bounds, there was a deposit of lead where the galena (the ore of lead) occurred in huge veins of calcite. Mined from 1834, the lead ore was found to be "nearly at the surface."[189] On the western bounds of Ballyhickey, a silver mine named Kilbreckan was opened in 1833 after the discovery of ore by men digging a drain in a bog (Fig. 3.19). The unusual ore, which when smelted produced a natural-type metal, was afterwards named Kilbrickenite.[190] To the north of Ballyhickey, in Moyriesk, a third mine was opened in the same period to explore indications of silver and lead.[191] Given the visibility of the ore before the modern mines were opened, any future archaeological investigations in

[189] R. Kane 1844 *The industrial resources of Ireland*, 202. Dublin. Hodges and Smith; Cole, *Memoir and map*, 119.

[190] Kane, *Industrial resources*, 201–2, 207, 221; Cole, *Memoir and map*, 119–20.

[191] Cole, *Memoir and map*, 120.

FIG. 3.19. The disused Kilbreckan lead and silver mine (photo E. FitzPatrick).

the environs of Ballyhickey should consider the possibility of encountering traces of smelting furnaces and lead/silver smelting slags.

Aside from the hypothesis that Ó hÍceadha mined the lead and silver as a resource of the bounds of his estate, he may alternatively, as the chief's physician and a leading member of a learned medical family,[192] have had need to access metal ores for the purpose of alchemy. The metals of alchemical medicine, which sought to purify the body, were gold, silver, lead, copper, iron, and tin. The practice had substantial overlap with metallurgy and was well established in later medieval and early modern European learned society.[193]

3.5 CONCLUSIONS

The estates of literati explored in this chapter were discrete landscapes, some of which were in the possession of the same kindreds for 250 to 300 years. Long-held

[192] The medical manuscript RIA MS 24 P 26 (1469, Reeves Collection. Dublin. Royal Irish Academy) is attributed to Donnchadh Óg Ó hÍceadha. Cunningham and Fitzpatrick, *Aon amharc ar Éirinn*, 41–3.

[193] M. Martinón-Torres and T. Rehren 2005 Alchemy, chemistry and metallurgy in Renaissance Europe: a wider context for fire-assay remains. *Historical Metallurgy* 39 (1), 14–28.

hereditary possession of estates cannot be assumed to have been a norm, but the attested presence of members of the Mac Fhirbhisigh kindred of historians at Lackan from the late fourteenth into the seventeenth century, the Ó Cléirigh poet-historians at Kilbarron between *c*.1400 and *c*.1641, and the Ó Dálaigh poets on the Sheepshead Peninsula from at least *c*.1300 to *c*.1600 implies that prominent literati maintained their estates from one generation to the next.

Some naming styles of estates, especially those that link topographical and settlement features and the term *baile* with the kindred name, appear to have been intended to generate a sense of deep rootedness and visibility in the lordships for leading learned men who were in fact mostly newcomers to the lands that Gaelic chiefs and Old English lords allocated to them, from the fourteenth century onwards.

With obligations to provide food for their families, guests, and schools, and with a need for animal membrane to produce parchment for their manuscripts, the keeping of cattle and other livestock by literati, and access to deer, would have supported hospitality, provisioning of schools, and maintaining a steady supply of parchment for manuscript production. Chronicle references to herds on the estates of literati, especially in the context of raids, and literary allusions to the gifting of livestock in return for learned services, indicate that sometimes large herds of cattle were maintained on their lands.

The equal importance of tillage is underscored by the incorporation of a glacial valley containing ploughable soil and its division into small plots at Cahermacnaghten, and by the recovery of cereal grains dominated by oats during excavations at Ballyegan and Cahermacnaghten. It is also suggested by references to tilling, harvesting, and improving land—and by the keyhole-type cereal-drying kilns found on the estates of the Mac Aodhagáin lawyers of Ballyegan and the Ó Duibhdábhoireann brehon lawyers of Cahermacnaghten, albeit that their precise period of use has not been pinned down.

References to the term *páirc* in Irish sources confirm that it had meaning in a Gaelic context before the intensive emparkment that occurred with English-style demesnes in the seventeenth and eighteenth centuries. Investigation of Park in Corca Mogha, Lackan in Tír Fiachrach, and Ardkyle in West Clann Chuileáin have revealed evidence for those estates as parkland, at least in the late sixteenth and turn of seventeenth century. Later emparkment of learned kindred lands, which happened extensively, suggests that they had previous histories as grazing for mixed herds, including deer, and were therefore highly desired for landed estates from the seventeenth century onward.

The hypothesis that learned kindreds may have exploited metal ores as an economic resource, or for the purposes of alchemy, cannot be resolved without further field-based research. However, it is plausible that there was an awareness of important resources on estates, and that the presence of quarriable stone on the bounds of estates such as Ballygalley, Ballymacaward and Túath Ghlae, and minerals and metal ores at Ballyhickey, Ballysadare, Kilweelran, the Sheepshead Peninsula, and Túath Ghlae, reflect certain considerations in the allocation of estates to literati more widely. This perspective also offers a new portal through which approaches to mineral extraction, and mining and quarrying culture, might be further explored in Gaelic lordships.

4

Dwellings of Literati

4.0 INTRODUCTION

The domestic environments of literati between *c*.1300 and 1600 might at first suggest that they were culturally conservative if not atavistic in their choice of dwellings. This chapter explores evidence to demonstrate that in repurposing earlier settlement forms, they refashioned them to reflect their status and to facilitate their needs. This process is largely seen in relation to the *caisel* (stone enclosure) and the *crannóg* (lake-island dwelling) and less commonly the promontory fort. The *caisel* of Cahermacnaghten in the lordship of Boireann, the *crannóg* of Cró Inis on Lough Ennell in the midland lordship of Fir Tulach, and the promontory fort at Kilbarron in the southern borderland of Tír Conaill are the core studies of repurposed early medieval settlement enclosures. The presence of lake-island dwellings on the estates of learned *airchinnigh* between Upper and Lower Lough Erne in Fir Mhanach is also considered in relation to their roles as keepers of guest-houses during the fifteenth and sixteenth centuries.

Learned kindreds of poets and lawyers, and servitors such as harpers, are recorded on landholdings with the place name *pailís* (palace) during the fifteenth and sixteenth centuries. The *pailís* emerged as a Gaelic aristocratic settlement form in the fourteenth century and appears to have been a chief's feasting hall enclosed within a moated site or a *ráth*. The relationship between literati and the *pailís* is interpreted through explorations of Pallis Hill in the lordship of Uí Cheinnsealaigh, the celebrated *Pailís Cluain Fraoich* in Machaire Chonnacht, *Lios Mór* in Uí Mhaine, and *Pailís Még Cárthaigh* in Iar Mhumhain.

The tower-house, a customary fortified residence of elites between *c*.1400 and 1650, was the dominant dwelling type of literati during the sixteenth century and the early seventeenth, but few were built by this class, they were for the most part allocated to them by the ruling families they served. Among those described is the modest tower-house on the estate of the Ó hUiginn kindred of poets, at Kilcloony in the lordship of Conmhaicne Mac Fheóruis, which is presented in its landscape setting, with a view to determining how the building might have served the kindred.

Landscapes of the Learned: Placing Gaelic Literati in Irish Lordships 1300–1600. Elizabeth FitzPatrick, Oxford University Press.
© Elizabeth FitzPatrick 2023. DOI: 10.1093/oso/9780192855749.003.0004

4.1 SETTLEMENT ENCLOSURES: *CAISEL, RÁTH, LIOS*

There is an unequivocal association between a *caisel* and the Ó Duibhdábhoireann learned kindred of brehon lawyers at Cahermacnaghten (3.2.2) in the uplands of the lordship of Boireann (Fig. 4.1). Before describing the *caisel* and interpreting how it was adapted to meet their needs and status, some reflection is necessary on the archaeology of medieval settlement enclosures of circular plan in Ireland. The *caisel*, or *cathair* as it is termed in the west of Ireland, has various readings in the Irish language as stone enclosure, rampart or stone fort, and dwelling.[1] In archaeological literature *caisel* came to be regarded as a "stone-built" enclosure, and *lios* and *ráth* as an "earthen fort."[2] *Ráth* originally meant the surrounding earthen bank and its accompanying fosse, but in the later medieval period it represented, in addition, the enclosed space and the house within.[3] It should be noted too that *ráth* in early and later

FIG. 4.1. A reimagining of the *caisel* of Cahermacnaghten (drawing D. Tietzsch-Tyler based on interpretation by E. FitzPatrick).

[1] Quin, *Dictionary*, 98:51, 103:88.

[2] S. P. Ó Riordáin 1953 (3rd ed.) *Antiquities of the Irish countryside*, 1–2. London. Methuen; FitzPatrick, Native enclosed settlement, 273–5.

[3] G. E. Daniel 1952 The Prehistoric Society: a report of the meeting held in Dublin. *Archaeology News Letter* 4 (5), 73.

medieval contexts was used of any earthen rampart enclosing a space.[4] The essential meaning of *lios* (OI *les*) is the garth or space containing a dwelling or dwellings, enclosed by a bank or rampart, but it can also refer to the enclosing bank or rampart itself.[5] The term *lios* has become exclusively used of settlement enclosures of both *caisel* and *ráth* type in modern scholarship, but as primarily an enclosed space, *lios* was applied to any expanse within an enclosure. For example, in a seventeenth-century source, the Ó Gnímh family of poets on the Ards Peninsula in east Ulster were attributed a *lios* as the site of their dwelling. Their estate was addressed as *Lios Toighe Uí Ghnímh* ("the enclosed space of the house of Ó Gnímh"), now Tullycarnan townland, Co. Down (Fig. 1.2).[6]

Until recently, the *caisel* and the *ráth* were reductively classified in Irish archaeology as "ring-forts" and ascribed an origin as homesteads of early medieval farming society.[7] However, both the terminology and interpretative framework for the early medieval *caisel* and the *ráth* have been revised, with "early medieval settlement enclosure" replacing "ring-fort" and their users now explored through the prism of dwelling practices and social identities.[8] Moreover, it has been suggested that later modifications to early medieval settlement enclosures should not be considered solely as evidence of their late use, but also as important indicators of social change in regions of late medieval Ireland.[9]

The presence of late medieval building fabric in the *caisel* of Cahermacnaghten has been interpreted as an anomalous survival of the "ring-fort" tradition in the west of Ireland, a reoccupation of long-abandoned sites by Gaelic chiefs or minor gentry in the fourteenth and fifteenth centuries during the fervor of "Gaelic revival."[10] However, the possibility that it is indicative of a more widespread regional practice of living in stone enclosures beyond the early medieval period has been strengthened by structural histories of nineteen other *caisel* sites in the Burren, which have shown that they were altered in different ways during the late medieval period.[11] Furthermore, Comber's excavations at Caherconnell, *c*.5 km east of Cahermacnaghten, have shown that the *caisel* had relatively continuous occupation from the tenth to the seventeenth century, with a later medieval house in the garth inhabited from the early fifteenth to the seventeenth century, and the entrance to the *caisel* also rebuilt within that time.[12]

---

[4] FitzPatrick, Native enclosed settlement, 274.

[5] Quin, *Dictionary*, 429:115; Ó Riordáin, *Antiquities*, 2; Daniel, Prehistoric Society, 73.

[6] Hughes, Land acquisitions, 83.   [7] FitzPatrick, Native enclosed settlement, 274–6.

[8] A. O'Sullivan and T. Nicholl 2011 Early medieval settlement enclosures in Ireland: dwellings, daily life and social identity. *PRIA* 111C, 59–90.

[9] FitzPatrick, Native enclosed settlement, 303.

[10] T. O'Keeffe 2000 *Medieval Ireland: an archaeology*, 24. Stroud. Tempus.

[11] FitzPatrick, Native enclosed settlement, 283–93.

[12] M. Comber 2016 The Irish cashel: enclosed settlement, fortified settlement or settled fortification? With evidence from ongoing excavations at Caherconnell, Co. Clare, western Ireland. In N. Christie and H. Hajnalka (eds), *Fortified settlements in early medieval Europe: defended communities of the 8th–10th centuries*, 6–10. Oxford. Oxbow.

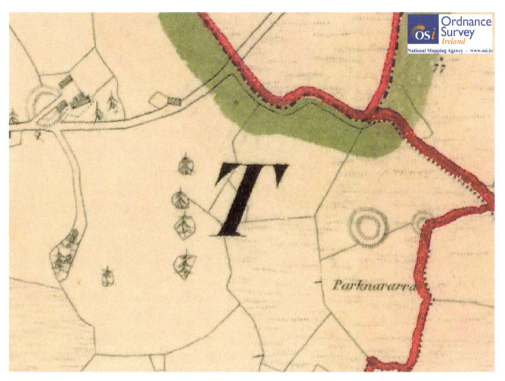

FIG. 4.2. Three *caisel* enclosures (top left, and right) and Parknararra, Caherclanchy (© Ordnance Survey Ireland/Government of Ireland Copyright Permit No. MP 002422).

The refashioning of Cahermacnaghten is therefore not atypical for the lordship of Boireann, but can use of medieval settlement enclosures by learned kindreds be argued more widely?

There are instances where historically traceable monument names link settlement enclosures with learned kindreds. On the estate of a branch of the Mac Fhlannchadha brehon lawyers in the lordship of Inse Uí Chuinn (Co. Clare), there are three *caisel* sites, two of which are associated with a large, enclosed field called Parknararra (3.3.1), and the third named Caherclanchy (*Cathair mhic Fhlannchadha*) after the family (Fig. 4.2). The three *caisel* sites are the only settlement features recorded in the landscape of Caherclanchy, and it is therefore probable that the one bearing the kindred moniker was a dwelling place of the family in the sixteenth century. The name of their *caisel* and landholding may have been influenced by naming practices in Túath Ghlae (3.4), the main estate of the kindred on the Atlantic coast of the lordship of Corca Modhruadh, where a *caisel* and associated landholding called Cahermacclancy (Fig. 3.15) was attributed to Cosnamach Mac Fhlannchadha in 1586.[13]

13 Nicholls, *Irish fiants*, ii, 737 [4876].

The hereditary historian Mac Craith seems to have made a distinction between *ráth* and *lios* in the *Caithréim Thoirdhealbhaigh* ("The triumphs of Turlough"), a fourteenth-century account of the civil wars among the Uí Bhriain of Tuadhmhumhain and their allies. In reference to the dwellings of the men of north Munster, he defined the *ráth* as the abode of every *ollamh* ("*gach ollam ina ráith*"), and the *lios*, the domicile of every layman or warrior ("*gach laoch ina lios*"). He implied that there was a difference in form and status between them, but his intention could also have been alliterative rather than instructive.[14] On the other hand, the poet Tadhg mac Dáire Mac Bruaideadha (1570–1652) later referred to the Ó Duibhdábhoireann *ollamh*'s *caisel* at Cahermacnaghten as "the lime-white *lios*" ("*ba aolta lios*").[15] Such nuanced interpretations of the nomenclature for medieval settlement enclosures by learned historians and poets, in different periods of time, could be the result of temporal or regional differences, but it may also have served a literary purpose. Gaelic texts such as the *Caithréim*, which was a triumphalist work recounting the battles in which the overlord of Tuadhmhumhain was the main protagonist, cannot be taken as direct evidence of contemporary living because, like much of later medieval Gaelic literature, it is laden with arcane allusions to earlier times.

This tendency can be further explored in the use of the term *lios* by the fourteenth-century poet Gofraidh Fionn Ó Dálaigh (d. 1387),[16] to describe where he was composing a long poem about the use of grammar—"I am Gofraidh grandson of Tadhg, of the south, from a smooth green height in Munster; there are few who know the answers to what I ask, from the *lios* where I lie."[17] As noted (2.3), Gofraidh lived in Ballydaly, a borderland estate of Iar Mhumhain overlooked by the hill of Claragh in the lordship of Dúthaigh Ealla. The identity of the *lios* where he lay might unhesitatingly be decided as one of six medieval settlement enclosures in Ballydaly, but mindful that *lios* applies to any enclosed space, a more cogent and credible environment for his poetic inspiration is the hillfort on the summit of Claragh (452 m OD). The idea that Gofraidh lay within the hillfort to compose his poem is made stronger by the attested associations between poets and memorialized hills in other lordships (2.3).

Remembrance of a heroic past was germane to the literary practice of the learned class, almost to the point of conceit, but it does not confer atavism in their lifeways. A telling instance of this is found in a fifteenth-century manuscript known as *Leabhar na Rátha* ("book of the enclosure") or the *Book of Pottlerath*. Compiled by scribes of the Mac Aodhagáin and Ó Cléirigh learned kindreds (among others), much of the writing

---

[14] O'Grady, *Caithréim Thoirdhealbhaigh*, i, 134, ii, 117.

[15] <https://bardic.celt.dias.ie/displayPoem.php?firstLineID=1504> (accessed March 10, 2022); Macnamara, O'Davorens, 204, 209.

[16] M 1387.4, iii, 18–19.

[17] "*Is mé Gofraidh mac meic Thaidhg/a-ndeas ón Mhumhain mhíonaird;/tearc trá ón lios i luighim/ gá dtá fios a bhfiafruighim.*" L. McKenna 1947b A poem by Gofraidh Fionn Ó Dálaigh. In S. Pender (ed.), *Féilsgríbhinn Torna*, 66–76. Cork University Press.

happened at Pottlerath in the southern bounds of *Magh Airbh* (barony of Crannagh, Co. Kilkenny).[18] It formed part of the *Saltair* of Edmund mac Richard Butler, who was a cousin of the earl of Ormond.[19] The observation has been made that Edmund, who embraced Gaelic customs, engaged in "conscious historicism" in commissioning *Leabhar na Rátha*—it contains material typical of earlier high-medieval Gaelic miscellanies, and employed antiquated ornamentation of that period.[20]

In an adroit elicitation of the past in Edmund's book, one of the scribes stated his place of writing:

> Today is the Saturday after Christmas and we are in Pottlerath...And all the new writing in this book was written for Edmund son of Richard in the Fort of Óengus mac Nad Froích which is now called Pottlerath.[21]

Here, the scribe invokes the *ráth* of an early historic king of Munster as the original name of Pottlerath. The place name Pottlerath (*Ráth an Photaire*, "*ráth* of the pot-makers") was derived from a modest *ráth* apparently used by potters in the townland.[22] That still leaves the identity of the "Fort of Óengus mac Nad Froích" to be established. There is a church in Pottlerath called "Templenaraha" (*Teampall na Rátha*, "church of the earthen enclosure"), which implies that it stood within a *ráth*, an interpretation supported by local knowledge of a former enclosure around it, but of which there is now no surface trace. *Teampall na Rátha* was built in the fifteenth century by Edmund Butler, whose castle (no longer standing) was situated just *c*.80 m to the south.[23] Consistent with the self-conscious alignment of his identity with the Gaelic past recognized in other areas of his cultural activities,[24] Edmund may have deliberately chosen the "Fort of Óengus mac Nad Froích" as the setting for his new church. The church has two entrances, one midway along the south wall and the other in the west gable. A window above the doorway and another at the west end of the south wall, point to a two-story west-end accommodation separate from the nave. Such quarters are a feature of churches that had learned incumbents elsewhere (5.2). The historic place name of the church, the tradition of an enclosure around it and provision of

---

[18] J. O'Donovan (ed. and tr.) 1841 The circuit of Ireland by Muircheartach mac Néill. *Tracts relating to Ireland*, i, 39–40. Dublin. Irish Archaeological Society; FitzPatrick, *Ollamh, biatach, comharba*, 181.

[19] B. Ó Cuiv 2001 *Catalogue of Irish language manuscripts in the Bodleian Library at Oxford and Oxford College Libraries*: part 1, descriptions, 62–87. Dublin Institute for Advanced Studies.

[20] K. Ralph 2014 Medieval antiquarianism: the Butlers and artistic patronage in fifteenth-century Ireland. *Eolas: The Journal of the American Society of Irish Medieval Studies* 7, 26.

[21] MS Laud Misc. 610, The book of the White Earl, fo. 61v. Oxford. Bodleian Library; Byrne, *A thousand years*, 26.

[22] W. Carrigan 1905 *The history and antiquities of the diocese of Ossory*, iii, 434. Dublin. Sealy, Bryers and Walker.

[23] Carrigan, *The history and antiquities*, iii, 433–4.   [24] Ralph, Medieval antiquarianism.

non-liturgical space within it, suggest that *Teampall na Rátha* was where the scribes of *Leabhar na Rátha* conducted their work.

4.2 CAHERMACNAGHTEN: RESIDENCE OF A LEGAL KINDRED

The *caisel* residence of the Ó Duibhdábhoireann learned family of secular lawyers in the lordship of Boireann was *Cathair mhic Neachtain* ("stone enclosure of the son of Neachtain"). An early historical king of that name is cited in a twelfth-century genealogy as one of the ancestors of Lochlann (d. 983) and Conchobar (d. 1003), from whom the later Ó Lochlainn and Ó Conchobhar chiefs had their descent.[25]

The results of a survey of the structure, combined with historical references to the family, suggests that the Ó Duibhdábhoireann lawyers were responsible for alterations and additions to the early medieval *caisel* in the late fifteenth century or early decades of the sixteenth (Fig. 4.1).[26] Aodh Ó Duibhdábhoireann's account in 1606 of the *ceann áit* ("head place") of his family, which contains some details of their *caisel* residence, is an important component of the suite of evidence for his family's occupancy of Cahermacnaghten (3.2.2).[27] How the upstanding remains of the *caisel* relate to the description of it in 1606 is included in the discussion of the structural history (4.2.1).

The *caisel* has sometimes been loosely referred to as the school of the Ó Duibhdábhoireann lawyers, but the word *sgoilteagh* (school-house), which is cited in Gaelic Irish manuscripts of the sixteenth century for the building in which learned men conducted their schools (6.0), is not used in the 1606 deed to describe any of the buildings in the garth. Moreover, the results of survey and excavation conducted in the building known as *Teach Breac*, southwest of the *caisel*, suggests that it was a purpose-built school-house (6.1.1).

4.2.1 A structural history of the caisel

The *caisel* of Cahermacnaghten is on elevated ground overlooking the glacial valley that runs through the western and central part of Cahermacnaghten townland (Fig. 4.3). As suggested (3.2.2), the valley was the spine of the estate, providing a natural routeway and, quite importantly, a depth of soil for small fields and gardens (Fig. 3.4). The local domestic watcr supply was a natural sinkhole in the karst on the western side of the *caisel* (Fig. 4.3), recorded in the deed of 1606 as "*tobar an bhaile*," ("well of the home place"). Macnamara observed *c*.1912 that it was "an ancient looking well,

---

[25] M. A. O'Brien (ed.) 1962 *Corpus genealogiarum Hiberniae*, 254–5. Dublin Institute for Advanced Studies.

[26] FitzPatrick, Antiquarian scholarship, 60–63; FitzPatrick, Native enclosed settlement, 290–99.

[27] Macnamara, O'Davorens, 90–1.

FIG. 4.3. The *caisel*, valley gardens, well, and park wall, Cahermacnaghten (photo E. FitzPatrick).

which dries up in summer."[28] It survives as a marshy area of ground without any well-house or enclosure.

The circular *caisel* (diameter 30 m) consists of a drystone walled enclosure, vestiges of a gate-house, and wall-footings of five buildings in the garth (Fig. 4.4). It was entered at east-southeast. The enclosing wall is *c.*2.5 m thick, composed of external and internal facing-stones with a substantial rubble core 1 m thick. It survives to a maximum height of 3 m over surrounding ground level and is constructed of large, roughly squared blocks of limestone, some of which, towards the base of the wall, are outwardly as large as 2.1 m by 0.5 m. However, massive blocks are the exception, the average range of block size is 0.5 m–1 m by 0.35 m–0.5 m. The smoother face of the stone is turned outward, appearing as well-fitted blockwork (Fig. 4.5). The base of the wall projects out, forming a slight batter. The accumulation of collapsed masonry and occupation debris in the garth is level with the top of the wall.

The *caisel* was altered in the late medieval period. A gate-house was built into the original entrance and five buildings were constructed in the garth. The wall fabric of the enclosure was secured with mortar where it flanked the gate-house and the entire circuit may have been harled or at least limewashed, so that it stood out against the gray limestone of the upland (Fig. 4.1). A single course of levelling stones near the top

[28] Macnamara, O'Davorens, 67, 87, 91.

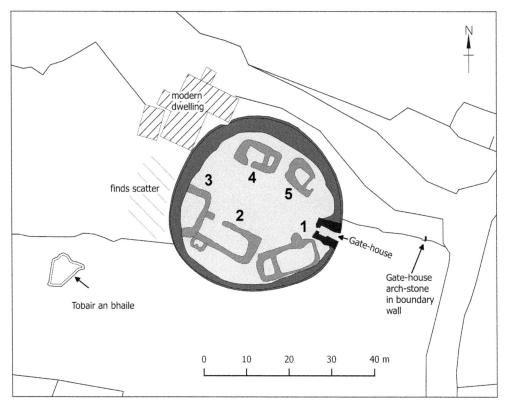

FIG. 4.4. Cahermacnaghten *caisel* and garth buildings, and the well of the homestead (drawing R. Clutterbuck).

of the wall suggests that the height of the enclosure was raised along parts of its circuit as part of the remodeling of the structure (Fig. 4.5a).

4.2.2 The gate-house

In the lordship of Boireann, late medieval alterations to the entrances of early medieval *caisel* enclosures have been identified at four sites, with the most elaborate of those changes made to the entrance of Cahermacnaghten.[29] A two-story gate-house was erected in the thickness of the wall at east-southeast. The addition of this structure suggests a concern with updating the *caisel* in line with architectural developments of the time. The entrance is borrowed from gate-houses of the bawns of tower-houses. A strong *caisel* would have served the same function as the bawn wall of a tower-house in defining a courtyard area for buildings and providing a measure of protection.

The upper floor of the *caisel* gate-house was dismantled or had collapsed before the nineteenth century. What remains at ground-floor level are the north and south

---

[29] FitzPatrick, Native enclosed settlement, 283–97.

(a)

(b)

FIG. 4.5. (a) Levelling stones in the upper courses of the *caisel* wall and (b) a break-line between the drystone *caisel* wall and mortared wing-wall, the gate-house, Cahermacnaghten (photos E. FitzPatrick).

side-walls, as well as some fixtures for the upper floor and architectural fragments of arched entrances. The gate-house, as it survives today (Fig. 4.4), consists of a lobby area that leads into a small, ground-floor space. A rectangular recess midway along the south wall suggests that there were steps at that point, leading to the first floor. The gate-house projected westward into the garth, beyond the internal face of the *caisel*. The north wall survives to a height of 2.2 m, the south wall has partly collapsed. Typical of late medieval wall construction, the fabric is roughly coursed limestone with a mortared rubble core, which was probably rendered with a lime-based plaster (Fig. 4.1). To support the two-story superstructure, the flanking walls of the *caisel* on the immediate north and south sides of the entrance had to be taken down and rebuilt using mortar to bind the masonry. This is proven by a vertical break-line in the facing-stones of the *caisel* wall on the south side of the entrance, combined with fragments of mortar in the interstices, and punch-dressed quoins (Fig. 4.5).

The earliest known sketches of the *caisel*, made by Ferguson in 1868, reflect these observations.[30] In his accomplished annotated elevation of the eastern half of the enclosure, and his plan of the gate-house, he noted that the masonry flanking the south side was "mortared and hammer-dressed," while the rest consisted of unmortared stones, corroborating that the wing-wall had been rebuilt to support the gate-house (Fig. 4.6).

Architectural fragments, identified during a survey of the *caisel* and its site for this study, have informed the reconstruction drawing of it as imagined *c.*1500 (Fig. 4.1). Among them is a punch-dressed arch-stone that was lodged in a modern boundary wall extending east of the *caisel* (Figs 4.4, 4.7).[31] Its size suggests that it is one of a pair that formed a semi-pointed external entrance to the gate-house lobby. Cut-stone features in situ date the gate-house entrance to the late medieval period. There are two punch-dressed stones projecting out from the north side wall, which are part of the frame of a former cut-stone doorway leading from the small lobby into the ground-floor chamber (Fig. 4.8). A punch-dressed pivot-stone, which held the upper pintle of a door-hinge, has collapsed from the south side of the lobby door frame (Fig. 4.7). In the ground-floor chamber, two punch-dressed corbels project out from the north wall of the gate-house. These and two others (not in situ) on the opposite wall supported beams for the first floor. Ferguson's plan of the gate-house (Fig. 4.6b) shows one corbel in the north wall and three in the south wall, in addition to parts of the lobby door frame and its pivot-stone.

A matching pair of cut and dressed arch-stones from a semi-pointed doorway were found in a garden on the north side of the *caisel* (Fig. 4.7). These once belonged either to the entrance in the west wall of the gate-house leading to the *caisel* garth or to a building in the garth.

---

[30] NLI PD 2040 TX, Samuel Ferguson, "Cahir Mic Craughteen—Meenaughteen," May 1868.
[31] During rebuilding of the drystone boundary wall *c.*2021, the arch-stone was removed to the front garden of the house adjoining the *caisel*.

(a)

(b)

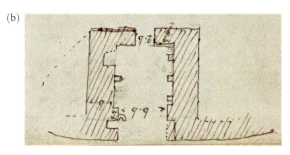

FIG. 4.6. (a) Ferguson's annotated drawings of the eastern façade and gate-house of Cahermacnaghten, and (b) plan of the gate-house, May 15, 1868. NLI PD 2040 TX, 2-3 (courtesy of the National Library of Ireland).

4.2.3 Buildings of the garth

The wall-footings of five buildings in the garth are ranged around the perimeter wall, leaving a small central courtyard (Figs 4.1, 4.4). Three of them have internal divisions and the two largest structures have projections, perhaps for hearths, on their long walls. The buildings and their precise positions in relation to each other and the enclosing wall of the *caisel* were cited as part of the inheritance of Aodh and Cosnamach Ó Duibhdábhoireann, sons of the *ollamh*, in the partition deed of 1606 (3.2.2). The deed also noted that the houses, along with the two cartrons of land that the brothers inherited from their father, Giolla na Naomh Óg, and agreed to divide up between them, had been the property of their grandfather, Giolla na Naomh Mór.[32] On that basis, the houses within the *caisel* cannot have been built any later than the sixteenth century.

The deed of 1606 was a witnessed and signed legal document of land division. It would have been important to enunciate properties on the land accurately, which is reflected in the synonymy between the documentary descriptions of the buildings

---

[32] Macnamara, O'Davorens, 86–7, 90–1.

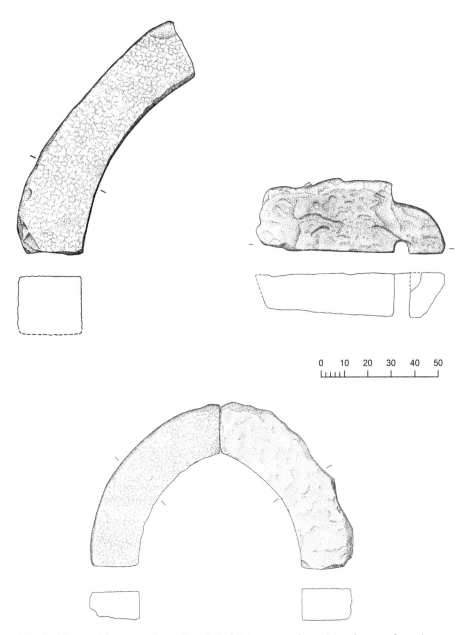

FIG. 4.7. Architectural fragments from the *caisel* of Cahermacnaghten: (a) arch-stone from the entrance to the gate-house, (b) pivot-stone, (c) pair of arch-stones from a doorway (drawing A. Gallagher).

within the *caisel* and the visible building footprints in the garth. The relevant extract from the 1606 deed (Corofin manuscript) as translated by Henebry for Macnamara reads:

And this is the partition of the home division [*ceann áit*]…the place of the big house of the *cathair* within [*teach mór na cathrach*; Building 2], together with the place of the kitchen house [*teach na cistineach*; Building 3] to the said big house of the *cathair* within,

FIG. 4.8. The north wall of the gate-house (photo E. FitzPatrick).

and the place of the house of the cells or graves [*teach na reilge*; Building 6] on the western side of the *cathair*... And the house [*teach*; Building 5] which is between the front of the big house and the door of the *cathair* and the place of another house [*teach*; Building 4] at the northwestern side of the *cathair* within; and the big house [*teach mór*; Building 1] which is at the eastern side of the door of the *cathair*.[33]

Buildings 1 and 5 in the garth are the only ones that were not qualified in 1606 as being the "place" (*áit*) of a house, which might mean that they remained upstanding and occupied while the others were already in a ruinous state.

Westropp made two sketch plans of the *caisel*, the first in 1895 and the second in 1911. The first (Fig. 4.9) shows a large house "the walls 3 feet thick," occupying the southern half of the garth and "another building with three rooms" in the northern sector. He indicated traces of a third building on the west side of the garth and of a fourth in the southeast quadrant, abutting the east gable of the large house.[34] His sketch of 1911 greatly revised the 1895 plan and remains broadly representative of what can be seen in the *caisel* today (Fig. 4.9). He replaced with two separate buildings what he had initially observed as a single three-roomed structure in the northern half of the garth.[35]

[33] Macnamara, O'Davorens, 86–7, 90–1.
[34] Westropp, Prehistoric stone forts, 121, 122.
[35] Westropp's sketch plan of 1911 was published in Macnamara, O'Davorens, 68.

(a)

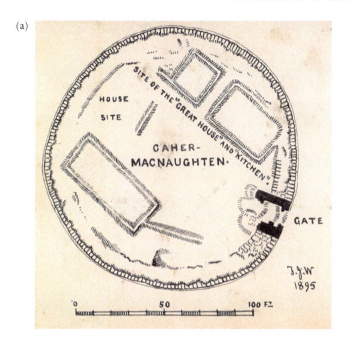

(b)

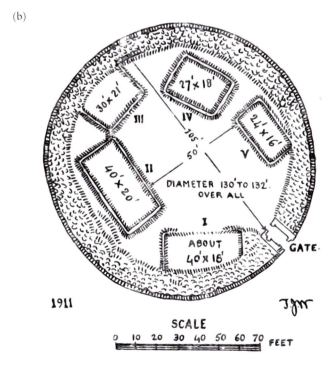

FIG. 4.9. (a) Westropp's plan of Cahermacnaghten, 1895 (published in Westropp, Prehistoric stone forts, 121, 122) and (b) his revised plan of 1911 (published in Macnamara, O'Davorens, 68).

The current plan of the garth shows that *teach mór na cathrach* (Building 2) dominated the southern half of the interior of the *caisel* (Fig. 4.4). The fact that it was qualified as "the big house of the *cathair* [*caisel*]" implies that it was the main building of the settlement enclosure. The long axis of the house is aligned east-northeast–west-southwest. It has internal dimensions of 12 m by 5 m and the long walls and gables are 0.95 m–1.1 m thick. An entrance is positioned towards the western end of the northern long wall. Next to it is *teach na cistineach*, the kitchen house (Building 3), mentioned as belonging to the big house. It is a small structure, 10 m by 6 m externally, adjoining the *caisel* wall. Both the big house of the *caisel* and the kitchen house (Buildings 2 and 3) were allotted to Aodh Ó Duibhdábhoireann as part of the 1606 agreement. The house of the cells or graves, *teach na reilge* (Building 6), is puzzling. It was, as the deed explains, outside and west of the *caisel*, and it too was part of Aodh's inheritance.[36] Macnamara presumed that this building was *Teach Breac*, the proposed school-house of the Ó Duibhdábhoireann lawyers, situated 1 km southwest of the *caisel* (6.1.1).[37]

Returning to the garth of the *caisel*, the deed notes a house (Building 5) positioned between the front of the big house (Building 1) and the door of the *caisel*. This is the small, ill-defined structure close to the enclosing wall in the northeast quadrant of the garth (Fig. 4.4). The place of another house (Building 4) is identifiable as degraded wall-footings of a small structure in the northwest quadrant of the garth. Finally, Building 1, cited as a big house, is *c.*11 m by 6.2 m internally, positioned nearest to the *caisel* entrance. Its dimensions are comparable to the principal house of the *caisel* (Building 2), but with the difference that the south long wall and east gable appear to adjoin the *caisel* wall. It may be the case that the wall face of the *caisel* was squared off to accommodate it. Buildings 1, 4, and 5 were enumerated in 1606 as the inheritance of Cosnamach.[38]

A magnetic susceptibility survey was conducted in the garth as part of the investigation of the *caisel* (Fig. 4.10).[39] The results show that Buildings 2 and 3 display only marginally enhanced magnetic susceptibility values in comparison to Buildings 4 and 5, which have noticeably distinct localized areas of enhanced values (S4 and S5) in their floor areas. This is also the case with Building 1, where, however, the focus of the anomaly (S6) is not in the floor area but in the southwest end of the structure. It is possible that the intense areas of susceptibility indicate hearths that were positioned directly on the floor. It might be expected that the kitchen house (Building 3) would indicate significant anomaly indicative of burning, but that was not the case. Ash from a domestic hearth and oven may have been cleaned out regularly and deposited outside

---

[36] Macnamara, O'Davorens, 86, 90.   [37] Macnamara, O'Davorens, 7.

[38] Macnamara, O'Davorens, 86–7, 91.

[39] J. Fenwick 2008 A preliminary report on the magnetic susceptibility survey of the cashel of Cahermacnaghten (08R179). National University of Ireland Galway.

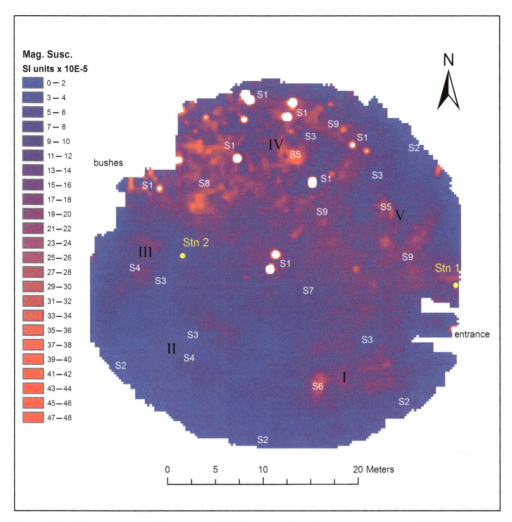

FIG. 4.10. Magnetic susceptibility survey of Cahermacnaghten (survey image J. Fenwick).

the enclosing wall of the *caisel*. Some corroboration of that practice is provided by material consistent with a kitchen midden recovered in 2006 arising from ground-works in the field immediately west of the *caisel* and next to the location of the kitchen house. Mechanical excavation had stripped and spread the topsoil, exposing burned stone and charcoal, animal bone, and oyster shells, and sherds of early modern Bellarmine ware and later pottery, across an area *c*.50 m by 40 m (Fig. 4.4).[40]

The deed of 1606 indicates the domestic nature of the *caisel* through reference to the presence of the kitchen house. This allows for an initial interpretation of the other four buildings as living quarters. The *caisel*, in its late medieval phase, housed

---

[40] E. FitzPatrick 2006 Report to the Department of Environment, Heritage and Local Government in the aftermath of topsoil removal at Cahermacnaghten, Co. Clare. Dublin.

an innovative modular settlement, reimagined in the reconstruction drawing (Fig. 4.1). The *caisel* wall functioned as a bawn, with the gate-house controlling access to the garth and protecting the occupants and property within.[41]

Are there any useful comparisons that can be made between the houses of the *caisel* and those associated with Gaelic learned professionals elsewhere? In Scotland there is just one location connected with a family of lawyers that has been the subject of archaeological investigation. Settlements traditionally associated with the Ó Muirgheasáin (Morison), *Sliochd a' Bhritheimh* (the Brieve's kindred), of Ness, in the north of the Isle of Lewis, have been explored by R. and C. Barrowman, with excavations at *Dùn Èistean* by the former and archaeological survey by the latter at Habost (1.0.1).[42] The family of Ó Muirgheasáin were *britheamhan* or lawmen to the MacLeod lords of Lewis during the fifteenth and sixteenth centuries, until the MacKenzies assumed control over the island in 1609–11.[43] Both the Ó Duibhdábhoireann and Ó Muirgheasáin lawyers held their roles in a hereditary capacity and provided services in law to Gaelic chiefs. However, the Ó Muirgheasáin *britheamhan* were purely practitioners of law. Unlike the Ó Duibhdábhoireann kindred of Cahermacnaghten, they did not keep a school, nor is it clear what the practice of law on Lewis involved prior to the seventeenth century.[44]

The Ó Muirgheasáin kindred are linked in local tradition with the diminutive tidal island of *Dùn Èistean*, situated just off the east coast of Ness at the northern tip of Lewis. There is no known authoritative record connecting them with *Dùn Èistean*, but their presence in Ness is well attested for the sixteenth and seventeenth centuries.[45] Excavations revealed that the cliff-bound island was not occupied continuously. It had three episodes of use between the late fifteenth century and the early nineteenth. The structures and materials from the first and second episodes, extending between the late 1400s and early 1600s, suggest that it was essentially a stronghold with a watchtower, frequented sporadically as a place of refuge. The houses relating to that period were built from low stone and earth walls and roofed with turf.[46] Barrowman concluded that their short-lived occupations and the archaeological evidence for conflict and destruction on the site, combined with the historical background and traditions relating to the Ó Muirgheasáin *britheamhan*, point to a role for *Dùn Èistean* as a refuge for the kindred, but also as a place of power with an important symbolic

[41] FitzPatrick, Native enclosed settlement, 290–3, 298–300.

[42] Barrowman, *Dùn Èistean*; C. S. Barrowman 2015 *The archaeology of Ness: results of the Ness Archaeological Landscape Survey.* Stornoway. Acair.

[43] A. MacCoinnich 2015 Dùn Èistean and the "Morisons" of Ness in the lordship of Lewis: the historical background, *c.*1493–*c.*1700. In Barrowman, *Dùn Èistean*, 41, 44–5, 66.

[44] MacCoinnich, Dùn Èistean and the "Morisons," 44–50.

[45] MacCoinnich, Dùn Èistean and the "Morisons," 41.   [46] Barrowman, *Dùn Èistean*, 380–91.

value.[47] It was abandoned by the mid-seventeenth century and only occasionally used as a temporary shelter thereafter.

The second settlement linked with the Ó Muirgheasáin kindred lies southwest of *Dùn Èistean*, at Habost, on Ness Machair. The earliest documented association of the *britheamhan* with Habost is for the year 1572.[48] Their dwelling was a building of turf and stone which, since the seventeenth century, has been known as "*An Taigh Mòr*" ("the big house") and "*Taigh a' Bhritheimh*" ("the brehon's house"). It is identified with certainty as an Ó Muirgheasáin house by 1643 when the lawyers had Anglicized their name to Morison and reinvented themselves as ministers in the kirk of Ness.[49] Gradiometry and resistivity surveys of the building revealed the Habost house as a rectangular structure, *c*.8 m by 6.5 m internally, the long axis of which is aligned east–west, with a partitioned east end. The stone-lined walls (2 m thick) had an earthen core. Sherds of hand-built pottery of sandy texture, some with grass- and seed-impressed decoration, dated to the late and post medieval periods, were recovered from archaeological features associated with agriculture, extending north and east of the house.[50]

What do the use of the terms *taigh mòr / teach mór* ("big house"), in the respective seventeenth-century descriptions of the dwellings of the Ó Muirgheasáin and Ó Duibhdábhoireann lawyers, mean? "Big" appears to have signified that the largest buildings were the primary dwellings in a composite settlement. In that regard, "the big house of the *cathair*" (Building 2) in Cahermacnaghten may have distinguished the family's principal living quarters in the southern half of the garth. It had a floor plan of 60 m², in comparison with the smallest structures, which have a floor capacity of just *c*.38 m². The Habost house, with a floor space of *c*.52 m², was not situated in an enclosure, but there were two other buildings to the south of it, which were recorded by the Ness survey as "very ephemeral linear mounds."[51] There is no dating evidence for those structures, but their degraded condition and proximity to *An Taigh Mòr* suggests that they were integral to the brehons' settlement.

By 1585 members of the Ó Duibhdábhoireann kindred had upgraded to a tower-house residence in the townland of Lissylisheen southeast of Cahermacnaghten (Fig. 3.4).[52] The *ollamh* Giolla na Naomh Óg and his son Cosnamach are recorded as residing there in 1601.[53] His eldest son, Aodh, categorized as a "yeoman" in 1601, lived in the *caisel* of Cahermacnaghten.[54] In 1606 the Cahermacnaghten lands and the *caisel* were shared out equally between Aodh and Cosnamach (3.2.2). The division of the property reflects the more systemic problem of partible inheritance of land and property in Gaelic lordships during the sixteenth and early seventeenth centuries (4.5).

---

[47] Barrowman, *Dùn Èistean*, 411–14. [48] MacCoinnich, Dùn Èistean and the "Morisons," 50.

[49] MacCoinnich, Dùn Èistean and the "Morisons," 44, 66–8.

[50] Barrowman, *Archaeology of Ness*, 180–3. [51] Barrowman, *Archaeology of Ness*, 258.

[52] Freeman, *Compossicion booke*, 7. [53] Nicholls, *Irish fiants*, iii, 506 [6562].

[54] Nicholls, *Irish fiants*, iii, 505 [6562].

To conclude, the alterations made to the *caisel* of Cahermacnaghten can be dated to the second half of the fifteenth century or to the early decades of the sixteenth, based on the standing late medieval fabric and surviving fragments of architectural features. The modifications included raising the enclosing wall, adding a gate-house, and constructing five buildings in the garth, one of which was the main dwelling with an attached kitchen house. Current evidence suggests that the association of the Ó Duibhdábhoireann kindred with the lands at Cahermacnaghten began with the *ollamh* Giolla na Naomh Mór and that it was he who altered the *caisel* to meet his status and needs as *ollamh* in brehon law to the Ó Lochlainn chief of Boireann. However, it cannot be determined from the upstanding remains whether all the changes and additions, especially the buildings in the garth, relate to a single period or to longer-term developments between the late fifteenth/early sixteenth century and 1606.

4.3 THE LEARNED COURT OF THE CHIEF'S *PAILÍS*

At the beginning of the fourteenth century, the *pailís* made an appearance in Gaelic poetry as an elaborate timber hall, fit for a king.[55] The Irish *pailís* is variously translated as a castle and a palace, a palisade, and a stockaded enclosure. The process by which this loanword was first adopted in Ireland is unclear, but its introduction was probably due to Anglo-Norman influence.[56] The *pailís* is best perceived in the context of its symbolic role during the dynamic period of transition from Gaelic kingship to lordship in Ireland, and the corresponding formation and consolidation of lordships throughout the fourteenth century.[57] Ferguson, in his discussion of the place name, has suggested that it may have specifically designated a banqueting hall of rectangular plan.[58] As a settlement form, about 40 percent of *pailís* locations have been identified as moated sites and a further 36 percent as enclosures of *ráth* type; the remainder present no surface traces to determine their form.[59]

Pardons issued to members of the learned class in the sixteenth and seventeenth centuries provenance some of them to *pailís*-named places and to estates adjoining them.[60] The records are simply by way of names and address. For instance, two members

---

[55]   L. McKenna (ed. and tr.) 1923 Poem to Cloonfree Castle. *Irish Monthly* 51 (606), 644; E. C. Quiggin (ed. and tr.) 1913 O'Conor's house at Cloonfree. In E. C. Quiggin (ed.), *Essays and studies presented to William Ridgeway on his sixtieth birthday, 6 August 1913*, 336, 337. Cambridge University Press; K. Simms 2001 Native sources for Gaelic settlement: the house poems. In Duffy, Edwards, and FitzPatrick, *Gaelic Ireland*, 257.

[56]   P. J. O'Connor 2001 *Atlas of Irish place*-names, 122–3. Newcastle West. Oireacht na Mumhan; D. Flanagan, and L. Flanagan 1994 *Irish place names*, 130. Dublin. Gill and Macmillan; Quin, *Dictionary*, 494:172.

[57]   Simms, *From kings to warlords*; FitzPatrick, Last kings, 201–11.

[58]   K. Ferguson 2001 Castles and the Pallas placename: a German insight. *The Irish Sword* 22 (89), 47.

[59]   FitzPatrick, Last kings, 206–7, 210–11.   [60]   FitzPatrick, *Ollamh, biatach, comharba*, 188.

of the ruling family of Mac Eochagáin are cited as being of Pallas (Co. Westmeath) in 1569 and 1581.[61] Pallas (*Pailís*) is also noted as the domicile of Melaghlin Ó Dálaigh in 1570–1.[62] His profession is not stated in the pardon, but the context of his address suggests that he was a member of the Ó Dálaigh poetic kindred. It is only when Pallas is explored in the field that the importance of the location becomes clear. It is distinguished by a moated site, and it is situated a short distance from *Cnoc Buadha*, the inauguration site of the Mac Eochagáin chiefs (2.2).[63] Both of those high-status monuments were situated in a borderscape of the lordship, where it met the neighbouring lordships of Uí Fhailge and Fir Cheall (Fig. 1.2).

The *pailís* sites referred to here, are by way of a sample. The purpose is to find out why members of the learned class are found in *pailís* landscapes and what their presence there represented. References to people in conjunction with *pailís* locations are not plentiful, but where they occur, they provide insight to the relationship between the learned and the place of the *pailís* in late medieval Ireland.

Members of the Mac Aodhagáin legal kindred, who served Mac Cárthaigh Mór, chief of Iar Mhumhain, are found living at Pallis (Co. Kerry), west of Killarney in Munster, in 1585–6 (Figs 1.1, 1.2).[64] In 1601, the poet Muiris Mac Dháibhí Dhuibh, who composed praise-poems for Mac Cárthaigh Mór, was also provenanced to Pallis where he lived with his family.[65] Pallis was the location of a tower-house residence of the chief, which was cited in the chronicles as "*caislén na Pallíse*" ("castle of the Palace") and "*Pailís Még Cárthaigh*" ("Mac Cárthaigh's palace"), for the years 1510 and 1514.[66] It was also recorded as "The Castle of the Pallice" in a Tudor survey of the lands of Mac Carthaigh Mór commissioned in 1597, which implies that the castle and the *pailís* were distinctive structures.[67] Writing in 1580 the Tudor captain, Edward Fenton, was left unimpressed by his encounter with Mac Cárthaigh's residence and hospitality—"called the Palace, a name very unfit for so beggarly a building, not answerable to a mean farmer's house in England, and his entertainment much like to his dwelling."[68] The proximity of the large *ráth* that lies *c.*70 m south of the site of the destroyed tower-house suggests that it was the *pailís*, an esteemed earlier feature of this landscape that had been incorporated within the tower-house settlement (Fig. 4.11). Just the southern half of the *ráth* remains, indicating a garth *c.*55 m in diameter, enclosed by a substantial earthen bank. The environs were emparked with

---

[61] Nicholls, *Irish fiants*, ii, 183 [1422]; ii, 522 [3775].

[62] Nicholls, *Irish fiants*, ii, 238 [1771].   [63] FitzPatrick, Gaelic political assemblies, 68.

[64] Nicholls, *Irish fiants*, ii, 655 [4576]; ii, 739 [4888]; O'Rahilly, Irish poets, 96–7.

[65] Nicholls, *Irish fiants*, iii, 446 [6515]; O'Rahilly, Irish poets, 96.

[66] ALC 1510.4, ii, 208, 209; AConn 1510.10, 614, 615; M 1514.5, v, 1326, 1327.

[67] Carew Ms 625, fo. 21r. The Clancarthy Survey from the Carew Collection. Lambeth Palace Library.

[68] R. Bagwell, 1890 *Ireland under the Tudors: with a succinct account of the earlier history*, iii, 49. London and New York. Longmans, Green, and Co.

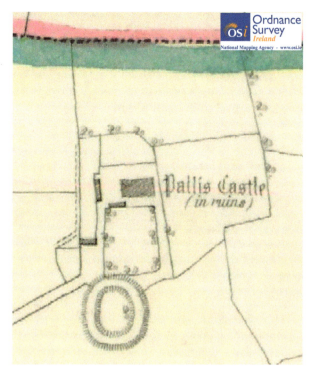

FIG. 4.11. The large *ráth* and site of "Pallis Castle", Co. Kerry (© Ordnance Survey Ireland/Government of Ireland Copyright Permit No. MP 002422).

the creation of Beaufort House demesne in the eighteenth century. Where in Pallis did the lawyer-poet Mac Aodhagáin, and the poet Mac Dháibhí Dhuibh and his family, live? The upstanding settlement evidence in Pallis townland suggests that it can only have been in a building of the tower-house courtyard or in the garth of the once-impressive *pailís* enclosure. With the advent of tower-houses in the fifteenth century, the *pailís* may have become redundant as a feasting hall and was perhaps repurposed thereafter as a dwelling-place for learned persons of Mac Cárthaigh Mór's court.

The people associated in the sources with *pailís* sites include chiefs and members of their families, servitors such as horsemen,[69] and learned professionals. The harper Seán Ó Maolfhachtna was living in 1602 in the landscape of the *pailís* of Ó Fearghail Buidhe, chief of the lordship of southern Anghal (Co. Longford).[70] Ó Fearghail of Pallas had surrendered his lands and had them returned to him to hold of the Crown in 1587.[71] Standing medieval settlement in Pallas is sparse, which narrows the options for the harper's dwelling. Bounded to the north and west by the Inny River, Pallas contains a large *ráth*, which is the most likely site of the *pailís*. Hugging the south bank of the river, opposite an eel weir, there are the remains of a fortified residence

[69] Nicholls, *Irish fiants*, iii, 8 [4980].   [70] Nicholls, *Irish fiants*, iii, 569 [6658].
[71] Nicholls, *Irish fiants*, iii, 37 [5091].

that appears to have been a castle of Ó Fearghail Buidhe. There were other members of the learned class living in the landscape of Ó Fearghail's *pailís*. The chief's lawyers were a branch of the Mac Aodhagáin kindred. Their estate at Ballymackeagan lay southwest of Pallas (3.3.1).[72] The presence of a harper and a lawyer in the environs of Pallas intimates that learned service providers of chiefs cohered around *pailís* sites, a phenomenon repeated elsewhere.

In southeast Leinster, the hereditary poets of the chiefs of the lordship of Uí Cheinnsealaigh were members of the Mac Eochadha kindred. They also held the office of inaugurator of the chief-elect, a role that was expressed in the place name of the assembly site of the ruling family, *Leac Mhic Eochadha* ("Mac Eochadha's flagstone or quarried stone") at Loggan near the county boundary of Wexford and Wicklow.[73] The townlands of Pallishill and Pallis Upper and Lower formerly constituted their estate. In 1601, eleven male members of the Mac Eochadha kindred, six of whom have been identified as poets, were living in the denomination of Pallis.[74] The poet Aonghus Ó Dálaigh was resident there too, as recorded in 1598 and 1601.[75] In 1619 there was a cluster of four houses and a watermill recorded on the east bank of the Bann River which demarcated the western bounds of Pallis.[76] There are also three settlement enclosures in Pallis, two of which are moated sites and the third a standard *ráth*.[77] They are all situated on the south-facing downslope of Pallis Hill and within a short distance of each other (Fig. 4.12). A flat-topped mound enclosed by a fosse lies east of the three enclosures. Classified as a motte, the tradition of urn burials there suggests that it may have been a Bronze Age funerary monument in origin.[78] The larger of the two moated enclosures was perhaps the site of the *pailís*, which, together with the other enclosures on the southern slope of Pallis Hill, and the group of houses on the Bann River, may have constituted settlements of the Mac Eochadha and Ó Dálaigh poets. The role of the landscape of Pallis as a place of territorial significance in the lordship of Uí Cheinnsealaigh is compounded by the literature and lore associated with the hill of Formoyle (*Formaoil*, 2.3), *c.*2 km south of Pallis (Fig. 4.12). It was the legendary *Formaoil na Fiann* ("bare-topped hill of the warrior-band") of

[72] Ballymackegan, Co. Longford, is represented in the fiants by "Currabeg" and "Corribegge" now Carrickbeg townland which formed part of the estate; Nicholls, *Irish fiants*, iii, 290 [6108]; iii, 569 [6658]; FitzPatrick, *Ollamh, biatach, comharba*, 168–70.

[73] AConn 1399.12, 374, 375; P. S. Dinneen (ed. and tr.) 1914 *Foras feasa ar Éirinn: the history of Ireland by Geoffrey Keating*, iii, 14–15. London. Irish Texts Society; FitzPatrick, *Royal inauguration*, 91–2, 104.

[74] Nicholls, *Irish fiants*, iii, 452–3 [6517]; O'Rahilly, Irish poets, 91–2. O'Grady, *Catalogue of Irish manuscripts*, 502.

[75] Nicholls, *Irish fiants*, iii, 326 [6232], iii, 452 [6517]; O'Rahilly, Irish poets, 99–100.

[76] Griffith, *Patent rolls of James I*, 362.

[77] M. J. Moore 1996 *Archaeological inventory of County Wexford*, 107. Dublin. The Stationery Office.

[78] G. H. Kinahan 1879–88 Sepulchral and other prehistoric relics, Counties Wexford and Wicklow. *PRIA* 2, 153, 159.

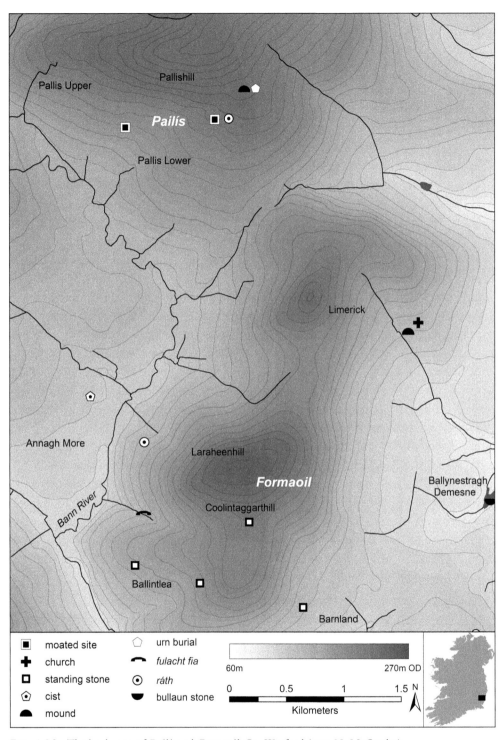

FIG. 4.12. The landscape of *Pailís* and *Formaoil*, Co. Wexford (map N. McCarthy).

the province of Leinster (2.3), gifted by the king of Leinster to Fionn mac Cumhaill and to Dubthach Maccu Lugir, chief poet of Ireland.[79]

The most celebrated *pailís* in fourteenth-century Gaelic poetry was that of *Cluain Fraoich*, built between 1293 and 1306 for Aodh Ó Conchobhair, chief of Machaire Chonnacht.[80] The full title of the site is referenced as "Palishclonfrey" (*Pailís Cluain Fraoich*) in a pardon dated 1594.[81] It translates as "palace of Fraoch's meadow." Recalling the legendary hero who is the central figure of the early medieval prose tale *Táin bó Fraích*, it mirrors the name of the Ó Conchobhair inauguration site *Carn Fraoich* ("Fraoch's cairn or mound") situated 9.5 km to the west.[82] The landscape of the *pailís* was focused on the three lakes of Cloonfree Lough, Fin Lough, and Ardakillin Lough (Co. Roscommon). A curious comment by the poet Aonghus Ó Dálaigh in his early fourteenth-century poem praising Aodh Ó Conchobhair's house at *Cluain Fraoich* intimates that *Pailís Cluain Fraoich* represented a new power center of the Ó Conchobhair dynasty, as chiefs of Machaire Chonnacht rather than kings of the province of Connacht. The poet appears to justify Ó Conchobhair's break with the long tradition of Connacht dynasts residing at ancient *Cruachu* (Croghan), the provincial capital of Connacht:

> Or do I decry yonder Croghan's ráth which has come to grassy Cloonfree? To the west there is only its phantom, to the east we see its semblance... to abandon Croghan's rampart for Cloonfree is no reproach to Aodh of fair-smooth locks.[83]

The new focus of power was established north of the shore of Cloonfree Lough in the townland of Cloonfree (*Cluain Fraoich*). It is identifiable as a moated site which has been known as "the King of Connaught's palace," from at least 1683.[84] No *pailís* site has yet been excavated, but poetic descriptions of timber halls have been used to try to inform its appearance and function. It has been argued that the morphology of the moated site concurs in some respects with aspects of its description in the two fourteenth-century poems addressed to it.[85]

[79] P. S. Dinneen (ed. and tr.) 1908 *Foras feasa ar Éirinn: the history of Ireland by Geoffrey Keating*, ii, 330, 331. London. Irish Texts Society; FitzPatrick, *Formaoil na Fiann*, 101–2; FitzPatrick, Finn's wilderness, 138–9; Ó Muraíle, *Leabhar mór na ngenealach*, ii, 714, 715; Ó Riain, *Dictionary*, 330–1.

[80] FitzPatrick, Gaelic service families, 179; Simms, Native sources for Gaelic settlement, 257; McKenna, Poem to Cloonfree, 644; Quiggin, O'Conor's house, 336, 337.

[81] Nicholls, *Irish fiants*, ii, 242 [5888].

[82] W. Meid (ed.) 1974 *Táin bó Fraích*. Dublin Institute for Advanced Studies; FitzPatrick, *Royal inauguration*, 60–8.

[83] Quiggin, O'Conor's house, 343.

[84] RIA 14 F 9, Letters containing information relative to the antiquities of the county of Roscommon, collected during the progress of the Ordnance Survey in 1837–8, by J. O'Donovan and George Petrie, ii, 322, 323. Dublin. Royal Irish Academy.

[85] McKenna, Poem to Cloonfree Castle; Quiggin, O'Conor's house; T. Finan and K. O'Conor 2002 The moated site at Cloonfree, Co. Roscommon. *Journal of the Galway Archaeological and Historical Society* 54, 79, 80–1.

Attendant *lucht tighe* lands around *Pailís Cluain Fraoich* would have been required for the chief's service providers. The *pailís* landscape was already a long-lived location before Aodh Ó Conchobhair's house was erected, reflected in the density of *ráth* and *crannóg* sites across it and in the wealth of finds recovered from lake-islands in Ardakillin Lough.[86] There is no known record of the estates allocated to the chief's household in that period, but a wide range of kindred names, drawn from the hereditary providers of the ruling family of Ó Conchobhair, were found in the *pailís* landscape in the sixteenth century, according to a list of pardons dated 1594.[87] Among them was a "scholar" of the Ó Donnabhair kindred, from whom the chief poets of the early medieval province had been drawn.[88] He lived in Cloonfinlough (Fig. 1.2) on the south side of Cloonfree, which was distinguished by the lake known as *Fionn Loch* ("white lake"). Members of the Ó Maoilchonaire kindred were also domiciled to Cloonfinlough in 1594. Their professions are not stated, but the hereditary poets and historians to the Ó Conchobhair ruling family, who had held the privileged office of inaugurating the chief-elect at *Carn Fraoich*, were drawn from that kindred.[89] If the presence of members of learned kindreds and other service providers was continuous in the *pailís* landscape from the fourteenth to the end of the sixteenth century, it ought to be reflected in the settlement archaeology of the region, a matter that can only be addressed through excavation of the moated site at Cloonfree and *ráth* and *crannóg* sites in the townlands where service providers are known to have lived.

In east Connacht, a moated site in the townland of Pallis (Co. Galway), in the lordship of Uí Mhaine, carries the name *Lios Mór*, implying a large, enclosed space (Fig. 4.13). It is enhanced by its setting at the northern end of a ridge, where it looks north towards the river and wood of Clonbrock Demesne (3.3.1), and eastward over an extensive marsh. The commanding location of the moated site and its landscape setting suggest that it is the *pailís* of the townland name. This is compounded by the fact that learned kindred estates can be identified immediately south of Pallis.[90] Furthermore, a strong case can be made for the *pailís* landscape as the setting for a Christmas feast hosted for the learned class in 1351 by Uilliam Ó Ceallaigh, chief of Uí Mhaine.

An account of the families and customs of the lordship of Uí Mhaine, preserved in the *Book of Lecan* (1397–1418), includes hereditary service kindreds of the Ó Ceallaigh chief's court. Among those listed are the chief's harper, Ó Longargain, who was living in Ballynabanaba, south of Pallis, at the time the *Book of Lecan* was compiled.[91] There

---

[86] B. Shanahan 2008 Ardakillin royal centre: a report on recent fieldwork carried out by the Discovery Programme at the royal centre of Ardakillin Co. Roscommon. *Group for the Study of Irish Historic Settlement Newsletter* 13, 7–13.

[87] Nicholls, *Irish fiants*, ii, 242 [5888].

[88] M 1101.13, ii, 971, 972.

[89] FitzPatrick, *Royal inauguration*, 181.

[90] FitzPatrick, The last kings, 204.

[91] O'Donovan, *Tribes and customs*, 93.

FIG. 4.13. View looking north to Clonbrock Wood over the moated site of *Lios Mór* on the long ridge in *Pailís*, Co. Galway (photo P. Naessens).

is also place-name evidence for the presence of the Ó Dubhagáin family of historians and poets in the *pailís* landscape.[92] Two townlands bearing their name, Ballydoogan (*Baile Uí Dhubhagáin*) and Cartrondoogan (*Cartrún Uí Dhubhagáin*), lie between the *pailís* and Ó Longargain's landholding at Ballynabanaba (Fig. 1.2).[93] Collectively, such references signal the presence of a chief's learned retinue adjacent to his *pailís*.[94]

Ó Ceallaigh's Christmas feast in 1351 was a spectacular event, recorded in the chronicles and celebrated in the poem *Filidh Éireann go haointeach* ("The poets of Ireland go to one house tonight") by Gofraidh Fionn Ó Dálaigh.[95] It involved building an enclosure ("*dún*") and establishing a temporary hospitality village, with a street for each learned profession, and sleeping booths ("*loingthighe leabtha*") and peaked hostels ("*bruighean corr*") erected as shelters.[96] Two sites have been proposed as the location of the feast—Castle Blakeney, Co. Galway and Castle Galey on the west shore of Lough Ree, Co. Roscommon.[97] The suggestion that it was set at Galey [*Gáille*]

[92] FitzPatrick, The last kings, 204; FitzPatrick, *Ollamh, biatach, comharba*, 168, 188.

[93] <https://www.logainm.ie/en/20280?s=Ballydoogan> (accessed April 3, 2022).

[94] Following my identification of Ballydoogan and Cartrondoogan, in *Ollamh, biatach, comharba*, 168, 188, and in The last kings, 204, additional service family landholdings were identified by D. Curley 2021 Uilliam Buide Ó Cellaig and the late medieval renaissance of the Uí Maine lordship, 39–40. In McInerney and Simms, *Gaelic Ireland (c.600–c.1700)*, 35–6. Dublin. Wordwell.

[95] U 1348.6, 493, 494; E. Knott 1911 Filidh Éreann go haointeach. *Ériu* 5, 50–69.

[96] Knott, Filidh Éreann, 56, 57, 58, 59.

[97] Knott, Filidh Éreann, 50, 51; Curley, Uilliam Buide Ó Cellaig, 35–6. Dublin. Wordwell.

beside Lough Ree is based on the presence of a ringwork on the lake shore combined with the poet's allusion to "The fortress of fair Gáille's chieftain [*dúna flatha Fionngháille*]." However, the poet did not say that the "fortress" was in *Gáille*.[98] The presence of the estates of the chief's key service providers in the landscape of the *pailís* of *Lios Mór*, combined with certain details of the poet's description of the setting of the event, make a stronger case for that landscape as the location of Ó Ceallaigh's famous hospitality.

The poet's detailed observation of the infrastructure prepared for the gathering suggests that he was present, "…for those who come to the house, there has been built…a castle fit for apple-treed Emain" ("*dún in Eamhna abhlaighe*").[99] "Castle" is a loose translation of what the chief built. The poet used the term *dún* to describe it and praised it as worthy of *Eamhain Macha* (Navan Fort, Co. Armagh), a late prehistoric mound and ditched enclosure encompassed by an earthwork, mythologized in early Irish literature as the ancient capital of Ulster and the royal abode of its king.[100] Medieval poets made favorable comparisons between *Eamhain* and the constructions of their patrons. In 1387 the Gaelic ruler of Tír Eoghain, Niall Óg Ó Néill, in a practice comparable to that of the Ó Ceallaigh chief in 1351, exploited the cultural capital of *Eamhain* by building a house there, to entertain the learned of Ireland.[101]

Dún translates as "fort" and applies to a royal earthen or stone enclosure of considerable extent.[102] Ó Ceallaigh's *dún* was, according to the poet, a stone and timber structure, built for the occasion above the brink of a lake called "*Loch na nÉigeas*" ("lake of the learned").[103] A survey conducted in 2016 for this study identified an ovoid enclosure known as "Doon Fort" in the townland of Doon (*An Dún*), as the strongest candidate for Ó Ceallaigh's *dún*. In the historical geography of this landscape, it lay between the estates of Ó Dubhagáin and Ó Longargáin (Fig. 4.14). The *dún* of the name is a platform (*c*.60 m × 50 m internally) defined by a scarp of earth and stone, quite precipitous in places, with external stone cladding visible in the eastern half. This curious monument, formed out of the ridge on which it sits (thereby requiring less effort to construct), overlooks a seasonal lake to the southwest, now known as Boggaun Lough in reference to its marshy ground. The tendency for the lower ground immediately to the south, east, and north of the *dún* to flood in winter and spring suggests that the monument would have been partly surrounded by water at the time of the Christmas feast. South of the lake, the ground rises again to a long ridge on which there are seven small enclosures. The Ó Ceallaigh ruling family had an enduring association with Doon. A "castle" attributed to Tadhg Ó Ceallaigh was

---

[98] Knott, Filidh Éreann, 60–1.   [99] Knott, Filidh Éreann, 56, 57.

[100] J. Waddell 2014 *Archaeology and Celtic myth*, 82–3. Dublin. Four Courts Press.

[101] U 1387, iii, 18, 19; K. Simms 1983 Propaganda use of the *Táin* in the later Middle Ages. *Celtica* 15, 142–3.

[102] Quin, *Dictionary*, 256:449.   [103] Knott, Filidh Éreann, 60, 61.

FIG. 4.14. The tree-clad *dún* and seasonal lake in summer, Doon Upper, Co. Galway (photo P. Naessens).

recorded there in 1574.[104] The Ordnance Survey of 1838 noted that it had stood within the enclosure but that "no part of the walls is now standing."[105] The nineteenth-century Doon House replaced it (Fig. 4.14).

The symmetry between the poet's mid-fourteenth-century description of the *dún* and its setting at *Loch na nÉigeas*, and the morphology of "Doon Fort" overlooking

---

[104] Nolan, Galway castles, 120.

[105] RIA 14 C 20, Letters containing information relative to the antiquities of the county of Galway, collected during the progress of the Ordnance Survey in 1838, by J. O'Donovan and T. O'Conor, 625. Dublin. Royal Irish Academy.

a seasonal lake at the heart of the lands of the chief's learned retinue, is considerable. It makes a strong case for "Doon Fort" as the enclosure erected by him to dispense his largesse to the literati of Ireland in 1351.

4.4 LEARNED KINDREDS AND LAKE-ISLANDS

Natural and artificial islands (termed *crannóg*) are found on estates occupied by learned kindreds between the fourteenth and seventeenth century. A *crannóg* was usually made by dumping layers of stone, soil, and brushwood into a shallow or marshland bordering a lake. Large, wooden, vertical piles were driven into the foundation and a timber platform erected and palisaded to accommodate a dwelling or more than one building. The historical use of this settlement form extended over the long period from *c.*500 CE to the seventeenth century, with some continuously occupied over a millennium.[106]

Offering hospitality to guests was a long-standing cultural practice among hereditary churchmen in the Irish monastic tradition, and one that continued with late-medieval learned men who held the offices of *comharba* and *airchinneach*.[107] The terms *fear tighe aoidheadh* (guest-house keeper) and *biatach* (food provider/hospitaler) are frequently used in the chronicles to describe those who provided hospitality.[108] For the pre-Norman period, the term *lios* (4.1) has an important application in defining monastic guest enclosures, with the term *lis-aiged* used in several instances to describe the enclosed space set aside for guests in monastic settlements.[109] At Armagh, the role of a monastic official tending to the needs of guests was defined on his death in 1004 as *airchinneach* of "*Lis-oigedh*," steward of the guest enclosure. He also happened to be an *ollamh* in poetry and history.[110] After the twelfth century, the prefix *lios* is not used to describe the place where guests were accommodated. It was replaced by *teach/ tigh* (house) in the many chronicle entries to the role of the *fear tighe aoidheadh* (guest-house keeper) for the late medieval period, which included secular learned men, especially poets. It had been an expectation of poets in early medieval society to offer hospitality in return for the generosity they received from hosts.[111] Exactly what forms of dwelling constituted guest-houses on the estates of learned kindreds remains

---

[106] See Drumclay, northeast of Enniskillen, in Foley and McHugh, *Archaeological survey*, i, part 2, 607–9; A. O'Sullivan 1998 *The archaeology of lake settlement in Ireland*, 37–177. Discovery Programme monograph 4. Dublin. Royal Irish Academy.

[107] O'Sullivan, *Hospitality*, 120–63.

[108] O'Sullivan, *Hospitality*, 120–1, notes that the term *biatach* "denoting one who supplies food to another, also appears quite frequently . . . to describe not only the hospitaller, but also the various other types of guesthouse-keepers in medieval Ireland."

[109] O'Sullivan, *Hospitality*, 26.   [110] U 1004, i, 510, 511.

[111] O'Sullivan, *Hospitality*, 141–2, 158–9.

to be proven beyond doubt, but there is already justification to propose that the *crannóg* served that purpose for some kindreds.

4.4.1 Learned churchmen, guesting, and lake-island dwellings

An opportunity to investigate lake-island dwellings in the context of literati who were *airchinnigh* on church land is presented by a striking cluster of learned clerics' estates on both sides of the River Erne between Upper and Lower Lough Erne, in the south-Ulster lordship of Fir Mhanach (Fig. 1.5). The topography of the estates is part of what is known as the "Drumlin belt" of south Ulster, a mass of oval-shaped hills of glacial drift with lakes in the hollows between them.

The Ó Luinín kindred of historians, poets, and physicians were *airchinnigh* of Arda (3.1) and sometimes held the office of *ollamh* in *seanchas* to Mág Uidhir.[112] At least one member of the kindred, the *ollamh* Matha Ó Luinín (d. 1588), is also recorded as a guest-house keeper.[113] The *airchinnigh* of the Erne had obligations to dispense hospitality. This aspect of their lifeways is acknowledged in chronicle entries. Others attributed the role of *fear tighe aoidheadh* in the drumlin country of the Erne include Tadhg Ó Breasláin (d. 1478), *ollamh* in law to the Mág Uidhir chief and arch-*airchinneach* of Derryvullan, and Gilla Chríost Ó Fiaich, who was a learned priest of the parish church of Derrybrusk and kept a house of general hospitality on his estate lands before his death in 1482 (Fig. 1.5).[114]

The exact extent of the Ó Luinín kindred's estate, *Fearann na hArda Muintire Luinín*, is not known, but the townland of Arda on the south bank of the river, and Tawnyreagh on the opposite side, constituted a major part of it.[115] During the fifteenth century the kindred also held a third part of the extensive *airchinneach* lands of Derryvullan, but which third is unknown.[116] The other two-thirds were occupied by the kindreds of Ó Breasláin and Ó Banáin.[117] The preference for lake-island dwellings in the late medieval and early modern landscape of the River Erne narrows the focus of the search for the settlement of the Ó Luinín *airchinneach* and *ollamh* of Arda. The townland of Arda contains two drumlins and two lakes, Arda Lough and Drumhirk Lough, while Tawnyreagh is dominated by two drumlins and Lough Raymond, sharing the lake with the adjoining townlands of Derrybrusk and Cappy. A *crannóg* close to the southwest shore of Lough Raymond is pertinent to informing the learned kindred settlement picture along the Erne because scientific dating indicates that it was in use

---

[112] U 1528.8, iii, 573; M 1478.12, iv, 1106, 1107; M 1396.2, iv, 743, 743.

[113] SAF 1588.1, 7.

[114] M 1482.2, iv, 1118, 1119; U 1482.10, iii, 280, 281, claims that he had maintained his guest-house for forty years; Foley and McHugh, *Archaeological survey*, i, part 2, 746–50. Derrybrusk church had two-story west-end quarters for the use of the *comharba*.

[115] M 1396.2; U 1512.11; U 1512.11, iii, 504, 505.

[116] Ó Scea, Erenachs, erenachships, 294.   [117] O'Sullivan, *Hospitality*, 160.

during the Ó Luinín occupancy of the Arda estate lands. Wooden piles forming "four close-set concentric circles" and a submerged flat oak beam were recorded on the western side of the stony surface of the island. Radiocarbon dating of a wood sample obtained from one of the piles produced an age range of CE 1480–1665.[118]

Sherds of Ulster coarse pottery found on the south and west shores of the Lough Raymond *crannóg* provide further dating evidence for its occupation. Ulster coarse pottery was hand built, unglazed, decorated, and predominantly cooking ware. It has been found in such great abundance on *crannóg* sites that it has acquired the alternative name *crannóg* ware. McSparron has identified at least two distinct types of this ware. The earliest form was current in the thirteenth and fourteenth centuries in eastern Ulster, and the later form, distinguished by thick-walled vessels, is datable to the fifteenth to seventeenth centuries and more widespread across Ulster.[119] There are concentrations of finds of Ulster coarse pottery in the drumlin country along the Erne. The sherds from the *crannóg* on Lough Raymond include two decorated rim sherds and a plain body sherd that relate to domestic occupation of what was either an early *crannóg* modified during the fifteenth to seventeenth century or one first built in that period for the use of the Ó Luinín kindred.[120] A second *crannóg* on the Ó Luinín estate survives as a stony surface close to the southeast shore of Drumhirk Lough in Arda townland. The Fermanagh survey noted a horizontal timber visible on the eastern shore of the *crannóg* and a basin stone was recovered from the northern shore.[121] There is no dating evidence from this site, but since artificial lake-islands were so essential to the settlement infrastructure of the region, it must have served a purpose on the Ó Luinín estate. The presence of two *crannóg* settlements on the core lands of their estate suggests roles for them as dwellings and/or guest-houses of the Ó Luinín *ollamh* and *airchinneach*.

The fact that hospitality was dispensed on the Ó Luinín estate from a guest-house raises an important point about the archaeological identity of the *teach/tigh aoidheadh* in late medieval Ireland. The role of guest-house keeper among learned churchmen, both *airchinnigh* and *comharbai*, involved running hospices. The recipients of this hospitality were, apart from fellow churchmen and members of the learned class, travelers, the sick, and the poor, who were, traditionally, the beneficiaries of monastic hospitality. Dozens of hospices were noted in the 1590s in south Ulster. The lordship of East Bréifne (Co. Cavan) alone had forty-six "hospitals" associated with churches,

---

[118] Foley and McHugh, *Archaeological survey*, i, part 2, 633.

[119] C. McSparron 2001 The medieval coarse pottery of Ulster. *The Journal of Irish Archaeology* 20, 101–2.

[120] B. Williams and S. Gormley 2002 *Archaeological objects from County Fermanagh*, 120. Northern Ireland archaeological monographs: 5. Belfast. Blackstaff Press.

[121] Foley and McHugh, *Archaeological survey* i, part 2, 588–9.

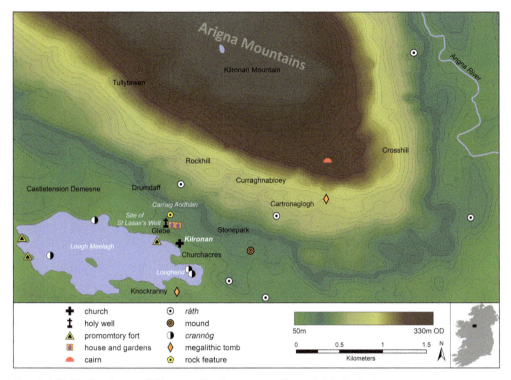

FIG. 4.15. The landscape of Kilronan, Co. Roscommon (map N. McCarthy).

among them Templeport on St Mogue's Island (*Inis Breacmhaigh*), which was a center of learned activity from at least the fifteenth century (Fig. 1.2).[122]

An insight to the role of the *crannóg* as a hospice for the weary, sick, and dying is conveyed at Kilronan (Fig. 4.15), in the Connacht lordship of Magh Luirg, where members of the Ó Duibhgeannáin kindred of learned historians who dominated the office of *comharba* of Kilronan parish church, for much of the late medieval period, were lauded by the chroniclers as guest-house keepers. In the chronicle record of his death, for the year 1398, David Ó Duibhgeannáin was addressed as "Cowarb [*comharba*] of the Virgin St. Lassar [Lasair], McDermott's chiefe Chronicler and his great favourite, a Common housekeeper for all comers of Ireland."[123] The cult of St Lasair was maintained by the *comharba*, and a life of the saint was compiled in 1670. According to the *Life*, Lasair was allegedly the daughter of Rónán, after whom the parish church was named.[124] Considering the obligation placed on the Ó Duibhgeannáin *comharba* and *ollamh* to provide hospitality, the question arises as to where guests were housed on his ecclesiastical estate.

---

[122] Gwynn and Hadcock, *Medieval religious houses*, 344–5; R. Flower 1926 *Catalogue of manuscripts in the British Museum*, ii, 538–9. London. British Museum.

[123] AClon 1398, 320.   [124] L. Gwynn 1911 The life of St Lasair. *Ériu* 5, 95.

In the *Life* of Lasair, she and her father Rónán built a house when they arrived to settle at Lough Meelagh: "And they blessed the blue-pooled full-fruitful shore of the lake, and erected a house for their use and dwelling,"[125] perhaps on "*Inis Mór Máothla*" ("big island of Meelagh"), one of two islands cited in the *Life*. The second, "*Inis na Naomh*" ("Saint's Island"), features poignantly as the place to which the saint took her sick father to die:

> Then Lasair...set forth with him across to the island on the stepping-stones, and did thus daily for a very long time, till Rónán grew heavy and aged...he could neither go out nor come in, since his time and days were spent...She [Lasair] stayed long after that, sad and sorrow-weary on Inis na Naomh and Loch Mór Máothla from that time until the beginning of the summer.[126]

There are two *crannóg* sites in an inlet of the eastern shore of Lough Meelagh, a short distance south of the parish church of Kilronan (Fig. 4.15). One of them is now called Loughend Island, situated *c*.120 m from the lake shore (Fig. 4.16). The other, consisting of a cairn of stones, is submerged in shallow water *c*.50 m from the lake shore.

FIG. 4.16. Loughend Island *crannóg* on Lough Meelagh, Kilronan (photo E. FitzPatrick).

---

[125] Gwynn, Life of St Lasair, 91.   [126] Gwynn, Life of St Lasair, 96, 97, 98, 99.

They are both in a landscape that was familiar to Ó Duibhgeannáin, author of the *Life*, and may therefore be the islands mentioned in the text.[127]

The value of the *Life* of Lasair is that it communicates, from the perspective of its learned author, some of the key settlement features of Kilronan—namely the church and the two lake-islands. The role of *Inis na Naomh*, as the location to which the ailing Rónán retired and died, implies a place of retreat, a hospice.

4.4.2 *The* crannóg *as poet's residence and guest-house*

A relationship between a residence and guest-house of an *ollamh* and a former retreat of kings can be seen in relation to *Cró Inis*, now Cormorant Island, in the southwest of Lough Ennell (Co. Westmeath) to which the Ó Cobhthaigh poets of the midland lordship of Fir Tulach are securely linked in the late medieval period (Fig. 4.17).

Cró Inis is situated *c*.300 m off the east shore of Dysart townland in the west of the lordship of Fir Tulach. The landscape of Lough Ennell constituted a key borderland between the three lordships of Magh Breacraighe, Cineál bhFiachach, and Fir Tulach.

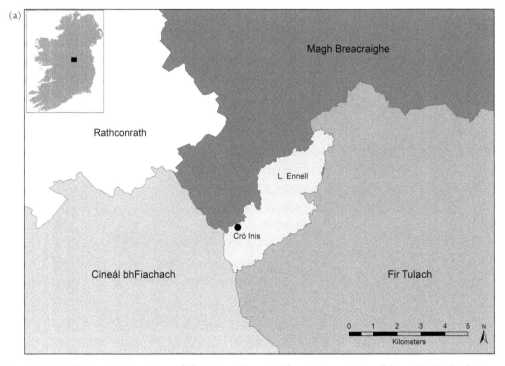

FIG. 4.17a. The territorial setting of *Cró Inis* at Dysart (*Díseart*), Lough Ennell (map N. McCarthy).

---

[127] Gwynn, Life of St Lasair, 73.

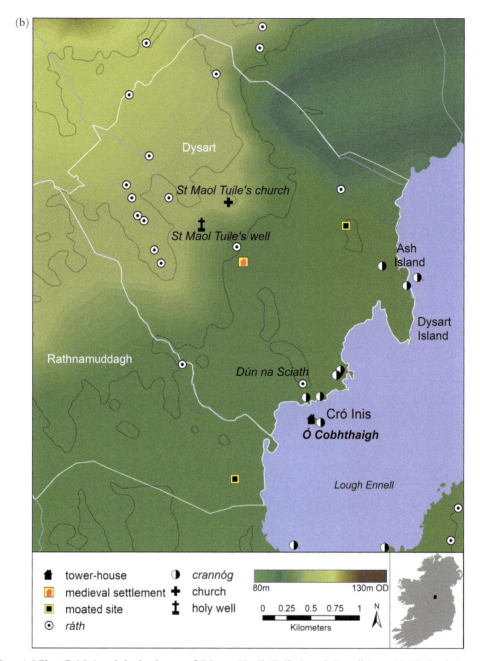

(b)

FIG. 4.17b. *Cró Inis* and the landscape of *Díseart Maoile Tuile*, Lough Ennell (map N. McCarthy).

The relationship of the Ó Cobhthaigh kindred with Fir Tulach and *Cró Inis* is noted in the chronicles for the fifteenth century. In 1446 Domhnall Ó Cobhthaigh, along with his two sons, was killed "in his own house" on *Cró Inis* by members of the neighboring families of Ó Maoilsheachlainn and Mac Eochagáin. Domhnall was described as "a man of wide accomplishment" and his house as "an open guest-house."[128] For the year 1452, the chronicles record the death from plague of the poet Aodh Mac an Chlasaigh Ó Cobhthaigh. He too was accorded the keeping of a house of hospitality in Fir Tulach, presumably on *Cró Inis*.[129]

Cró Inis is a high-cairn *crannóg* (*c*.50 m in diameter) situated in a visible location on the lake.[130] The word *cró* has a range of meanings, principal among which are enclosure or fold, but also hut or cell.[131] Underwater investigations in 1989 revealed a complex double- and triple-layered palisade of mostly birch timbers off the shoreline of the *crannóg*, which is possibly the *cró* referenced in the place name. Birch posts from the offshore palisade were radiocarbon dated to the second quarter of the ninth century, and dendrochronological dates obtained from oak planks suggested a construction or refurbishment date in the first quarter of the twelfth century for the palisade on the southwest side of the island. Stray finds, dating to the eleventh/twelfth century, were recovered from the surface.[132] The early medieval phase of the *crannóg* is identified with the royal residence of the Clann Cholmáin kings of the Southern Uí Néill.[133]

There is reason to expect a late medieval dwelling on *Cró Inis*, based on the chronicle entries concerning the role of the Ó Cobhthaigh poets as guest-house keepers. During the progress of the Ordnance Survey of Westmeath in 1837, O'Conor visited *Cró Inis* finding "a very small portion of a wall covered with ivy, about the centre of the island." He could not determine what it was, but he collected some local traditions that variously described the remains as a "monastery" and a "castle." The "castle" was recalled as having "a great height of the walls" standing until *c*.1787 when it was robbed out to build a cottage on another island.[134] In the 1930s, Macalister excavated a structure at the center of *Cró Inis* that appears to have been part of the "castle," but which he dismissed as a pyramidal folly. What he recorded was 4 m

[128] A Conn 1446.2, 490, 491; M 1446.14, iv, 948, 949.

[129] M 1452.21, iv, 984, 985; The historic function of the Ó Cobhthaigh kindred as dispensers of hospitality is recalled in a portrayal of group drinking vessels (methers) on a wall memorial (1684) to a family member, in the parish church of Lynally, a center of learning in the fifteenth century (Co. Offaly). See E. FitzPatrick 2021 A learned identity: monuments to Thomas Coffy, at Lynally, Co. Offaly. In T. Dooley, M.A. Lyons, and S. Ryan (eds), *The historian as detective: uncovering Irish pasts*, 141–3. Dublin. Four Courts Press.

[130] A. O'Sullivan 2012 The archaeology of early medieval settlement and landscape in Westmeath. In P. Stevens and J. Channing (eds), *Settlement and community in the Fir Tulach kingdom: archaeological excavation on the M6 and N52 road schemes*, 18. Dublin. National Roads Authority.

[131] Quin, *Dictionary*, 159:536–8.

[132] R. Farrell 1991 The Crannog Archaeology Project (CAP): archaeological field research in the lakes of the west midlands of Ireland. In C. Karkov and R. T. Farrell (eds), *Studies in insular art and archaeology*, 100–1, 103. Oxford, Ohio. American Early Medieval Studies and the Miami University School of Fine Arts; E. P. Kelly 1991 Observations on Irish lakes. In Karkov and Farrell, *Studies in insular art*, 89–91.

[133] O'Sullivan, Archaeology of early medieval settlement, 18.

[134] RIA 14 G 14, Letters containing information relative to the antiquities of the county of Westmeath, collected during the progress of the Ordnance Survey in 1837–8, by J. O'Donovan and T. O'Conor, ii, 37–9. Dublin. Royal Irish Academy.

square in plan internally, with walls *c.*1.5 m thick, entered through a narrow doorway at the north end of the east wall. All four walls had a pronounced batter, the masonry was crude, but at least two of the corners were finished with cut quoins. A deep recess was built into the northwest corner. Animal bones were the only recorded finds from the excavation and no dating evidence emerged.[135] The consensus is that what Macalister uncovered was probably a tower-house (or part of), erected at the center of the island on the earlier *crannóg* of the Clann Cholmáin kings.[136]

Why the late medieval Ó Cobhthaigh *ollamh* in poetry resided on *Cró Inis* is partly answered by the continuity of Lough Ennell as an important borderscape, but it is perhaps also because the island was a former early medieval royal center of the over-kingdom of Mide, the kingship of which was dominated by the Southern Uí Néill dynasty of Clann Cholmáin between the eighth and eleventh centuries.[137] The Ó Cobhthaigh kindred were deeply connected with the old overkingdom, having pro-vided military services to the household of the king of Mide at least as early as the eleventh century.[138] *Cró Inis* is especially associated with royalty in the eleventh and twelfth centuries.[139] The twelfth-century *Life* of St Colmán of Lynn speaks of the entitlement of the king of Mide to "a lad for his horses when he is in Cró-Inis."[140] The death of the king in 1022, one month after he had been victorious in battle, occurred on *Cró Inis*.[141] The *Annals of Clonmacnoise* provide the important detail that he died "in Croinnis upon Logh Innill neere his house of Doone Sgiath."[142] The *dún* referred to as the king's house is the onshore *ráth* of *Dún na Sciath*, which lies directly north of the island in the townland of Dysart on the western shore of Lough Ennell (Fig. 4.17b). Commenting on the pairing of the *crannóg* and the *ráth*, Warner surmised that the island "seems to have been some sort of adjunct, perhaps a second-ary dwelling, a personal retreat."[143]

The withdrawal of the Clann Cholmáin king of Mide to *Cró Inis* after battle, and his death there within a month, suggests that it was in fact a place of retreat, a *bruiden* (hostel) or guest-house to the onshore royal residence of *Dún na Sciath*. This percep-tion of lake-islands as places of retreat for aged and ailing elites was earlier mentioned (2.1.1) in relation to *Inis Saimér* in the Erne Estuary of Tír Conaill. The same practice is attributed to St Ronán of Kilronan in his withdrawal to *Inis na Naomh* when approaching death. Since *Cró Inis* was integral to the monastic landscape of Dysart, it is probable that it was a monastic hostel in origin, maintained by churchmen for the

---

[135] R. A. S. Macalister 1937–8 On an excavation conducted on Cro-Inis, Loch Ennell. *PRIA* 44C, 248–52.
[136] A. O'Sullivan 2004 The social and ideological role of crannogs in early medieval Ireland, ii, 87, Fig. 2.31. PhD diss. National University of Ireland Maynooth; Kelly, Observations on Irish lakes, 89–90.
[137] Ó Corráin, *Ireland before the Normans*, 21.   [138] M 1030, ii, 820, 821.
[139] Byrne, *Irish kings*, 87.   [140] Cited in Byrne, *Irish kings*, 143.
[141] M 1022.2, ii, 800, 801.   [142] AClon 1022, 171.
[143] R. Warner 1994 On crannogs and kings, part 1. *Ulster Journal of Archaeology* 57, 63.

Clann Cholmáin kings. Obligations of monastic hostels included compassionate care of the weary and sick traveler.[144]

Living on an island where, historically, the overkings of Mide had resorted for respite was entirely appropriate for an *ollamh* of one of the constituent territories of the former overkingdom. By providing hospitality on *Cró Inis*, the Ó Cobhthaigh *ollamh* memorialized the role of the island as a place of royal retreat.

4.5 TOWER-HOUSES AND FORTIFIED SETTLEMENTS OF LITERATI

Tower-houses, built in large numbers in Ireland, were commonplace residences of elites from *c.*1400 through to the end of the seventeenth century. It was during the sixteenth century that the tower-house became the dwelling of distinction for members of the learned class. Most of them were built by ruling families and allocated to members of their learned courts. However, in his study of the tower-houses of professional lineages in Co. Clare, Tierney has pointed to some that were built by those of means. Drawing on a sixteenth-century list of castle-builders, he identified five tower-houses, among which was the castle of Urlan (3.3.1), erected by the Mac Fhlannchadha brehon lawyers in the lordship of West Clann Chuileáin.[145] Making a useful comparison between the residences of the Mac Fhlannchadha lawyers and the Ó Maoilchonaire poets in the same lordship, he found that the poets appear not to have had sufficient material wealth to construct their own castles and instead lived in tower-houses provided to them by ruling families, such as Rossmanagher built by the Mac Conmara chief.[146]

Structurally, there is nothing obvious that differentiated a tower-house known to have been constructed by a learned family from a tower-house lived in by nobility. However, there are aspects of the tower-house and bawn that would have suited an *ollamh*. It afforded the possibility of more defined and controlled use of space, with the separation of areas for guests from private chambers.[147] The protective bawn would also have been useful for controlling access to the goods of the family, including their manuscript collections.

The allocation of tower-houses by chiefs to *ollamhain* was a widespread practice in the sixteenth century and the early years of the seventeenth. Redwood Castle, built by Ó Cinnéide, chief of Urumhain, was assigned to the Mac Aodhagáin brehon lawyers

---

[144] A. Anderson and M. O. Anderson (eds and trs) 1961 *Adomnán's life of Columba*, 87 i. 48. London. Nelson; St Maol Tuile of Dysart is known for wonder-making. The Mac and Ó Maoltuile physicians share his name.

[145] Tierney, Tower houses and power, 221–2; M. Breen 1995 A 1570 list of castles in County Clare. *North Munster Antiquarian Journal* 36, 132.

[146] Tierney, Tower houses and power, 223.   [147] FitzPatrick, *Ollamh, biatach, comharba*, 182.

c.1600 (3.3.1; 6.1.3).[148] The symbolism of the borderland location of the building is inherent in the talismanic figure of a female exhibitionist positioned on the east wall, facing towards the lordship of Éile Uí Chearbhaill (2.0.1).

From *c*.1585, members of the Ó Duibhdábhoireann kindred were living in Lissylisheen tower-house, southeast of Cahermacnaghten (4.2.3). Lissylisheen was not listed among the hereditary lands of the kindred in the Ó Duibhdábhoireann deed of 1606. It is possible that it was newly acquired because of the Composition of Connacht in 1585.[149] The original owner-occupiers of the tower-house are unknown, but it must have been a castle of Ó Lochlainn or of Ó Briain, leased to the Ó Duibhdábhoireann *ollamh*. The Uí Bhriain ruling family were particularly acquisitive in the late sixteenth century, pushing into the lands of minor kindreds and controlling where and how they lived in the Burren region. This pattern is typical of early modern developments in land-based social relationships in Ireland, reflecting movement away from tradition-bound Gaelic society to a landlord–tenant society, which in the lordship of Boireann was driven by the Uí Bhriain after the Composition of Connacht.[150]

In east Connacht, the tower-house of the Ó hUiginn poets on their estate at Kilcloony (Co. Galway) was originally built in the fifteenth century by the de Bermingham lord of Conmhaicne Mac Fheóruis, a family of Anglo-Norman descent (Fig. 4.18). In what became typical practice, Kilcloony Castle was assigned to the Ó hUiginn poets. They are first referenced as being of Kilcloony in 1574, when the

FIG. 4.18. View north from Kilcloony tower-house to Knockmaa (photo E. FitzPatrick).

---

[148] Curtis, *Calendar of Ormond deeds*, 244.
[149] Freeman, *Compossicion booke*, 7.   [150] Nugent, *Gaelic clans*. 191–3.

ollamh, Domhnall, was listed as the occupant of the castle at "Kilclune," and again in an indenture of 1585.[151] Their association with Kilcloony in the sixteenth century is poetically recorded in a poem written between 1550 and 1591 by Tadhg Dall Ó hUiginn, the Sligo kinsman of the Kilcloony branch of the kindred, in which he referred to seventeen poets from Ulster having studied their art at Kilcloony.[152]

The tower-house and lands of Kilcloony lay at the junction of three medieval parishes in what had been the early medieval territory of Conmaicne Cenél Dubáin, over which the Anglo-Norman de Bermingham family gained control.[153] The settlement at Kilcloony was a complex of buildings and earthworks extending over the greater part of the townland of the name, the central focus of which was the tower-house with an accompanying bawn wall.[154] There are three striking aspects of the tower-house. Foremost among them is the view north and the landscape setting of the building (Fig. 4.18). It looks out towards the great expanse of flat land that extends southwest to Knockmaa, a celebrated landmark hill of the early medieval kingdom of Mag Seóla and, in Gaelic literature, the domain of the mythological figure Findabair and his seven sons.[155] The view north was facilitated by the setting of the tower-house on a prominent spur of land, a natural promontory (*c.*60 m OD), which is straight sided and steep on its west side (Fig. 4.19).

The tower-house survives to first-floor level only (Fig. 4.20). Construction of the building can be dated to the fifteenth century on the basis of the rounded, punch-dressed quoin-stones that survive on the southeast and southwest corners, and which are found in other Co. Galway tower-houses securely dated to that period, including Claregalway Castle of the Clanrickard Burke family, which has been assigned to the first half of the fifteenth century.[156] The remaining architectural features of Kilcloony tower-house include a base batter, a barrel vault that supports the first floor, a garde-robe chute at the north end of the east wall, window embrasures that preserve substantial traces of wickerwork centering, and fragmentary decorative window heads on the south wall of the first floor and on the route of the former mural staircase. The small and compact nature of the discrete spaces of the tower-house were created by a vertical cross-wall that separates the main rooms of the building from the narrow chambers on the south side.

[151] Nolan, Galway castles, 117; Freeman, *Compossicion booke*, 65.

[152] E. Knott (ed. and tr.) 1922 *A bhfuil aguinn dár chum Tadhg Dall O'Huiginn (1550–1591)*, i, 82. London. Irish Texts Society; E. Knott (ed. and tr.) 1926 *The bardic poems of Tadhg Dall Ó Huiginn (1550–1591): translation, notes, etc.*, ii, 54. London. Irish Texts Society.

[153] MacCotter, *Medieval Ireland*, 135–6.

[154] E. FitzPatrick and N. McCarthy 2019 Kilcloony: a settlement of the Uí hUiginn poets and its landscape setting, Kilcloony, County Galway. Cill Chluaine, Conmhaicne Mac Fheóruis. Report for the Milltown Heritage Group. Milltown.

[155] MacNeill, *The festival of Lughnasa*, 593; O'Grady, *Silva Gadelica*, ii, 225.

[156] R. Sherlock 2011 The evolution of the Irish tower-house as a domestic space. *PRIA* 111C, 121, n. 12.

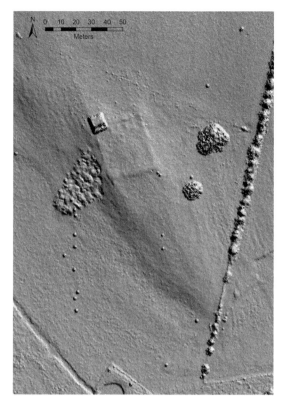

FIG. 4.19. LiDar image of Kilcloony tower-house, bawn and bawn buildings, showing its setting on a spur of high ground (LiDAR data courtesy of Transport Infrastructure Ireland).

Another significant aspect of the tower-house is that its architecture expresses a concern with controlling access to the building. There is a concentration of security features at the main entrance in the south wall and at the entrance to the eastern chamber that led into the main ground-floor chamber and to the staircase (Figs 4.20a, 4.21). The doorway of the tower-house has been removed from the south wall, but door-bar holes, a yett-hole, and a gun-loop remain in situ. It is unclear whether those features, reflective of a threat to life and property, were contemporary with the fifteenth-century construction of the tower-house or added during the Ó hUiginn occupancy of the building.

For a ruling family, it was imperative to have the court physician near at hand (2.0.1).[157] For that reason, physicians were usually allocated estates, often distinguished by tower-house residences, within easy reach of the chiefry castle. The Ó Conchubhair medical kindred, *ollamhain* in medicine, keepers of a school, and physicians to the Mac Giolla Phádraig chiefs of Osraighe in the sixteenth century, had a tower-house residence at Aghmacart (Co. Laois). It was situated just *c.*3 km west of Cullahill

---

[157] FitzPatrick, *Ollamh, biatach, comharba*, 175.

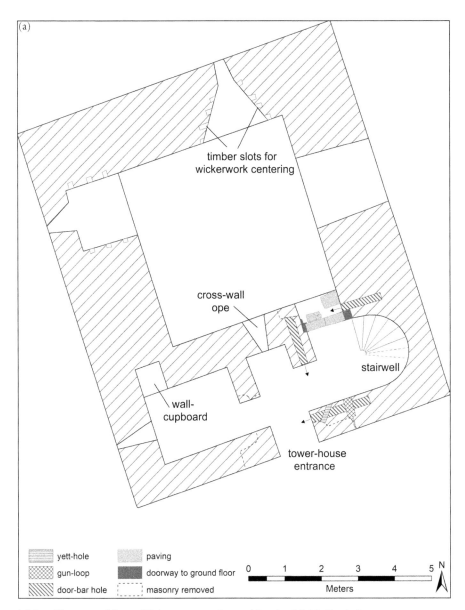

FIG. 4.20a. The ground floor, Kilcloony tower-house (drawing N. McCarthy).

Castle, which was the principal seat of Mac Giolla Phádraig.[158] The chief's physician is first securely cited in connection with Aghmacart in the late sixteenth century. Donnchadh Óg Ó Conchubhair is recorded as official physician to Fínghin Mac Giolla Phádraig in a transcription of the *Liber pronosticorum*, compiled at Aghmacart and

---

[158] Nic Dhonnchadha, Medical school of Aghmacart, 11.

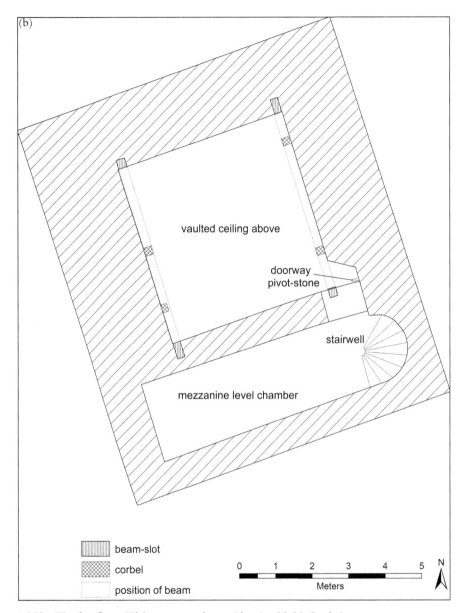

(b)

vaulted ceiling above

doorway
pivot-stone

stairwell

mezzanine level chamber

beam-slot

corbel

position of beam

0 1 2 3 4 5

Meters

N

FIG. 4.20b. The first floor, Kilcloony tower-house (drawing N. McCarthy).

dated 1590.[159] The modest tower-house and bawn was situated south of the Augustinian priory overlooking the River Goul. It is now a vulnerable ruin, consisting of the north façade and northeast corner (Fig. 4.22).

The widespread use of tower-houses by learned kindreds during the sixteenth century and early seventeenth may have been influenced to a degree by the debilitating

---

[159] Nic Dhonnchadha, Medical school of Aghmacart, 13–14.

F IG. 4.21. North façade of Kilcloony, showing security features of the former entrance (photo E. FitzPatrick).

Gaelic practice of partible inheritance of property. Put simply, the tower-house enabled more kin to have their own discrete living spaces under the same roof, in the manner of a tenement. There was particularly extreme partitive division of the property of the Mac Aodhagáin brehon lawyers of Park in the early seventeenth century (3.3.1). Standing remains of their tower-house consist of just the northeast corner of the base of the structure, with an attached portion of bawn wall. In 1618 seven family members received fragments of land as diminutive as one-twelfth of the estate and shares of Park tower-house as small as a third of the building.[160]

Notwithstanding the obvious decline of the family's means, the lawyer Cormac Mac Aodhagáin made a bold statement in 1627 by having a fireplace keystone, believed to be from Park tower-house,[161] inscribed with two panels of an Irish-language dedication in Gaelic hand and an intertwined sacred trigram representing the holy name of Jesus (Fig. 4.23).[162] In translation, the inscription reads, "Cormac Mac Aodhagáin made this work at the time of the age of the Lord, one thousand six

[160] Griffith, *Patent rolls of James I*, 414; Costello, Ancient law school of Park, 97.

[161] RIA 14 C 20, Letters, County Galway, 102.

[162] H. Blake, G. Egan, J. Hurst, and E. New 2003 From popular devotion to resistance and revival in England: the cult of the Holy Name of Jesus and the Reformation. In D. Gaimster and R. Gilchrist (eds), *The archaeology of Reformation 1480–1580*, 175–6, 190–1. Society for Post-Medieval Archaeology monograph: 1. Leeds. Maney.

FIG. 4.22. Aghmacart tower-house (photo E. FitzPatrick).

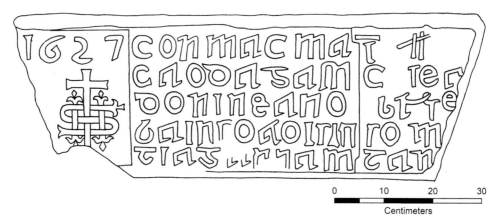

FIG. 4.23. The inscribed fireplace keystone from Park tower-house (photo E. FitzPatrick, drawing A. Gallagher).

hundred and twenty seven."[163] It has been suggested that, by the late sixteenth century, the Irish language was a central part of Gaelic identity and used as a form of resistance to English colonialism.[164] The combination of the sacred trigram with the Gaelic inscription on the Park stone declared the political outlook of Mac Aodhagáin and, more widely, suggests an alignment of some learned men with Counter-Reformation ideals in later sixteenth- and seventeenth-century Ireland.

Learned kindreds who had the resources to construct substantial stone buildings did not always choose conventional tower-houses. The dwelling of the Ó Cléirigh *ollamh*, on his estate at Kilbarron, is referred to as "Kilbarron Castle," but it is more aptly described as a modular settlement consisting of a modest gate-house keep and two rectangular houses constructed up against a curtain or bawn wall on the perimeter of a promontory fort (Fig. 4.24). In that sense the approach to creating a domestic space was not unlike the Ó Duibhdábhoireann lawyers' manipulation of the *caisel* at

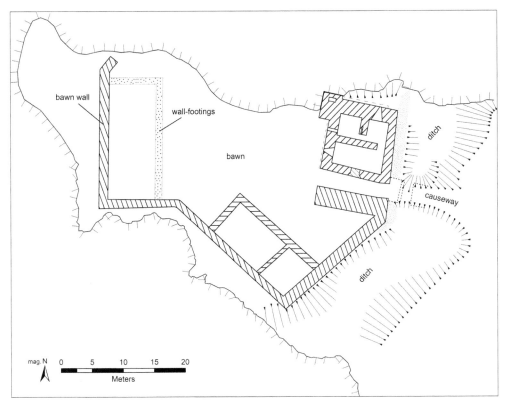

FIG. 4.24. Plan of the gate-house keep, bawn, standing garth buildings, and landward defenses of the promontory fort, Cloghbolie, Kilbarron (drawing N. McCarthy, after M. Casey, in Lacey 1983).

[163] Costello, Ancient law school of Park, 98.

[164] P. Palmer 2001 *Language and conquest in early modern Ireland: English Renaissance literature and Elizabethan imperial expansion*, 181–5. Cambridge University Press.

Cahermacnaghten, with its gatehouse and buildings disposed to the perimeter of the enclosing wall (4.2.1). In keeping with that, the Ó Cléirigh fortified settlement was not marked as a castle but as the "ruines of a stone house" on the seventeenth-century Down Survey parish map of Kilbarron.[165]

Projecting into Donegal Bay, the rather savage but beautiful sea point on which the Ó Cléirigh family lived has the essential characteristics of a promontory fort—a coastal headland, the seaward sides of which are defended by cliffs and protected from the landward side by one or more curved ramparts of earth and stone and accompanying fosses (Fig. 4.24). Current knowledge suggests that coastal promontory forts origi- nated in the Iron Age, but six of the nine excavated sites in Ireland also had periods of medieval and later use.[166]

The Ó Cléirigh promontory fort has sheer cliffs on the north and south long sides and is cut off from the landward side by a deep fosse which was faced with flagstones on the west side. This revetment is best seen in French's photograph taken between 1865 and 1914 (Fig. 4.25). The building stone of the site is the local Mullaghmore

CASTLE RUINS. NEAR BALLYSHANNON. 5527. W.L.

FIG. 4.25. French's view of Kilbarron Castle, 1865–1914. The stone facing on the fosse can be seen to the right (courtesy of the National Library of Ireland).

---

[165] <http://downsurvey.tchpc.tcd.ie/down-survey-maps.php#bm=Tirhugh&c=Donegal&p=Kilbarran+and+ Inishmacsaint> (accessed June 7, 2019).

[166] E. FitzPatrick 2005 Promontory forts. In S. Duffy (ed.), *Medieval Ireland*, 389–91.

sandstone, perhaps quarried out along the coastline south of the promontory fort, where there is visible evidence of past quarrying. A causeway crosses the landward defenses, and a strong masonry curtain wall encloses the promontory at the west, at the south, and on the east line of the fosse, making a right-angled turn west along the south side of the causeway. The compact gate-house keep protected the northeast edge of the promontory (Fig. 4.24). Internally, the ground floor was subdivided into three diminutive rooms and there was a garderobe on the first floor that discharged over the cliff.

The settlement on the promontory replaced an earlier fortified building of *c*.1400, reputedly of the Ó Sgingín learned kindred, who had preceded the Ó Cléirigh family as court historians to the Ó Domhnaill.[167] It was a target in the attacks and raids along the southern borderland of Tír Conaill and had been assailed in 1390 by the Ó Conchobhair-Sligo chief of Cairbre.[168]

4.6 CONCLUSIONS

Investigating the residences of members of literati in different regions of Ireland has revealed variety, intention, continuity, and social change in the dwellings allocated to them, or which, less commonly, they chose to build for themselves. While learned kindreds carried the weight of the history of the ruling families they served, they were not bound by it in their quotidian lives. The built heritage associated with them in thirteenth- to seventeenth-century Ireland indicates that the professional needs of this group had an impact on architectural developments in the lordships. Their dwellings expressed a concern to be forward-looking by adapting traditional enclosed settlement forms to contemporary architectural fashion (4.1, 4.3). This is seen in the reuse of the *caisel* (stone enclosure) and the *crannóg* (artificial lake-island dwelling), both of which had early origins. By the sixteenth century, most *ollamhain* resided in tower-houses allocated to them by their chiefs and overlords (4.5). As seen at Kilcloony, that practice was undoubtedly beneficial, both to literati as a physical expression of their standing in society and to chiefs as visible reminders of their power in the landscape of lordship. However, a darker side of the widespread use of the tower-house by this class of society in the later sixteenth/early seventeenth century is that it also reflects the consequences of partible inheritance of property, as experienced among the Mac Aodhagáin lawyers at Park, whereby several members of the kindred shared the tower-house space. In that context, the erection of the inscribed fireplace keystone that declared the political and religious outlook of the family in 1627 was a measure of their cultural resilience.

[167] Simms, Bardic schools, 36.
[168] AConn 1390.10, 362, 363; M 1390.8, iv, 720, 721.

It is where literati adapted earlier settlement forms to contemporary living that the type of spatial arrangement and buildings that were favorable to their domestic needs is best seen. In manipulating earlier settlement enclosures as their domestic space, they contributed to architectural innovation in late medieval Ireland. When the Ó Duibhdábhoireann lawyers were granted the half-quarter of Cahermacnaghten, they refashioned a *caisel* to suit their needs as members of a learned elite serving the court of the Ó Lochlainn chief. For a family whose members had held the office of *ollamh* in brehon law of Corca Modhruadh, from at least as early as 1364, the decision to live in an early medieval *caisel* named after a historic king of that territory, Nechtain, was perhaps carefully contrived when they were first granted their estate.[169] While their motivation for living in a *caisel* might at first suggest atavistic tendencies, the significant remodeling of the early enclosure and the construction of contemporary late medieval houses in the garth portray a progressive kindred assuming the architectural fashion of the period, but within their means as a minor legal family.

The Ó Cléirigh *ollamh* did not build a conventional tower-house and bawn. He chose a modular settlement (at least in its final form) consisting of a gate-house keep to control access to the garth, and living and perhaps guesting quarters constructed against a strong curtain wall. The sea-point setting of the Ó Cléirigh residence in *c*.1400 was significant. It was a prominent headland of his coastal estate and therefore a highly visible statement of the presence of the Ó Domhnaill chief's *ollamh* in the southern borderland of Tír Conaill.

The *crannóg* was a commonplace settlement form in the estate landscapes of the many learned *airchinnigh* families concentrated between the upper and lower lakes of the River Erne in the lordship of Fir Mhanach. The recovery of fifteenth- to seventeenth-century occupation evidence in the form of a dated wooden pile and sherds of Ulster coarse pottery from the Lough Raymond *crannóg*, situated on the estate of the Ó Luinín *ollamh* and *airchinneach* of Arda, suggests that occupation of late medieval lake dwellings may be found among *airchinnigh* of south Ulster where the culture of keeping guests was usual. The occupancy of a *crannóg* by the Ó Cobhthaigh poets of *Cró Inis* on Lough Ennell can be related to the need for visibility of the chief's *ollamh* in a premier borderland, a role which Lough Ennell had for the lordship of Fir Tulach. It can also be linked with the fact that Lough Ennell had been a former early medieval royal center of the overkingdom of Mide, with the island functioning as a retreat for the overking. Historically important *crannóg* sites were occupied by some literati in the late medieval period, as a form of continuity of their predominant early historic roles as retreats and hospices for elites.

Poets and harpers were especially documented as living in *pailís*-named places in the sixteenth and seventeenth centuries, in the lordships of Cineál bhFiachach, Iar Mhumhain, Southern Anghal, and Uí Cheinnsealaigh. It has been proposed that they

---

[169] The *caisel* had possibly been an Ó Lochlainn dwelling beforehand; FitzPatrick, Native enclosed settlement, 303.

may have resided in *pailís* enclosures of *ráth* and moated-site type that had been vacated by ruling families with the advent of tower-house facilities for feasting.[170] In Machaire Chonnacht and Uí Mhaine, learned kindreds are recorded on their own landholdings in *pailís* landscapes, with some, such as the harper of the Ó Ceallaigh chief, linked to his landholding as early as the late fourteenth or early fifteenth century. These relationships may be interpreted as indications of the presence of a chief's court, with the probability that the predecessors of poets and harpers lived in *pailís* landscapes as part of the formation of the estates of householders, at emerging lordship centers used for feasting in the fourteenth century.

[170] FitzPatrick, Last kings, 209.

Church Space for Learned Occupations

5.0 INTRODUCTION

The role that the Church played in providing space for learning from the twelfth century onward is well known. Church schools, especially those attached to cathedrals, were common in northern Europe.[1] Bishops, monasteries, cathedral chapters, and parish priests had oversight of schools and controlled the appointment of teachers. The long-standing association between churches and schools in urban environments continued into the sixteenth century. Grammar schools were often physically attached or adjacent to parish churches, even where they were no longer controlled by a parish or chapter.[2]

In late medieval Ireland, providers of conventional education included colleges attached to cathedrals and parish churches, and the *studia* of the Mendicant orders established by the end of the thirteenth century to teach arts, grammar, philosophy, and theology to the pre-ordained.[3] Chantry colleges of canons, patronized by families of Anglo-Norman origin and established in several of the towns during the fifteenth and early sixteenth centuries, were primarily concerned with maintaining the daily divine office and offering masses in intercession for deceased members of the founders' kindreds, but they also performed the social role of educators.[4] Typical of these were the chantry colleges at Ardee (Co. Louth), Cashel and Clonmel (Co. Tipperary), Howth (Co. Dublin), and Slane (Co. Meath).[5] College buildings were used to house the canons, but parts of them must also have been used as school-rooms.

[1] Orme, *Medieval schools*, 136; Willemsen, *Back to the schoolyard*, 23–4; K. Salonen 2019 Reformation and the medieval roots of the Finnish education. In K. Sinnemäki, A. Portman, J. Tilli and R.H. Nelson (eds), *On the legacy of Lutheranism in Finland: societal perspectives*, 103–4. *Studia Fennica Historica* 25. Helsinki. Finnish Literature Society.

[2] Willemsen, *Back to the schoolyard*, 92–3, 261–4.

[3] C. Ó Clabaigh 2012 *The friars in Ireland 1224–1540*, 271–84. Dublin. Four Courts Press.

[4] C. Lennon 2008 The parish fraternities of County Meath in the late Middle Ages. *Ríocht na Midhe* 19, 95–6.

[5] J. Bradley 1989 The Chantry College, Ardee. *Journal of the County Louth Archaeological and Historical Society* 22 (1), 6–19; R. Moss (ed.) 2014 *Art and architecture of Ireland, i, medieval Ireland, c.400–c.1600*, 171–2. Dublin. Royal Irish Academy.

Landscapes of the Learned: Placing Gaelic Literati in Irish Lordships 1300–1600. Elizabeth FitzPatrick, Oxford University Press. © Elizabeth FitzPatrick 2023. DOI: 10.1093/oso/9780192855749.003.0005

There are many links between Gaelic literati and buildings on church land cited in the chronicles, papal registers, and ecclesiastical taxations for the late medieval period. A vacant benefice or impending vacancy was apparently viewed as an opportunity for a learned man to acquire both a living and a building that he could use for his professional occupations.

In this chapter, investigations of the archaeology of churches and chapels, directly associated with Gaelic learned clerics, suggest that their use as space for scholarship, including schools, may have been a widespread phenomenon in Ireland, especially during the fifteenth and sixteenth centuries. In that period, representatives of learned kindreds were still finding their way into the offices of *airchinneach* and *comharba* on church lands, which is reflected in the names of learned individuals in clerical roles cited in ecclesiastical records, and arguably in corresponding changes to the fabric of church buildings where learned clerics were the incumbents. It is important to reiterate the point that in the medieval Irish Church, *comharbai*, while technically abbots, were not necessarily required to be ordained, their roles as heads of churches being largely administrative. The *airchinnigh* were generally unordained lay men who, as tenants of church land, had obligations to act as stewards of its property. Just how many of the literati were ordained priests is difficult to determine. But it appears to have been the case that they were mostly not ordained, and that where they are recorded in the papal registers as perpetual vicars, lassitude was deemed a problem among them. For instance, in 1487–8, the worldly Cairbre Mac Aodhagáin, of the Mac Aodhagáin kindred of brehon lawyers, was the incumbent of the parish church of Kilglass (Co. Sligo), on the western edge of the Ó Dubhda lordship of Tír Fiachrach. He was accused of simony, "notorious fornication," and "turning to his evil uses the goods of the said vicarage." Although he was under sentence of excommunication, he had "celebrated divine offices in contempt of the Keys, thereby contracting irregularity."[6]

It is unsurprising that literati were drawn to Kilglass—it was just a kilometer east of Lackan, the estate of the Mac Fhirbhisigh kindred of historians who are associated with Lackan as early as the fourteenth century (3.3.1; Fig. 3.12). In 1590, Maicnia Mac Con Midhe, a member of the west Sligo branch of the Mac Con Midhe learned kindred of poets, was living in Kilglass. Several of his kin were resident in the parishes of Kilglass and Castleconor in the late sixteenth century and early seventeenth.[7] None of the Mac Fhirbhisigh kindred appear to have held the offices of *comharba* or *airchinneach* of Kilglass in any period. However, it is possible that they had secular proprietorship of the church lands (3.3.1).

There are several unusual features in the architecture of Kilglass that suggest a role for the parish church other than providing pastoral care. The accusation, in 1487–8,

[6] J. A. Twemlow (ed.) 1960 *Calendar of papal registers relating to Great Britain and Ireland, xiv, 1484–92,* 216. London. HMSO.
[7] O'Rahilly, Irish poets, 107, 108.

that Cairbre Mac Aodhagáin had behaved badly and used the goods of the vicarage inappropriately, implies that pastoral care may not have been a priority of some incumbents. The anomalies of Kilglass church are obvious. It is a long building (21 m × 6.4 m internally) with suggestions of former two-story quarters incorporated into the west end. It has an uncommon number of windows for a church. Aside from the east window, there are three others towards the eastern end of the south wall in the chancel area, and two more lighting the west end of the nave. A large recess or wall-cupboard occupies the east end of the south wall of the chancel. The fifteenth-century doorway is positioned at the west end of the south wall and was the only entry point to the building. A door-bar hole running deep into the west side of the embrasure indicates a concern with controlling access to the building. Dedicated to the local saint, Molaise, there is no early medieval fabric in the church. The succession of learned clerics who held it during the late medieval period may have made some modifications, if not entirely rebuilt the church to facilitate their learned occupations, in collaboration with the Mac Fhirbhisigh *ollamh* of Lackan.

In general, what survives of church buildings associated with learned *airchinnigh* and *comharbai* is often insubstantial, and therefore the focus is placed in this chapter on case studies of those that have standing walls, preserve readable architectural features, or for which there are previous records. They include the churches of Inishmore and Killerry in the borderland between the north Connacht lordships of West Bréifne, Cairbre, and Tír Oilella-Corran (2.1.3), Kilbarron in the southern borderland of the Ulster lordship of Tír Conaill (2.1.1), and St Breacán's Chapel at Toomullin, which is proposed as the law school of the Mac Fhlannchadha brehon lawyers in the Ó Conchobhair lordship of Corca Modhruadh (3.4). As a counterpoint to church sites with historically attested links to literati in Gaelic lordships, the efficacy of material culture in pointing to a church that may have been a seat of learning in the culturally hybrid borderland of the Pale, during the late medieval period, is investigated at Smarmore (Co. Louth).

5.1 THE PROBLEM OF SPACE FOR LEARNING IN EARLY MEDIEVAL CHURCHES

The question naturally arises as to whether there were buildings dedicated to learned activity in pre-twelfth-century monasteries that might have exerted an influence on how church space was used by later medieval Gaelic literati who held ecclesiastical offices. There is a tentative argument for a "school-house" in the early medieval monastery of Nendrum, founded in the seventh century on Mahee Island, Strangford Lough, Co. Down.[8] The monastery of St Molaise on Inishmurray in Sligo Bay,

---

[8] T. McErlean and N. Crothers 2007 *Harnessing the tides: the early medieval tide mills at Nendrum Monastery, Strangford Lough*, 306–11. Belfast. Environment and Heritage Service.

reputedly founded in the sixth century, is also attributed a school-house.[9] An early medieval school at *Túaim Drecain*, Tomregan (Co. Cavan), which is identified with the site of a monastic church in the uplands of west Co. Cavan (Fig. 1.2), was reputedly founded by Bricc or Bricín ("little speckled one").[10] It was alleged to have had three separate schools where Latin, law, and poetry were taught.[11]

During his excavations at Nendrum (1922–4), Lawlor uncovered the foundations of a rectangular stone building in the western half of the middle enclosure of the monastic complex, which he interpreted as a school-house. His surmise was based on the recovery of a range of finds from the building.[12] He did not record any of the stratigraphy of the areas of the site that he excavated.[13] The wall-footings of the building have been preserved and indicate a structure with an east–west alignment, internal dimensions of 14.3 m by 4 m, and walls *c.*0.75 m thick. In the early stages of the excavation, roofing materials in the form of straw and partially burned roof beams and roofing nails were recovered from the low mound that represented the outline of the building. The surviving walls were clay bonded, and there was evidence for a wooden door at the east end of the north wall in the form of a door-hinge and handle and nailed planks.[14] The size of the structure and its relatively thin walls are more typical of a late medieval building. Therefore, doubt has been expressed about Lawlor's statement that a range of early medieval artefacts were recovered from its floor. The finds are more likely to have been related to "an occupation layer or structure below the rectangular building."[15] What is certain, however, is that early medieval material culture associated with literacy and learning was recovered at Nendrum, in the form of thirty slate motif pieces, three of which have traces of lettering, along with a possible arm from a set of dividers, and four styli suggesting that wax tablets for writing were used at the site.[16] Mortars and pounders found outside of the rectangular building during Lawlor's excavation were posthumously identified as items that may have been used for making pigments.[17] All of this material is indicative of learned activity, but it does not necessarily predicate a school-house at Nendrum.

The presence of material culture associated with literacy and learning, and the corresponding absence of a school-house or scriptorium, is a conundrum of other monastic sites where excavations have taken place. Survey and excavation (1999–2004)

---

[9] J. O'Sullivan and T. Ó Carragáin 2008 *Inishmurray: monks and pilgrims in an Atlantic landscape, i, archaeological survey and excavations 1997–2000*, 8–12. Cork. Collins Press.

[10] Ó Riain, *Dictionary*, 110.   [11] Ó Riain, *Dictionary*, 118.

[12] H. C. Lawlor 1925 *The monastery of Saint Mochaoi of Nendrum*, 143–9. Belfast. Natural History and Philosophical Society; C. Lowe (ed.) 2008 *Inchmarnock: an early historic island monastery and its archaeological landscape*, 257–63. Edinburgh. Society of Antiquaries of Scotland.

[13] U. O'Meadhra, 1987 *Early Christian, Viking and Romanesque art: motif-pieces from Ireland*. Theses and papers in North-European archaeology: 17, 71–3. Stockholm. Almqvist and Wiksell International.

[14] McErlean and Crothers, *Harnessing the tides*, 375–6; O'Meadhra, *Motif-pieces*, 73.

[15] McErlean and Crothers, *Harnessing the tides*, 376.

[16] O'Meadhra, *Motif-pieces*, 73.   [17] O'Meadhra, *Motif-pieces*, 73.

on the small monastic island of Inchmarnock, west of the Isle of Bute in the estuary of the River Clyde in western Scotland, uncovered about a hundred pieces of incised slate, ranging in date over the long medieval period, the majority of which are motif pieces. The corpus also includes eight text-inscribed slate fragments that have been assigned dates between the seventh and ninth centuries. These have been described as "evidence of instruction in literacy, the teaching of basic skills in forming letters, writing Latin, and copying text."[18] On the basis that seventh-century text-inscribed slate fragments were recovered from the area west and north of the church, Lowe suggested that a monastic school-house could have been positioned somewhere in the northwest quadrant of the island monastery, west of the church and outside the inner enclosure that encompasses the church and cemetery, although "we only see it through the debitage of its day-to-day activity."[19] In support of that suggestion, he drew on the similarity of the spatial arrangement of the Nendrum and Inishmurray "school-houses," which lie west of the churches and outside of the *sanctissimus* enclosures at both sites. However, these analogies are problematic because of the buildings concerned at Nendrum and Inishmurray.

During Wakeman's survey of St Molaise's Monastery on Inishmurray Island *c*.1886, he recorded a building locally named "*Túr Uí Bhreanaill*" ("Ó Brenaill's tower") and the "school-house."[20] A sketch-plan had earlier been made of it in 1794 by Cooper (Fig. 5.1). The "school-house," one of four beehive-shaped drystone cells on the island, is situated in the western division of the monastic enclosure. It is circular in plan, with a corbeled roof; the entrance is a square-headed doorway formed by large jamb-stones at the north point of the building. A single window is positioned at the south, opposite the doorway. In the western half of the interior, there are two keeping-holes and a stone bench set against the wall.[21] The term *clochán* is given to this distinctive beehive structure in archaeology and vernacular architecture. However, it is a modern application of the term, the original meaning of which is a paved road or causeway.[22] Perhaps a historically more accurate word for the beehive shelter is *both* meaning cell or hut (3.1, 6.3).[23]

The simple beehive cell of circular plan had extraordinary continuity and various uses in different parts of Ireland, ranging from early medieval monastic and lay domestic buildings to sweathouses, pig-sties, hen-houses, storage for milk and turf, and dwellings of communities involved in the seasonal movement of livestock.[24] However, they are

---

[18] K. Forsyth and C. Tedeschi 2008 Text-inscribed slates. In Lowe, *Inchmarnock*, 128, 132.

[19] Lowe, *Inchmarnock*, 257.

[20] W. Wakeman 1885 Inis Muiredeach, now Inishmurray, and its antiquities. *Journal of the Royal Historical and Archaeological Association of Ireland* 7 (64), 203–5.

[21] O'Sullivan and Ó Carragáin, *Inishmurray*, 139–40.

[22] Quin, *Dictionary*, 123:249; An Roinn Oideachais, *Gearrfhoclóir*, 138.

[23] Quin, *Dictionary*, 80:149.

[24] E. E. Evans 1942 *Irish heritage: the landscape, the people and their work*, 81–4. Dundalk. Dundalgan Press; F. H. A. Aalen 1964 Clochans as transhumance dwellings in the Dingle Peninsula, Co. Kerry. *JRSAI* 94 (1), 39–45.

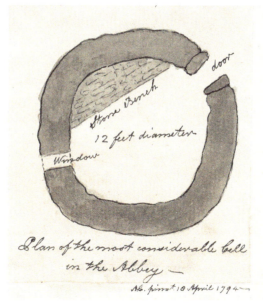

FIG. 5.1. The cell known as the "school-house" on Inishmurray, photographed *c.* 1900 by Robert Welch (BELUM.Y.W.18.01.35, courtesy of National Museums of Northern Ireland), and Cooper's plan of the "most considerable cell," Inishmurray, 1794 (courtesy of the National Library of Ireland).

particularly concentrated in monastic contexts, especially in peninsular Co. Kerry, where radiocarbon analysis of cattle bones from a drystone corbeled hut of circular plan, on the monastic island of Illaunloughaun, dated its construction to between 775 and 961 CE.[25]

Why the Inishmurray beehive cell was attributed use as a school-house is unknown. Cooper's sketch-plan indicates that the cell was there in 1794, but Wakeman's record of 1886 was the first to document it as a school-house. The attested versatility of the beehive cell means that it could have been adapted for use as a space for poetic composition (6.3). A branch of the Ó Dálaigh poets had a connection with Inishmurray. The poet Maoileoin Ó Dálaigh was interred on the island in 1612, which implies that his kindred had burial rights there.[26] Speculatively, the kindred's association with Inishmurray may have included using it as a retreat for poetic composition.

It would seem, then, that space for learning within monastic sites can be identified from distribution patterns of finds relating to knowledge production, but, as yet, the nature of the buildings in which that activity happened in early medieval Ireland remains elusive.

The early medieval geography of the school attributed to St Bricín at *Túaim Drecain* places it in Magh Slécht, a district associated with the legendary pre-Christian god Crom Crúaich, in the northeastern borderland of the overkingdom of Uí Briúin Bréifne (Fig. 2.11).[27] It was cited as a boundary place of the province of Connacht in a fourteenth-century poem describing the pre-Norman topography of the northern half of Ireland.[28] The church, of which there are no upstanding remains, was situated at the butt of a low ridge, in Church Meadow, east of Togher Lough, in Mullynagolman townland. Slievebrickan, a hill northwest of Mullynagolman, was interpreted by O'Donovan as Breacán's mountain (*Sliabh Breacáin*).[29] When recorded in 1948, traces of the foundations of the church and a round tower were visible as "slight grassy banks," and "much mortar" was spread across the site. Fragments of a rotary quern, iron slag, and a possible furnace-bottom were also recorded, but no finds indicative of learned practices. The church clearly had late medieval alterations or rebuilding, as a mullion, an arch-stone, and gable copingstones were recovered at the site.[30] The remarkable "Tomregan stone," which appears to have formed the apex of a church doorway, or perhaps a tympanum, is believed to be from Mullynagolman. Classified as an exhibitionist figure, it is a representation in sandstone of a torso-less male, showing the head with moustache and beard, extended and splayed limbs, outward-turned buttocks, and scrotum. The figure holds a small object with a human

---

[25] J. White Marshall and C. Walsh 2005 *Illaunloughan Island: an early medieval monastery in County Kerry*, 37–42. Bray. Wordwell.

[26] ALC 1612, ii, 517.   [27] J. P. Dalton 1921–4 Cromm Cruaich of Magh Sleacht. *PRIA* 36C, 23–67.

[28] Carney, *Topographical poems*, 20.

[29] <https://www.logainm.ie/en/3983> (accessed March 21, 2022).

[30] O. Davies 1948 The churches of County Cavan. *JRSAI* 78, 116–17.

face, in one hand, and a horseshoe-shaped object, in the other. Late medieval exhibitionist figures in borderland contexts have been noted elsewhere in this study (2.0.1; 4.5).

The expertise of St Bricín of *Túaim Drecain* as a physician is conveyed in a late narrative of the law tract "Judgments of inadvertence" (*Bretha étgid*), which concerns Cenn Fáelad, an early medieval learned man (*sapiens*), who was the son of Ailill of the Cenél nEógain dynasty of Ulster.[31] His death was recorded for the year 679.[32] Later traditions about Cenn Fáelad's life allege that he received a head injury at the battle of Mag Roth in 637 and was taken to *Túaim Drecain*, to the house of the physician Bricín, who removed his "brain of forgetfulness." As a result, Cenn Fáelad could memorize everything he was taught in all three schools by Bricín and he wrote down in lime chalk (*i cailc liubhair*; 3.4) all that he remembered.[33] It is probable that the seventh-century Cenn Fáelad attended the *Túaim Drecain* school, but the narrative of the removal of his "brain of forgetfulness" has been adjudged "a later accretion to the tradition, using Cenn Fáelad as a prototypal learned figure" and the three schools as an allegory "for what was probably a wide variation in actual practice."[34]

5.2 LITERATI AND CHURCHES FROM PARISH FORMATION TO PROTESTANT REFORMATION

It is during the period of the formation of parishes in the late twelfth and early thirteenth century that we find clues to the beginning of the allocation of church land and church buildings to kindreds who were practitioners of the Gaelic arts. One of those pointers is the place name *Nuachongbháil*, which signified a new holding or new settlement on church land and associated church buildings. It is an uncommon place name, with just nine recorded as parish, townland, or church names in the Anglicized forms Noughaval/Nohaval and Oughaval.[35] Most of the churches of this name had early medieval antecedents, and at least five of the nine can be linked with kindreds of lawyers, poets, and physicians, and/or with learned activity, at different moments in time.

The involvement of learned kindreds with *Nuachongbháil* places is quite consistent, to the extent that it cannot be mere coincidence. Nohavaldaly (*Nuachongbháil Uí Dhálaigh*) in Co. Kerry was the landholding of a branch of the Ó Dálaigh poets who

[31] Breatnach, *Corpus iuris Hibernici*, 381.   [32] U 679, i, 144, 145.

[33] Breatnach, *Corpus iuris Hibernici*, 381.

[34] F. Qiu 2021 Law, law-books and tradition in early medieval Ireland. In T. Gobbitt (ed.), *Law book culture in the Middle Ages*, 138. Explorations in medieval culture: 14. Leiden and Boston. Brill; E. Johnston 2013 *Literacy and identity in early medieval Ireland*, 57. Woodbridge. Boydell Press.

[35] See, for instance, entry for Nohaval, Co. Kerry, in Placenames Database of Ireland. https://www.logainm. ie/en/1117 (accessed 5 August, 2019).

served the Mac Cárthaigh Mór chief of Iar Mhumhain (4.3). They were tenants of the land associated with the parish church of Nohaval, of which there are no upstanding remains. The name of their church estate is variously cited in ecclesiastical records as "Nochuayilalla" in 1471 and "Nocwhayllalla" in 1481.[36] A papal register of 1500 recorded that Bernard Ó Dálaigh had detained the vicarage of Nohavaldaly without title "for some time" and he was to be removed.[37] The Ó Dálaigh poets were deeply imbedded with the parish church and its lands, a relationship which probably began with the elevation of the pre-twelfth-century church to parish status and the creation of the new parish settlement from the late twelfth or thirteenth century.

The Connacht medical kindred of Ó Fearghusa are associated with Oughaval parish church in Churchfield (Co. Mayo). In the colophon of a medical manuscript dated to 1563, a member of the family noted that he had written it at his father's house at "Bale [*baile*] na Uachamhala," which is Oughaval in the northeast borderland of the lordship of Umhaill (Figs 1.1, 1.2).[38] The standing remains of Oughaval parish church, dedicated to St Columcille, consist of the west gable, the south long wall, and the western end of the north long wall (Fig. 5.2). A gabled cross-wall separates west-end

FIG. 5.2. The view west to Croagh Patrick from Oughaval (photo E. FitzPatrick).

[36] O'Connell and Costello, Obligationes pro annatis, 17, 29.
[37] A. P. Fuller (ed.) 1994 *Calendar of entries in the papal registers relating to Great Britain and Ireland, xvii, part 1, 1492–1503*, 226–7. Dublin. Irish Manuscripts Commission.
[38] Gillespie, Scribes and manuscripts, 15–16.

quarters from the nave of the church. This space is entered from the west gable through a sandstone doorway of trabeate form, which is now the only visible remains of the early medieval foundation. The numinous view west from the church is directly to Croagh Patrick.

The difficulty in connecting families with the initiation of new ecclesiastical settlements linked to parish formation is that the documentary records for their presence on church lands referred to as *Nuachongbháil* tend to be intermittent. The earliest record of members of the Ó Duibhdábhoireann lawyers on the church lands of Noughaval (mensal land of the bishop of Kilfenora in the lordship of Boireann) is for the fifteenth century.[39] The respective entries in the papal registers relating to Dermot Ó Duibhdábhoireann in 1455 and John Ó Duibhdábhoireann in 1460 suggest that Dermot was an *airchinneach* and confirm that John had been a priest or *comharba* of Noughaval Church:

> To the precentor, the chancellor and the official of Kilfenora (*Fynnaboren.*). Mandate to collate and assign to Donald Olochlynd, priest, of the diocese of Kilfenora, the perpetual vicarage of the parish church of Noua *alias* Mougaual [Noughaval] in the said diocese, value not exceeding 3 marks sterling, void by the death of John Odubgaborynd [Ó Duibhdábhoireann].[40]

The Ó Duibhdábhoireann kindred's relationship with the church and its lands continued well into the seventeenth century (5.2.1), the churchyard becoming their burial place. Ní Ghabhláin identified pre-twelfth-century cyclopean masonry in the south wall of Noughaval (Fig. 5.3). It indicates that earlier fabric was incorporated into the construction of the parish church, which can be dated to *c*.1200 by a late Romanesque doorway added to the west end of the south wall and a chancel arch of the same period.[41] A settlement cluster, and eventually a marketplace, developed around the parish church.[42] Considering that the association of the Ó Duibhdábhoireann kindred with Cahermacnaghten was quite late (3.2.2, 4.2.1), it is plausible that they were allocated their first estate in the lordship, as brehon lawyers and *airchinnigh* of the episcopal mensal lands of Noughaval *c*.1200.

In one instance a *Nuachongbháil* site can be linked to the compilation of a manuscript. The parish church of Oughaval, Carricksallagh (Co. Laois), was where the Book of Leinster (*Lebar na Núachongbála, c*.1100–35) is believed to have been partly,

---

[39] McInerney, Clerical and learned lineages, 164–5.

[40] J. A. Twemlow (ed.) 1921 *Calendar of papal registers, Britain and Ireland, xi, 1455–1464*, 206. London. HMSO; J. A. Twemlow (ed.) 1933 *Calendar of papal registers, Britain and Ireland, xii, 1458–1471*, 131. London. HMSO.

[41] S. Ní Ghabhláin 1995 Church and community in medieval Ireland: the diocese of Kilfenora. *JRSAI* 125, 65.

[42] E. Campbell 2013 Exploring the medieval and early modern settlement of Noughaval in the Burren. *The Other Clare* 37, 12–17.

FIG. 5.3. The parish church of Noughaval, Burren, with remains of the late-Romanesque doorway (left), south wall (photo E. FitzPatrick).

if not wholly, written and where it is known to have been housed in the fourteenth century (Fig. 1.2).[43]

Two additional church sites with the designation *Nuachongbháil* are situated on the estates of families of lawyers and poets. They are Nohaval (Co. Kerry) on the estate of the Mac Aodhagáin lawyers of Ballyegan (3.3), and Oughaval, on the lands of the Ó hUiginn kindred of Kilmacteige (Co. Sligo) where the church is no longer standing but an early medieval graveslab has been recorded.[44]

5.2.1 *The churches of Inishmore and Killerry*

It has previously been argued (2.1.3) that the presence of the learned kindreds of Ó Cuirnín and Mac an Óglaigh in Calraighe and Clann Fhearmhaíghe served to embolden the claim of the Ó Ruairc chief of West Bréifne over both *túatha* inclusive of Lough Gill (Fig. 2.9). Here, the churches linked to them at Inishmore and Killerry are described and proposed as space that supported their roles as literati.

Inishmore is an island of 41 acres at the approximate center of Lough Gill. A church that is one of the best-preserved buildings associated with a Gaelic learned kindred in Ireland is situated in a small clearing at the east end of the island (Fig. 5.4). It was positioned to take advantage of the natural harbor 35 m to the south, where a

---

[43] R. I. Best, O. Bergin, and M. A. O'Brien, 1954 *Book of Leinster, formerly Lebar na Núachongbála*, i, xi–xv Dublin. Dublin Institute for Advanced Studies.

[44] The Sligo branch of the Ó hUiginn poets may originally have been *airchinnigh* of the episcopal mensal land of Oughaval parish church in Kilmacteige townland.

FIG. 5.4. St Lomán's Church, Inishmore, Lough Gill (photo P. Naessens).

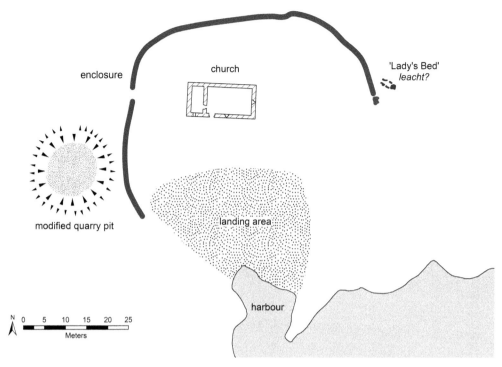

FIG. 5.5. Site plan of St Lomán's (drawing N. McCarthy and P. Naessens, based on survey by E. FitzPatrick and P. Naessens).

former landing site is identifiable. From the shoreline, the view south across the lake is to Killerry Mountain. The church is surrounded on the landward side by an earthen enclosure and open to the shore elsewhere (Fig. 5.5).[45] As ostensibly a parish church, Inishmore would have required a fenced graveyard. However, despite the presence of the enclosure and a claim by Francis Grose (1791) that "in former ages" the church site was the burial place of the parish and *túath* of Calraighe, there is no trace of any grave-markers of any age within or outside of the enclosure.[46]

The foundation of the first church on Inishmore is attributed to St Lomán, the pyx-bearer or *hostiarius* of St Patrick, whose feast day was celebrated on 11 October.[47] Outside the enclosure at the northeast, there is a small, rectangular area surrounded by stone settings, which may be the remains of a *leacht* (memorial cairn). In local tradition, pregnant women entered it and turned thrice round as a protection against dying in labor (Fig. 5.5). It was integral to a pattern performed on the saint's feast day. St Lomán's Church had the status of a parish church, probably as early as the

---

[45] The survey of the site and church building was undertaken in 2016.

[46] F. Grose 1791 *The antiquities of Ireland*, i, 58–9. London. S. Hooper.

[47] Ó Riain, *Dictionary*, 401.

(a)

(b)

FIG. 5.6. (a) St Lomán's, showing the cross-wall that separated the nave from the west-end quarters (photo E. FitzPatrick), and (b) ground plan of St Lomán's (drawing N. McCarthy and P. Naessens, based on survey by P. Naessens and E. FitzPatrick).

thirteenth century. During the fifteenth century it was variously documented under the names Inishmore, Calry, and Clogher in the papal registers.[48]

Members of the Ó Cuirnín hereditary kindred of poets and historians held the office of *comharba* of the island church while also serving as *ollamh* to the chief of West Bréifne, and sometimes to the chief of Cairbre (2.1.3). The role of *ollamh* of Bréifne is attributed to various members of the kindred in chronicle entries from the mid-fourteenth century to the second half of the fifteenth.[49] Their association with Inishmore is documented for the fifteenth century only, and specifically in relation to a fire in the church, cited in the chronicles for 1416 (2.1.3).[50] Changes to the architecture of the building during that century suggest that it remained the headquarters of the *ollamh* after the conflagration of 1416.

The roofless church has internal dimensions of 14.5 m by 6.1 m (Fig. 5.6), the gables and long walls standing to their full height. It is entered through a cut-stone doorway positioned towards the west end of the south long wall. A two-story apartment occupies the west end of the church, separated from the nave by a cross-wall. The east gable is dominated by a large, lancet-style window, and the south façade contains a small lancet and two single-light windows on the ground and first floor of the west-end quarters (Fig. 5.7). There are no features in the north long wall.

There are three antiquarian accounts of the church on Inishmore. The earliest known description is by Grose in *The antiquities of Ireland* (1791). He wrote, "the church is an oblong, with a few loophole windows, which most of the very old Culdean edifices have. There is a recess at one end, lighted by a similar window. The door has some rude carvings like dentils."[51] His cursory description was accompanied by an equally unedifying, romanticized illustration of the interior by the engraver Bigari.[52] In 1904 Fennell published a more detailed description of the site, including plans of the church and sketches of some of its architectural features.[53] Bigger (1907) followed up Fennell's report with a short observation about the building, suggesting that "the lintel of a cyclopean west door" (indicative of early medieval church architecture) was preserved in the west gable.[54] However, the narrow lintel stone is not convincing as the head of a former early medieval trabeate doorway.

An analysis of the architecture of the parish church indicates two phases of building: the first *c.*1200 and the second, a major refurbishment of it in the fifteenth century, probably in the decades after the fire of 1416 (2.1.3). There are several architectural features that support a date of *c.*1200 for the construction of the parish church on

---

[48] Twemlow, *Calendar of entries in the papal registers*, xviii, 6.

[49] See: M 1347.13, iii, 588, 589; AConn 1399.15, 374, 375; AConn 1400.12, 376, 377; M 1429.12, iv, 876, 877; M 1459.12, iv, 1004, 1005.

[50] AConn 1416.23, 430, 431; M 1416.17, iv, 828, 829.   [51] Grose, *Antiquities of Ireland*, 58–9.

[52] Grose, *Antiquities of Ireland*, plate between 58 and 59.

[53] W. J. Fennell 1904 Church Island or Inishmore, Lough Gill. *Ulster Journal of Archaeology* 10 (4), 168; F. J. Bigger 1907 Inishmore, Church Island, Lough Gill. *Ulster Journal of Archaeology* 13 (3), 143.

[54] Bigger, Inishmore, 143.

FIG. 5.7. The south façade, showing (left to right), the upper- and lower-floor windows of the west-end quarters, the entrance to the church, and a single-light window in the nave (photogrammetry P. Naessens).

FIG. 5.8. The east window, St Loman's, *c.*1200 (photo E. FitzPatrick).

Inishmore. The east gable is dominated by a single-light window of lancet form constructed of fine sandstone ashlar masonry that carries traces of diagonal tooling, a type of stone dressing largely used during the twelfth and thirteenth centuries (Fig. 5.8). The reveal of the wide-splaying embrasure is finished in ashlar and the sill is stepped. Light was also admitted to the chancel through a similar ashlar lancet of *c.*1200 in the south wall. The alternating long and short quoins on all four corners of the church, and especially where they are most intact on the northwest and southwest corners, terminate in plain gable corbels that are chamfered on the underside. In churches of the twelfth and thirteenth centuries, gable corbels are skeuomorphs, which is the case at Inishmore.[55]

---

[55] T. Ó Carragáin 2010 *Churches in early medieval Ireland: architecture, ritual and memory,* 30. London and New Haven. Yale University Press; Fennell (Church Island, 168) noted "the existence of corbel stones projecting from the gables with apparently no useful purpose."

0   0.25   0.5   0.75   1
Meters

FIG. 5.9. The south doorway of St Loman's showing the cusped arch (photogrammetry P. Naessens).

The extent of the damage that the fire of 1416 caused to the church on Inishmore is unknown. However, the replacement of the church doorway and the refurbishment, if not rebuilding, of the west end happened between 1416 and *c.*1500. The round-headed limestone doorway is decorated with half-round tracery cusps and the jambs terminate in bases with pointed, chamfered stops (Fig. 5.9). It was an unusual choice of door form in a period when the semi-pointed arch was commonplace. It may have been designed to recall a late Romanesque predecessor contemporary with the *c.*1200 phase. Late Gothic half-circle cusped tracery is more usually found on arcades, such as those of the fifteenth-century cloister walk at Holycross Abbey, Co. Tipperary and, closer to Inishmore, the Ó Croidheáin tomb in the Dominican priory at Sligo, dated by an inscription to 1506.

Earlier architectural fragments from a doorway of *c.*1200 are incorporated into the west side of the door embrasure. The east side carries a partial Irish-language inscription which is quite eroded, but five letters "MIRUI" of what may be a personal name can be distinguished.[56] The embrasure would have been rendered with plaster and the inscription was probably not intended to be seen after the new doorway was inserted.

Inishmore is not alone in having an ornamental doorway in a church where the incumbent was a learned cleric. It is noteworthy that several west-of-Ireland parish churches, where the *comharba* or *airchinneach* was also an *ollamh*, are distinguished by ornamental doorways. The late Romanesque doorway in the parish church of Noughaval, in the lordship of Boireann, has already been noted (5.1). A Romanesque doorway is positioned towards the west end of the south wall of St Feichin's Church, in the townland of Kilboglashy at Ballysadare (Fig. 5.10). It was previously observed (3.4) that the *airchinneach* of the church in the mid-twelfth century was Ua Dúilendáin, an *ollamh* in law.[57] The twelfth-century doorway is in two orders, with a plain, chamfered hood-molding and a tympanum supported by a lintel. Lions are

FIG. 5.10. Medland's view of St Feichin's at Kilboglashy, Ballysadare, 1791, showing the Romanesque doorway in the south wall (courtesy of the National Library of Ireland).

---

[56] Fennell, *Church Island*, 169; the inscription was confirmed as "MIRIU" during the survey of the building by the author in October 2016.

[57] Ó Corráin, *Nationality and kingship*, 62n.; M 1158.2, ii, 1128, 1129.

carved on the large capitals of the first order, while the arch of the second order is decorated with human heads and a single beaked animal head. The doorway appears to be original to the south wall,[58] but it has all the appearances of having been reassembled. Because of internecine war among the sons of the king of Connacht in 1228, when "all Connacht was ruined between them and turned into a continuous desert from Ballysadare southward," the church may have been damaged and rebuilt thereafter.[59] It is probable that the Romanesque portal was first built during Ua Dúilendáin's period as *airchinneach* and when the Rule of the Canons Regular of St Augustine was adopted.[60] He would have had the means to do so, as he was also a *taísech túaithe* (3.4).

The parish church of Kilronan, on the north shore of Lough Meelagh (Co. Roscommon), has a late Romanesque sandstone doorway at the western end of the south wall (Fig. 5.11). It consists of a hood-molding and a single order of

(a)

0.5m

FIG. 5.11a. The late Romanesque doorway, Kilronan (photogrammetry K. Karlinski).

---

[58] T. O'Keeffe 2003 *Romanesque Ireland: architecture and ideology in the twelfth century*, 149. Dublin. Four Courts Press.

[59] AConn 1228.3, 29.   [60] Gwynn and Hadcock, *Medieval religious houses*, 160–1.

(b)

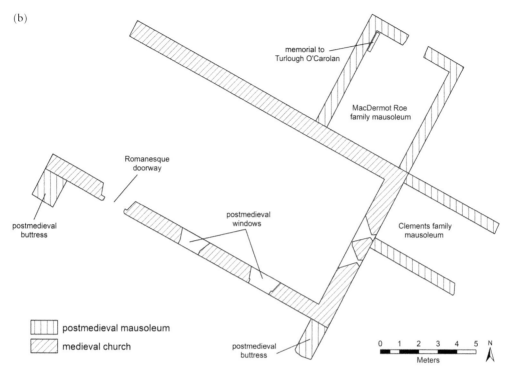

FIG. 5.11b. Plan of Kilronan showing the position of the doorway. The west end of the church has not survived (drawing N. McCarthy and K. Karlinski).

voussoirs decorated with cylinders arranged alternately horizontal and vertical. The Ó Duibhgeannáin *ollamh* in *seanchas* to the Mac Diarmada chief of Magh Luirg was the *comharba* of St Lasair of Kilronan—an association that reached back to at least 1339, when the chronicles record that Fearghal Ó Duibhgeannáin had the church made.[61] There was an earlier church on the site, indicated by the late Romanesque doorway. The Kilronan doorway has been assigned a date of *c*.1210. Since it is lacking capitals and bases, and the decorative voussoirs of the arch order are mismatched, the suggestion has been made that it was rebuilt at some point, possibly in 1339, or perhaps even as late as the seventeenth century, when the cult of St Lasair became a focus of Catholic pilgrimage at Kilronan.[62] However, the church was burned in 1340 and re-erected in 1347.[63] The single-ordered doorway either survived the fire of 1340 or was remade during the rebuilding of 1347.

There are other examples of unusually ornamental doorways in parish churches run by learned kindreds. At Drumacoo (Co. Galway) in the south Connacht lordship of Aidhne (Fig. 1.2), there is a very fine late Romanesque doorway in the south wall of

---

[61] M 1339.7, iii, 564, 565; AConn 1339.9, 282, 283.
[62] Moss, Romanesque sculpture in north Roscommon, 141–4.
[63] M 1340.16, iii, 570, 571; M 1347.9, iii, 588, 589.

FIG. 5.12. The late Romanesque doorway of the parish church, Drumacoo (photo E. FitzPatrick).

the early thirteenth-century parish church (Fig. 5.12). The Drumacoo portal, which has been dated to *c*.1235,[64] with its "transitional" arch, limestone construction, and high-quality architectural sculpture, is more typical of west-of-Ireland late Romanesque architecture than the Kilronan doorway. The *comharba* of Drumacoo was Fachtna Ó hAllgaith (d. 1232).[65] He is described in the chronicles as a learned man who kept a "house of instruction for the kindred," as well as a guest-house and a house for the sick. The date of the erection of the fine doorway probably lies within the years before his death.[66]

What can be concluded about the contexts in which such doorways were created? Moss has suggested that the late Romanesque Kilronan doorway (or surviving parts of it)

[64] B. Kalkreuter 2001 *Boyle Abbey and the School of the West*, 71. Bray. Wordwell.

[65] O'Sullivan, *Hospitality in medieval Ireland*, 155.

[66] AConn 1232.9, 45; M 1232.1, iii, 259, 260.

was possibly built into the parish church of 1339 to emphasize the antiquity and importance of St Lasair's foundation and, by association, the Ó Duibhgeannáin kindred of historians.[67] O'Keeffe has suggested that Drumacoo bears out his hypothesis that the late Romanesque in thirteenth-century parish churches in the west of Ireland is, perhaps, an architectural expression of parish formation.[68] To both of those theories it must be added that, in the west of Ireland, ornamental doorways tend to occur where a church was also a seat of learning and where the *comharba* or *airchinneach* was a learned person. A bespoke ornamental doorway may have signified a parish church where learning took place and the status of its incumbent *comharba* or *airchinneach* as a learned person, when parish churches in the western dioceses of Ireland were established from *c.*1200 onward. Continuity of the role of the portal as a signifier of space used by learned kindreds, especially at parish churches, is perhaps also reflected in the ornate late medieval south doorway of the church on Inishmore.

The focus of the third phase of construction on Inishmore included what appears to have been a workspace with a private room overhead at the west end of the church, and the south doorway entering the nave (Fig. 5.13). There is no reason to believe

FIG. 5.13. Looking towards the west-end quarters of St Loman's, Inishmore (photo E. FitzPatrick).

[67] Moss, Romanesque sculpture in north Roscommon, 141–4.

[68] T. O'Keeffe 2006 The built environment of local community worship between the late eleventh and early thirteenth centuries. In E. FitzPatrick and R. Gillespie (eds), *The parish in medieval and early modern Ireland: community, territory and building*, 142. Dublin. Four Courts Press.

that this was not in place before the fire of 1416, but a finely punch-dressed ogee-headed window in the south wall of the west-end quarters suggests a period of refurbishment in the second half of the fifteenth century. The two-story quarters, providing a total of 37.2 m² in floor space, may well have been designed to accommodate the needs of the *comharba–ollamh*. Two-story west-end quarters of churches have been identified more widely as priests' residences.[69] When such additions are found at churches where pastoral care had lapsed for periods of time and *airchinnigh* and unordained *comharbai* who were literati controlled them, the remit of west-end lodgings may have included facilitating professional activities.

The west-end space in Inishmore was relatively well lit and screened off from the nave of the church by a cross-wall (0.85 m thick) that is not bonded into the long walls of the building. It is entered at the south end of the partition, through a round-headed limestone doorway complete with a threshold. The doorway is a patchwork of chamfered, punch-dressed, and plain architectural fragments from at least two opes, suggesting prudent re-use of building fabric (perhaps after the fire of 1416).

The ground-floor chamber was lit from the south wall by a single-light window sitting in a deep, linteled embrasure that is slightly splayed to funnel light in. A squint in the cross-wall admitted light into the chamber too, but it was also positioned to enable a view into the nave. The west face of the partition is busy with fixtures, including two deep wall-cupboards north of the doorway and another set slightly lower to the ground and positioned immediately south of the doorway (Fig. 5.14). There is a curious feature lying directly beneath the squint and between two wall-cupboards, which Fennell misread as another squint.[70] It is a channeled drainage stone set into an ope (0.25 m²) that runs for 1.55 m at a northwest–southeast angle through the partition wall. It discharged into the nave. The very narrow groove in the drainage stone suggests that this was not for kitchen slops but for finer liquid runoff (Fig. 5.15).

The upper story of the west gable had a timber floor, as indicated by the rows of joist-holes in the east and west walls. As noted, it was lit from the south wall by a single-light ogee-headed window (Fig. 5.16). This window form is one of the more datable features of the west-end apartment. It was a popular window type in Irish tower-houses, churches and religious houses during the fifteenth century and has been described as a "hallmark" of the period.[71] The very fine punch dressing on the ogee-headed window at Inishmore compares, for instance, to that on the ogee-headed windows in the tower-house at Carlingford Mint, Co. Louth, *c.*1467, which date to

[69] H. Bermingham 2006 Priests' residences in later medieval Ireland. In FitzPatrick and Gillespie (eds), *The parish in medieval and early modern Ireland*, 168–85; E. FitzPatrick and C. O'Brien 1998 *The medieval churches of County Offaly*, 134–9. Dublin. Government of Ireland.

[70] Fennell, Church Island, 167.

[71] H. G. Leask 1960 *Irish churches and monastic buildings, iii: medieval Gothic, the last phases*, 114. Dundalk. Dundalgan Press; M. Ní Mharcaigh 1997 The medieval parish churches of south-west County Dublin. *PRIA* 97C, 251.

Fɪɢ. 5.14. West face of the cross-wall, St Loman's, showing the first-floor entrance from the nave, joist-holes for the upper floor, and ground-floor wall-cupboards, a squint, an ope for runoff, and the doorway to the nave (photogrammetry P. Naessens).

FIG. 5.15. Aperture for the channeled stone, angled in the cross-wall, St Lomán's, Inishmore (photo E. FitzPatrick).

the second half of the fifteenth century. There are apertures for a shutter visible in the lower half of the internal face of the Inishmore window and, like the ground-floor window in the same wall, the embrasure is linteled and splayed to maximize light in the interior. In the west gable there is a recess with cut-stone sides and a rough relieving arch that appears to have been a large wall-cupboard.

Partial remains of an ope, wide enough to have been a doorway (0.5 m), positioned just above the joist-holes at the north end of the partition wall, suggests that the first floor was reached by a ladder from the nave (Fig. 5.14). The separate entrances to the ground and first floors of the west-end quarters have implications for how that area was used. They suggest that both levels were discrete spaces serving different purposes. The plentiful wall-cupboards, the channeled stone, and the squint to view the nave from the cross-wall imply that the ground-floor chamber was the *ollamh*'s workspace and perhaps where inks and pigments were made. Fennell's earlier interpretation of this space reimagined it as a library.[72] The squint suggests that some adjacent activity in the nave needed to be observed from the ground-floor room, perhaps a school of

[72] Fennell, Church Island, 167.

FIG. 5.16. Windows in the south wall of the west-end quarters, St Lomán's (photo E. FitzPatrick).

poetry. The upper room, reached from the nave at first-floor level, was designed to be more private.

In the same year (1416) that Ó Cuirnín's church caught fire, his neighbor on the south side of Lough Gill, Tómas Mac an Óglaigh, chief professor of law in Connacht and *airchinneach* of the medieval parish church of Killerry, died (Fig. 5.17).[73] Killerry (*Cill Oiridh*) was in the bounds of the lordships of West Bréifne and Tír Oilella-Corran (2.1.3; Fig. 2.9). The learned kindred of Mac an Óglaigh were associated with the church at least as early as 1333.[74]

The ruined church of Killerry looks west to Slishwood and to the mountains north of Lough Gill (Fig. 5.18). It was built on the site of an early medieval monastic foundation, which is attested by a surviving cross-inscribed grave-slab of that period re-used as a grave-marker in the northeastern area of the walled graveyard (Fig. 5.19). The east face of the slab is decorated with a deeply incised Latin cross with expanded

[73] M 1416.4, iv, 824, 825; AConn 1416.8, 428, 429.   [74] M 1333.1, iii, 551, 552.

FIG. 5.17. View south from the harbor at Inishmore to Killerry Mountain (photo E. FitzPatrick).

FIG. 5.18. The parish church, Killerry, looking south (photo E. FitzPatrick).

terminals. A fragment of another slab bearing a Latin cross lies nearby. Seven water-rolled stones rest on a broken flagstone (Fig. 5.19). They are locally believed to have had curative properties bestowed on them by St Patrick.[75] Dating the origins of spherical stones that have duality as harbingers of cures and curses is difficult unless they are

[75] H. S. Crawford 1913 Notes on stones used as a cure at Killerry, near Dromahair, and on certain bullauns. *JRSAI* 3 (3), 267–8.

(a)

(b)

FIG. 5.19. (a) An early medieval cross-inscribed grave-slab, and (b) A group of cursing/curing stones, Killerry (photos E. FitzPatrick).

inscribed. The best known and most closely datable cursing/curing stones are the *clocha breaca* ("speckled stones"), a large collection of water-rolled stones sitting on a *leacht* on Inishmurray Island (6.1). Fourteen of them carry early medieval carvings.[76] The use of the *clocha breaca* as cursing stones is believed to have "roots in liturgical cursing by early medieval clergy, as a sanction against enemies and oath-breakers," and the imprecatory ritual associated with them continued into the later medieval period.[77] The modern practice is to turn one of the stones clockwise for curing and anti-clockwise for cursing. The attested associations of the speckled stones on Inishmurray with liturgical cursing raises the possibility that the Killerry stones are of some antiquity and were, perhaps, used by Mac an Óglaigh in his capacity as hereditary law *ollamh*, in sanctioning enemies of the lordship of West Bréifne and the province of Connacht in a significant borderland setting.

There is no ostensibly early medieval wall fabric and no pre-twelfth-century fixtures in Killerry parish church, nor have the windows or doorway survived (Fig. 5.18). The building is 17.7 m east–west by 5.7 m north–south internally. A former cross-wall closed off accommodation for the *airchinneach–ollamh* (5.8 m by 5.7 m) at the west end of the building.[78] The north wall is the best-preserved fabric of the church. In the modern period, the upper half of the east gable was rebuilt and the east window was replaced. The south wall was incorporated into the graveyard boundary and much of it was thinned out. Grassed-over wall-footings indicate the line of the west gable. It is expected that the doorway of the church was in the position typical of late medieval parish churches—at the west end of the south wall leading into both the nave and chancel and the west-end chamber. If, as the former cross-wall suggests, the west end was the apartment of the Mac an Óglaigh *airchinneach–ollamh*, then there must originally have been a small doorway in the cross-wall to allow access to and from the nave of the church.

5.2.2 Saint Bairrfhionn's borderland church at Kilbarron

Bairrfhionn, a saint of the southern borderland of Tír Conaill, was integral to the identity of Kilbarron (*Ceall Bhairrfhionn*) where the Ó Cléirigh kindred lived and kept a school (2.1.1; Fig. 2.1). The saint is attributed other foundations in borderland settings, such as Drumcullen at Knockbarron (*Cnoc Bhairrfhionn*, Co. Offaly; Fig. 1.2), in the frontier between the early historic provinces of Mide and Munster.[79]

The parish of Kilbarron in Tír Conaill had been united to the Cistercian abbey of Assaroe between 1424 and 1427. As rector, the abbot received two-thirds of the

[76] O'Sullivan and Ó Carragáin, *Inishmurray*, 103.
[77] O'Sullivan and Ó Carragáin, *Inishmurray*, 335–41.
[78] T. O'Rorke 1890 *The history of Sligo town and county*, ii, 318–19. Dublin. James Duffy and Co.
[79] E. FitzPatrick 1998 The early church in Offaly. In W. Nolan and T. P. O'Neill (eds), *Offaly: history and society*, 117–18. Dublin. Geography Publications; Ó Riain, *Dictionary*, 83–4.

church tithes in kind and was responsible for bearing two-thirds of the costs of repairing and maintaining the church. The bishop of Raphoe was due one-third of the tithes and carried one-third of the charges for upkeep of the church.[80]

The Ó Cléirigh *airchinneach–ollamh* had two buildings on his estate of episcopal mensal land—the gate-house keep and bawn buildings in the promontory fort that was the kindred's residence from the fifteenth century (4.5), and a small church known as *Ceall Bhairrfhionn* ("Bairrfhionn's Church") situated 1.5 km east of the promontory fort.[81] The founding of the church is attributed to the late sixth-century St Bairrfhionn, whose staff was reputedly recovered from the sea along the coast of the parish by a miracle of St Columcille.[82]

The unconventional layout and architectural details of St Bairrfhionn's church suggest that it served an additional purpose for the Ó Cléirigh *ollamh*. For a building that was intended to provide pastoral care, there is a curious absence of any upstanding archaeological evidence in the form of grave-slabs, and no obvious sign of a premodern graveyard there. In the modern period the church ground was used for burial of unbaptized children, which is commemorated at the site by the local community.[83]

St Bairrfhionn's lies low in the coastal landscape. The views from it, across Donegal Bay, draw the eye to the cliffs of Slieve League, to the high peak of Slievetooey to the northwest and to the uplands of Crownarad, Mulnanaff, and Crocknapeast to the northeast. Kings Mountain dominates the view from the church to the south side of the bay. St Bairrfhionn's is a compact rectangular building, 10.3 m by 4.9 m internally (Fig. 5.20). All four walls are standing, but in variable condition. The north and south long walls (0.85 m thick) reach their full height at *c*.3 m above the floor. The west gable (1 m thick) has lost its apex, but it retains a loft window. The east gable and its window have partly collapsed. Elevations of the walls sketched by Lockwood *c*.1903 indicate that they are in much the same condition now as they were over a century ago.[84]

The church sits on bedrock of the Mullaghmore Sandstone Formation (sandstone, siltstone, and shale),[85] which was the source of the building stone. The north wall rests on a plinth that was necessary to create a level construction surface (Fig. 5.21). Surviving architectural features include two doorways—one at the east end of the north wall and the other towards the western end of the south wall—a plain, single-light

[80]   Costello, *De annatis Hiberniae*, i, 260, 276, 278; Mac Neill and Hogan, *A booke of the kings lands*, 185.

[81]   Ó Riain, *Dictionary*, 83–4; Gwynn and Hadcock, *Medieval religious houses*, 388.

[82]   O'Kelleher and Schoepperle, *Betha Colaim Chille*, 134, 135.

[83]   Noted as "Children's Burial Ground" on 25-inch Ordnance Survey, 1897–1913; See E. Murphy 2011 Children's burial grounds in Ireland (*cillíní*) and parental emotions toward infant death. *International Journal of Historical Archaeology* 15 (3), 410–11.

[84]   F. W. Lockwood 1903 Kilbarron castle and church, Co. Donegal. *Ulster Journal of Archaeology* 9, 115.

[85]   Long, *Geology of south Donegal*, sheet 3 and part of sheet 4.

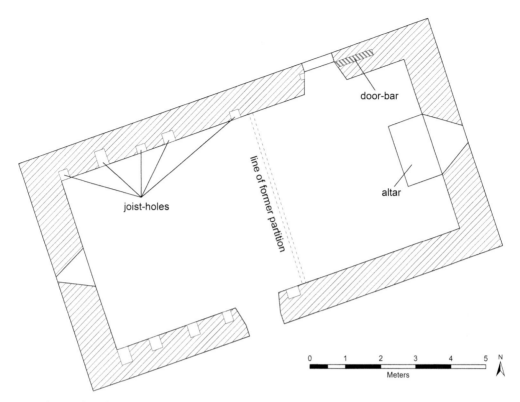

Fig. 5.20. Plan of the church of St Bairrfhionn, Kilbarron, showing joist-holes in the long walls for the upper floor (drawing N. McCarthy).

Fig. 5.21. The north façade of St Bairrfhionn's (photo E. FitzPatrick).

FIG. 5.22. The eccentric arch-stones of the south doorway, St Bairrfhionn's (photo E. FitzPatrick).

window in the west gable, and the remains of a stone platform for an altar against the east gable.[86]

Both doorways have semi-pointed cut-stone arches and threshold-stones. The south doorway has an eccentric appearance, the arch-stones having been cut at a straight angle externally and not shaped to a semi-pointed form as they are internally (Fig. 5.22). The jambs are crude, an extension of the wall fabric, except for a single block on the east side dressed with diagonal punch dressing. Particular attention was paid to the stonework of the wide-splaying embrasure, which has a linteled head, a paved floor, and sides neatly finished with quoins, some of which are punch dressed. The north doorway leading into the east end of the building is smaller and has a more accurately shaped punch-dressed, semi-pointed arch and alternating long and short cut-stone jambs (Fig. 5.21). The embrasure was formed in the same style as that of the south doorway, with a linteled head, and sides finished with quoins. Some of the former doorway fixtures remain, including a door-bar hole, 1.07 m deep, which suggests a concern with security and controlling access to the building. Kilbarron would

---

[86] B. Lacey 1983 *Archaeological survey of County Donegal: a description of the field antiquities of the County from Mesolithic period to the 17th century* AD, 276. Lifford. Donegal County Council.

have had a dark interior unless the doors were left open to admit light. There are no windows at all in the long walls, but there may have been opes in the cross-wall.

The building had a curious layout (Fig. 5.20). Approximately 5.3 m was partitioned off from the east end, implying non-liturgical use of the western part. Joist-holes, ranging along each of the north and south long walls, supported beams for an upper floor. The west end had its own discrete entrance in the south wall, confirmed by a joist-hole on the east side of the doorway and another opposite it in the north wall (Fig. 5.23). The eastern end of the building was entered through the north wall doorway. Presumably, the two parts had distinct roles—the east end for cure of souls, with separate quarters in the west end comprising a dark ground floor and an upper floor lit by a single-light window. The allocation of half of the space to non-liturgical purposes is unusual and suggests that as a learned man and *airchinneach* of the church, the Ó Cléirigh *ollamh* may have used Kilbarron for activities associated with his learned role as a poet-historian. It is even possible that the building was constructed with that function largely in mind.

In Lockwood's record of Kilbarron, he noted what he believed were the remains of several buildings both to the north and west of this church.[87] However, what he saw extending northward from the church is a modern, thick drystone enclosure with

FIG. 5.23. The west end of St Bairrfhionn's (photo E. FitzPatrick).

[87] Lockwood, Kilbarron castle and church, 115.

internal divisions (Fig. 5.21). Why such a substantial partition of that space was required is unknown, but it did not constitute a building, nor is there any evidence that it was used for burial. Its two parts may relate to later use of the grounds for cultivation.

Where the period of origin of St Bairrfhionn's is concerned, Allingham suggested that it belonged to the thirteenth or fourteenth century, while Lockwood assigned it to the later fourteenth century based on the plainness of the two doorways and their arrangement in the building.[88] Others have suggested a date in the fifteenth or sixteenth century.[89] There are reasons why the date of construction can be fixed to the first quarter of the fifteenth century. There are no architectural features of the building that can be securely dated after the fifteenth century. The parish church is cited in the papal taxations (*obligationes pro annatis*) for 1424–7.[90] The historical context of the establishment of the Ó Cléirigh kindred at Kilbarron also suggests that the church was constructed in that period. They built their dwelling within a coastal promontory fort where an earlier residence of their predecessors had been destroyed in 1390 (4.5).[91] The construction, by the Ó Cléirigh *ollamh*, of both a residence and a church facilitating a school, within the first quarter of the fifteenth century, would have served to consolidate his place as poet-historian and chronicler to the Ó Domhnaill in the southern borderland of Tír Conaill.

5.2.3 Saint Breacán's Chapel at Toomullin

A chapel dedicated to St Breacán in the townland of Toomullin, east of the village of Doolin (Co. Clare), is sequestered in the valley of the Aille River, which looks west to the Atlantic at Doolin Bay (Fig. 5.24). In the sixteenth century it was situated on the land of Aodh Mac Fhlannchadha, a many-sided learned man who is described in the record of his death in 1575 as "the head of a school [*oide*] of the Feineachas [brehon law] and of poetry, and a purchaser of wine, by no means the least distinguished of the lay brehons of Ireland."[92] A strong case can be made for St Breacán's as Aodh's school in the sixteenth century, and of the kindred perhaps as early as the fourteenth century.

Toomullin was integral to Túath Ghlae, the large estate of the Mac Fhlannchadha lawyers (Fig. 3.15). Knockfin, the estate *ceann áit*, is a kilometer north of Toomullin (2.3; Fig. 3.15). It has been suggested that Túath Ghlae was originally church land, a view that is supported by the proprietorship which the Mac Fhlannchadha kindred had of the lands attached to the sinecure chapels on their estate, including Toomullin.[93] Their proprietorship of Toomullin implies that they controlled the benefice and that

---

[88] Allingham, *Ballyshannon*, 16; Lockwood, Kilbarron castle and church, 115.
[89] Lacey, *Archaeological survey*, 276.   [90] Costello, *De annatis Hiberniae*, i, 260.
[91] M 1390.8, iv, 720, 721; Simms, *Gaelic Ulster*, 380.   [92] M 1575.6, v, 1682, 1683.
[93] McInerney, *Clerical and learned lineages*, 153.

FIG. 5.24. St Breacán's Chapel in the valley of the Aille River, Toomullin, looking west to the Atlantic (photo N. Grundy).

the lands attached to the chapel became part of their hereditary estate as brehon law-yers. That was certainly the case by the later sixteenth century, when Aodh Mac Fhlannchadha was living at Toomullin.[94] His residence is recorded as the castle of "Tomeleny" (Toomullin) in a list of castles compiled in 1570,[95] and identifiable as the remains of a tower-house northwest of St Breacán's Chapel.

The immediate landscape of the chapel is enclosed to the north, east, and south by contiguous ridges that form a protecting arm around the eastern end of the site (Fig. 5.25). Those to the south and southwest bear the names Knockagowan and Knockastoolery and are distinguished by a remarkable concentration of Bronze Age barrows and a standing stone with a possible ogham inscription (Fig. 3.15).[96] From

[94] Additional family members are provenanced to Toomullin later, such as "Donogh M'Clanchye, of Tomolyne" pardoned in 1586. Nicholls, *Irish fiants*, ii, 737 [4876].

[95] M. Breen 1995 A 1570 list of castles in County Clare. *North Munster Antiquarian Journal* 36, 134.

[96] Ferguson, *Ogham inscriptions*, 54.

Fig. 5.25. Ridges form a natural protection around St Breacán's. The ruins of the phosphate factory to the right (photo N. Grundy).

the northern ridge there is a clear view to Knockfin and the medieval parish church of Killilagh. The ridges also afford an unimpeded view west to the sea and to the Aran Islands. For a purveyor of wine, the setting of Aodh Mac Fhlannchadha's settlement at Toomullin had the advantage of visibility and proximity to the sea.

The chapel sits in a pronounced meander of the Aille River. The river flows through rock cliffs, hence the name Aille (from *aill*, cliff). The meander is a point at which the dark shale of the Clare Shale Formation meets grey siltstone and sandstone (Fig. 5.26). On its course further northwest, but within the denomination of Toomullin, the river is also a meeting point for the black shale, with cherty limestone containing crinoids.[97] St Breacán's Chapel was built on the dark shale. Breac or Breacán is a name attributed to several local holy men in medieval Ireland. It is a personification of *breac*, conferring something speckled or variegated on saints of the name.[98] The Dál Cais overkingdom was the early medieval center of the cult of St Breacán and therefore he had a strong and enduring presence in the region.[99] He is also found on the western edge of the estate of the Ó hÍceadha physicians at Ballyhickey in the lordship of Clann Chuileáin (3.4).

---

[97] Mcnamara and Hennessy, *The geology of the Burren*, 5, 6, 15–16.

[98] Quin, *Dictionary*, 82:168. *Breac* can also mean trout, in reference to its speckled skin; Ó Riain, *Dictionary*, 110.

[99] Ó Riain, *Dictionary*, 112.

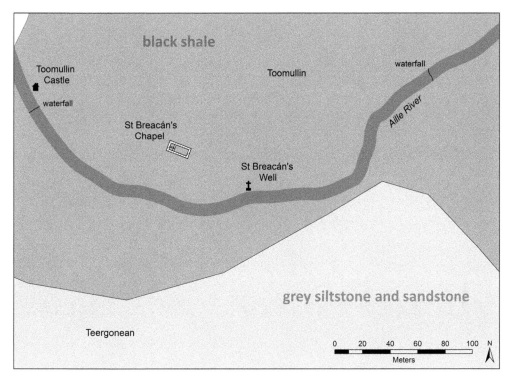

FIG. 5.26. St Breacán's and the bedrock geology along the Aille River (drawing N. McCarthy).

The Kilbreckan silver mine recalls the name of the saint's church, *Cill Bhreacáin*, which is situated in the townland of Noughaval, west of Ballyhickey (Fig. 3.18).[100]

The immediate environs of the chapel were greatly altered *c*.1924–47 because of opencast mining for phosphates. The shale bedrock was removed from the river and from the adjacent land to reach the phosphate layer. As the mining enterprise developed, accessing the phosphates involved continuously diverting the course of the river by constructing earthen dams.[101] A holy well commemorating St Breacán on the north riverbank was a casualty of those works. High embankments now close off the view to the river from the chapel. A photograph taken by French, between 1865 and 1914, of one of three waterfalls on the river in Toomullin, reveals the former natural beauty of the discrete landscape of Breacán's Chapel, which was open to the river (Fig. 5.27).

The chapel has an ambiguous identity.[102] The design, history, and setting of St Breacán's strongly suggest that members of the Mac Fhlannchadha learned kindred

---

[100] T. J. Westropp 1900–2 The churches of County Clare and the origin of the ecclesiastical divisions in that county. *PRIA* 6C, 103, 147.

[101] P. J. Cronin 2001 Mid 20th century mines in the Doolin area, Co. Clare, Ireland. *Proceedings of the University of Bristol Spelaeological Society* 22 (2), 226.

[102] Westropp, Ancient remains near Lisdoonvarna, 154.

FIG. 5.27. French's view of the waterfall on the Aille River, with the west gable of St Breacán's visible in the background, 1865–1914 (Lawrence Photograph Collection, courtesy of the National Library of Ireland).

either contrived it as a law school with a minor role as a chapel at the beginning of the fourteenth century, or gradually transformed it from a sinecure chapel into a school during the fifteenth century.

Kelly has noted that the Mac Fhlannchadha legal kindred were not involved to any great extent in the transcription of the Old Irish law texts and did not confine themselves to law but branched out into literature and poetry.[103] As a teacher of brehon law and poetry, the sixteenth-century Aodh Mac Fhlannchadha of Toomullin would have needed a school-house. He was the son of Baothghalach Mac Fhlannchadha, *ollamh* in brehon law to the overlord of Tuadhmhumhain. His wife Honoria and son Baothghalach (named after his grandfather) are mentioned in an inquisition of 1589, which claimed that Aodh had died on 5 October 1579, at which time he was "the owner in fee of the castle of Toomullin, and of certain lands which he rented from the Bishop of Killaloe."[104] It is argued here that St Breacán's on Aodh's landholding

---

[103] Kelly, *Guide to early Irish law*, 256.

[104] Frost, *History and topography*, 271–2. The chronicles note his death four years earlier in 1575. See M 1575.6, v, 1682, 1683.

provided the space for his learned occupations. The fact that he had an independent tower-house residence is in keeping with the general trend during the sixteenth century for secular learned kindreds to have a separate dwelling from the school-house (6.0), usually but not exclusively a tower-house (4.5).

Although St Breacán is mainly known for his association with Inishmore (the largest of the Aran Islands, Co. Galway), the medieval genealogy ascribed to him places him in the main line of the early medieval Dál Cais dynasty of Munster, the center of his cult.[105] A more appropriate saint could not have been chosen for a chapel on the estate of a legal kindred whose leading member was attributed the hereditary title "*ollamh* Dál gCais in jurisprudence" by the chroniclers.[106]

The value of the building at Toomullin as a chapel was listed at ten shillings and twelve pence in the papal taxation of 1302.[107] The building has a developed west end, the combined nave and chancel is small in size, it lacks an accompanying graveyard that would otherwise be indicative of pastoral care, and it is not mentioned in the papal registers for the late medieval period.[108] Ní Ghabhláin concluded from her survey of the building that its small size and the absence of a graveyard, combined with the fact that it received one of the lowest valuations in 1302 for the diocese of Kilfenora (to which it belonged), means that it could never have served as a parish church.[109] It was the church of Killilagh that served the parochial community of the Mac Fhlannchadha estate. St Breacán's must therefore have been a small, proprietary church that functioned as a sinecure chapel. A closer study of the building and its associations suggest an additional role for it.

The combined nave and chancel has an internal footprint of *c*.52 m² (Fig. 5.28). A cross-wall at the west end of the nave demarcates a small (2.8 m by 5.45 m) two-story apartment. The east and west gables, the cross-wall, and the north wall (Fig. 5.29) of the building stand to their full height, but the south wall is quite ruined, especially towards the east end (Fig. 5.30). The wall fabric throughout the building is roughly coursed limestone and sandstone with black shale in the mortared core. Both O'Donovan, writing in 1839, and Westropp, writing in 1906, believed that the cross-wall was the original west gable of the fourteenth-century chapel, to which the west-end quarters were later added,[110] but a detailed inspection for this study confirmed that, while the west end was altered, it is original to the building and not an extension.

Despite its unstable condition, the collapsed masonry, and overburden of vegetation, several datable features of the chapel are visible and accessible. There are no architectural

[105] Ó Riain, *Dictionary*, 112.   [106] M 1576.4, v, 1684, 1685.
[107] Sweetman and Handcock, *Calendar of documents relating to Ireland*, 299.
[108] Westropp (Ancient remains near Lisdoonvarna, 156) noted that the church at Toomullin lacked burials.
[109] Ní Ghabhláin, Church and community, 72; S. Ní Ghabhláin 1996 The origin of medieval parishes in Gaelic Ireland: the evidence from Kilfenora. *JRSAI* 126, 40.
[110] RIA 14 B 23, 322, 323; Westropp, Ancient remains near Lisdoonvarna, 156.

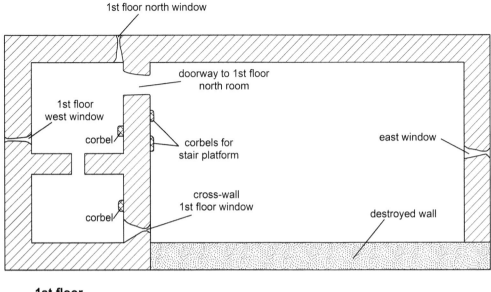

1st floor

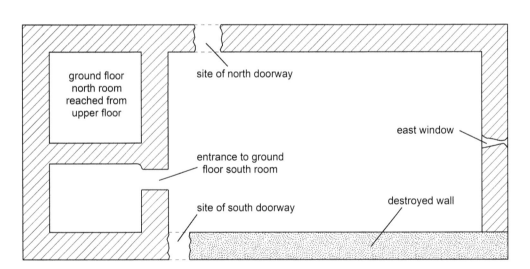

ground floor

Fɪɢ. 5.28. Ground- and upper-floor plans of St Breacán's (drawing N. McCarthy incorporating features of Ní Ghabhláin's plan 1996).

FIG. 5.29. The north façade of St Breacán's (photo N. Grundy).

FIG. 5.30. Features of St Breacán's viewed from south (photo E. FitzPatrick).

features surviving from the fourteenth-century phase—the windows and doorways are of the fifteenth century and later.

The entrance to the chapel has not survived but, according to O'Donovan, in 1839 it had two doorways "reduced to formless breaches" positioned opposite each other, one in the north and the other in the south wall "at the distance of 2.0 feet from the original west gable" (Fig. 5.27).[111] The chapel was lit by a cusped, ogee-headed lancet, centrally placed in the east gable. Externally, this window is finished with an ogee arch. Triquetra knots, typical of the interlaced patterns used by Irish masons in the fifteenth century, decorate the spandrels.[112] Overhead, it has a hood-molding with L-shaped stops (Fig. 5.31).

FIG. 5.31. Decorative ogee-headed window, east gable, St Breacán's (photo N. Grundy).

[111] RIA 14 B 23, 322, 323.

[112] C. Hourihane 2003 *Gothic art in Ireland, 1169–1550: enduring vitality*, 144–7. New Haven and London. Yale University Press.

The two-story quarters at the west end of the chapel contained three discrete spaces, separated from the nave by a gabled cross-wall. The ground floor was entered through a typical late medieval-style semi-pointed doorway positioned at the south end of the cross-wall (Fig. 5.32). The doorway is punch dressed and retains the pivot-stone for the door-hinge. There are two small rooms on the ground floor, separated from each other by a narrow partition wall aligned east–west, which is now no more than 0.4 m high and covered with collapsed masonry and vegetation. A plan made of the building twenty-five years ago, when it was in better condition, indicated a doorway in the partition wall, on the first floor, between the two rooms (Fig. 5.28).[113] Neither of the rooms had windows, depending for light on an open door.

The upper floor was a more commodious single room with its own entrance at first-floor level in the north end of the cross-wall. The entrance has a depressed arch set into an embrasure with a wide splay that would have facilitated ease of movement into the room (Fig. 5.33). While the sides of the doorway are well cut and punch dressed, the head is quite crude, as though wrought by an inexpert

FIG. 5.32. The ground-floor entrance to the west-end quarters, St Breacán's (photo E. FitzPatrick).

[113] Ní Ghabhláin, Church and community, 69.

FIG. 5.33. Entrance to the first-floor room of the west-end quarters, St Breacán's (photo E. FitzPatrick).

hand. This is unlike the fine workmanship of the ground-floor doorway and suggests masonry of the last phase of alterations to the building. The same crudity can be seen in the production of the spandrels above the round-headed window in the west gable of the first-floor room (Fig. 5.34), which seems to have been inserted at the same time as the first-floor doorway. It is as though the mason was trying to emulate the earlier work in the building to make a visible link with the historic past of the chapel but lacked the expertise to do so. In this last phase of alteration, connecting the new work with the old may have been important to preserving the identity of St Breacán's.

The first-floor room was well lit in its final phase. There was an additional single-light window at the south end of the cross-wall and a large, rectangular window (which possibly had a frame of four lights) at the east end of the north wall. This, again, is quite late work. There is evidence for the floor itself in the form of joist-holes and corbels in the west face of the cross-wall (Fig. 5.28). The surviving corbels are of different types, suggesting that some of them were reused from an earlier phase of the building.

As with the first-floor room of St Lomán's Church on Inishmore (5.2.1), the upper floor of St Breacán's was apparently a self-contained, private space, reached from the nave by a ladder or timber stairs. Two corbels projecting out from the east

Fig. 5.34. The west gable window with crudely cut spandrels, St Breacán's (photo E. FitzPatrick).

face of the cross-wall suggest that there may have been a small platform at the top of the stairs (Fig. 5.28).

In any interpretation of this late work in St Breacán's Chapel it must be considered that, during the Protestant Reformation in Ireland, some late medieval churches were repurposed for worship. An important consequence of this was that a number of Gaelic learned men became Church of Ireland ministers, perhaps mainly as a means of retaining their lands and access to church buildings. In a list of the clergy of the diocese of Kilfenora compiled for a visitation of the diocese in 1615, "Murtogh O Daveryn [Ó Duibhdábhoireann] minister and an Irishe-man" was recorded as vicar of Toomullin and of Noughaval in the Burren where the Ó Duibhdábhoireann kindred had been long-standing church tenants (5.2).[114] This confirmation that St Breacán's Chapel had become a center of the Protestant faith by 1615, suggests that, arising from its conversion, the latest alterations to the chapel were made to facilitate the incumbency of the Ó Duibhdábhoireann minister. The apex of the cross-wall gable is crowned by a bellcote for a single bell (Fig. 5.29), which may have been installed for his ministry. The arrangement whereby a member of the Ó Duibhdábhoireann learned

[114] Dwyer, *The diocese of Killaloe*, 98.

kindred of Noughaval in the Burren served the Protestant chapel of St Breacán on the lands of the Mac Fhlannchadha lawyers in Toomullin, reflects how Gaelic literati carefully negotiated a changed world. It preserved St Breacán's and Noughaval as places of pedigree for their Gaelic communities and the long tradition of scholarly links between the two legal families, at least until 1623 when a new vicar was appointed to Noughaval.[115]

The collective evidence suggests that St Breacán's was a building adapted to special purposes over the long period of its use. There are two artefacts from the site that are potentially indicative of activities related to the Gaelic arts. A medieval bronze harp peg was discovered in 1935 by a man "digging a potato garden by the wall of the ruined church."[116] The harp to which it once belonged may have been used for liturgical purposes, but harps were also possessions of poets (2.1.3). What appears to be a shale trial piece or work surface was found at the foot of the north wall of the chapel recently. The object has one straight side, which is quite smooth from being handled. It is rounded at its broadest end and narrows at the other end, where it was worked to an angle. Flakes of shale were removed from the rounded top and along the angled edge, where one of the flaked-off areas contained an ammonoid fossil. There is an artificial groove at the broad end. Across the surface of both faces there are multiple very light linear incisions, some of which are natural abrasions, but most are artificial score marks made with a sharp-pointed tool. This dark shale is a compact material that breaks away in relatively thin, flat planes. It must therefore have been ideal as a work surface for inscription. It is plentiful in the immediate area of St Breacán's Chapel and used as filling stones in the wall fabric of the building.

The dedication of the chapel to Breacán, the saint of the pre-Norman Dál Cais overkingdom, implies a concern to make a visible connection between the overkingdom and the late medieval overlords of Tuadhmhumhain, whom the Mac Fhlannchadha lawyers served. The architectural analysis has revealed a building with a complex history—constructed no later than the fourteenth century, refurbished in the fifteenth, and again in the late sixteenth or early seventeenth, to accommodate the Ó Duibhdábhoireann Gaelic minister. The focus of the alterations was the west-end quarters, which were integral to the building and not an addition as had been suggested by some antiquaries.[117] The patronage of this work may be attributed to the Mac Fhlannchadha legal kindred who were well established on their Túath Ghlae estate by the mid-fourteenth century and continued to live there in reinvented capacities into the seventeenth century.[118]

---

[115] Griffith, *Patent rolls of James I*, 563. Patrick Lesaight was made both chancellor of Kilfenora Cathedral ("Finebore") and vicar of Noughaval, which was vacant by 1623 "by lapse or forfeiture, and in the King's gift".

[116] D. F. Gleeson 1935 Find of harp peg at Toomullin, Co. Clare. *JRSAI* 5 (1), 148; J. Raftery 1941 A bronze zoomorphic brooch and other objects from Toomullin, Co. Clare. *JRSAI* 11 (2), 56–60.

[117] Westropp, Ancient remains near Lisdoonvarna, 156.   [118] Hardiman, Ancient Irish deeds, 38, 42.

FIG. 5.35. The west face of the cross-wall in St Breacán's Chapel, Toomullin. The fabric of the bellcote at the apex of the gable incorporates reused late medieval architectural fragments (photo E. FitzPatrick).

5.2.4   The parish church of Smarmore in a march of the English colony

The churches that have been discussed thus far were situated in Gaelic lordships. The special circumstances of churches in the marches between Gaelic territories and lands under the control of the English Crown elicit questions about the identity of their incumbents.[119] One such church was the medieval parish church of Smarmore (Co. Louth). Inscribed slates found there suggest that it was a center of knowledge in plant-based medicine and music, at least during the fifteenth century.[120]

Smarmore is situated on the modern county boundary between Louth and Meath (Fig. 5.36). In the political geography of late medieval Ireland it was in the march of the "four obedient shires"—Dublin, Kildare, Louth, and Meath. Booker, in her work

---

[119] B. Smith 2013 *Crisis and survival in late medieval Ireland: the English of Louth and their neighbours, 1330–1450.* Oxford University Press.

[120] A. J. Bliss 1967 An inscribed slate from Smarmore. *Notes and Queries* 14 (3), 85; A. J. Bliss 1965 The inscribed slates at Smarmore. *PRIA* 64C, 33–60; A. J. Bliss 1961 Smarmore inscribed slates. *Journal of the County Louth Archaeological and Historical Society* 15 (1), 21–2; D. Britton and A. J. Fletcher 1990 Medieval Hiberno-English inscriptions on the inscribed slates of Smarmore: some reconsiderations and additions. *Irish University Review* 20 (1), 55–72.

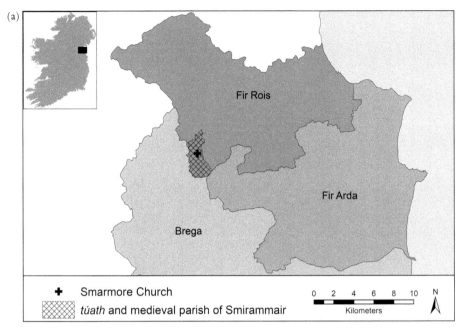

FIG. 5.36a. The early medieval geography of Smarmore (map N. McCarthy).

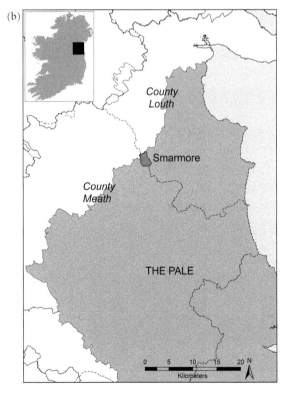

FIG. 5.36b. The late medieval borderland location of Smarmore relative to the Pale and the counties of Louth and Meath (map N. McCarthy).

on defining that region, explains that the four shires had "sheltered inner parts" collectively referred to as the "Maghery" (from *machaire*, a plain) and borderlands called "marches," where raiding and petty warfare were endemic.[121] The exact bounds of the "loyal" parts of the four shires are impossible to identify because they were dynamic, and descriptions of them are imprecise.[122]

The term "Pale" was first used by the Irish parliament in the late fifteenth century to describe an aspiration for a more clearly defined border around the loyal portions of the four shires. This involved some digging of ditches to prevent cattle raids, although O'Keeffe has argued that the Pale boundary earthwork was probably not completed.[123] The Pale boundary was that very loosely described for the Maghery in 1488.[124] In the context of what is known about the route of the boundary, Smarmore lay at the inner edge of the march (Fig. 5.36b).

A borderland status was not new to Smarmore in the fifteenth century. The Gaelic *túath* of Smarmore (upon which the medieval parish and Anglo-Norman manor of Smarmore were based) was situated on the southwest boundary of the *trícha cét* of Fir Rois, which belonged to the Ulster overkingdom of Airgialla, where it met the kingdom of Fir Arda and the overkingdom of Brega (Fig. 5.36a).[125]

The place name Smarmore is a corruption of (OI) *Smirammair*, which translates as "a mash of bone marrow." This peculiar term occurs in the epic tale *Táin bó Cúalnge* ("The cattle raid of Cooley"), from the Ulster cycle of tales preserved in the twelfth-century *Lebar na Núachongbála*, in which Fíngin Fáithlíaig ("seer-physician") organizes a marrow-mash as a cure for the wounds of Cethern mac Fintain, an Ulster warrior and ally of the hero Cú Chulainn:

> So then Fíngin Fáithlíaig asked Cú Chulainn for a marrow-mash to cure and heal Cethern mac Fintain...And Cethern was placed in the marrow-mash for the space of three days and three nights, and he began to soak up the marrow-mash which was about him. And the marrow entered into his wounds and gashes, his sores and many stabs. Then after three days and three nights he arose from the marrow-mash, and thus it was that he arose: with the board of his chariot pressed to his belly to prevent his entrails from falling out.[126]

---

[121] S. Booker 2018 *Cultural exchange and identity in late medieval Ireland: the English and Irish of the four obedient shires*, 26–7. Cambridge University Press.

[122] Booker, *Cultural exchange and identity*, 26.

[123] T. O'Keeffe 1992 Medieval frontiers and fortification: the Pale and its evolution. In F. H. A. Aalen and K. Whelan (eds), *Dublin city and county, from prehistory to present: studies in honour of J. H. Andrews*, 57–78. Dublin. Geography Publications.

[124] Booker, *Cultural exchange and identity*, 28–9.

[125] P. Gosling 2015 Placing names in *Táin Bó Cúalnge*. *Journal of the County Louth Archaeological and Historical Society*, 28 (3), 320–1; D. Mac Iomhair 1962 The boundaries of Fir Rois. *Journal of the County Louth Archaeological and Historical Society* 15 (2), 179.

[126] C. O'Rahilly (ed. and tr.) 1970 *Táin bo Cúalnge: from the Book of Leinster*, 104–5, 240. Dublin Institute for Advanced Studies.

In other medieval literature, *Smirammair* is the place where Cethern is wounded and where the marrow-mash cure is administered to him. A mnemonic verse by the poet Cinaeth húa hArtacáin (d. *c.*975) laments, "Cethern son of Fintan from the east has fallen at *Smirammair*."[127] A version of the *Táin* preserved in the late medieval *Yellow Book of Lecan* refers to Smarmore as *Imorach Smiromrach*, "brink or border of the marrow-bath."[128] The circumstances in which this curious place name came to be used of the *túath*, parish, and church of Smarmore are uncertain. Much of the *Táin* is set in Louth. Was *Smirammair* a place already known for the art of healing and mythologized in the *Táin* because, historically, it lay in borderland between the Ulster overkingdom of Airgialla and the midland overkingdom of Brega? Or did it originate with the *Táin* episode in which the marrow-mash features? That question cannot be answered definitively. However, an investigation of the medieval church and the corpus of inscribed slates found there suggests that there were practitioners of plant-based medicine at Smarmore in the late medieval period. The meaning of the place name and its mention in early medieval literature hold the possibility that the site was associated with healing in an earlier period too.

The warrior Cethern is associated with a holed standing stone situated in farmland north of Smarmore (Fig. 5.37). Called the "hurl stone," it is a large slab of sandstone and shale, standing 1.8 m tall in the townland of Hurlstone (Fig. 5.38). An origin myth relates it to the *Lia Toll* ("hole or hollow stone") cited in the *Yellow Book of Lecan* version of the *Táin*. In that version, the furious Cethern drives his sword and fist through the stone, thereby creating the centrally placed hole, large enough for a hand to fit through.[129] It was recorded in a plea roll of 1301 as "Thorledestone."[130] The borderland context of the stone in the western bounds of Fir Rois and the late medieval march, and its proximity to the parish church of Smarmore, suggest that historically it had a totemic role in this landscape. It recalls *Cloch Breac*, ("speckled stone"), Co. Sligo, an impressive standing stone *c.*2 m tall, with an oblong perforation at its base (Fig. 5.39).[131] It stood alongside a well called *Tobar na bhFiann* ("the well of the Fiann"), referencing the warrior band of Fionn mac Cumhaill, on the bounds of the estate of the Ó Dubhagáin historians at Ballydoogan, a junction of three medieval parishes and four townlands, in the lordship of Cairbre.[132] Speckled stones and holed stones belong to the category of objects used for curing, cursing, swearing

---

[127] W. Stokes 1902 On the deaths of some Irish heroes. *Revue Celtique* 23, 306, 307.

[128] J. Strachan and J. G. O'Keeffe (eds) 1912 *The Táin bó Cúailnge, from the Yellow Book of Lecan: with variant readings from the Lebor na huidre*, 95: 2742–3. Dublin. Royal Irish Academy.

[129] Strachan and O'Keeffe, *Táin bó Cúailnge*, 3315; Gosling, Placing names, 322.

[130] D. Mac Iomhair 1965 Townlands of County Louth in AD 1301. *Journal of the County Louth Archaeological and Historical Society* 16 (1), 45.

[131] W. Frazer 1896 On "holed" and perforated stones in Ireland. *JRSAI* 6 (2), 165–6; Borlase, *Dolmens of Ireland*, i, 179; Holed stones occur in Cornwall, for example at Mên-an-Tol and Tolvan.

[132] Borlase, *Dolmens of Ireland*, i, 174; O'Rahilly, Irish poets, 117.

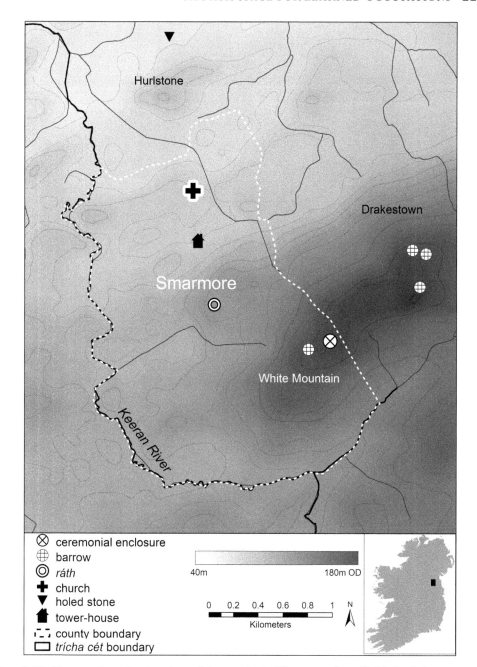

FIG. 5.37. Topography and archaeology of the townland of Smarmore (map N. McCarthy).

oaths, and making agreements.[133] The "hurl stone" perhaps facilitated some or all of those acts in the bounds of Fir Rois.

The church of Smarmore is on a low hill bounded on its east side by a wooded valley, at the northern end of Smarmore townland (Fig. 5.37). Its setting on the

[133] Frazer, On "holed" and perforated stones, 169.

FIG. 5.38. The "hurl stone" or *Lia Toll* (photo E. FitzPatrick).

boundary between two types of bedrock (Fig. 5.40) probably relates to the original allocation of the church lands, which would have included access to resources in the form of different types of soils and stone (5.2.3). The Keeran River, which delimits the western and southern sides of Smarmore townland, was an important defining element of the boundary of the local medieval kingdom of Fir Rois and the borderland of the Airgialla–Brega overkingdoms and later territorial denominations including the Louth–Meath border (Fig. 5.37). A hill called "White Mountain" (160 m OD), the focus of funerary and ritual activity in prehistory, is at the southeast end of the townland and dominates the view south from the church (Fig. 5.37).

There are remarkably few extant historical references to Smarmore and its church. It lay within the medieval diocese of Armagh and was a possession of the Augustinian abbey of St Mary at Navan (Co. Meath).[134] The earliest official record of the church is contained in the register (1361–80) of the archbishop of Armagh, where it is listed among the procurations and synodals of the English part of the diocese of Armagh as

[134] M. C. Griffith 1991 *Calendar of inquisitions formerly in the office of the chief remembrancer of the exchequer prepared from the MSS of the Irish Record Commission*, 109. Dublin. The Stationery Office.

Fig. 5.39. *Cloch Breac*, Ballydoogan–Derrydarragh, Co. Sligo, photographed by Robert John Welch (1859–1936) (BELUM.Y.W.18.01.13, courtesy of the Ulster Museum Collection, National Museums Northern Ireland).

"Ecclesia de Smermore" in "Decanatus de Atrio" ("deanery of Ardee").[135] The only known record of the name of a priest associated with Smarmore is for the seventeenth century. James Hussey (Ó hEódhasa), priest and scholar, served Smarmore until his death *c*.1635.[136] However, Booker's observation that there were Gaelic Irish as well as English priests in the marches, and that "extensive bilingualism" prevailed, is important in terms of understanding the potential for hybridity at church sites in the region during the late medieval period.[137] She has determined that in the fifteenth century there were "a great many Irish clerics serving in and near Ardee, one of the important markers of the maghery and of the pale boundary in Louth."[138] The church at Smarmore, just 7.5 km southwest of Ardee, belonged to the deanery of Ardee, and

[135] B. Smith (ed.) 1996 *The register of Milo Sweetman, archbishop of Armagh 1361–1380*, 250 [fo. 52v]. Dublin. Irish Manuscripts Commission.

[136] L. P. Murray 1936 The will of James Hussey of Smarmore, Co. Louth, "priest" (AD 1635). *Journal of the County Louth Archaeological and Historical Society* 8 (4), 303–21.

[137] Booker, *Cultural exchange and identity*, 216–17, 247–8.

[138] Booker, *Cultural exchange and identity*, 120, 215.

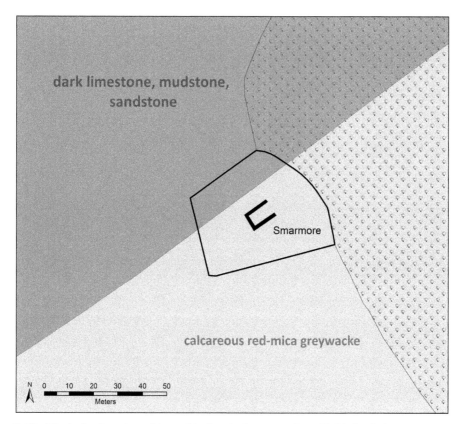

FIG. 5.40. The bedrock setting of the parish church, Smarmore (map N. McCarthy).

therefore may have been served by priests of Gaelic Irish origin who spoke English as well as Irish. Multilingualism was not unusual in march areas. In fifteenth-century Wales, the speaking of both Welsh and English, and exchange between the two cultures, was common in the borderland or march with England.[139]

There was acculturation between Gaelic and Anglo-Norman communities of Louth. In the fourteenth century the Anglo-Norman de Bermingham earl of Louth patronized Maelruanaidh Cam (squint-eyed) Ó Cearbhaill as his court musician. Ó Cearbhaill conducted a school in the art of the stringed instrument known as the *tiompán* (2.1.3).[140] Along with his patron and several of de Bermingham's retinue and family, Ó Cearbhaill and twenty student *tiompán*-players were slain in 1329 in de Bermingham's house at

---

[139] H. Fulton 2019 The Red Book and the White: gentry libraries in medieval Wales. In A. Byrne and V. Flood (eds), *Crossing borders in the insular Middle Ages*, 38. Medieval texts and cultures in northern Europe series: 30. Turnhout. Brepols.

[140] It has been suggested that the *tiompán* can be best classed with the northern European family of lyres and that it was the Irish counterpart of the Welsh *crwth* and the English *crowd*. See A. Buckley 1978 What was the tiompán? A problem in ethnohistorical organology: evidence in Irish literature. In J. Kuckertz (ed.) *Jahrbuch für Musikalische volks und völkerkunde* 9, 80, 81. Cologne. Musikverlag Hans Gerig.

Braganstown on the northern boundary of Fir Rois.[141] The exact location of Ó Cearbhaill's school is unknown, but its very existence underscores the vibrancy of the Gaelic arts in an Anglo-Norman polity in the first quarter of the fourteenth century.

The name of the church at Smarmore and its dedication were recorded in the nineteenth century as *Teampull Smearmaid* ("church of the marrow-mash") and All Saints.[142] It would be difficult to argue for an early medieval origin for it but for the fact that the archaeology of the site reveals a more complex past. Two of three cross-inscribed grave-slabs recorded in Smarmore graveyard in 1943 confirm an early medieval origin for the foundation, and the third, in situ, is later medieval and decorated with a plain Latin cross with expanded terminals.[143]

The proportions of the building are in keeping with those of a twelfth-century or earlier church.[144] However, since the walls were largely rebuilt, its exact footprint remains uncertain. Among the cut stones there are diagonally tooled fragments of doorways and windows that corroborate a twelfth- or very early thirteenth-century phase for the church. There are also several late medieval cut and dressed arch-stones, jamb-stones, a mullion, and stoup.

The surviving half of a sandstone mortar (Fig. 5.41) and a large basin-stone embedded in the ground at the entrance to the church are of particular interest because of the evidence from the slate inscriptions for learned expertise in plant-based medicine at Smarmore during the fifteenth century. The making of plant remedies would have required crushing plant matter in a mortar or a basin. Sandstone was a preferred material for grinding and pounding.[145] Stone basins have been recorded in association with Gaelic kindreds of physicians in Scotland, in at least two instances. On the west coast of Islay, there are four fixed basins carved into the corners of the socket-stone of the Kilchoman high cross that dates to the fourteenth or early fifteenth century. A Latin inscription in Lombardic hand, on the east face of the cross shaft, commemorates a physician and his son who are also figuratively represented holding books in the panel above the inscription. They have been interpreted as representations of members of the Islay branch of the Mac Bethadh medical family who served Clann Domhnaill.[146] It has not been established whether the mortars are contemporary

---

[141] AClyn 1329, 192–5; J. F. Lydon, 1977 The Braganstown Massacre, 1329. *Journal of the County Louth Archaeological and Historical Society* 19 (1), 5–16.

[142] RIA 14 D 23, Letters containing information relative to the antiquities of the county of Louth, collected during the progress of the Ordnance Survey in 1835–6, by J. O'Donovan, T. O'Conor, and P. O'Keeffe, 172. Dublin. Royal Irish Academy.

[143] V. M. Buckley and P. D. Sweetman 1991 *Archaeological survey of County Louth*, 279. Dublin. The Stationery Office.

[144] Buckley and Sweetman, *Archaeological survey*, 259.

[145] C. Rynne 2018 Milling of cereals in Gaelic and Anglo-Norman Ireland *c.* 1200–1500: technology and cultural choice. In Campbell, FitzPatrick, and Horning, *Becoming and belonging in Ireland*, 51.

[146] The Royal Commission on the Ancient and Historical Monuments of Scotland 1984 *Argyll: an inventory of the monuments volume 5: Islay, Jura, Colonsay and Oronsay*, 196–203. Edinburgh.

FIG. 5.41. A sandstone mortar, Smarmore (photo by E. FitzPatrick).

with the cross, but the tradition relating to them is that "expectant mothers would grind out such hollows with a pear-shaped pestle, in order to try and secure male offspring."[147] A garden of medicinal plants and "a cup in a rock...[that] served as a mortar in which to pound them' were still known in the nineteenth century at the house of the Ó Conchubhair physicians of Ardoran on the north side of Lough Feochan, Lorn.[148]

It was during the removal of earth from the church at Smarmore in 1959 that the text-inscribed slates came to light. Forty-nine of them were recovered from excavation spoil and deposited in the National Museum of Ireland.[149] Lucas established that they had been found "at an uncertain depth in surface soil along the inside of the north wall" of the church, together with sherds of medieval pottery and glass, stone, and metal finds.[150] In 1962 Bliss conducted a licensed excavation in two areas within the graveyard where he recovered three more slates.[151]

---

[147] The Royal Commission, *Argyll*, 5, 196–203.

[148] D. MacKinnon 1912 *A descriptive catalogue of Gaelic manuscripts in the Advocates Library Edinburgh and elsewhere in Scotland*, 64. Edinburgh. William Brown.

[149] NMI 1961: 8–56.

[150] A. T. Lucas 1963 National Museum of Ireland archaeological acquisitions in the year 1961. *JRSAI* 93 (2), 128.

[151] NMI 1963: 89–91; Bliss, Inscribed slates at Smarmore, 33–4.

FIG. 5.42. A pestle used with four basins or mortars in the socket-stone of the Kilchoman high cross, Rhinns of Islay. A work of the Iona School, the late medieval cross is associated by inscription with a physician (SC 416799 © Crown Copyright: HES.).

The slate was sourced locally, possibly at Drakestown, east of Smarmore, where olive-colored slate was quarried (Fig. 5.37).[152] Slate is also dominant in the bedrock of the Collon area southeast of Smarmore. Three of the olive-colored slates were re-used roof slates.[153] The surface damage to them confirms that they were inscribed after they had been discarded as roofing material.[154] This observation is important to authenticating the secondary use of the slates as writing rather than roofing materials at Smarmore. The language of the inscriptions is predominantly late medieval Hiberno-English, with some Latin and a single Gaelic word.[155] There is content relating to plant-based medicinal recipes, some of which are vulneraries used in the healing of wounds.[156] Others are ecclesiastical in content and four are inscribed with polyphony or musical notation.[157] The Hiberno-English hand has been dated to the early years of the fifteenth century and the style of the musical notation on four of the slates to the third decade of the fifteenth century.[158]

The quantity and content of the Smarmore slates suggests that *Smirammair*, "marrow-mash"/ *Imorach Smiromrach*, "border of the marrow-bath," was a notable place of learning during the fifteenth century, where learned clerics practiced the arts of plant-based medicine and music.

5.3 CONCLUSIONS

Learned kindreds in their various capacities as *airchinnigh*, *comharbai*, and secular proprietors of church land, had access to ecclesiastical buildings to support their learned occupations. Inishmore and Kilbarron are documented as parish churches, but the developed west ends of both buildings and the absence of late medieval graveyards suggest an additional purpose for them, combining liturgical and learned space for the Ó Cuirnín and Ó Cléirigh *ollamhain*. As seen, the architecture and ecclesiastical records for Kilbarron indicate a construction date for the church in the first quarter of the fifteenth century, when the Ó Cléirigh learned kindred had established themselves in the southern borderland of Tír Conaill. The singular plan of the building with two doorways, one entering what was essentially a diminutive chapel, the other leading into two-story quarters that occupied half the length of the building, suggests that Kilbarron was purpose built by the Ó Cléirigh *ollamh* to suit his learned

---

[152] Bliss, Inscribed slates at Smarmore, 34 and n. 2. [153] NMI 1961: 10, 16, 22.

[154] NMI 1961: 10 has a perforation at one end. It was a broken roof slate that was re-used for writing.

[155] Bliss, Inscribed slates at Smarmore, 35–7.

[156] Britton and Fletcher, Medieval Hiberno-English inscriptions, 59–60.

[157] Bliss, Inscribed slates at Smarmore, 35; NMI 1961: 12, 24, 34, 41.

[158] Bliss, Smarmore inscribed slates, 21; Bliss, Inscribed slates at Smarmore, 35; see musical notation on NMI 1961: 12, 24, 34, 41; Britton and Fletcher, Medieval Hiberno-English inscriptions, 55–72.

activities. In short, it was perhaps not so much a church adapted for use by an *ollamh*, but space for a learned occupation that facilitated some degree of liturgical use.

The involvement of clerical learned men in the construction and refurbishment of churches may have been usual, as suggested by those situated on church land named *Nuachongbháil*. It is more directly indicated in the case of the Ó Duibhgeannáin *ollamh and comharba* of Kilronan, who is recorded as having built the parish church in 1339 and re-erected it in 1347. Secular learned kindreds who assumed proprietorship of church land, which became their hereditary estates as professional families, involved themselves in building or renovating sinecure chapels too. The argument has been made that the Mac Fhlannchadha lawyers had St Breacán's Chapel at Toomullin built *c.*1300, as secular proprietors of the lands attached to it, and that they used it for their learned purposes—especially during the lifetime of Aodh Mac Fhlannchadha, the teacher of brehon law and poetry who lived at Toomullin in the sixteenth century. The incumbency of an Ó Duibhdábhoireann Gaelic minister at Toomullin, in the changed circumstances of the early seventeenth century, does not predicate an immediate end to learned activity there, but a new opportunity to maintain scholarship among professional families.

The need for space in which to write, teach, and dwell means that churches had to be adapted to serve multiple functions for their learned occupants. Inishmore, Killerry, Kilbarron, Toomullin, and Smarmore had west-end quarters separate from their naves. Of those, the west-end quarters at Inishmore and Toomullin still have standing remains that indicate purposeful design in their layout. Lacking a source of heat and without much light, none of them could be described as commodious.

At Inishmore and Toomullin, the ground- and first-floor rooms had separate entrances reached from the nave, implying that they were discrete spaces serving different functions, and that the upper room in each case was private. The concentration of fixtures in the cross-wall of the ground-floor room on Inishmore suggest that the Ó Cuirnín *comharba–ollamh* continued to use the church long after the fire of 1416 and hint strongly at an *ollamh*'s workspace.

The layout and features of some of the churches suggest that their naves may have been used as school-rooms communicating with the ground-floor rooms of west-end quarters. The separate entrances from the nave to the ground and upper floors at Inishmore and Toomullin imply a purposeful dialog between them. Apart from admitting light to the ground-floor room, the squint in the cross-wall at Inishmore allows a direct view into the nave. Furthermore, the large number of inscribed slates from the church at Smarmore suggests that it served a school and not just a learned cleric's scholarship, with perhaps the nave used as teaching space and the west end reserved as the incumbent's private quarters.

Learned kindreds carried the weight of the past of the Gaelic ruling families they served, but they were not bound by it. In the churches that they built or altered for their own needs, they contributed to innovation in the architecture of later medieval

Ireland. As seen at Ballysadare, Kilronan, and Drumacoo, Romanesque doorways of the twelfth century and *c.*1200 are found in parish churches of the western dioceses of Ireland where the *comharba* or *airchinneach* was a learned person. It has been argued that portals of newly created parish churches were signifiers of seats of learning, a message also reflected later, in the fine doorway at Inishmore.

6

Designated School-Houses

6.0 INTRODUCTION

Writing in Gaelic schools of law and medicine in the sixteenth century, learned scribes used the terms "*sgoilteagh*" and "*tigh na scoile*" ("school-house") to describe their place of work.[1] Aggregated learned communities of established and student scribes frequented school-houses within their networks during this period, to learn their art and to transcribe material for signature manuscripts under the direction of *ollamhain*. In this chapter, school buildings of secular kindreds of lawyers, physicians, and poets, who did not hold church offices, are investigated as both purpose-built space for learned occupations and opportunistic re-use of existing structures. Attention is also given to how different professional needs of literati influenced the buildings in which they learned their art, and what the localized settings of schools reveal about their intellectual practices.

As buildings with a discrete purpose, school-houses were the focal points of secular Gaelic learned activity during the late medieval and early modern period. As such, they are potentially rich sources of knowledge about the environment of schooling and behaviors of the groups that used them. Finding the school buildings of secular literati in the Irish landscape is challenging. The field-based research discussed in this chapter suggests that some were situated on grange lands of religious houses and made use of grange buildings, both before and after the Dissolution, while others were purpose-built and may have been based on the layout of churches with late medieval west-end quarters that have been investigated in Chapter 5. It is also proposed that by naming the buildings in which they worked as school-houses, and through proactive networking, sixteenth-century schools of law and medicine gave status and visibility to their culture of knowledge. This may have been a conspicuous response to the introduction of Tudor parochial and grammar schools.

---

[1] RIA MS D v 2, 72r sup.; BL Egerton MS 88, fo. 33; RIA MS 23 Q 6, Section D, 42 Law text. Dublin. Royal Irish Academy; Nic Dhonnchadha, Medical school of Aghmacart, 13–14; FitzPatrick, *Ollamh, biatach, comharba*, 187.

Landscapes of the Learned: Placing Gaelic Literati in Irish Lordships 1300–1600. Elizabeth FitzPatrick, Oxford University Press.
© Elizabeth FitzPatrick 2023. DOI: 10.1093/oso/9780192855749.003.0006

6.1 SCHOOL-HOUSES OF LEGAL KINDREDS

The Jesuit priest Edmund Campion provided an apparent eyewitness account of the interior of a law school in his *A historie of Irland* (1571):

> I have seene them where they kept schoole, ten in some one chamber, groveling upon couches of straw, their bookes at their noses, themselves lying flatte prostrate, and so to chaunte out their lessons by peece-meal, being the most part lustie fellowes of twenty five yeares and upwards.[2]

He did not identify the location of this school and provided few details of the building other than that the students lay together on long seats of straw in one room.

To begin to address the form of Gaelic law-school buildings, findings from archaeological investigations of *Teach Breac* ("speckled house") on the Ó Duibhdábhoireann estate at Cahermacnaghten, in the lordship of Boireann, and the remains of a building on the estate of the Ó Deóradháin brehon lawyers at Ballyorley (Co. Wexford), in the lordship of Uí Cheinnsealaigh, are presented. A location for the *sgoilteagh* of the Mac Aodhagáin *ollamh* in law in the estate landscape of Park, in Corca Mogha (Co. Galway), is proposed, and the identity of what was described in the fifteenth century as "the capital of Brehon law of Ireland" is explored in relation to the Mac Aodhagáin legal kindred of Ballymacegan and Redwood (Co. Tipperary), in the north Munster lordship of Urumhain.[3]

6.1.1 Teach Breac *on the Cahermacnaghten estate*

While copying manuscript material in summer, Cosnamach Ó Duibhdábhoireann, son of the *ollamh* Giolla na Naomh Óg, addressed a comment to a fellow scribe explaining that he had carried out his work both on the estate of the Ó Deóradháin lawyers at Ballyorley and in the school-house (*tigh na scoile*) at Cahermacnaghten.[4] Written in the top margin of a manuscript page, his note is invaluable primary textual evidence for a school-house on the Ó Duibhdábhoireann kindred's lands. The year in which Cosnamach was writing is not mentioned in the text, but as earlier noted (4.2.3), in 1601 he and his father were living in the family's tower-house at Lissylisheen, just southeast of Cahermacnaghten.[5] Another family member, Oilibhéar Ó Duibhdábhoireann, is cited in the same manuscript, and provenanced to Lissylisheen

---

  [2] Campion, *Historie of Irland*, 26.
  [3] RIA MS 23 P 16, 206; Ó Longáin and Gilbert, *Leabhar breac*, ii, 38.
  [4] RIA MS D v 2, 72r sup. "*a Cathair Micc Nechtaig dam a tigh na scoile in cetla do mí medon ant samraid*". "I am in Cahermacnaghten, in the school-house, on the first day of the month of June". I am grateful to Professor Liam Breatnach for this reference.
  [5] Nicholls, *Irish fiants*, iii, 506 [6562].

in an inquisition of 1585.[6] It is a reasonable assumption, therefore, that Cosnamach was writing in the school-house at Cahermacnaghten sometime between the late sixteenth century and the turn of the seventeenth. In 1552, the scribe Forandan, from the Mac Fhlannchadha law school in the neighboring lordship of Corca Modhruadh, had visited the Ó Duibhdábhoireann school to copy the *Amrae Coluim Chille*, but he did not specify where on the Cahermacnaghten estate he had conducted the work.[7]

The text-based evidence for an active Ó Duibhdábhoireann law school is for the second half of the sixteenth century, when manuscript comments by learned men testify to the scholarly networks between the Ó Duibhdábhoireann school and those of the Mac Fhlannchadha, Mac Aodhagáin, and Ó Deóradháin brehon lawyers.[8] The school had its golden age during that period, and it is not mentioned after the sixteenth century. Aodh Ó Duibhdábhoireann, in the text of the land-division deed of 1606 (3.2.2), claimed that Ó Duibhdábhoireann occupancy of the Cahermacnaghten estate extended back to the lifetime of his grandfather, Giolla na Naomh Mór, and not before then. The fifteenth- or early sixteenth-century alterations made to the *caisel* of Cahermacnaghten (4.2) fit well with that family tradition, raising the possibility that the school-house was also part of a program of building on the estate in that period.

Where was the Ó Duibhdábhoireann school-house? The settlement directly associated with the kindred is the *caisel*. As shown (3.2.2), Aodh, the eldest son of the *ollamh*, was living there by 1601, and in 1606 he and his brother Cosnamach made an agreement to divide the lands and *caisel* between them.[9] The findings of a detailed survey and two excavations undertaken in 2008 and 2010 at *Teach Breac* suggest that it was the school-house of the Ó Duibhdábhoireann kindred from *c*.1500 until *c*.1600, with the *caisel* used as the family residence until the *ollamh* moved to the tower-house nearby at Lissylisheen between *c*. 1585 and 1601 (4.2).[10]

Teach Breac was situated in Kilbrack, a subdivision of the Cahermacnaghten estate, *c*.1 km to the southwest of the *caisel* (Fig. 6.1). It is sequestered and difficult to reach without knowledge of the local landscape.[11] Although it lies in a settlement corridor and was not remote from neighboring landholdings in the past, it is insulated by precarious limestone pavements containing deep grykes. Dineley, writing of the dangers of the pavements in 1681, remarked:

> …a traveler passing over this Barony his horse's leg chanced to stick in an hole between two rocks and to leave one of the shoos, which he alighting and searching for it, drew up

---

[6] RIA MS D v 2, 72r end; Freeman, *Compossicion booke*, 9.

[7] Bisagni, *Amrae Coluimb Chille*, 11–12; RIA MS D v 2, 72r fo. 72.

[8] Especially Domhnall Ó Duibhdábhoireann's school. His brother was perhaps Giolla na Naomh Mór of Cahermacnaghten; See Macnamara, The O'Davorens, 79; O'Sullivan, The book of Domhnall, 288–9; BL Egerton MS 88; NKS MS 261 b 4°, Law text. Copenhagen. Royal Library; RIA MS 23 Q 6, 33–52.

[9] Macnamara, O'Davorens, 86–93.

[10] FitzPatrick, Cahermacnaghten, 41–3; FitzPatrick and Clutterbuck, Cabhail Tighe Breac Cahermacnaghten, 26–7.

[11] FitzPatrick, Antiquarian scholarship, 64; FitzPatrick, *Ollamh, biatach, comharba*, 187.

FIG. 6.1. The low-slung south façade of *Teach Breac*, Cahermacnaghten, with grass-covered limestone pavement in the foreground (photo E. FitzPatrick).

out of the same place above 30 shoos; this is modestly thought the least number, for some undertake to say 30 dozen.[12]

For the unwary, a journey to or from *Teach Breac* would have been arduous on horseback and tediously slow on foot. However, for those who lived and worked in this landscape, the terrain would not have been an impediment to making paths through it to access water, tend livestock, and to travel in and out of the settlement. In that respect, the glacial valley *c*.170 m north of *Teach Breac* is a natural route that connects it with the *caisel* and hence it is germane to understanding how the building might have been reached in the past (3.2.2; Fig. 3.4). Walking the route from the *caisel*, *Teach Breac* is not visible until nearing the southwest end of the valley. At that point, the north façade emerges prominently into view to the south. Conversely, from a southern approach the building appears low-slung, with just the tops of the walls visible. An upright stone, wedged into position in the limestone pavements on that side of the building, may have functioned as a marker announcing its presence across the karst (Fig. 6.2).

A profile through *Teach Breac*, taken after excavation, revealed that the original floor level was *c*.1.5 m lower than the surrounding limestone pavement on the south side of the building (Fig. 6.3). The visual impact from the south was therefore

---

[12] Shirley, Extracts from the journal, 193.

FIG. 6.2. Upright stone marker in the limestone pavement, with *Teach Breac* in the background (photo E. FitzPatrick).

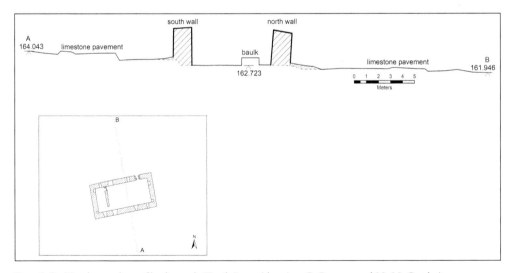

FIG. 6.3. North–south profile through *Teach Breac* (drawing C. Bruton and N. McCarthy).

deliberately reduced by the choice of site. For those within its walls, it was positioned so that it was largely concealed and so that distraction from movement in the surrounding landscape was minimized. The location of *Teach Breac* and the fact that it is hard to reach are two factors that lend themselves to an interpretation of the building as one with a special purpose, fulfilling a need for an undistracted environment in a sequestered place, away from the concourse of daily life.

Teach Breac sits within a settlement that extends over an area of 1,600 m², incorporating the wall-footings of three other rectangular buildings, two of which to the east and west of *Teach Breac* postdate its construction and primary phase (Fig. 6.4).[13] The settlement also includes a kiln (3.3), a *clochán*, several pens and enclosures, and small plots and fields.

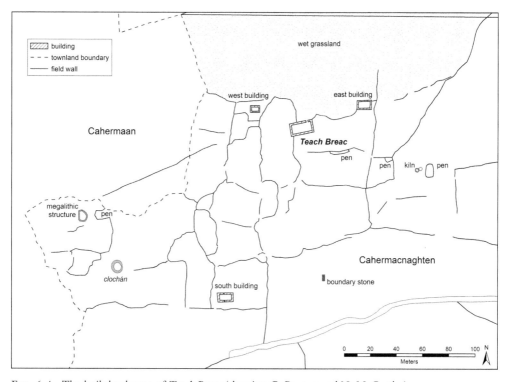

FIG. 6.4. The built landscape of *Teach Breac* (drawing C. Bruton and N. McCarthy).

[13] The east building was excavated in 2007 (License No. 07E0395). It was found that a doorway pivot-stone had been taken from *Teach Breac* and reused in this building. E. FitzPatrick 2007 Archaeological excavation of a building at Cahermacnaghten, Burren, Co. Clare (07E0395). Report to the Department of Environment, Heritage and Local Government; The west building (License No. 10E146) was excavated in 2010. E. FitzPatrick and R. Clutterbuck 2013b Cahermacnaghten: post-medieval dwelling (10E146). In I. Bennett (ed.) *Excavations 2010: summary accounts of archaeological excavations in Ireland*, 24–5. Dublin. Wordwell; The south building was not excavated but its features suggest that it is also late.

Over its lifetime, *Teach Breac* had different uses, with intermittent periods of abandonment. Based on the results of archaeological excavation and architectural analysis, a case can be made both for its origin as a school-house in the late fifteenth or early sixteenth century and conversion of the building into a dwelling in the early to mid-seventeenth century. During the eighteenth and nineteenth centuries it was mostly abandoned, with possible occasional re-use. Much of the upper wall fabric of the building collapsed during the nineteenth and twentieth centuries.

Various identities—castle, church, and school-house—were assigned to *Teach Breac* by nineteenth- and early twentieth-century antiquaries. When O'Donovan directed the Ordnance Survey sappers to document both the *caisel* and "castle" of Cahermacnaghten on the six-inch map of the area in 1839, the "castle" to which he was referring was a building that had been listed in 1574 as a stronghold of the Ó Lochlainn chief at "Cahiricnacty."[14] Following O'Donovan's information, the Ordnance Survey designated the *caisel* as the "Site of O'Loughlin's Castle," while *Teach Breac* was classified as "Church (in ruins)."[15] Frost, in his brief account of Cahermacnaghten,[16] proposed that the Ó Duibhdábhoireann school had been based in the *caisel* and, without any supporting evidence, it was designated as "O'Davoren's School (site of)" by the Ordnance Survey of 1915.[17]

It was Macnamara who first suggested that *Teach Breac* might relate to the learned activities of the Ó Duibhdábhoireann lawyers (Fig. 6.5). He proposed that it belonged

Fig. 6.5. *Teach Breac, c.*1910 (Macnamara Photographic Collection, courtesy of Clare County Library).

[14] R. W. Twigge 1909–11 Edward White's description of Thomond in 1574. *Journal of the North Munster Archaeological Society* 1, 82; RIA 14 B 23, i, 235.

[15] Ordnance Survey Ireland 1839 First-edition six-inch map, sheet ix, County Clare. Dublin. Ordnance Survey Office; Reference to the *caisel* as an Ó Lochlainn "castle", implies they used it before passing it to their lawyers.

[16] Frost, *History and topography*, 17–21.

[17] Ordnance Survey Ireland 1916 Second-edition six-inch map, sheet ix, County Clare. Dublin. Ordnance Survey Office.

"to the same period as the first establishment of the school at Cahermacnaghten i.e. circa A.D. 1500" and furthermore that it was built by the Ó Duibhdábhoireann family "as a hostel for the accommodation of their pupils...or it was the school-house itself, the kindred using the caher [*caisel*] as a residence only."[18] In 1902 he recorded the local Irish name for the building as "*Cabhal Tigh Breac*" ("ruin of the speckled house").[19] Perhaps influenced by his work, and that of Westropp who accompanied Macnamara during his investigations at Cahermacnaghten in 1902, the classification of the building as a church was dropped and the Anglicized name "Cowelteebrack" was ascribed to it by the Ordnance Survey of 1915.[20] Writing about *Teach Breac* in 1911, Westropp declared "whatever the real nature of the building may be, I am more than doubtful that it ever was a church. If so, it must have been carefully designed to conceal its character from the outer world."[21]

That the name of the building, as recorded by Macnamara, is of some antiquity is supported by seventeenth-century documentary evidence. The place name "Kiltebrack," which appears to derive from the Irish *Coill Tighe Breac* ("wood of the speckled house"), was cited in a survey of the lands of the earl of Thomond in 1625.[22] In the *Books of survey and distribution* for 1637–8, "Kilbrack" was specified as an alias for Cahermacnaghten,[23] and it was documented as such in 1787 on Henry Pelham's Grand Jury map of Co. Clare.[24] The earliest mention of what appears to be this land denomination occurs in *Suim cíos Ua Bhriain* ("O'Brien rental", compiled perhaps as early as the mid-fourteenth century), where *Coill Breac* ("speckled wood") in the lordship of Boireann is cited as *lucht tighe* or mensal land of the Ó Briain overlord.[25] None of the aforementioned versions of the place name appear in the land-division deed of 1606 (3.2.2). However, the place name "*áit tighe na reilge*" is mentioned in that deed.[26] Both Macnamara and Westropp surmised that it might be synonymous with *Teach Breac*. They took "*na reilge*" to mean "of the graves," from Irish *reilig*, meaning grave or cemetery, and were therefore perplexed by the absence of any evidence for burials in the vicinity of *Teach Breac*.[27] However, "*reilge*" could also derive from *reiclés*, which has a broader meaning as an oratory, church, or cell.[28]

The attribution *breac* ("speckled, spotted, or variegated") to *Teach Breac*, and to the denomination of *Coill Breac* (Kilbrack) in which the building was historically

---

[18] Macnamara, O'Davorens, 69–70.   [19] Macnamara, O'Davorens, 70.

[20] Ordnance Survey Ireland, Second-edition six-inch map, County Clare.

[21] T. J. Westropp 1911 Prehistoric remains (forts and dolmens) in the Burren, Co. Clare. *JRSAI* 1 (4), 367.

[22] NLI P4769, Petworth Collection, C 27/A/34, 1626, An abstract of such rents and revenues as do belonge to the right Hon:ble Earle of Thomond...Dublin. National Library of Ireland.

[23] Simington, *Books of survey and distribution*, iv, 465.

[24] H. Pelham 1787 *The county of Clare in the province of Munster and Kingdom of Ireland: surveyed and drawn by order of the Grand Jury of the county.* London. Henry Pelham.

[25] Hardiman, Ancient Irish deeds, 39, 43.   [26] Macnamara, O'Davorens, 86–7, 90–1.

[27] Westropp, Prehistoric remains, 366, 367.   [28] Quin, *Dictionary*, 503:31.

situated, requires some explanation. It was erected on crinoidal limestone, just 150 m north of a thin stratigraphic unit of dark limestone and shale, which separates the limestone from cherty mudstone shale (Fig. 6.6).[29] The descriptor *breac*, as it applies to the name of the building, and to the land denomination, may refer to the different types of bedrock in the vicinity, but it could more specifically allude to a striking quality of the crinoidal limestone, which contains fossilized crinoids, especially their stems that produce a speckled or variegated appearance. A relationship between St Breacán and the variegated bedrock of the Aille River was previously discussed in relation to his chapel in Toomullin (5.2.1). It is conceivable that bedrock had a metaphysical role in the formation of appropriate surroundings for the work of schools, with variegated and brecciated stone possibly reflecting learned activity as a transitory state.

Teach Breac was built on the northern edge of a low karst cliff that drops down to wet grassland (Fig. 6.4). With a rectangular plan (15.5 m east–west by 5.8 m north–south internally) and a total floor area of *c*.90 m², the roofless ruin has proportions usually associated with a late medieval parish church, which, together with the east–west alignment of the building, contributed to the earlier opinion that it was a church (Fig. 6.3). It is a single-story structure with a loft. The loft floor was supported by a series of stone corbels, some of which remain in place in the gables (Fig. 6.4), with others recovered during excavation (Fig. 6.7). The roof of the building was probably thatched and of cruck construction, with the timbers springing from the top of the thick walls.

The external walls were made inordinately strong (*c*.1.3 m thick) because they had no foundations and sat directly on the limestone pavement that inclines from east to west (Fig. 6.3). To compensate for the incline, leveling stones and packing material were used in raising the first masonry courses of the walls. A firm red clay was also used to fill the natural grykes in the limestone pavement and to iron out irregularities to make a smoother floor.[30]

The walls of *Teach Breac* were constructed from the local limestone, and apart from the west gable, they are in poor condition. The wall structure consists of facing stones between which there is a heavily mortared rubble core. The masonry style is best seen on the west gable (Fig. 6.8). Most of the facing stones are narrow, rectilinear blocks, with some larger stones randomly placed between them. Small flat stones were used to level rows. All four corners of *Teach Breac* were finished with punch-dressed quoin-stones, most of which were robbed out over time for use in the construction of nearby drystone walls. A view of the building in the 1900s shows the intact quoins of the northwest and southwest corners placed alternately long and short (Fig. 6.5).[31]

[29] Mcnamara and Hennessy, *The geology of the Burren*, 5, 6, 16.
[30] FitzPatrick, Cahermacnaghten, 43.
[31] MN_CL235841, Macnamara Collection, Cabhail Tighe Breac. Ennis. Clare County Library.

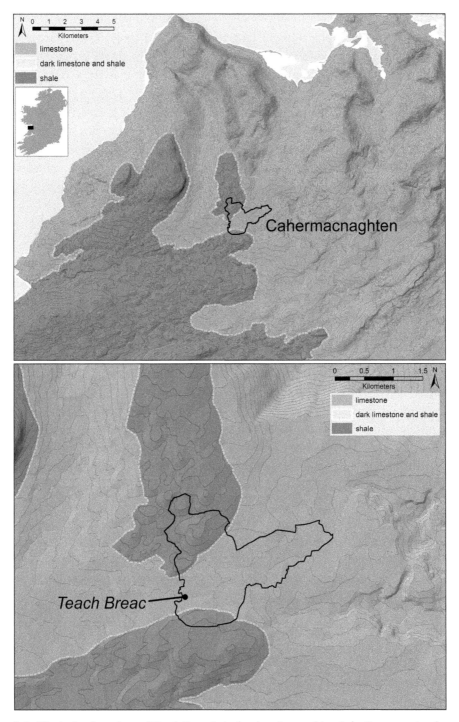

FIG. 6.6. The bedrock geology of *Teach Breac*, in its local setting, and (top) the Burren region (map N. McCarthy).

FIG. 6.7. Wall cupboard and corbels for the loft floor, east gable, *Teach Breac* (photo E. FitzPatrick).

FIG. 6.8. External face of the west gable, *Teach Breac* (photo E. FitzPatrick).

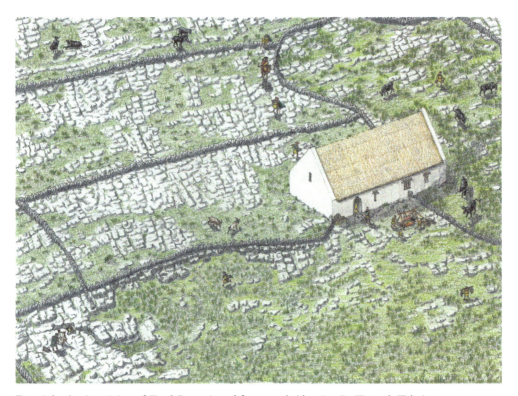

FIG. 6.9. A reimagining of *Teach Breac* viewed from north (drawing D. Tietzsch-Tyler).

Analysis of the mortar used in the wall core of the west gable confirmed that it was derived from the limestone, with the aggregate consisting of poorly sorted limestone pebbles, granules, and sand sourced from a stream bed.[32] The walls were rendered with lime plaster, and perhaps whitewashed externally and internally (Fig. 6.9).

The entrance to *Teach Breac* was positioned at the east end of the north wall, which was the façade of the building. It had collapsed by 1902.[33] A matching pair of arch-stones and two jamb-stones from the doorway were recovered as surface finds (Fig. 6.10).[34] It had a semi-pointed arch, the large stones of which were hewn from local limestone of poor quality, prone to fracturing. The masons worked with the natural imperfections of the stone, ensuring that any surface flaws faced inward. The arris was finished with a molding consisting of a half-roll flanked by quirks or angular incisions. This form of angle-roll was very common in early and high Gothic[35] and continued to be used in Ireland in the late Gothic period.

---

[32] P. Cox and M. L. McCarthy 2009 Cabhail Tighe Breac, Burren, Co. Clare: mortar analysis, 3–7. Dublin. Carrig.
[33] Macnamara, O'Davorens, 69.   [34] FitzPatrick, Cahermacnaghten, 42.
[35] R. K. Morris 1992 An English glossary of medieval mouldings. *Architectural History* 35, 11.

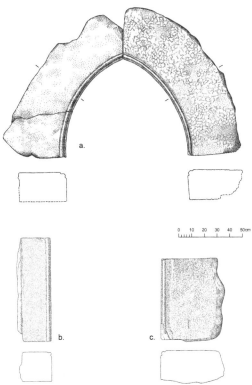

FIG. 6.10. Parts of the doorway to *Teach Breac*, including (a) pair of arch-stones and (b–c) jamb-stones (drawings A. Gallagher).

Outside of urban environments, such detail is usually reserved for the portals of religious houses and parish churches in Ireland. The angle-roll is used in combination with other moldings on the very late medieval doorways of the parish churches at Carran and Drumcreehy, which belong to a period of renewal in church architecture in the lordship of Boireann reflected elsewhere in Ireland between *c.*1450 and the Henrician Reformation (1537).[36] The mason may have consciously borrowed it for *Teach Breac* from the distinctive molded style of the doorways of parish churches.

Teach Breac had seven windows on the ground floor, three in the north wall, and four in the south wall, with narrow single-light windows in the east and west gables of the loft (Fig. 6.11). The ground-floor windows were positioned approximately at waist level above the original floor surface precluding any distant views from within, especially to the south where, as previously noted, the exterior ground level was

[36] H. A. Jeffries 2010 *The Irish Church and the Tudor reformations*, 15–22. Dublin. Four Courts Press; H. A. Jeffries 2006 Parishes and pastoral care in Ireland in the early Tudor era. In E. FitzPatrick and R. Gillespie (eds), *The parish in medieval and early modern Ireland: community, territory and building*, 225–7. Dublin. Four Courts Press.

north wall

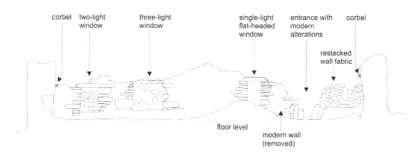

west wall   **east wall**

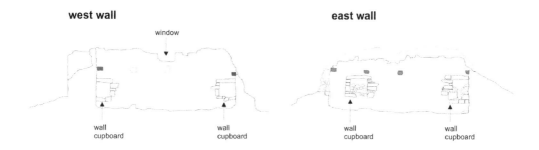

south wall

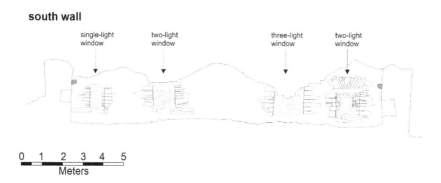

FIG. 6.11. Internal elevations of the walls of *Teach Breac* based on LiDAR survey (drawing R. Clutterbuck and N. McCarthy; LiDAR survey images The Discovery Programme).

considerably higher (Fig. 6.3). According to Westropp, the central west ope in the south long wall was another entrance to the building.[37] The authors of plans of the building made in 1989 and 1995 concur with him.[38] However, a survey for this study

[37] Westropp, Prehistoric remains, 367.

[38] Ní Ghabhláin planned the building in 1989 (unpublished) and dismissed the idea that it had been a church or that it in any way incorporated the fabric of an earlier church. The 1995 plan was made during Ristéard Ua Cróinín's survey of the castles and tower-houses of Co. Clare.

confirmed that the ope concerned was formerly a window that matched a triple light directly opposite it in the north wall (Fig. 6.11).

Knowledge of the window forms is based on the surviving cut-stone frame of the two-light window at the west end of the south wall, architectural fragments recovered from the site, and the field records of Macnamara and Westropp. The two-light window originally had a hollow-chamfered hood-molding with L-shaped stops that was still in place when Westropp observed it as "a plain hood with stepped ends" in 1911 (Fig. 6.12).[39] The hood style of the windows is confirmed by a frame fragment from another double-light that retains the attached hollow-chamfered hood (Fig. 6.13). The window mullions were of half flat-splay chamfered type, which can be found elsewhere in the Burren—in the south wall of the parish church at Noughaval (5.1) and the south wall of the chancel of the cathedral at Kilfenora.

The window frames had no glazing-bar holes and no grooves for glass. In the embrasure of the surviving two-light window, there are notches to receive shutter-hinges, and a deep aperture for a bar that secured the closed shutters. There are also notches in the collapsed frame of the three-light window in the north wall, and a small pivot-stone

FIG. 6.12. Embrasure and frame of a formerly two-light window, south wall, *Teach Breac* (photo E. FitzPatrick).

[39] Westropp, Prehistoric remains, 367.

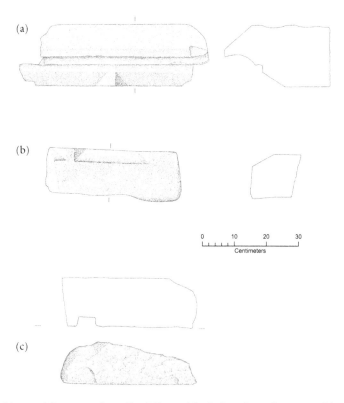

FIG. 6.13. Architectural fragments from *Teach Breac*: (a) window-frame fragment with attached hollow-chamfered hood and mullion footprint; (b) window-frame fragment with partial mullion footprint; (c) pivot-stone for a door-hinge (drawings A. Gallagher).

for a hinge in the sill-stone of a narrow single-light window immediately west of the doorway in the north wall. It can be concluded that the windows of *Teach Breac* were shuttered and not glazed and that they conformed to the Tudor Late Gothic style (1485–1603) of flat-headed, mullioned windows.[40]

The surviving internal architectural fixtures of the building include four deep wall-cupboards built into the thickness of the gables and placed towards the corners (Figs 6.7, 6.14).

During the excavation of 2008 a cross-wall aligned north–south was uncovered in the interior of *Teach Breac*, 2.7 m east of the west gable (Figs 6.14, 6.15).[41] It sat directly on the limestone pavement, confirming that it was contemporary with the construction and primary use of the building. Like the cross-walls erected in churches

[40] M. Airs 1989 Architecture. In B. Ford (ed.), *The Cambridge cultural history of Britain, iii: sixteenth-century Britain*, 59. Cambridge University Press.

[41] FitzPatrick, Cahermacnaghten, 43; FitzPatrick and Clutterbuck, Cabhail Tighe Breac, Cahermacnaghten, 26–7.

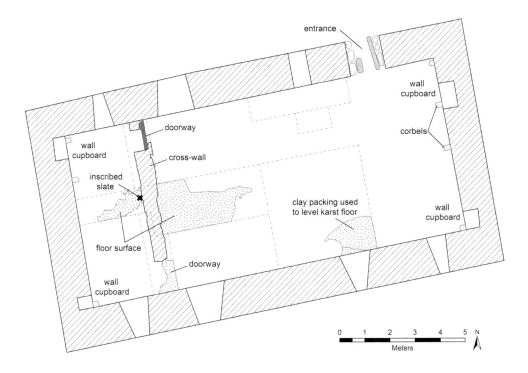

FIG. 6.14. (top) Plan of Phase 1, *Teach Breac* (drawing C. Bruton, E. Campbell and N. McCarthy) and (bottom) view looking west across the building during excavation in 2008, showing the Phase 2 east partition wall and fireplace in foreground (photo E. FitzPatrick).

FIG. 6.15. Threshold, jamb-stones, and pivot-stone of the doorway in the west cross-wall of *Teach Breac*, revealed during excavation, 2008 (photo E. FitzPatrick).

to create west-end quarters, it partitioned off a west-end room (perhaps the *ollamh*'s quarters) from the rest of the building when *Teach Breac* was first constructed. The room was entered through a narrow doorway at the north end of the cross-wall, the punch-dressed sill-stone, a single jamb-stone, and the lower pivot-stone of which were found in situ (Fig. 6.15). A pair of punch-dressed and chamfered arch-stones, removed from the building in the modern period and recovered as surface finds 40 m northwest of *Teach Breac*, appear to have belonged to it, as together they form a semi-pointed arch that fits the door span (Fig. 6.16). A gap uncovered at the corresponding south end of the cross-wall (Fig. 6.14) suggested that there was a second doorway into the west-end room, the masonry of which had been robbed out some time after *Teach Breac* was abandoned. Two entrances into that space presuppose that it was subdivided into a northern chamber, lit by the single-light window at the west end of the north wall, and a southern chamber, lit by the surviving twin-light window in the south wall, but excavation did not reveal any evidence of a stone or more ephemeral dividing wall on the east–west axis of the room.

No evidence of a permanent or temporary hearth relating to the primary occupation of *Teach Breac* was found during excavation. The possibility that Gaelic school-houses were not heated is suggested in other respects. A scribe working between 1564 and 1570 on the book of Domhnall Ó Duibhdábhoireann complained of having cold

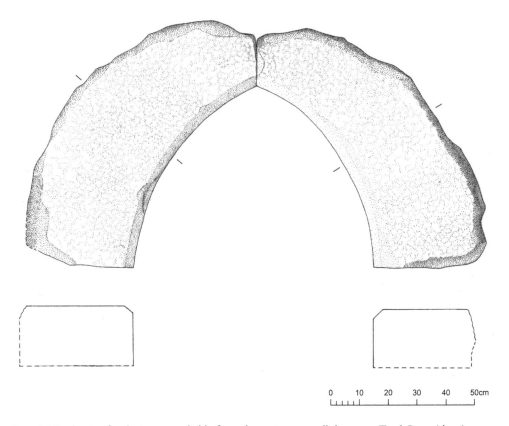

F‌IG. 6.16. A pair of arch-stones, probably from the west cross-wall doorway, *Teach Breac* (drawing A. Gallagher).

hands in the Park school-house of the Mac Aodhagáin brehon lawyers.[42] No hearth was found during the excavation of the proposed law-school building of the Ó Deóradháin kindred at Ballyorley (6.1.2). The evidence for hearths in late medieval schools elsewhere is variable. The fifteenth-century schoolrooms of Eton, Magdalen, and Winchester, for instance, did not have fire-pits or fireplaces.[43] However, archaeological and pictorial evidence for open fires and stoves, glazing, and straw-covered floors in late medieval schools of the Low Countries, and the many depictions of tiled stoves in sixteenth-century German prints of school interiors, suggest that there was a concern with keeping students warm in some school cultures. Willemsen points out that window glass has been recovered in the fourteenth-century school of Liège in Belgium and in Gorinchem and Zwolle in Holland.[44] A miniature in the manuscript known as the *Hours of Catherine of Cleves*, compiled at Utrecht *c*.1450, shows a school interior with the floor covered in straw for warmth, and students seated on straw benches by

---

[42] BL Egerton MS 88, fo. 81v, col. 2, bottom line; O'Grady, *Catalogue of Irish manuscripts*, 132.
[43] Orme, *Medieval schools*, 145.   [44] Willemsen, *Back to the schoolyard*, 266.

the wall.[45] The windows of *Teach Breac* were not glazed. The shutters must therefore have remained closed during cold and inclement weather, darkening the interior. If Campion's description of the inside of a law school (1571) is an eyewitness account, the straw couches that he mentions would have afforded some warmth and comfort (6.1).[46]

An AMS radiocarbon age range of 1488–1603 was obtained for faunal remains recovered from a deposit in the entrance gap of the north doorway in the west cross-wall.[47] The deposit related to fixing irregularities in the bedrock floor, in order to facilitate construction of the entrance. Since *Teach Breac* had an afterlife as a dwelling, small finds from its primary period of use were few. However, a small fragment of inscribed slate, potentially diagnostic of school activity, was recovered west of the cross-wall, from a mortar-rich floor deposit related to the primary occupation of the west-end room (Figs 6.14, 6.17).[48]

The excavations revealed that *Teach Breac* also had an east cross-wall, which gave the building a tripartite plan in its final form (Fig. 6.14). However, it was not original to the building, it related to a second phase of its use in the seventeenth

FIG. 6.17. A fragment of inscribed slate recovered from the west room, *Teach Breac* (photo M. Stansbury).

---

[45] Willemsen, *Back to the schoolyard*, 46–7.   [46] Campion, *Historie of Irland*, 26.

[47] UBA-13601, 96.4 (2 sigma) cal AD 1488–1603: FitzPatrick and Clutterbuck, Cabhail Tighe Breac, Cahermacnaghten, 26.

[48] FitzPatrick, Cahermacnaghten, 43.

century.[49] A large fireplace with cut-stone pillars and corbels was uncovered in the west face of the cross-wall. Perhaps of stone-canopy type, it warmed the central room, which was the largest space in the building in the seventeenth century. Excavation at the north end of the east cross-wall revealed that it was constructed on top of a clay layer including refuse, in the final phase of the primary use of the building. The deposit contained shell, a quantity of charred oat grains and some hulled barley as well as animal bone, both domestic (cattle, sheep) and wild species including deer antler. That the cross-wall post-dated the external walls was also suggested by the fact that, at its full height, it would have partly blocked a single-light window in the north long wall. In Macnamara's understanding of the plan of *Teach Breac*, the north end of the east cross-wall cleared the window and there was a "bench" between the outshot of the fireplace and the north long wall.[50] Excavation proved that the window would have been partly occluded by the cross-wall and that Macnamara's "bench" was just a large block of collapsed building fabric.[51] This result further confirmed that the east cross-wall postdated the construction of the building.

The significant phase of refurbishment represented by the east cross-wall appears to have transformed the building into a dwelling (Fig. 6.14). A refuse deposit broadly relating to that phase was recovered from the southwest corner of the room on the east side of the cross-wall. It contained animal bone, some seashell, a significant quantity of oat grains, and three small finds including the top of a knife, a small fork, and a sherd of pre-modern glass. A rental of the earl of Thomond, dated 1626, indicates that there were no tenants on the lands of Kilbrack in 1626.[52] However, by *c*.1637–8, Kilbrack was in the possession of "Turlough O'Bryen" and it was perhaps during his ownership of the property that *Teach Breac* was refurbished as a dwelling.[53]

The archaeology, architecture, setting, and place name of *Teach Breac* indicate that it was not built as a church or a dwelling.[54] When it was first built and occupied, the dimensions, east–west orientation, and internal layout of the space, divided by a cross-wall into a large room and a small room, resembled those of parish churches and sinecure chapels with separate west-end quarters (5.1). Certain features of the first-phase building—the facility of four wall-cupboards, the entrance with its angle-roll molding, no evidence of a hearth, and the lack of an accompanying bawn or defensive features of any type—point to a building contrived for a special purpose. Although small finds relating to the primary occupation of the building were few, the fragment of inscribed slate recovered in the west-end room is material culture normally related to writing and learning in a school context (Fig. 6.17).

---

[49] FitzPatrick, Cahermacnaghten, 43; FitzPatrick and Clutterbuck, Cabhail Tighe Breac, Cahermacnaghten, 27.

[50] Macnamara, O'Davorens, 69.

[51] FitzPatrick and Clutterbuck, Cabhail Tighe Breac, Cahermacnaghten, 27.

[52] NLI P476, Petworth Collection, C 27/A/34, 1626.

[53] Simington, *Books of survey and distribution*, iv, 465.   [54] Macnamara, O'Davorens, 86–7, 90–1.

The period in which *Teach Breac* was first built can be narrowed down using a combination of scientific dating, architectural details, and knowledge of the optimum period of learned activity in the Ó Duibhdábhoireann school. Having examined the architectural features of the building, Westropp believed that it was "at the latest of the early seventeenth century."[55] Macnamara offered a more precise date of *c*.1500, based on his reading of the building and his understanding of two texts. The first, as previously noted (4.2.2), is a genealogical poem *Ní crann aontoraidh an uaisle* ("Nobility is not a tree of just one fruit") composed by Tadhg mac Dáire Mac Bruaideadha (1570–1652) and principally addressed to his contemporary, Giolla na Naomh Óg Ó Duibhdábhoireann, who was *ollamh* in the late sixteenth century and at the turn of the seventeenth.[56] The second is a genealogy by Muircheartach Ó Briain of Ballyportry, Co. Clare, compiled in 1754, that attributed the founding of the Cahermacnaghten school to Giolla na Naomh Mór, father of Giolla na Naomh Óg, *c*.1500.[57] The radiocarbon age range of AD 1488–1603 broadly informs the construction period of the building. Both the angle-roll molding on the north doorway and the windows of Tudor Late Gothic form fit comfortably within that range.

Based on the combination of its landscape setting, current dating, plan and architectural details, and the inscribed slate find, *Teach Breac* can credibly be proposed as the school-house of the Ó Duibhdábhoireann *ollamh*, where Cosnamach Ó Duibhdábhoireann was writing sometime between the second half of the sixteenth century and the turn of the seventeenth.[58]

The Tudor Composition of Connacht (1585), which introduced a new socio-political and economic order into the lordship of Boireann, was driven by the family of the earl of Thomond who became increasingly acquisitive, buying up portions of estates.[59] In such circumstances it is probable that the Ó Duibhdábhoireann school had declined by *c*.1606.

6.1.2 *Law school-houses at Park and Ballyorley*

Between 1564 and 1570, Domhnall Ó Duibhdábhoireann and his associates were frequently based in Corca Mogha, to copy material for Domhnall's book from the manuscript collection of the Mac Aodhagáin law school at Park (3.3.1).[60] Copying also happened at two other locations in that period, Ardkyle in the lordship of West Clann Chuileáin and Ballyorley in the lordship of Uí Cheinnsealaigh (Fig. 6.18). Most of the work for the book, however, was conducted at Park, as testified by the

[55] Westropp, Prehistoric remains, 367.   [56] Macnamara, O'Davorens, 204, 209.
[57] Macnamara, O'Davorens, 157.   [58] RIA MS D v 2, 72r.
[59] Nugent, *Gaelic clans*, 192–3.   [60] O'Sullivan, Book of Domhnall, 283–7.

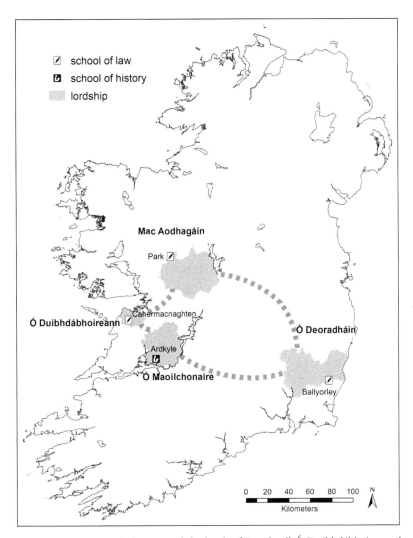

Fig. 6.18. The scholarly network that created the book of Domhnall Ó Duibhdábhoireann between 1564 and 1570 (map N. McCarthy).

comments of the scribes themselves, dated 1564, 1567, and 1568.[61] The environment of their task, over a period of seven years, was typical of Gaelic learned practice, as Corca Mogha was an in-between place, a premier borderland between Uí Mhaine and Clann Conmhaigh (Fig. 3.10). Domhnall and the members of his peripatetic school had a very specific purpose—to make a book that would distinguish the

[61] BL Egerton MS 88, fo. 12b, col. 2, fo. 14, col. 1; O'Grady, *Catalogue of Irish manuscripts*, i, 111: "The Park is my quarters. Written by Manus for Domhnall, who is himself travelling all over Ireland A.D. 1567"; BL Egerton MS 88: *anno domini 1568. in Páirc mo log*; O'Grady, *Catalogue of Irish manuscripts*, i, 140, "A.D. 1568. The Park is my location"; TCD H.3.18, MS 1337/3 Miscellanea, p. 450 (see also pp. 443, 445, 452, 454). Trinity College Dublin: *A bpáirc damh* 1564; O'Grady, *Catalogue of Irish manuscripts*, i, 139: "I am at Park. 1564."

Ó Duibhdábhoireann legal kindred. This was not unusual—several learned kindreds made books that were closely identified with them. Domhnall's book, which contained legal material, tales, and grammar, has survived in three parts, in three different repositories, at Copenhagen, Dublin, and London.[62] Other books particular to learned kindreds have been less fortunate. The *Leabhar gearr* or "Short book" of the Ó Cuirnín family of Inishmore is only known from the moment of its destruction by fire in 1416 (2.1.3).[63] Extant in 1636, *Leabhar Mic Bruaidheadha*, compiled by the poet Maoilín Óg Mac Bruaideadha, and *Leabhar Chloinne Uí Maoilconaire* of the Ó Maoilchonaire poets and chroniclers, were lost thereafter.[64] These were significant works particular to the *ollamhain* of learned kindreds. The convening of Domhnall Ó Duibhdábhoireann's school specifically to produce a book, and the devotion of his learned scribes to that end, is a salient example of a practice shared by other Gaelic schools.

Park in the 1560s was by all accounts a busy center of learning that was also frequented by members of the Mac Fhirbhisigh, Mac Fhlannchadha, Ó Ceandamháin, Ó Deóradháin, and Ó Maoilchonaire learned kindreds.[65] Where did they do their work on the Park estate? Maghnus Ó Duibhdábhoireann, in a comment he wrote in a margin of a page of Domhnall's book *c.*1566, noted the *sgoilteagh* as his place of writing (Fig. 6.19).[66] The school-house at Park was evidently a building set apart for learned activity.

The Mac Aodhagáin *ollamh* had a tower-house residence in Park (4.5), his occupancy of which is confirmed in the list of castles in Co. Galway made for Lord Deputy Sir Henry Sidney in 1574 (4.5).[67] In 1618, "a stone house" was recorded within the bawn.[68] While it is tempting to suggest that the stone house was perhaps the school-house, there is a convincing case for the separation of residences from school-houses in other secular learned kindred settlements. Cahermacnaghten *caisel* and Lissylisheen tower-house are apart from but convenient to *Teach Breac* (6.1.1); the Ó Dálaigh school-house at Dromnea was separate from but adjacent to the family's tower-house residence in Farranamanagh (6.3.1); and the tower-house of the Ó Maoilchonaire *ollamh* was at Rossmanagher, while the business of his school was conducted nearby in Ardkyle (3.3.1).[69] The Ardkyle school building has not been identified with certainty, but some premodern building fabric recorded at Deerpark House, in Deerpark

---

[62] NKS MS 261 b 4°; RIA MS 23 Q 6, 33–52; BL Egerton MS 88.

[63] AConn 1416.23, 430, 431.　　[64] J. O'Donovan (ed. and tr.) 1856 *Annála*, vol. 1, lxv, lxvi.

[65] O'Grady, *Catalogue of Irish manuscripts*, i, 119, 125, 130, 134; O'Sullivan, Book of Domhnall, 286.

[66] BL Egerton MS 88, fo. 30r: "*Is minic tic Gerailt do túr luderim don sgoilteagh uchán*"; O'Grady, *Catalogue of Irish manuscripts*, 120: "Gerald keeps on coming too often to the school-house in quest of certain girls of mine."

[67] Nolan, Galway castles, 122.　　[68] Costello, Ancient law school, 97.

[69] B. Ó Dálaigh 2008 The Uí Mhaoilchonaire of Thomond. *Studia Hibernica* 35, 35–68; O'Rahilly, Irish poets, 109. Members of the kindred were pardoned in 1577 and 1603; BL Egerton MS 88, fo. 75v.

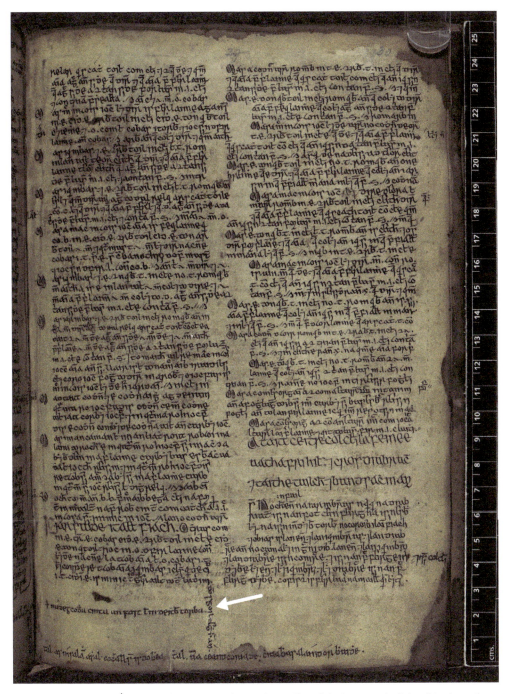

F<small>IG</small>. 6.19. Maghnus Ó Duibhdábhoireann refers to the *sgoilteagh* (written vertically) as his place of writing (BL Egerton MS 88, fo. 30r, courtesy of the British Library).

townland, south of Ardkyle, holds the possibility that the school was situated there. Such a juxtaposition of key buildings to each other on learned kindred lands suggests that the Park school-house might be found at a distance from the tower-house. A suitable setting for it can be pointed out at the northern end of the Park estate, which consisted of a large tract of bogland. In that bogland there is a small but distinctive island, reached by a track north of Park tower-house (Fig. 3.11). There was a roofed rectangular building (15 m × 6 m) aligned east–west on the west side of the island in the nineteenth century.[70] Its relative isolation is contrary to the otherwise agglomerated nineteenth-century settlements of the district, but typical of the separate sequestered settings preferred for Gaelic secular school-houses. It was comparable in scale and alignment to *Teach Breac* (15 m × 7 m), but no more than that can be ascertained. Investigation of the island for this study revealed that the building had been completely quarried out, perhaps as early as the late nineteenth or early twentieth century since it was not subsequently marked by the Ordnance Survey.

Practicalities of the work that took place in the school-house at Park during the sixteenth century are captured in remarks made in the margins of Ó Duibhdábhoireann's book. The scribe Aodh chided the *ollamh* Domhnall for requesting an initial letter of him when he had not been provided with ink: "bad luck to you that are driving me distracted, requiring a head-letter of me, and I not having so much as a drop of ink to help me out with the job."[71] Maghnus, who contributed several folios of writing, struggled with the materials provided to him at Park *c*.1565.[72] He lamented, "My writing equipment is bad. A soft spiky pen and foxy thick ink and stony-green parchment and grief!"[73] He referred to his writing material as "*memrum*" (parchment).[74] The reason why it was stony-green was probably because blemishes had not been fully abraded and sufficiently whitened with chalk or lime (3.4). The quality of the parchment in the section that contains his work varies considerably.[75]

The compilation of Domhnall Ó Duibhdábhoireann's book also involved sojourns by him and his school on the estate of the Ó Deóradháin lawyers in the lordship of Uí Cheinnsealaigh in southeast Leinster, a distance of *c*.300 km from Park.[76] The name

[70] Ordnance Survey Ireland 1839 First-edition six-inch map, sheet xviii, County Galway. Dublin. Ordnance Survey Office.

[71] O'Grady, *Catalogue of Irish manuscripts*, i, 131.

[72] O'Sullivan, Book of Domhnall, 284.

[73] BL Egerton MS 88, fo. 29v, top margin: "*ní maith meidh mo scríbhinn. Penn bog gér ocus dubh ruadh righin ocus memrum clochglas ocus maoithe*". O'Grady, *Catalogue of Irish manuscripts*, i, 120.

[74] Quin, *Dictionary*, 459:98; M. Carver and C. Spall 2004 Excavating a *parchmenerie*: archaeological correlates of making parchment at the Pictish monastery at Portmahomack, Easter Ross. *Proceedings of the Society of Antiquaries of Scotland* 134, 186, 188.

[75] For instance, pp. 14, 15, 63–70 and 80–1 of BL Egerton MS 88 are very thick and unpliable, while pp. 17, 18, 45, 46, 48, and 72–8 are quite thin.

[76] O'Sullivan, Book of Domhnall, 283–7.

of their estate was cited as *Baile Uí Dheóradháin* ("landholding or settlement of
Ó Deóradháin"), in a marginal comment by Cosnamach Ó Duibhdábhoireann, who,
as previously noted (6.1.1), was there to copy a text.[77] The lands that constituted the
Ó Deóradháin estate, in the medieval parish of Kilcormick and northern borderland
of the old *tricha cét* of Síl Mella,[78] can be reassembled through different textual
sources. It constituted at least a quarter of land that can be identified in the modern
landscape through townland names. Domhnall Ó Duibhdábhoireann recorded his
presence in the Ó Deóradháin school-house on Shrove Tuesday *c.*1566—"I am
Domhnall in the school-house at Ballyorley today" (*Misi Domhnall a dtig na scoile
dam.i. a mBaile Orlaith aniu*).[79] Ballyorley, southeast of the village of Ferns, was
recorded in a seventeenth-century land survey of Co. Wexford as 351 acres of good
arable, suitable for growing rye and oats.[80] Tomnaboley, adjoining the east side of
Ballyorley, is cited as the provenance of a member of the Ó Deóradháin kindred in
a pardon of 1612 and again in an inquisition dated 1627.[81] The denomination of
Garrybrit was also integral to *Baile Uí Dheóradháin*. Described in 1640 as 200
acres of land that had been held "as the inheritance of Brean O Doran [Ó Deóradháin]
Protestant," it adjoined the west side of Ballyorley.[82] Furthermore, Gabrial Ó Deóradháin
located himself at a place called *An Ghráinseach* ("the Grange") in a colophon written
and dated by him to 1575.[83] Reference to this place survives in the local landscape as
Grange, a townland situated immediately west of Garrybrit. A land-block consisting
of Ballyorley, Tomnaboley, Garrybrit, and Grange can be proposed as the minimum
extent of the former estate of *Baile Uí Dheóradháin*.

The fact that additional Ó Deóradháin and Ó Duibhdábhoireann scribes referred
to *An Ghráinseach* as their place of work intimates that it was where the school-house
was situated (Fig. 6.20).[84] The place name implies an out-farm of a religious house.
Grange townland does not contain a settlement with a monastic farm, but there is
a complex of settlement features consistent with a grange in nearby Ballyorley.
Augustinian granges in Ireland are under-researched. Cistercian granges are better
understood, especially because of recent excavations at the site of Beaubec Grange,
Co. Meath.[85] Research on granges in Britain has shown that they tended to include
elements of different type and function, among them moated sites and mottes, barns,

---

[77] RIA MS D v 2, 72r sup.   [78] MacCotter, *Medieval Ireland*, 254.

[79] BL Egerton MS 88, fo. 27.

[80] R. C. Simington (ed.) 1953 *The civil survey* AD *1654–56, County of Wexford*, 79. Dublin. The Stationery
Office.

[81] Griffith, *Irish patent rolls*, 391; Hardiman, *Inquisitionum in officio*, i, 468.

[82] Simington, *Civil survey, Co. Wexford*, 79.   [83] RIA MS 23 Q 6, A, p. 5 b *i*.

[84] RIA MS 23 Q 6, A, p. 1 a *i*; RIA MS 23 Q 6, D, p. 42 a *i*.

[85] G. Stout 2015 The Cistercian grange: a medieval farming system. In M. Murphy and M. Stout (eds),
Agriculture and settlement in Ireland, 26–68. Dublin. Four Courts Press.

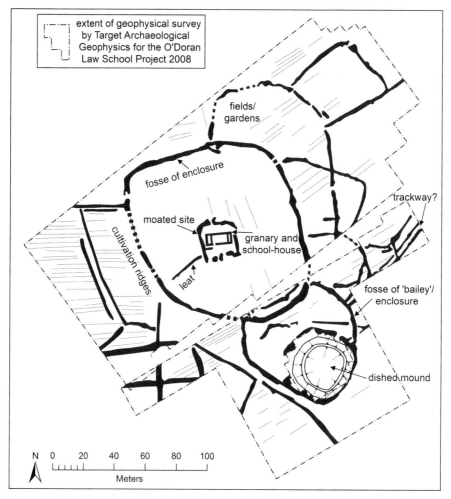

FIG. 6.20. The proposed grange settlement revealed by geophysical survey, Ballyorley, with updated annotations (survey Target Archaeological Geophysics, courtesy of the O'Doran Law School Project 2008).

house platforms, and chapels.[86] The complex in Ballyorley consists of a moated site encompassed by a subcircular enclosure containing 2.85 acres of land. The enclosure is defined by a fosse. Geophysical survey of the site revealed additional features. An entrance gap on the northeast side of the enclosure leads into a nest of fields that extend over *c*.1.1 hectares, some of which contain premodern cultivation ridges (Fig. 6.20).[87]

---

[86] R. Roberts 2014 *GGAT 129: Cistercian granges in Glamorgan and Gwent*, 18. Swansea. Glamorgan-Gwent Archaeological Trust.

[87] J. Nicholls 2008 Geophysical survey report: Ballyorley Upper, County Wexford, license 08R103. Target Archaeological Geophysics, for the O'Doran Law School Research Committee; FitzPatrick and Ó Drisceoil, Landscape and law school, 400–7.

Outside and to the south of the large enclosure there is an earthwork in the form of a subcircular mound with a dished summit. A broad fosse surrounds it. Classed, variously, as a motte, a ringwork castle, and a *ráth*, it is separated from the large enclosure to the north by an intervening bow-shaped enclosure defined by a continuous fosse (Fig. 6.20).[88] It presents the appearance of a bailey, but the geophysical survey did not reveal any features within it. The discovery of "cinerary burials" within the bounds of Ballyorley holds the possibility that the earthwork is a modified prehistoric barrow.[89] This may find some support in the word *tuaim*, in the townland name Tomnaboley (*Tuaim na Buaile*). The exact meaning of Old Irish *túaim* is uncertain in this context, but it has been given various readings as tumulus, mound, and hillock, which might render the name "tumulus of the milking place" in reference to the adjacent mound in Ballyorley.[90] The earthwork had a special meaning, locally. A folklore record of 1939 notes that a large block of stone referred to as the "Moate Stone" lay at the edge of the earthwork. It was frequented by local men, who each attempted to lift and pitch it in a test of their strength.[91] What the earthwork represented in the Ó Deóradháin settlement is unknown, but it merits consideration as the possible inauguration site of the Mac Murchadha chief, *Cnoc an Bhogha* ("hill of the bow"), which has otherwise been unsatisfactorily speculated as the hill of Knockavocka west of Ballyorley.[92] Spatial relationships between estates of literati and assembly places of Gaelic chiefs find expression elsewhere (2.2).

There are wall-footings of a stone building, 14.6 m by 5.2 m, aligned east–west, on the northern half of the platform of the moated site (Fig. 6.20). The building, which is regarded in local tradition as the Ó Deóradháin school-house, was unscientifically excavated in 1948, during which the line of all four walls, the doorway, and what was described as a "vestry" containing a circular hollow, were uncovered.[93] A quernstone and a jug were among the finds but there is no surviving report on the excavation in 1948, and where the finds were subsequently housed has not been established. A plain Latin cross made of granite is held to have been recovered from the building and re-erected *c*.200 m to the south in a roadside bank, sometime between 1845 and 1848.[94] It is 0.80 m as it now stands, but since the shaft was broken at some point, it must have been longer implying that it was not a roof finial but a self-contained monument with a base. It has been speculatively assigned an eighteenth-century date.[95]

[88] FitzPatrick and Ó Drisceoil, Landscape and law school, 407–9.

[89] FitzPatrick and Ó Drisceoil, Landscape and law school, 389.

[90] Quin, *Dictionary*, 611:335–6.

[91] NFC 0890, 108. National Folklore Collection, University College Dublin. A story collected from local men, Ballyorley and Tomnaboley, Co. Wexford, 1939.

[92] FitzPatrick and Ó Drisceoil, Landscape and law school, 388–9; FitzPatrick, *Royal inauguration*, 25, 227.

[93] FitzPatrick and Ó Drisceoil, Landscape and law school, 394–6.

[94] NFC 0890, 107. National Folklore Collection, University College Dublin. A story collected from a local man, Ballyorley, Co. Wexford, 1939.

[95] Moore, *Archaeological inventory*, 147.

However, the plainness and crudity of the cross do not necessarily confer a modern origin. By comparison with *Crois an Ollamh* ("the *ollamh*'s cross") in the settlement of the Scottish Mac Bethadh physicians of Pennycross, overlooking Loch Scridain in Mull, it can be rehabilitated as a potentially important symbolic feature of the Ó Deóradháin period of occupancy of *An Ghráinseach* at Ballyorley. *Crois an Ollamh* in Pennycross is a plain Latin cross, rough-hewn from Moine granulite. It originally stood at least *c*.1.85 m tall. The shaft is inscribed with the date 1582 and what have been interpreted as the initials of Gille Coluim Mac Bethadh and his son Domnall.[96]

An excavation to recover the plan of the Ballyorley building was conducted in 2009.[97] It confirmed that the 1948 excavation had destroyed the stratigraphy of the site. The shale rubble foundations of the building were clay bonded and *c*.1.2 m thick. Doorway fixtures, including a threshold slab and half of the top-stone of a quern-stone, repurposed as the pivot for a door-hinge, indicated the former entrance at the west end of the south wall. Two internal cross-walls, 0.85 m wide, were found to divide the interior into three rooms. None of the partitions was tied into the long walls of the building; nevertheless, the same clay bonding was used in both the partition and structural walls, suggesting that they may be broadly contemporary. In its final form, the partitions subdivided the building into a centrally placed main room and two very small rooms at the east and west ends, with a shallow recess in the north wall of the western room (Fig. 6.20). An unstratified quernstone fragment recovered in the western room was the only artefact found during the 2009 excavation.

Several interpretations of this complex site have been proposed.[98] However, revision of the collective evidence from the site, for this study, suggests that the Ballyorley building originated either as a chapel or granary of a monastic grange of the Augustinian priory at Ferns and may have been altered to suit the professional needs of the Ó Deóradháin lawyers. In favor of an origin as a granary, the site in its entirety has the profile of an agricultural settlement and a seventeenth-century historical land-use record as arable suited to oats and rye. Moreover, the presence of quernstones in the building at least implies that grain was being ground within its walls, even if the lost stratigraphy of the site has precluded knowing when.

In medieval Ireland, the term "grange" was used to describe an independent out-lying farm of a religious house, inclusive of its land as well as buildings, the purpose of which was to supply the mother-house with processed grain and other agricultural goods. The nearest religious house to the Ó Deóradháin estate was the Augustinian priory of Ferns.[99] In an extent of the monastic lands of Ferns taken in 1541, the

---

[96] Royal Commission on the Ancient and Historical Monuments of Scotland 1980 *Argyll: an inventory of the monuments volume 3: Mull, Tiree, Coll and northern Argyll*, 159–60. Edinburgh.

[97] FitzPatrick and Ó Drisceoil, Landscape and law school, 394–400.

[98] Moore, *Archaeological inventory*, 116–17; FitzPatrick and Ó Drisceoil, Landscape and law school, 400–3.

[99] Gwynn and Hadcock, *Medieval religious houses*, 175–6.

obsolete place name "Ballyntogher," and "Ballyhoury" (also "Ballyhowry"), perhaps a corruption of Ballyorley, are cited as priory lands.[100] Ballyntogher, from the Irish *Baile an Tóchair*, means "place or settlement of the causeway or trackway." A *tóchar* is mentioned in connection with Ballyorley in a description of the "meetes and bounds" of the medieval parish of Kilcormick in 1654–5. The bounds of the parish began "at the Togher [*tóchar*] of Balliorlmore [Ballyorleymore] thence along the river."[101] The geophysical survey located what may be part of that trackway on the southeast side of the site (Fig. 6.20).

The earliest secure historical record connecting the Ó Deóradháin lawyers with Ballyorley and *An Ghráinseach* is for the sixteenth century. Whether the family had been tenants of the Augustinian grange from the thirteenth or fourteenth century or were assigned it in the sixteenth century, following the dissolution of the priory, has not been established.[102] The destruction of the stratigraphy of the building proposed as the school-house means that it cannot be dated more closely than the later medieval period, based on the plan and structure of the walls. However, there are precedents for other kindreds of literati as tenants of granges before the dissolution. A branch of the medical family of Ó Fithcheallaigh occupied a grange of the Cistercian abbey and hospital of Aghmanister (Co. Cork), Corca Laoighdhe, in the lordship of Uí Bhána. Recorded *c.*1496 as "*Granseach Muintere Fithcheallaigh*" ("grange of the people of Ó Fithcheallaigh") by the medical scribe Connla Mac an Leagha, who was there to copy manuscript material for a medical treatise, it is identifiable in the modern landscape as the townlands of Grange Beg and Grange More, south of Aghmanister.[103]

Irrespective of when the Ó Deóradháin lawyers were allocated their estate, the inclusion of a grange was entirely in keeping with the lifeways of Gaelic learned kindreds. It was noted (3.3) that cultivation of land for the production of food was considered an important task of an *ollamh*, with Domhnall Ó Duibhdábhoireann, for instance, swapping the pen for the reaping hook to bring in the harvest.[104] With the Ballyorley building compartmentalized into three discrete spaces, grinding grain would not have been incongruous with the work of the various Ó Deóradháin and Ó Duibhdábhoireann scribes who recorded their place of writing as *An Ghráinseach* in the sixteenth century.

---

[100] N. B. White (ed.) 1943 *Extents of Irish monastic possessions, 1540–41*, 371–2. Dublin. The Stationery Office.

[101] Simington, *Civil survey, Co. Wexford*, 25.

[102] Gwynn and Hadcock, *Medieval religious houses*, 176.

[103] RIA MS 24 B 3, 94; D. Hayden 2019 Attribution and authority in an Irish medical manuscript. *Studia Hibernica* 45, 27, fn 31; Ó Muraíle, The hereditary medical families, 88, 108.

[104] O'Grady, *Catalogue of Irish manuscripts*, i, 128; BL Egerton MS 88 fo. 58.

6.1.3 Ballymacegan and the capital of brehon law

In comments made in the margins of the early fifteenth-century *Leabhar breac* (1.1), the scribe, Murchad Ó Cuindlis, twice cited *Cluain Lethan* ("broad meadow") as his place of writing between 1408 and 1411.[105] To it he attributed the lofty title "Capital of Brehon Law of Ireland" (*"Ardchathair Fénechais Érenn"*), noting that it had been plundered on the feast of St John the Baptist.[106] *Cluain Lethan* was situated in the lordship of Urumhain in north Munster, but Ó Cuindlis described it, as being situated in "Múscraige Tíre," which, by the fifteenth century, was an obsolete political territory. This kind of archaism in references to Gaelic polities is normal in commentaries by learned scribes, who often cited pre-conquest geographies to elevate the status of the places in which they were writing or the patrons whom they served (1.2.1). Before the twelfth century, the landmass of the late medieval lordship of Urumhain, and, it has been argued, the small territory of Mag Ua Farca north of the Little Brosna River (Fig. 6.21), had constituted the kingdom of Múscraige Tíre.[107]

An important point that needs to be made from the outset is that from the mid-sixteenth century, *Leabhar breac* was in the keeping of the Duniry branch of the Mac Aodhagáin kindred in the Connacht lordship of Clann Uilliam Uachtair (Figs 1.1, 1.2), where it became known as *Leabhar mór Dúna Doighre*, in reference to Duniry.[108] The Mac Aodhagáin kindred clearly coveted the book, which has prompted the opinion that their Munster branch, who lived in the River Shannon borderland of the lordship of Urumhain, had been involved in writing it with Ó Cuindlis at *Cluain Lethan*.[109]

Finding *Cluain Lethan* involves, in the first instance, setting out the extent of the estate lands of this branch of the Mac Aodhagáin kindred. Sixteenth-century English administrative documents and land surveys of the mid- to late seventeenth century provide an overview of them, at least in those periods. The estate lands of the kindred were orientated on a chain of hills that extend northeast—southwest between the townlands of Redwood and Portland in the northern tip of the lordship, bounded by the River Shannon, Lough Derg, and the Little Brosna River (Fig. 6.21). They gave topographical unity to the landholdings.

The earliest unequivocal association between a member of the Mac Aodhagáin learned family of brehon lawyers and land in the northern border of the lordship was recorded in the state papers for 1591, at which time the *ollamh* Cairbre Mac Aodhagáin was cited as living at "Bally McEgan" (*Baile Mhic Aodhagáin*), the place name giving

---

[105] RIA MS 23 P 16, 42, 206.

[106] RIA MS 23 P 16, 206; Ó Longáin and Gilbert, *Leabhar breac*, ii, 38.

[107] P. Byrne 2014 The northern boundary of Múscraige Tíre. *Ériu* 64, 112–19.

[108] Royal Irish Academy 1948 *Catalogue of Irish manuscripts in the Royal Irish Academy*. Dublin. Royal Irish Academy.

[109] Ó Concheanainn, Scribe, 65.

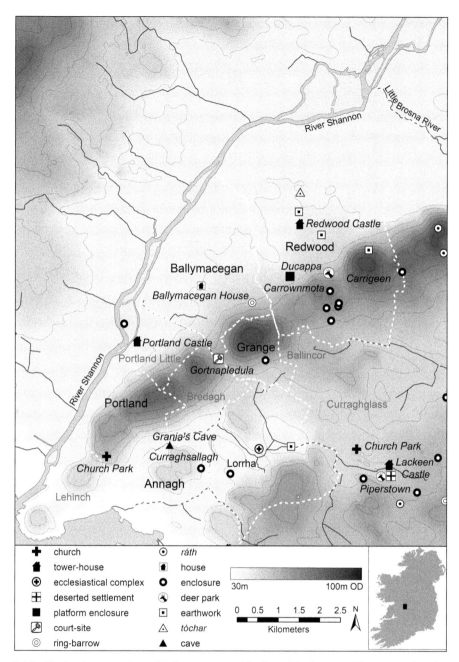

Fig. 6.21. The landscape setting of Ballymacegan and Redwood in the River Shannon and Little Brosna River borderland of Urumhain (map N. McCarthy).

him visibility in the border landscape of the lordship (3.5).[110] Ballymacegan was situated 4 km to the west of Lorrha, an early medieval monastic foundation with Augustinian and Dominican religious houses, where Ó Cuindlis also copied text for the *Leabhar breac* in the early fifteenth century.[111]

Cairbre Mac Aodhagáin's son Donnchadh was slain in 1602 in the vicinity of Redwood, which is represented in the modern landscape by the townland of that name adjoining the east side of Ballymacegan.[112] Redwood Castle became the residence of the family during the late sixteenth century, having been allocated to them by Ó Cinnéide, chief of Urumhain.[113] Cairbre's grandson Cosnamach surrendered his lands to the Crown in April 1611 and was regranted them to hold of the Crown.[114] His estate in 1611 included Carrownmota and Dromod in addition to Ballymacegan. In the modern landscape, Ballymacegan survives as a townland of that name, the boundaries of which have remained unchanged from its seventeenth-century descriptions. Dromod was a parcel of land within the townland of Bredagh. Carrownmota, from the Irish *Ceathramadh an Mhóta* ("quarter of the mound or moat"), also known as Moatfield, was part of Redwood townland and consisted of 64 acres of mostly arable, some meadow, pasture, and shrubby wood. A "thatch house" was noted within it.[115] The Civil Survey of 1654–6 recorded three other land denominations that belonged to members of the family in fee by descent from their ancestors. These included Annagh, Redwood, and Grange, adjoining the southeast boundary of Ballymacegan (Fig. 6.21).[116] Grange, as its name implies, was probably an out-farm of the nearby Augustinian priory at Lorrha. No monastic extents survive for Lorrha and therefore there is no written record of an association between the priory and the denomination of Grange.[117] However, as will be seen, a church building in Portland, south of Grange, is a good candidate for a grange chapel.

The Mac Aodhagáin lawyers had an open-air court site on their estate lands, documented by the Down Survey of the seventeenth-century as "Gornapledula [*sic* Gortnapledula]," It constituted 15 acres of land lying between Bredagh and Grange, the ownership of which, ironically, was described as "in controversie" between members of the Mac Aodhagáin kindred.[118] Gortnapledula is a corruption of the Irish

---

[110]   Hamilton, *Calendar of the state papers*, 426; O'Rahilly, Irish poets, 97.

[111]   T. Bolger, C. Moloney, and C. Troy 2012 Archaeological excavations at Lorrha, Co. Tipperary. *The Journal of Irish Archaeology* 21, 113–37.

[112]   M 1602.14, vi, 2314, 2316.

[113]   Curtis, *Calendar of Ormond deeds*, 244 (Deed 294); Simington, *Civil survey, Co. Tipperary*, ii, 322.

[114]   C. Mac Hale 1990 *Annals of the Clan Egan*, 38. Enniscrone. Conor Mac Hale.

[115]   Simington, *Civil survey, Co. Tipperary*, ii, 316.

[116]   Simington, *Civil survey, Co. Tipperary*, ii, 317, 318, 322.

[117]   Bolger, Moloney, and Troy, Archaeological excavations at Lorrha, 119; Gwynn and Hadcock, *Medieval religious* houses, 185.

[118]   <https://downsurvey.tchpc.tcd.ie/down-survey-maps.php#bm=Lower+Ormond&c=Tipperary> (accessed March 12, 2014).

Gort na Pléadáile ("field of the pleadings"), which refers to the site where the Mac Aodhagáin brehon lawyers listened to pleas and made judgments. Its location as given by the Down Survey is sloping pastureland without any standing archaeology, but which affords panoramic views north over Ballymacegan and Redwood. The nineteenth-century Ordnance Survey marked the court site in the townland of Portland, south of Ballymacegan (Fig. 6.21).[119] However, the venues for brehons' courts tended to be earthwork enclosures, particularly prehistoric barrows as seen in relation to the "Brehon's Chair" in the borderscape of Ballaghmore in the lordship of Osraighe (2.0.1) and *Suidhe Adhamhnáin* in the western bounds of the lordship of Cineál bhFiachach (2.2). About 1 km northeast of Gortnapledula, in the southeast corner of Ballymacegan, there were formerly two ring-barrows, one of which has survived in remarkably well-preserved condition. It is on a north-facing slope and consists of a circular flat-topped mound enclosed by a broad, flat-bottomed fosse cut out of the underlying bedrock. Given the differing opinions about the location of Gortnapledula, it is possible that the Ballymacegan ring-barrow marked the site of the court of the Mac Aodhagáin brehons. Alternatively, there may have been more ring-barrows in this now intensively farmed landscape including the denomination designated Gortnapledula by the Down Survey.

Apart from the ring-barrows, the surviving archaeology of the Mac Aodhagáin estate lands is sparse.[120] There are no upstanding monuments of medieval date in Ballymacegan. In Redwood, there is a tower-house that was accompanied by two thatched houses in the seventeenth century, a routeway running between the tower-house and the River Shannon, and several earthen enclosures, including a raised platform in the subdenomination of Carrownmota (Fig. 6.21).

There is a perception of *Cluain Lethan* as a lost place, somewhere in the vicinity of Ballymacegan and Redwood.[121] Equipped with knowledge of the sizeable block of lands that the Mac Aodhagáin kindred occupied during the sixteenth and seventeenth centuries, two candidates emerge for the fifteenth-century school.

A geographical connection between Redwood and *Cluain Lethan* is implied in a marginal comment in *Leabhar breac*, in which the scribe expressed his relief that he and his companions had not fallen into a cave while passing through Redwood, presumably on their way to or from the law school at *Cluain Lethan*. "God gave protection to us in the night when passing through Coill in Ruad [Redwood], so that we did not go into the cave."[122] This comment implies that *Cluain Lethan* was situated in the

---

[119] Ordnance Survey Ireland 1837 First-edition six-inch map, sheet iv, County Tipperary. Dublin. Ordnance Survey Office.

[120] E. FitzPatrick 2014 The cultural landscape of the Mac Aodhagáin brehons of Ballymacegan and Redwood, Lower Ormond, Co. Tipperary. Report for Clann Mac Aodhagáin.

[121] Ó Longáin and Gilbert, *Leabhar breac*, xvii–xviii; Ó Concheanainn, Scribe, 65; Herbert, Medieval collections, 35; Bolger, Moloney, and Troy, Archaeological excavations at Lorrha, 118.

[122] RIA MS 23 P 16, 184.

Redwood area. No cave has been recorded within the bounds of Redwood townland, but Curraghsallagh ("dirty moor"), an area of marshland and bog southwest of Redwood in the townland of Annagh, contains a natural cave called "Grania's Cave," which is possibly the fearful hole to which the learned of *Cluain Lethan* were alert when journeying to or from the law school in the fifteenth century (Fig. 6.21).

There are two late medieval buildings situated to the south of the known lands of the Mac Aodhagáin lawyers. The first is in "Church Park" in the townland of Curraghglass, south of Redwood. It is on the east side of the monastery of Lorrha and 1 km northwest of the Ó Cinnéide chief's sixteenth-century tower-house at Lackeen and the deserted settlement of Piperstown (Fig. 6.21). The building has an unusual plan, no accompanying graveyard, and no saint association or history as a church. Gleeson suggested that it was a chantry of the Ó Cinnéide chief, attached to his tower-house settlement at Lackeen.[123] It consists of three structures forming a T-plan complex (Fig. 6.22). The main building (8 m × 4.45 m internally) is aligned east–west. There is an ogee-headed single-light window of fifteenth-century date in the east gable, which is the only standing wall. The long walls and the west gable have been reduced to their footings. Two other buildings orientated north–south adjoin the west end of the long walls of the main structure and survive as footings 1 m thick. The plan of the building complex, with rooms extending north and south of the main structure, suggests that it was adapted to another purpose.

The second candidate for *Cluain Lethan* is a late medieval building situated in a meadow, also called "Church Park," in the townland of Portland, southwest of Grange (Figs 6.21, 6.22). Grania's Cave in Annagh is a short distance east of it. There is an

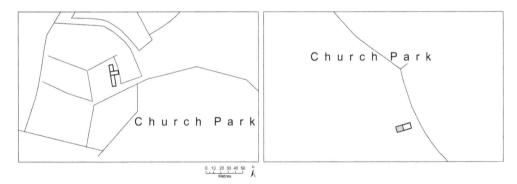

FIG. 6.22. Thumbnail plans of the buildings at Church Park, Curraghglass, and Church Park, Portland (drawing N. McCarthy).

[123] D. F. Gleeson 1951 Churches in the deanery of Ormond: Aradh and Ormond Lower. *North Munster Antiquarian Journal* 6 (3), 103.

extensive view south from Church Park to the Arra Mountains, Devil's Bit Mountain, the Silvermines, and Keeper Hill. Furthermore, Church Park lies towards the south-west end of the chain of hills that distinguished the estate lands of the Mac Aodhagáin lawyers, setting it apart from the residential hub of the family (Fig. 6.21).

The seventeenth-century landownership record for Portland indicates that most of it belonged to the Ó Cinnéide family, who had it in in fee by descent from their "ancestors."[124] The proximity of Grange to Portland and the character of the "Church Park" building suggest that it may have been grange land that the Ó Cinnéide chief acquired in the sixteenth century following the dissolution of the Augustinian priory at Lorrha.

The Church Park building has no name or dedication, there is no known ecclesiastical record for it, and it was never a parish church (Fig. 6.23). There was a graveyard attached to it until *c.*1800 where unbaptized children had been

Fig. 6.23. The building at Church Park, Portland, showing the east gable with ogee-headed window, and the barrel-vaulted west end (photo E. FitzPatrick).

---

[124] Simington, *Civil survey, Co. Tipperary*, ii, 319. The survey mentions Portland Castle, but not the Church Park building.

interred.[125] The suggestion has been made that Church Park was a chantry maintained by the Mac Aodhagáin lawyers, since their estate was situated nearby, but there is no evidence to support that function.[126] The anonymity of the building and its proximity to Grange intimates that either it was a grange chapel adapted for use as the Mac Aodhagáin law school or that it was constructed from the outset as a law school on grange land of Lorrha, at the beginning of the fifteenth century. An affiliation between *Cluain Lethan* and the monastery of Lorrha is supported by the content of the *Leabhar breac*, which is mainly ecclesiastical and hagiographical literature, suggesting that it was compiled for a religious community.[127] Interpretation of the architecture of the Church Park building in Portland is compromised by the fact that the long walls and west end were largely rebuilt and that some of the architectural features were replaced in the modern period. It is 15.9 m in length externally, 8.35 m wide at the east gable, and 9.1 m across the west gable, the greater width being attributable to a base batter (projecting *c*.0. 35 m from the wall-face), which supports a barrel-vaulted west-end chamber occupying 7.4 m of the overall length of the building. The long walls were rebuilt but the east gable, which has a wall thickness of 1.25 m, stands to its original height. It appears to be the only part of the building that was not heavily reconstructed (Fig. 6.23). The original punch-dressed quoins of the gable are in situ and it has a centrally placed single-light ogee-headed window of fifteenth-century type, with decorative spandrels. The window embrasure, with its round head and soffit constructed of finely cut and punch-dressed stone, is work datable to the sixteenth century.

A reproduction doorway leads into the building through the south wall, close to its junction with the barrel-vaulted chamber. The form of the doorway (if a faithful copy of the original), with its semi-pointed arch and pointed stops, belongs to the fifteenth century. The cross-wall separating the main body of the building from the vaulted ground floor has been rebuilt. It contains a cut-stone, semi-pointed doorway, with chamfered jambs and pointed stops. It is flanked on its immediate north and south sides by two narrow lights. These and the doorway itself are the only sources of light for the otherwise cavernous, vaulted ground floor. Nothing of the upper floor, which the vault and its battered walls supported, has survived (Fig. 6.23).

The understanding that emerges from this attempt to identify *Cluain Lethan* is that there are two late medieval buildings without saint associations or histories as churches, in Curraghglass and Portland, in the vicinity of the estate lands of the Mac Aodhagáin lawyers as they were known in the sixteenth and seventeenth centuries. They are both apart from the main medieval settlement nodes, in relatively isolated settings. However,

---

[125] Gleeson, Churches in the deanery of Ormond, 105.
[126] Gleeson, Churches in the deanery of Ormond, 106.
[127] Ó Concheanainn, Scribe, 65; W. Follett 2013–14 Religious texts in the Mac Aodhagáin library of Lower Ormond. *Peritia* 24–5, 216–21.

there are several aspects of Church Park in Portland that favor it over Church Park in Curraghglass as the locus of the *Cluain Lethan* law school. The former is situated towards the end of the chain of hills that formed the spine of the Mac Aodhagáin estate lands and just west of Grania's Cave; the substantial two-story west-end quarters of the structure conforms to the late medieval accommodations made elsewhere for learned incumbents of parish churches and sinecure chapels; and the proximity of the townland of Grange to it, connotes a grange building adapted for use as a school or constructed anew in the fifteenth century as a school on grange land. The Mac Aodhagáin kindred of this region of north Munster were secular. There is no evidence to confirm an ecclesiastical role for them, but that would not have precluded their tenancy or proprietorship of grange land.

The record of the collection of manuscripts in the possession of the Mac Aodhagáin lawyers of Ballymacegan and Redwood in the seventeenth century entails the continuance of their school in some capacity, from its earliest reference as the "capital of Brehon law of Ireland" in the early fifteenth century. There are records of the chronicler Ó Cléirigh consulting material at Ballymacegan in 1628–9, and the historian Mac Fhirbhisigh of Lackan transcribed manuscripts there in 1643.[128]

The historical profile of the family as practitioners of law for the Ó Cinnéide chief of Lackeen was foremost in the sixteenth and seventeenth centuries. The presence of the court site, *Gort na Pléadáile*, on their lands, lends credence to that view. The reason why their role as legal practitioners apparently dominated that of academic lawyers in the early modern period can be related to the role of Lackeen tower-house in the sixteenth century, which was intended to increase the visibility of the Ó Cinnéide chief and that of his court in the northern borderland of the lordship (Fig. 6.21). Lackeen possessed some of the lands of the dissolved monastery at Lorrha in the seventeenth century and perhaps, therefore, from the period of the Dissolution.[129] Members of Ó Cinnéide's court resided near the tower-house, a practice already noted in relation to the poets who served the Mac Cárthaigh Mór chief of Iar Mhumhain in the sixteenth century, at Pallis, Co. Kerry (4.3). The deserted settlement of Piperstown, from the Irish *Baile an Phíopaire* ("landholding or settlement of the piper"), the place "in which lived the retainers and minstrels of Lackeen Castle," extended over a large field south of the tower-house (Fig. 6.21) and was recorded in 1709 as "Gortnepipery," from the Irish *Gort an Phíopaire* ("field of the piper").[130] The role of the Mac Aodhagáin lawyers as providers of law services to the chief's household secured their continued status in this borderscape of Urumhain and increased their professional prestige in the sixteenth century.

---

[128] Cunningham, *Annals of the Four Masters*, 255.   [129] Simington, *Civil survey, Co. Tipperary*, ii, 315.
[130] <https://www.logainm.ie/en/46010?s=Abbeville> (accessed March 12, 2017); The piper's field was incorporated into the demesne of Abbeville House and transformed into a deer park between the seventeenth and nineteenth centuries.

6.2 A SCHOOL OF MEDICINE

The dissolution of religious houses *c.*1540 provided an opportunity for members of the learned class to acquire appropriate space to conduct schools, especially in circumstances where the lands of dissolved houses had been acquired by the ruling families they served. This is suggested in the case of the Ó Conchubhair physicians, who lived on lands of the Augustinian priory of Aghmacart, in the lordship of the Mac Giolla Phádraig, chief of Osraighe (Figs 1.1, 1.2). The Ó Conchubhair medical kindred conducted a school on their estate in the sixteenth century. They had a school-house, which is attested in a remark made by Risteard Ó Conchubhair in 1590 while he was transcribing a copy of the medical text *Liber pronosticorum*: "in the company of my master and kinsman in the school-house [*a ttech na sgoili*] in Aghmacart on the 6th day of March. And upon my word, I am thirsty and hungry. 1590."[131]

Aghmacart school-house was integral to a remarkable exchange in the late sixteenth century between the hereditary physicians of Ossory, Connacht, and western Scotland. Donnchadh Ó Conchubhair, known as Donnchadh Albanach, physician to the MacDougalls of Dunollie in Argyll, spent some of the period from St Patrick's Day 1596 until 30 May 1600 in the school-house, transcribing the medieval medical text known as *Practica seu lilium medicine* (1305) by the French physician Bernard of Gordon.[132] The other Scottish figure in this network was John Mac Bethadh, *an t-Ollamh Ileach*, of Ballinaby, Islay. In the 1560s, Mac Bethadh appears to have made a circuit of the Gaelic hereditary medical schools in Connacht, commissioning various medical manuscripts from the Ó Ceandamháin physicians in Iarchonnacht (3.3.1) among other long-standing medical practitioners in the west of Ireland.[133] The centrality of the Aghmacart school-house to early modern medical knowledge exchanges, accords it an important status.

The remains of Aghmacart priory consist of the east gable end of the church and a south transept that was converted for use as the parish church (Fig. 6.24). A former chapel or sacristy was aligned north–south at the east end of the south long wall. A residential tower for the canons, which collapsed *c.*1850, stood at the west end, adjoining the south transept, a view of which was presented by Newton in his drawing of the building complex in 1793 (Fig. 6.25).[134] The priory was suppressed in 1540. A monastic extent of it taken in 1541 did not state to whom it had been disposed, remarking only that there were no "superfluous buildings," with all those still standing "necessary for the farmer," including a watermill on the River Goul that formed the southern boundary of the monastic settlement. The parish church was acknowledged, and the lands of the priory were accounted for as 22 acres of arable, one acre of wood, and another of moor.[135] The chief of Osraighe, Sir Barnaby FitzPatrick, is recorded in

---

[131] Nic Dhonnchadha, Medical school of Aghmacart, 13–14.
[132] Nic Dhonnchadha, Medical school of Aghmacart, 30–1.
[133] Bannerman, *The Beatons*, 116–17.
[134] Carrigan, *History and antiquities of the diocese of Ossory*, ii, 238.
[135] White, *Extents of Irish monastic possessions*, 333.

FIG. 6.24. The eighteenth-century rebuilt parish church, the early modern mausoleum of the Mac Giolla Phádraig family, and east gable of the Augustinian priory church at Aghmacart (photo E. FitzPatrick).

FIG. 6.25. Newton's north view of Aghmacart Abbey, 1793, with Aghmacart tower-house in left background (courtesy of the National Library of Ireland).

1574 as holding a lease from the Crown "of the site of the monastery...the lands of Agmacarte and the tithe corn of the rectory of Agmacartye."[136]

The allocation of an estate at Aghmacart to the Ó Conchubhair physicians may have coincided with the successful appropriation of the Augustinian priory foundation and its lands by the ruling family of Osraighe between 1540 and 1574. As noted (4.5), Aghmacart tower-house became the residence of the Ó Conchubhair *ollamh* in medicine and appears to have been on grange land (Fig. 4.22).[137]

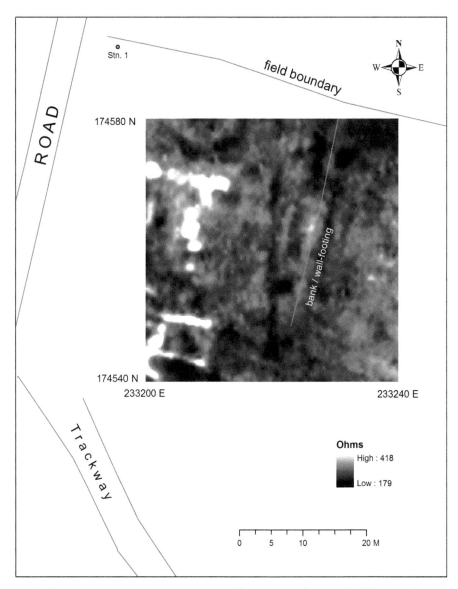

FIG. 6.26. Electrical-resistance survey, showing wall foundations of putative buildings, "infirmary field," Aghmacart (image J. Fenwick).

[136] Carrigan, *History and antiquities of the diocese of Ossory*, ii, 237.
[137] Carrigan, *History and antiquities of the diocese of Ossory*, ii, 239.

The exact location of the Ó Conchubhair school-house is, as yet, unknown, but with priory buildings at his disposal, the *ollamh* is likely to have adapted an existing building to that purpose rather than erecting a new one. At the beginning of the twentieth century a local tradition abided that there had been an infirmary attached to the priory and that its site could be identified as the "infirmary field" *c.*200 m north of the tower-house. It was noted that "in very dry summers, the foundations of houses may be distinctly traced here, beneath the surface."[138] An electrical-resistance survey was conducted, for this study, in the "infirmary field," based on the premise that the Ó Conchubhair physicians may have re-used a priory building for their medical practices and manuscript production. The survey confirmed the presence of foundations of at least two buildings lying within a walled garth, which lends some credence to the tradition that the infirmary of the priory had been in that field (Fig. 6.26).[139] The setting of the site on the northeastern edge of the priory settlement strengthens that case and the prospect that the Augustinian infirmary was repurposed as the school-house of the Ó Conchubhair medical kindred in the sixteenth century.

6.3 SCHOOLS OF POETRY

The work of secular professional poets and their training in the art of *filidheacht* was different from that of other branches of the literati. Therefore, it is to be expected that their needs were reflected in the environments in which they worked. An anonymous seventeenth-century poem "I am alone among men" ("*Aonar dhamhsa eidir dhaoinibh*"), which laments an emptied school, recalls the "three forges" in which the poet learned his art. They are described as the "house of memorizing" ("*teach meabhraighthe*"); the "house of reclining or composition" ("*teach luighe*"); and the "house of the critic" ("*teach breithimh*").[140] The poet refers to the first house as a place of collective activity where young poets gathered to recite what they had learnt. In contrast, he describes the second house as "*dánbhoth*," a poetic hut or cell that appears to have been for individual use, to prevent distraction or "beguilement" while composing. The third house was given to the examination of students' compositions.[141] There is some ambiguity as to whether the poem is alluding purely

---

[138] Carrigan, *History and antiquities of the diocese of Ossory*, ii, 239.

[139] J. Fenwick and E. FitzPatrick 2010 A report on the geophysical survey at the possible site of the Uí Chonchubhair medical school at Aghmacart, Cullahill, Co. Laois. Consent no. 10R44. School of Geography and Archaeology, National University of Ireland Galway.

[140] Bergin, *Irish bardic poetry*, 159–60, 286; D. McManus 2004 The bardic poet as teacher, student and critic: a context for the grammatical tracts. In C. G. Ó Háinle and D. E. Meek (eds), *Unity in diversity: studies in Irish and Scottish Gaelic language, literature and history*, 102–3. Trinity College Dublin.

[141] Bergin, *Irish bardic poetry*, 159–60, 282.

to the structure and process of learning *filidheacht* or to the buildings in which it happened, or to both. Nevertheless, the three defined activities of reciting, composing, and being examined predicate different environments, especially in relation to the first two.

The dark hut as the place of poetic composition is reflected in the writings of poets in the fifteenth and sixteenth centuries. Tadhg Óg Ó hUiginn (d. 1448), in his elegy on "The breaking up of a school" ("*Anocht sgaoilid na sgola*"), refers to the "mystic hut of poesy" ("*a bhoth fholamhsa*") where his brother and teacher, Fearghal Ruadh, trained him in the art of poetry. With the school ending, Tadhg regretted "the huts I might dwell in abide not" ("*ní mharad na botha a mbeinn*"), implying that they were temporary structures, taken down after use.[142] That the "hut of poesy" was a dark space, a small windowless shelter, is, according to Bergin, intimated by the poet's use of a metaphor from falconry—young hawks, like students of poetry, began their training in darkness.[143] This method of learning how to compose is also referred to in "This is comfortable" ("*Cuimseach sin*"), a sixteenth-century poem by Fear Flatha Ó Gnímh (fl. 1556), in which he chided a fellow poet for composing in the open air. The poet was adamant that "without a dark hut, without hardship" ("*gan boith ndiamhoir, gan deacoir*"), no art could be created. For him, the uninviting environment of darkness and austerity, not "a view of mountains" or an "airy prospect," was required for composition.[144] However, the fact that Ó Gnímh chastized his fellow poet for composing outdoors, implies that it was practiced by some. As earlier observed, the fourteenth-century poet Gofraidh Fionn Ó Dálaigh, by his own admission, composed his poem on the use of grammar, while reclining in an enclosed space ("*ón lios i luighim*"). As suggested (4.1), the *lios* concerned was perhaps Claragh hillfort that overlooked the poet's estate.[145] The implied use of the landscape, including monuments of the past, as a place of poetic inspiration, means that practices probably varied between schools of poets and over the long period from the fourteenth to the seventeenth century. Consequently, darkened huts may not have been a consistent aspect of their built environment.

The earlier-noted place name *Botha Muintire Fialáin* (Boho) in the lordship of Fir Mhanach (3.1), which references huts associated with the Ó Fialáin *ollamh* in poetry in the fifteenth century, strengthens the case for their use beyond poetic allusion.[146] Speculatively, the *ollamh*'s *botha* may have been circular drystone constructions, like the so-called "school-house" cell on Inishmurray Island (5.1). However, huts made of more ephemeral materials, such as the windowless and chimneyless post-and-wattle

---

[142] Bergin, *Irish bardic poetry*, 149, 150, 281, 282.
[143] Bergin, *Irish bardic poetry*, 7n., 281.   [144] Bergin *Irish bardic poetry*, 118, 265.
[145] McKenna, A poem by Gofraidh Fionn, 66–76.   [146] U 1498, iii, 426, 427.

cretach, usually of oval or circular plan and covered with scraws and rushes, and the still more basic beehive huts that feature on early modern English maps of Ireland, merit more consideration.[147] The idea of temporary structures renewed as required at the sites of poetic schools is not without precedent. Gaelic society was proficient in transitory living spaces, eloquently described by Nicholls as "erected with facility and abandoned without regret."[148] That versatility extended to "sleeping booths" ("*loingthighe leabtha*") and "peaked hostels" ("*bruighean corr*"), poetically recorded by Gofraidh Fionn Ó Dálaigh as the dwellings provided to the learned groups attending the Christmas feast of the chief of Uí Mhaine, in 1351 (4.3).[149]

There are some antiquarian accounts from the eighteenth and nineteenth centuries of the Gaelic poetic environment. One by the Scottish antiquary Martin Martin was based on vestiges of bardic cultural practice in the Outer Hebrides, which he recorded in 1703. The endurance of the bardic tradition there is attested as late as 1748 when a poet of the Mac Mhuirich learned kindred was recorded as serving Clanranald from his estate on South Uist (1.4).[150] Martin noted the "very singular" way in which poets typically composed in a "dark cell," shutting their doors and windows for an entire day, lying on their backs "with a stone upon their belly, and plads about their heads, and their eyes being cover'd they pump their brains for rhetorical encomium or panegyrick."[151]

In 1722 Thomas O'Sullevane published a description of a "poetical seminary," claiming knowledge of the local environment and buildings where Gaelic schools of poetry had been conducted. It has been suggested that his motivation for doing so was to try to achieve a framework for scholars to understand the practices of Gaelic lawyers and poets, while traces of the tradition remained.[152]

O'Sullevane outlined the setting:

Concerning the poetical seminary, or school…It was likewise necessary the place should be in the solitary recess of a garden, or within a sept or inclosure, far out of reach of any noise, which an intercourse of kindred might otherwise occasion.[153]

According to him, the school was convened in one building:

---

[147] J. H. Andrews 2004 The mapping of Ireland's cultural landscape, 1550–1630. In Duffy, Edwards, and FitzPatrick, *Gaelic Ireland*, 166–7.

[148] Nicholls, Gaelic society and economy, 403.

[149] Knott, Filidh Éreann, 56, 57.

[150] Dodgshon, *From chiefs to landlords*, 89.

[151] M. Martin 1703 *A description of the Western Islands of Scotland*, 116. London. Andrew Bell.

[152] E. Darcy 2021 "The footsteps of that custom…still remaining": medieval memory culture and Thomas O'Sullevane's portrayal of the Irish bardic tradition. *PRIA* 122C, 14.

[153] T. O'Sullevane, 1722 Dissertation. In U. de Burgh, *Memoirs of the Right Honourable the Marquis of Clanricarde, Lord Deputy General of Ireland,* clix. London. James Woodman.

a snug, low hut, and beds in it at convenient distances, each within a small apartment, without much furniture of any kind, save only a table, some seats, and a conveniency for cloaths to hang upon. No windows to let in the day, not any light at all us'd but that of candles, and these brought in at a proper season only.

Furthermore, he claimed that the students worked alone on their poems:

by himself upon his own bed, the whole next day in the dark, till at a certain hour in the night, lights been brought in they committed it to writing. Being afterwards dress'd and come together into a large room, where the masters waited, each scholar gave in his performance.[154]

O'Sullevane did not cite the sources from which he compiled his description. One school of thought suggests that he was a less than reliable authority on Irish matters.[155] Yet, the educational routine and conditions that he relates are believed by others to be "supported by the evidence of poetry,"[156] with the practice of excluding external distractions well founded elsewhere in medieval Europe in both recitation and composition.[157] That may be so, but he conflated the locus of composition and examination into a single, windowless, and compartmentalized building, whereas the impression from the poetry, cited above, is that composing happened in multiple individual huts.

Hyde's late nineteenth-century romanticized description of a bardic school may have been influenced by O'Sullevane's. The details differ somewhat, and his source is unattributed:

Very extraordinary these quarters were; for the college usually consisted of a long low group of whitewashed buildings, excessively warmly thatched, and lying in the hollow of some secluded valley, or shut in by a sheltering wood, far removed from noise of human traffic and from the bustle of the great world. But what most struck the curious beholder was the entire absence of windows or partitions over the greater portion of the house.[158]

The group activity of recitation would have required a building capable of accommodating the school at large, "a trysting-place for youthful companies," as noted in the seventeenth-century poem "I am alone among men."[159] The existence of such a building is intimated by Aenghus Ó Dálaigh (d. 1617) in *Tribes of Ireland*, in which

---

[154] O'Sullevane, Dissertation, clix.

[155] D. Ó Murchadha 1982 Is the O'Neill–MacCarthy letter of 1317 a forgery? *Irish Historical Studies* 23 (89), 66. Ó Murchadha points out that O'Sullevane forged at least one document and gave false information about the location of Irish manuscripts in Germany.

[156] McManus, The bardic poet, 121. Trinity College Dublin.

[157] Darcy, The footsteps of that custom, 19.

[158] D. Hyde 1899 *A literary history of Ireland: from earliest times to the present day*, 529. London. Fisher Unwin.

[159] Bergin, *Irish bardic poetry*, 159, 286.

he praises the house of his kinsman at Finavarra (Co. Clare), in the borderland between the lordships of Boireann and Uí Fiachrach Aidhne (Fig. 1.4): "The house of Ó Dálaigh, great its wealth, bestowing without folly at a white house [*brogh bán*]; It were a sufficiently loud organ to hear his pupils, reciting the melodies of the ancient schools."[160] There are no standing remains of this late medieval building at Finavarra.

It was earlier observed (2.1.2) that there is a building dedicated to St Mac Creiche at Ballynoe on the estate of the Mac Bruaideadha poet-historians of Slieve Callan. The wall foundations indicate that it was relatively small, *c*.9.5 m by *c*.4.5 m internally. There are no visible architectural features to help to date it, but the wall thickness (*c*.0.8 m) suggests that it is a late medieval construction. It has a similar footprint to St Bairrfhionn's at Kilbarron (10.3 m × 4.9 m) in Tír Conaill, where the unusual layout of the building intimates that it was constructed primarily to serve the learned occupations of the Ó Cléirigh *ollamh* and his school (5.2.2). St Mac Creiche's has been linked with a reference in a high-medieval *Life* of the saint, to a hermitage marked out by four stones, between *Formaoil* and the River Inagh in the landscape of Slieve Callan, to which he is reputed to have made a Lenten retreat.[161] This image of a place of reclusion, perhaps more so than its saint association, may have made it a suitable environment for poetic composition and for a building to facilitate the intellectual life of the Mac Bruaideadha poets and visiting *ollamhain* to *Formaoil* on their Slieve Callan lands (2.3).

It should be noted too that there is a building referred to as "Ballydaly Church" on the estate of the Ó Dálaigh poets in the borderland between Iar Mhumhain and Dúthaigh Ealla (2.3), which is now represented by a featureless drystone rectangular structure derived from the original building that stood there. Ballynoe, Kilbarron, and Ballydaly have, in common, a certain ambiguity about their sole designation as ecclesiastical buildings, which is compounded by the absence of formal graveyards. However, there are later burial grounds for unbaptized children associated with each of them. Interments in child burial grounds in Ireland occurred at deserted sites in borderland settings, and appear to belong mostly to the post-medieval period, with the earliest historically attested evidence for the practice emanating from Counter-Reformation policy of the seventeenth century.[162]

6.3.1 The Ó Dálaigh school of poetry at Dromnea

The survival of standing building fabric of late medieval secular schools of poetry is poor, but as a counterpoint to the poetic allusions to the spaces in which poets recited

---

[160] O'Donovan, *Tribes and customs*, 82, 83; MacCotter, *Medieval Ireland*, 144, 196.

[161] C. Plummer (ed.) 1925 *Miscellanea hagiographica Hibernica*, 13, 53. Subsidia Hagiographica 15. Brussels. Société des Bollandistes; McInerney, Lettermoylan of Clann Bhruaideadha, 85–6.

[162] Murphy, Children's burial grounds in Ireland, 410–11.

and composed, and to the unattributed modern accounts of O'Sullevane and Hyde, there is a nineteenth-century description for and fragmentary remains of a former late medieval building at Dromnea, on the south side of Sheepshead Peninsula, ascribed in local tradition of the nineteenth century to the Ó Dálaigh poets of Muinter Bháire (Fig. 6.27).[163]

The place name, Dromnea, has been officially rendered *Drom an Fhéich* ("hill of the debt"), but it had an earlier reading as *Drom an Fheadha* ("hill of the wood").[164] The hill has a distinctive profile, presenting the appearance of an island in the bay (Fig. 6.28). It rises to a height of 58 m OD and gradually declines southwest to the aptly named *Formaoil* where the sandstone bedrock is laid bare above Dunmanus Bay (2.3; Figs 6.27, 6.28).[165] The view south is dominated by Mount Gabriel on the Mizen Peninsula. In keeping with the generally prehistoric megalithic archaeology of hills classified as *formaoil*, there was a stone row consisting of an east-west alignment of three standing stones, one of which stood "16 feet high and about 6 foot broad" on the north side of the hill.[166] The scale of the monument recalls the stone row on the estate of the Mac Bethadh physicians at Ballinaby in the Rhinns of Islay (Fig. 7.1). Recorded by Pennant in 1772, it consisted of three stones, two of which remain in place, the tallest standing *c.* 5 m (16 ft).[167]

The archaeology of Dromnea includes a large *ráth* recorded as "LisDromnea," and a spring emanating from a cliff face, locally known as *Tobar na nDuanairidhe* ("well of the poets").[168] The remains of a building, much discussed as an "old college" during the progress of the first Ordnance Survey of Co. Cork in 1845, lie at the southwest end of a flat-bottomed valley on the north side of Dromnea. At the time of the first Ordnance Survey of the peninsula (1842), the sheltered valley contained a clachan, an informally arranged cluster of farmhouses and associated outbuildings and small infields that had colonized the site. Most of the clachan buildings were knocked down, modernized, or replaced over time. Clachans and dispersed farms typified the rural settlement pattern of the peninsula in the second half of the eighteenth century and during the nineteenth.[169] On the higher ground to the south of the valley, there is a separate group of four stone buildings. A survey of them in 2010 suggested that

[163] FitzPatrick, Landscape and settlements of the Uí Dhálaigh poets, 460–80.

[164] O'Donovan, *Tribes and customs*, 12; <https://www.logainm.ie/en/8594?s=Dromnea> (accessed March 21, 2022).

[165] Tierney, Dromnea bardic school, 9.

[166] Ordnance Survey memorandums for Co. Cork, ii, 457–8. First recorded by J. Beirne for the Ordnance Survey in 1845, there is now no trace of this monument; FitzPatrick, Landscape and settlements of the Uí Dhálaigh poets, 466.

[167] T. Pennant, 1776 *A Tour in Scotland MDCCLXXII*, ii, 224. 2nd edition. London. Benjamin White.

[168] Ordnance Survey memorandums for Co. Cork, ii, 457–8; B. O'Donoghue 1986 *Parish histories and placenames of west Cork*, 62. Cork.

[169] K. Hourihan 1991 Rural settlement and change near Bantry 1600–1846. *Bantry Historical and Archaeological Society* 1, 47, 50–1.

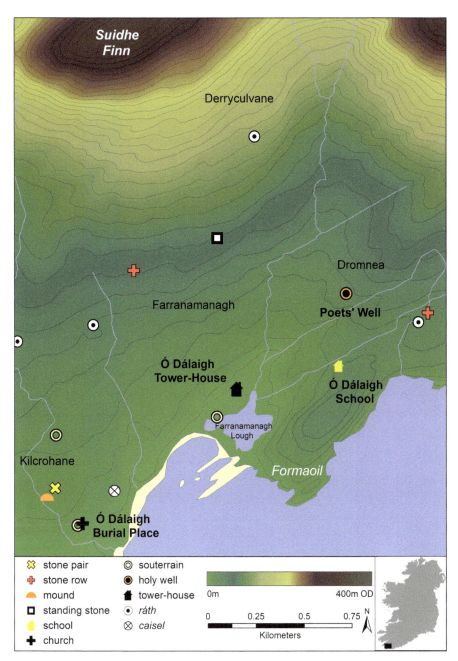

FIG. 6.27. The local landscape of the Ó Dálaigh school building and tower-house, Dromnea and Farranamanagh (map N. McCarthy).

FIG. 6.28. The western profile of Dromnea indicates that the hill in its entirety can be classed as a *formaoil* (photo Cillian Irish).

they merited further consideration as structures related to the Ó Dálaigh school.[170] However, on further investigation it became clear that this tight cluster and its adjoining field walls fit the profile of the clachan and dispersed farming settlements of the southern side of the Sheepshead Peninsula. The overall settlement evidence, combined with an analysis of the local environment, point to the valley on the north side of Dromnea as the central focus of the Ó Dálaigh school, but whether it had more than one building is unknown.

The valley is *c.*6 m deep where it closes at its northeast end. It broadens as it declines on its southwest route to the east shore of Farranamanagh Lough (Fig. 6.29). The lough is a small and shallow sedimentary lagoon, separated from the sea by a natural curved barrier of cobble. The stump of the modest tower-house residence of the Ó Dálaigh family is situated on the north shore.[171] Freshwater streams enter the lagoon from the north side. The brackish water of this special environment hosts a range of edible species that can tolerate salinity—eel, common goby, shore crab,

[170] FitzPatrick, Landscape and settlements of the Uí Dhálaigh poets, 471–2.
[171] Healy, *Castles of Co. Cork*, 200–1.

FIG. 6.29. The valley setting of the Dromnea school building, descending west to the tower-house and Farranamanagh Lough (photo Cillian Irish).

and brown shrimp.[172] It would have been an important and convenient food source in the immediate landscape of the tower-house and school.

The building on the valley floor recorded by the first Ordnance Survey of 1845 was sketched and described by Beirne in April of that year (Fig. 6.30):

> In the townland of Dromnea there stands the remains of an ancient edifice now incorporated within the dwelling house of George Nicholson [*recte* Nicholas] and said to be the remains of an old college. The northern side wall is about 10 feet [3.5 m] high and 25 feet [7.62 m] long in which there is a small window similar to one in the western end of Kilcrohan[e] old church. This ruin is evidently one of considerable antiquity, although I could not obtain any information from the gentry of this part of the country respecting it, except its being called by the peasantry "the old college".[173]

O'Donovan understood "old college" to mean a Gaelic school because he had already encountered traditions relating to those of other learned kindreds in counties Galway

---

[172] National Parks and Wildlife Service 2018 *Conservation objectives: Farranamanagh Lough (SAC 002189)*. Dublin. Department of Culture, Heritage and the Gaeltacht.

[173] Ordnance Survey memorandums, ii, 455–6.

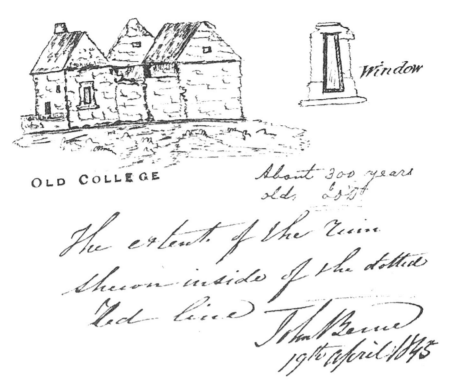

FIG. 6.30. In Beirne's sketch he remarked that the "old college" at Dromnea was "about 300 years old." He used a broken line to indicate "the extent of the ruin," which includes the north wall and a single-light window incorporated into farm buildings (Ordnance Survey memorandums, 1845).

and Clare. Commenting on Beirne's findings, he advised how the building should be documented on the Ordnance Survey map:

> Now, from the names which the peasantry give the ruins of the houses of the MacEgans [Mac Aodhagáin] of Galway and O'Dalys [Ó Dálaigh] of Corcomroe or Burren in Clare, I am inclined to believe that this is the ruin of O'Daly's house. Whatever name was applied to MacEgan's house at Duniry, Co. Galway might be safely used here.[174]

Dromnea was subsequently classified as a "bardic seminary."[175]

Commenting further in 1852, O'Donovan wrote:

> The "Old College House" still remains and forms the residence of a farmer, Mr. George Nicholas. The walls are well built, and cemented with lime and mortar, and from fragments

---

[174] Ordnance Survey memorandums, 458, 463.
[175] Ordnance Survey Ireland 1845 First-edition six-inch sheet, cxxxviii, County Cork. Dublin. Ordnance Survey Office.

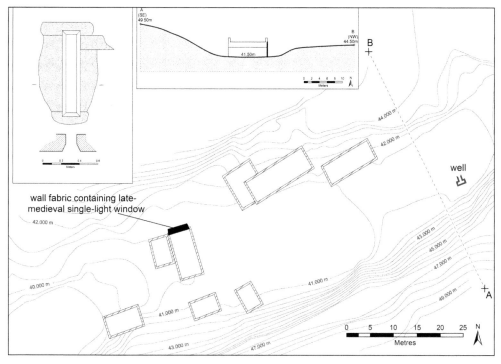

FIG. 6.31. Plan of the farm buildings in the valley at Dromnea showing the remains of the late medieval fabric of the "old college" and the domestic well (drawing C. Bruton and N. McCarthy).

of ruins still to be seen close to what remains, it may be inferred that it was once a house of some importance.[176]

He seems to imply that the school building was more extensive, but as he did not visit the site, Beirne's report and sketch of 1845 must be deemed the most reliable account of what remained in the nineteenth century.

What stands there now is considerably smaller than the structure recorded by Beirne (Fig. 6.31). A short length of the north wall contains a, clearly, reset single-light window, chamfered and punch dressed in a typical late medieval style.[177] There are other settlement features too. A long-abandoned spring well is situated towards the southern side of the valley floor (Fig. 6.31). The well chamber was hollowed out from the natural rock, topped with drystone walling, and roofed using large slabs in the ancient, corbelled style. The age of the well structure is difficult to determine (5.1), but both the school and the clachan that succeeded it would have needed a fresh water supply. The presence of springs must have been among the reasons why the valley floor was chosen for the school.

---

[176] O'Donovan, *Tribes and customs*, 12.
[177] Confirmed during a building inspection by the author, March 2010.

It may be concluded that the settlement of the Ó Dálaigh poets at Dromnea formed a discrete landscape carefully laid out to take advantage of the local topography and resources—the sequestered valley facilitating poetic endeavor and the lagoon serving as both a natural fishpond and a protective barrier from the sea for the kindred's tower-house. The standing remains of the "old college" building are insufficient to be certain that the structure was originally large enough to house a school of poets, or to assign it a precise function in the scheme of learning *filidheacht*, but viewed in its setting and against both the nineteenth-century tradition and the Ordnance Survey record of the structure, it has a justifiable claim to be the locus of the Ó Dálaigh school.

6.4 CONCLUSIONS

The terms *sgoilteagh* and *tigh na scoile*, as used by secular learned men who documented their places of writing in Gaelic schools of law and medicine during the sixteenth century, signified discrete buildings that were designated school-houses. A finding of the field-based inquiry is that purpose-built school buildings of the late medieval period, such as *Teach Breac* and Dromnea, may have been relatively uncommon among learned kindreds, with opportunistic re-use of granges and buildings of dissolved religious houses perhaps more the norm. However, this perspective must be tempered by the poor survival, and in some cases, absence, of standing building fabric for several former school-houses, among them Aghmacart medical school, Park law-school, and the Ardkyle school of *seanchas*, all of which played such key roles in knowledge exchanges between literati. Targeted archaeological excavation has the potential to inform the current picture.

There was a long tradition in other cultures of making use of almost any building for the purpose of schooling, from the halls of private homes to the chambers of gatehouses and former hospitals.[178] Irish literati appear to have been advantaged with access to grange land as well as buildings of dissolved religious houses. It has been argued that a favorable candidate for the renowned law school of *Cluain Lethan*, which existed at the time of the composition of the *Leabhar Breac* (1408–11), is a solitary building with no attached graveyard in Church Park at Portland, south of the core estate lands of the Mac Aodhagáin brehon lawyers of Ballymacegan and Redwood. Like so many of the church spaces at the disposal of learned *comharbai*, *airchinnigh*, and secular proprietors of church land, the building at Church Park has an ambiguous identity which is compounded by the fact that the branch of the Mac Aodhagáin lawyers in the lordship of Urumhain are not known to have held church offices. *Cluain Lethan*, alias Church Park, perhaps originated as a grange chapel, or a schoolhouse modeled on a chapel and built on grange land in the early fifteenth century.

---

[178] Orme, *Medieval schools*, 136–7.

Unequivocal occupation of a grange in the sixteenth century has been shown in respect of the Ó Deóradháin lawyers in the lordship of Uí Cheinnsealaigh. Along with members of the Ó Duibhdábhoireann legal kindred, they identified themselves as writing on their estate at *An Ghráinseach*, in Ballyorley. It has been argued that *An Ghráinseach* was an agricultural settlement of a monastic grange of the Augustinian priory at Ferns, containing a granary on a moated site platform, repurposed wholly or in part as the school-house of the Ó Deóradháin *ollamh* and perhaps distinguished by the plain Latin cross reputed to have been recovered from the site in the nineteenth century. *An Ghráinseach* was integral to a complex settlement that included a large earthwork, tentatively identified in this study as a candidate for the Uí Cheinnsealaigh inauguration site, *Cnoc an Bhogha*.

Grange land of the Augustinian priory of Aghmacart appears to have been allocated to the Ó Conchubhair physicians as their estate, sometime between 1540 and 1574 when the chief of Osraighe, who had benefited from the dissolution of the monasteries, held the priory lands. Properties of dissolved religious houses afforded opportunities to acquire land and buildings that could be repurposed as dwellings and school-houses. Aghmacart facilitated the professional needs of the Ó Conchubhair physicians by providing them with a tower-house residence, and a school-house that, possibly, re-used the dissolved priory infirmary.

Based on the scale of the buildings that have survived, the size of school-houses was modest, with *An Ghráinseach* and *Teach Breac* ranging between 76 and 90 m² of floor space, capable of accommodating ten to fifteen within their walls. The estimates are not at odds with Campion's observation of ten reclining students in one room of an Irish law school in the sixteenth century. O'Sullivan's study of the codicology of Ó Duibhdábhoireann's book suggests that approximately fourteen different scribes had worked on it in the Park law school, but how many of them were in the school-house at any one time is unknown.[179] Quarters for sleeping were perhaps provided in lofts of school buildings, and where *ollamhain* were tower-house users, bawn buildings need consideration as lodgings for visiting *ollamhain* and their retinues.

An understanding of the built environment of schools of poetry has been disadvantaged somewhat by romanticized modern accounts of the structures in which poets composed and by the paltry survival of buildings that can be authoritatively associated with secular poetic kindreds. However, the weight of literary and place-name allusions to *botha*, compliant with the apparent need of some schools of poets for darkness and austerity to facilitate composition, suggest that cells or huts are credible built heritage of poetic kindreds. Their lack of visibility in the landscape may be attributed to the probability that they were mostly temporary structures, built of ephemeral materials such as wattle and scraws, erected and dismantled seasonally as required by the schools. However, this perspective also needs to accommodate the idea that composition

---

[179] O'Sullivan, Book of Domhnall, 289.

practices differed among poets between the fourteenth and seventeenth centuries, with some eschewing the dark hut for open-air settings, as their places of inspiration.

The occurrence of stone buildings on the estates of some poets is a counterpoint to the invisibility of poetic *botha* and has been addressed as possible evidence for houses of recitation. The physical remains, and nineteenth-century Ordnance Survey record, of the bardic school at Dromnea is foremost amongst them, but Mac Creiche's hermitage at Ballynoe in Slieve Callan and the structure known as "Ballydaly Church," at the foot of the hill of Claragh, may have shared a similar purpose.

One certainty is that the settings of school buildings, whether for poetry, law or medicine, were contrived to provide a relatively separate and often a decidedly sequestered learned environment, apart from the formal residence of the *ollamh*.

The Gaelic *sgoilteagh* and the manuscripts compiled within its walls had greater visibility during the sixteenth century. But can the historical frame of reference, from the end of the fifteenth century to the second half of the sixteenth, bring more clarity to the establishment of the Gaelic school-house? The architectural details and the radiocarbon age range of 1488–1603 have broadly informed the construction and primary use period of *Teach Breac* on the Cahermacnaghten estate, suggesting that it originated *c*.1500. Its construction, however, could relate more closely to legislation for the establishment of parochial schools to promote the English language in Ireland from 1537.[180] The Tudor strategy to use schools as "a civilizing agency" had been initiated in Wales in 1536, with free grammar schools founded at Abergavenny, Bangor, and Brecon, among others, so that the Welsh would learn English.[181] In Ireland, such initiatives remained largely aspirational because they were dependent on the enthusiasm of local clergy, but they may have prompted a desire among Gaelic literati to legitimize their work during a period when the institutions of Gaelic lordships came under increasing scrutiny from the Tudor administration. A need to affirm autochthonous knowledge was experienced among learned kindreds elsewhere when confronted with change in different periods.[182]

Unlike most Gaelic poets, lawyers were not disabled by tradition, a fact underscored by how adept the Ó Duibhdábhoireann and Ó Deóradháin legal kindreds were at negotiating Tudor administrative reform on behalf of their chiefs, by modifying legal tradition in the second half of the sixteenth century.[183] During the 1570s, diocesan grammar schools that reflected the civilization of the English Pale began to be built to prepare young men for careers in state and church. Their mentality was one of Christian humanism, whereby youths would be "enured with a pure English tongue,

---

[180] Lennon, Pedagogy as reform, 46. [181] Orme, Education in medieval Wales, 640–1.

[182] Pryce, Lawbooks and literacy, 34–5.

[183] N. Patterson 1991 Gaelic law and the Tudor conquest of Ireland: the social background of the sixteenth-century recensions to the pseudo-historical prologues to the *Senchas már*. *Irish Historical Studies* 27, no. 107, 215; Patterson, Brehon law, 60.

habit, fashion, and discipline."[184] At the same time, there was increased activity in the Gaelic schools, especially in the law schools at Ballyorley, Cahermacnaghten, and Park, a development that has been attributed to the business of adapting Gaelic law to support the process of Anglicizing government during a period of rapid political change.[185] Contrary to the view that Gaelic lawyers of this period copied old legal texts simply for their antiquarian value, while the institutions of their society collapsed around them, Patterson has shown that Ó Duibhdábhoireann and Ó Deóradháin lawyers facilitated Crown demands for administrative reforms within the lordships during the 1560s and 1570s, and even used aspects of traditional law to support legal change in respect of primogeniture and capital punishment, for instance.[186]

The skill of such literati in negotiating the survival of their profession and supporting the needs of lordships in a time of great change implies a progressive and adaptive mindset that extended to the buildings which they resolutely called school-houses. But just how many of the school-houses active in the second half of the sixteenth century might have originated during and after the Dissolution, to facilitate the accommodation of Gaelic law to English administrative reform, and as a response to the new Tudor educational culture of parochial and grammar schools, is unknown. Answers require further archaeological investigation at the sites of identified secular schools and a refinement of the timeframe in which manuscripts associated with specific schools of this period were compiled.

---

[184] Lennon, Pedagogy as reform, 51. [185] Patterson, Gaelic law, 215.
[186] Patterson, Gaelic law, 194–5.

7

Conclusion

A Place for the Learned

In 1637, Sir Randall MacDonnell, 2nd earl of Antrim, granted an annuity of twenty pounds to Domhnall Ó Siadhail of Artigoran, Co. Antrim, to act as physician to him and his heirs and "to proceede in the science…of phisik."[1] Around the same time, he leased Toberdornan, near the north Antrim coast, to the historiographer Fearfeasa Ó Duibhgeannáin.[2] His favoring of both learned men was in keeping with an "Irish Scot" of Gaelic origin[3] retaining a core of learned people on his estate (Fig. 1.2). Toberdornan is distinguished by Dunmull, a hillfort on a striking volcanic rock, regarded as the inauguration site of a local early medieval dynasty.[4] Artigoran is situated on the east side of the River Bann within a short distance of the "parly hill" of Drumskea,[5] the summit of which is crowned by a mound. It sat in the landscape of a pre-Norman *óenach* assembly.[6] The pedigreed contexts of both landholdings in an erstwhile premier borderland are a remarkable late instance of the Gaelic practice of aligning literati with other manifestations of dynastic identity and power (2.2).

This study has created pathways to finding Gaelic literati in the lordships of Ireland and to reason where and why they were placed in those polities between 1300 and 1600. The result is a framework for recognizing and interpreting an archaeology of this class in Irish society. Some of the conclusions are necessarily provisional because of the nature of the material involved, but there are some clear signposts. A concept of "borderscape" has emerged, whereby estates of the learned are found relative to other tangible expressions of the political power of chiefs and overlords. The findings

---

[1] PRONI D2977/5/1/2/2 Grant by the earl of Antrim of an annuity of £20 to Donell O'Shyell. Belfast.

[2] Hughes, Land acquisition, 80–1.

[3] J. H. Ohlmeyer 1993 *Civil war and restoration in the three Stuart kingdoms: the career of Randal MacDonnell, marquis of Antrim, 1609–1683*, 43–8. Cambridge University Press.

[4] FitzPatrick, *Royal inauguration*, 115–16.

[5] Marked on Speed's map of Ulster (1610) as "Knock Mullagh." J. Speed, 1611/1612 *The theatre of the empire of Great Britaine: presenting an exact geography of the kingdoms of England, Scotland, Ireland*. London.

[6] Gleeson, Kingdoms, communities, and *óenaig*, 34.

Landscapes of the Learned: Placing Gaelic Literati in Irish Lordships 1300–1600. Elizabeth FitzPatrick, Oxford University Press.
© Elizabeth FitzPatrick 2023. DOI: 10.1093/oso/9780192855749.003.0007

about borderscapes support the view that literati had agency in the strategies of chiefs to preserve their lordships and to assert overlordship.

An insight of this study is that *ollamhain* in law, history, medicine, and poetry were integral to the creation of borderscapes during significant times for ruling families. Claims by Gaelic chiefs to borderlands with long histories and deep pedigrees needed to be continuously stated and made visible. The allocation of estates to literati in those spaces was an important approach adopted by ruling families. The fourteenth-century period of the ascendancy of Gaelic lordships, during which new boundaries were established and existing ones consolidated, is arguably one of the earliest contexts in which literati were mobilized in the formation of new chiefry borderscapes. This finds expression in the emergence of the *pailís*, perhaps primarily developed for feasting, with attendant designation of lands for literati. Creating new nodes of power during this period also appears to have involved hosting major hospitality events in *pailís* landscapes where learned kindreds had their estates, as suggested by the setting for the famed Christmas feast of 1351 proposed in this study (4.3).

The phenomenon of poets, lawyers, and harpers living on *pailís*-named lands during the sixteenth and seventeenth centuries may in certain instances represent continuity of earlier borderscapes, even where they had been eclipsed by the transfer of power to another part of the lordship. In that respect, the suggestion has been made that some literati took up residence in *pailís* enclosures vacated by ruling families with the advent of tower-house facilities for feasting (4.3). The provenance of literati and servitors to the environs of *pailíse* in the later period points to a deliberate renaissance of court culture by some Gaelic chiefs, among them the Mac Cárthaigh Mór, chief of Iar Mhumhain. His residence, *caislén na Pallíse* ("castle of the Palace") consisted of a tower-house and a large *ráth* regarded as the *pailís* of the name, and around which members of the Mac Aodhagáin legal family and the poet Muiris Mac Dháibhí Dhuibh were living in the late sixteenth century and at the turn of the seventeenth.

The consolidation of lordship borderlands in the fourteenth and fifteenth centuries evidently involved the incorporation, into emerging borderscapes, of prehistoric funerary landscapes that were designated as assembly places of ruling families (2.2). At centers of political power, the proximity of assembly sites to estates where learned kindreds were living in the sixteenth century is a relationship that is likely to have originated with the development of chiefry borderscapes from the fourteenth century onward. This paradigm has been proposed (2.2) in respect of the juxtaposition of Magh Adhair, the inauguration and *oireachtais* venue of the Ó Briain overlord and his vassal chief Mac Conmara of West Clann Chuileáin, to the estate of the physician Ó hÍceadha of Ballyhickey, as recorded in the sixteenth century. Similarly, a frame of reference for the sixteenth-century record of "Grange O'Mulchonry" in Magh Luirg may lie in a fourteenth-century relationship between the estate of a member of the Ó Maoilchonaire kindred of poets and the designation of prehistoric funerary monuments on Knockadoobrusna as an assembly place for the chiefs of Magh Luirg. Roles as keepers of assembly places have been envisaged for literati in such contexts (2.2).

Recognition of the link between learned kindred estates and active places of political assembly in the sixteenth century has highlighted institutional roles of the learned in premier borderscapes. The *tulach síodh*, as termed by the Ulster poet Eochaidh Ó hEódhasa, has been proposed as the essential locus of arbitration and agreement-making. An interpretation of *Suidhe Adhamhnáin* as a peace-mound where, in 1566, an agreement was forged between Cineál bhFiachach and Muintir Thadhgáin and witnessed by the poet-*ollamh* "of both countries," has made it possible to recompose an important western borderscape of the Cineál bhFiachach overlordship and to place the estates of literati among other manifestations of that space. The result is a premise for integrating literati estates with other signatures of chiefry borderscapes, with the prospect of rehabilitating the less-understood court sites, like Gortnapledula in Urumhain (6.1.3) and the anomalous category of "chairs" attributed to brehon lawyers, such as that on Kyle Hill in Osraighe (2.0.1).

Finding where several leading poets had their estates between the fourteenth and sixteenth centuries has established a firm association between them and an early boundary landmark of primordial character, the *formaoil* or bare-topped hill (2.3). Linked in the chronicles with medieval battles and violent actions and conveyed in the Finn cycle of tales as the quintessential domain of Fionn mac Cumhaill and his *fían*, this study has identified *formaoil* as indicative of a specialized borderscape that memorialized the heroic deeds of rulers and their ancestors. Mediated by poets, the immutable *formaoil* and its associated prehistoric monuments, is perhaps best conceived as a living museum of a chief's imagined heritage. The environment and connotations of this singular landform are superlatively exemplified by the *Formaoil* of the contested *túath* of Calraighe and its landscape of prehistoric monuments that incorporates traditions of the burial place of a sixth-century king of Connacht and the *óenach* of Lough Gill (2.1.3). The proximity of bare-topped hills to poets' estates, as seen in relation to Gofraidh Fionn Ó Dálaigh's land at the foot of the hill of Claragh, Dromnea of the Ó Dálaigh poets on the Sheepshead Peninsula, and Mac Bruaideadha's *Binn Formaoile* in the landscape of Slieve Callan, suggests that poets who eschewed the darkened hut for an "airy mountain prospect"[7] used these iconic hills and mountains as retreats to compose (2.3). It is conceivable that they were involved in curating the hillforts, standing stones, stone rows, stone circles, tombs and cairns, which mostly typify the archaeology of hills termed *formaoil*, and which may have been incorporated into poetic practices alongside border hunting and fighting.

In concluding that borderscapes distinguished by *formaoil* were specialized and set apart from those that were settled centers of power, it is important to emphasize that

---

[7] Bergin, *Irish bardic poetry*, 118, 265.

they could be activated in tandem with the pursuit of territorial claims. This is implicit in the late medieval settlement archaeology of the *túath* of Calraighe (2.1.3; 5.2.1), a borderscape periodically disputed between the lordships of West Bréifne and Cairbre.

Moving from the wider domain of borderscape to the particularity of learned kindred estates, some conclusions can be made arising from the range of estates that were surveyed (Fig. 1.2, Appendix). Literati held estates as church officials, secular proprietors of church land, secular occupants of *lucht tighe* lands, and occasionally as heirs of *túath* leaders. Hereditary possession over several generations is difficult to prove for most learned kindreds because their associations with specific places is not generally supported with sustained documentation. However, longevity on estates can be demonstrated in respect of the Mac Fhirbhisigh kindred of historians at Lackan in the lordship of Tír Fiachrach, the Ó Cléirigh poet-historians of Kilbarron in Tír Conaill, the Ó Duibhgeannáin historians of Kilronan in Magh Luirg, and the Ó Dálaigh poets of Sheepshead Peninsula in Fonn Iartharach. A reading of the settlement archaeology of the estates of these prominent kindreds of literati, combined with intermittent chronicle and other references over a period of at least 200 years, imply that they persisted on the lands first assigned to them.

It has been established that one means of locating literati in the landscape of Gaelic lordships is through a particular style of naming estates that incorporated kindred personal names and sometimes their professions (3.1). The Mac an Chrosáin poets of Ballymacrossan in the lordship of Clann Mhaoilughra and the two branches of the Ó Siadhail physicians of Ballysheil in the lordships of Dealbhna Eathra and Uí Eachach Cobha were readily identifiable by the titles of their estates (Fig. 1.2). Similar naming practices pertained to some church estates, with the huts or cells of Ó Fialáin of Boho (*Botha Muintire Fialáin*) distinguishing him as *airchinneach* of the medieval parish church and *ollamh* in poetry to the Mág Uidhir chief of Fir Mhanach. It is possible that this naming style arose to give *ollamhain* and their families more visibility, and to imply deep-rooted belonging, especially for those who were relative newcomers to their estates.

Where sources have allowed a record of Gaelic learned kindreds in relatively continuous occupation of their borderland estates, the fact of that continuity has enabled a view of the landscapes and built heritage of their landholdings and the cultural practices associated with them over the *longue durée*.

Estates varied considerably in size, from the entire Túath Ghlae of the Mac Fhlannchadha lawyers, and the Sheepshead Peninsula of the Ó Dálaigh poets, to the modest holdings of a *ceathramadh* or quarter of a *baile biataigh*, typically represented by the landholdings of Ó Cuindlis at Ballaghdacker and Ó Duibhdábhoireann at Cahermacnaghten (3.2). Some kindreds consolidated several landholdings in one area over time. By the seventeenth century, the extended family of the Mac Aodhagáin brehon lawyers of Ballymacegan had a mosaic of lands in the River Shannon borderland of the lordship of Urumhain (6.1.3).

Farming was fundamental to estate life for learned kindreds. It underpinned their roles as food providers, hospitalers, and keepers of schools. Readings of estate topographies and historic vegetation, chronicle and poetic references to herds of cattle and to horses received as payment for poems, to the raiding of livestock and to the perpetration of raids by literati, reflect the dominance of pastoral agriculture (3.3). However, a view of the importance of tillage to literati has also emerged in this study with both direct and circumstantial evidence for the cultivation of oats, barley and rye. Evidence for plot enclosure, and the presence of cereal-drying kilns at Cahermacnaghten and Ballyegan, as well as the deposits of refuse grains recovered during excavations in *Teach Breac* (6.1.1), indicate that grains were historically harvested in the environs of the lands that had constituted learned kindred estates. Also, occasional epistolary manuscript remarks by scribes about harvesting, and complaints from poets about the difficulty of tilling their estate lands, imply that cultivation of grain crops was expected on learned kindred landholdings (3.3). Moreover, the acquisition of a "Marl-hole field" by the learned family of Ó Maoilchonaire of Ardkyle entails knowledge of land improvement among literati in the sixteenth century. These points have much wider relevance for the practice of agriculture in late medieval and early modern Ireland.

There are two additional interrelated findings in respect of land organization and use. As seen, learned members of chiefs' courts and other service providers are provenanced to parks in sixteenth- and early seventeenth-century Gaelic and English records (3.3.1). It is clear that chiefs had parkland within which secular learned kindreds were allocated estates (3.3.1). The Mac Aodhagáin estate at Park in Corca Mogha, and that of the Ó Maoilchonaire historians at Ardkyle in West Clann Chuileáin, confirm the existence of parkland estates of literati in that period. Furthermore, modern emparkment of learned kindred lands as part of landed estates between the seventeenth and the end of the nineteenth century implies that they had previous histories as grazing for mixed herds, including deer. An estimated 70 percent of literati landholdings consulted for this study (Fig. 1.2; Appendix) eventually became part of modern landed estates, which suggests that their natural and cultural capital was deemed of high value by the landowning class (3.3.1).

Attention has been drawn to the occurrence of metal ores and quarriable stone in the environments of learned kindred estates that were situated on *lucht tighe* and church land (2.4, 4.2). Without targeted fieldwork to find evidence for premodern extraction of those resources, the idea that the learned class directly engaged with quarrying and mining remains unproven. However, the hypothesis that co-occurrences of earth materials with estates of literati predicates knowledge of material conditions shares a broader platform in the study of the medieval past. A new focus on the relationship between environmental factors and human agency in the shaping of medieval settlement and landscape has been advocated for Britain.[8] In that context, the presence

[8] T. Williamson 2013 *Environment, landscape and society in early medieval England: time and topography*, 1–5. Woodbridge. Boydell.

of valuable earth materials in the environs of learned kindred estates that had earlier profiles as royal lands (the *túath* of Magh Adhair of the Dál Cais dynasty), suggests that there was later medieval knowledge of them, perhaps even continuity of use, which influenced where chiefs established their borderscape centers of power. A promising direction for further research on this issue lies in the fact that on three estates explored in this study, metal ore deposits and quarriable stone occur at points along their boundaries. Silver and lead deposits (mined in the modern period) are found along the northern and western bounds of the physician's estate at Ballyhickey in the West Clann Chuileáin lordship (Fig. 3.18). A major source of coarse sandstone at Knocknalarabana on the estate of the Mac Fhlannchadha brehon lawyers of Túath Ghlae was a long-standing landmark of the southern boundary of their lands (Fig. 3.15), and a sandstone rock formation marking the southwesterly point of Ballymacaward estate, in southern Tír Conaill, was historically quarried for quernstones.

An equally auspicious signpost for ground-truthing a relationship between literati estates and mineral and metal resources lies in learned kindred estates that were on the lands of religious houses. Notable among these is the juxtaposition of the silver and lead deposits at Abbeytown, Ballysadare, to the Augustinian priory and the landholding of the brehon lawyers and *airchinnigh* of the parish church (3.4). It must also be considered that in a metaphysical context, the inclusion of the smith among the identities of Fionn mac Cumhaill may connote earth materials in the estate landscapes of the learned, as expressed, for instance, in the juxtaposition of the mountaintop of *Suidhe Finn* to the mineral-rich environment of the Ó Dálaigh poets on the Sheepshead Peninsula (2.3).

Turning from estates to their buildings, some key findings have arisen from the investigation of dwellings of literati. Although many *ollamhain* were living in towerhouses by the sixteenth century, several settlement forms were repurposed by this class. Where both secular and clerical kindreds were involved in constructing new dwellings, the late medieval evidence from the *caisel* of Cahermacnaghten (4.1) and from the promontory fort at Kilbarron (4.5) suggests that modular settlements were preferred. As living and perhaps guest quarters, the Ó Cléirigh *ollamh* opted for a gate-house keep and rectangular buildings constructed against a strong curtain wall. Both kindreds chose early settlement enclosures for their residences, which could be, reductively, interpreted as a reflection of a tradition-bound atavistic tier in the hierarchy of Gaelic society. However, such an interpretation would fail to see the more important fact that the mode in which they modified settlement sites (within the limits of their own resources) shows a desire to be fashionable and outward looking. The influence of tower-house architecture on aspects of their design is clear in respect of gate-houses controlling access to garth buildings. In repurposing earlier settlement forms, literati contributed to the development and expression of architecture in late medieval and early modern Ireland.

Late medieval use of lake-island dwellings, namely the *crannóg*, has been proposed among some of the learned *airchinnigh* kindreds situated between the upper and lower lakes of the River Erne, in the Ulster lordship of Fir Mhanach, where there was a strong culture of guest-houses. In addition, the adoption of historically important *crannóg* sites by poets, such as the Ó Cobhthaigh kindred who kept a guest-house on Lough Ennell, may be construed as an attenuated tradition of their predominant early historic roles as retreats and hospices for elites (4.4.2).

As already observed, the names of several learned kindreds appear in sixteenth- and very early seventeenth-century sources in association with the sites of *pailíse* that have been identified in the field, either as moated sites or *ráth* enclosures. Further archaeological investigation is needed to ascertain whether those late engagements of the learned with *pailíse* represent continuity from the fourteenth century or a return to them linked with a renaissance in court culture in the sixteenth century.

An etiology of borderscapes will automatically include early churches associated with learned activity, such as St Feichin's at Kilboglashy in Ballysadare, and Clonfert-Molua at Kyle, both of which remained active as churches in premier borderlands throughout the late medieval period (2.0.1). However, as seen (Chapter 5), many of the church buildings of literati who held the offices of *comharba* and *airchinneach* are later in origin.

Literati who were holders of church offices, between the fourteenth and sixteenth centuries, were mostly *airchinnigh*. In that capacity they had access to church land and buildings. Letters between the papal curia and Irish dioceses communicate an absence of ordained priests and some unlawful incumbencies by learned *airchinnigh*, especially during the fifteenth and early sixteenth centuries (5.2). The implication of this is that laymen usurped priests' positions, assuming almost total control over church property. The relative autonomy of literati who held church offices positioned them to establish communities of learning at their church sites. Cooperation in utilization of appropriate space for learned occupations is likely to have been widespread among them (5.0, 6.1.2).

A finding of the relationship between churches and learned *comharbai* and *airchinnigh* is that there is evidence to support their involvement in building and modifying churches to identify them as places of learning. This is strongly evinced by sites that have attested records of learned *comharbai* and *airchinnigh* in the late twelfth and early thirteenth century and corresponding church fabric datable to that period, especially Romanesque-style doorways (5.2.1). The dominance of learned kindreds in the late medieval period, at church sites that had been designated as new settlements in the twelfth and thirteenth centuries, by the place name *Nuachongbháil*, has been observed (5.2). Much of the standing fabric of the churches called *Nuachongbháil* has disappeared, but Noughaval in the lordship of Boireann, where a branch of the Ó Duibhdábhoireann legal kindred were church tenants, retains some of its late

Romanesque doorway. The association may reflect placement of literati in these new church-based land holdings when they first received that status.

Attention has been drawn to twelfth- and thirteenth-century ornamental doorways at churches securely linked to learned kindreds, including those of St Feichin's at Kilboglashy in Ballysadare, and Drumacoo in the lordship of Uí Fiachrach Aidhne (5.2.1). The use of an ornamental doorway as a signifier of the learned status of an incumbent is suggested too by the preservation of the Romanesque doorway within the parish church of Kilronan by the *comharba–ollamh*, when the church was re-erected *c.*1347 after a fire in 1340. The fifteenth-century round-headed late medieval doorway of Ó Cuirnín's church on Inishmore may have been an attempt to evoke a Romanesque predecessor after the fire there in 1416, while borrowing a new fifteenth-century fashion of openwork tracery.

West-end quarters in a parish church or chapel are not indicators of the presence of a member of the learned class *per se*. They were quarters for clerical incumbents, generally priests who provided pastoral care.[9] However, where the *comharba* or more usually the *airchinneach* of a church was a member of the literati, west-end quarters require interpretation in the context of the incumbent's needs for space to facilitate learned occupations. The well-formed two-story west-end quarters of Ó Cuirnín's church on Inishmore, with the unusual combination of fixtures in the cross-wall, implies a special purpose. The fifteenth-century inscribed slates recovered at the parish church of Smarmore indicate learned activity there (5.2.4). More tentatively, the shale trial piece and the harp peg from St Breacán's Chapel, Toomullin, have been included as material evidence of learned activity at the Mac Fhlannchadha law school in the lordship of Corca Modhruadh (5.2.3). With learned *airchinnigh* exercising control over church buildings in late medieval Ireland, it is plausible that the need for facilities to support their learned occupations incentivized development of west-end quarters in parish churches and sinecure chapels. The fifteenth century in Ireland has been identified as a period of "great rebuilding" of churches, especially parish churches.[10] The extent to which this was an even phenomenon on the island is questionable, but it is a fact that several parish churches and sinecure chapels were either rebuilt or greatly modified during that century. Where churches became central to programs of rebuilding in the fifteenth and sixteenth centuries, it may not necessarily have been to augment their spiritual roles but to convert them into workspace for literati, and dwelling space where needed.

One of the indicators of a church or chapel building constructed for or adapted to the needs of the learned appears to be the absence of a formal graveyard with premodern grave markers or other signs of medieval use. A finding of this study is

---

[9] Bermingham, Priests' residences, 168–85.
[10] Jeffries, *The Irish Church and the Tudor reformations*, 15–22; O'Keeffe, Built environment, 145–6.

that post-medieval burial grounds for unbaptized children are in several instances found at sites formerly occupied by learned kindreds. The occurrence of childrens' burial grounds at St Bairrfhionn's, Kilbarron, St Mac Creiche's, Ballynoe, Church Park, Portland, and at "Ballydaly Church" beside the hill of Claragh, is a recognition of the historically marginal locations of these deserted sites and their suitability as unconsecrated ground.

The process of repeatedly enriching borderscapes involved the physical manifestation of learned occupations. A conclusion of this study is that to facilitate their arts and networks of learning, secular lawyers, physicians, and poets built and repurposed buildings on their estates during the sixteenth century. The development of school-house buildings by literati is in keeping with two tendencies elsewhere in Europe. Schools adapted all kinds of buildings as their venues,[11] and "purpose-built—and thus recognizable schools" are relatively late, with the Latin schools of the Netherlands, for instance, not constructed until the sixteenth century.[12] In respect of the first trend, *An Ghráinseach*, the school-house of the Ó Deóradháin lawyers of Ballyorley in the sixteenth century, appears to have been a repurposed grange building, erected on a moated site in a monastic grange of Ferns Abbey (6.1.2). It has been proposed, too, that the Ó Conchubhair physicians may have used the infirmary of the Augustinian priory of Aghmacart as their school-house in the sixteenth century (6.2). Both imply opportunistic re-use of religious buildings. This was more especially the case in the period of the dissolution of religious houses between 1539 and the mid-sixteenth century, during which approximately 40 percent of Ireland's abbeys were dissolved and the undissolved left vulnerable to acquisitive land speculators.[13] However, Gaelic chiefs were among the beneficiaries of dissolved religious houses, which would have positioned them to allocate monastic property, both land and buildings, to the learned men of their courts (6.2).

The results of detailed survey and excavation at *Teach Breac* on the Cahermacnaghten estate has suggested that it was purpose-built *c.*1500 and that it can be credibly identified as the *sgoilteagh* of the Ó Duibhdábhoireann lawyers (6.1.1). In consideration of the background to this period, it has been argued that its construction could be closer to *c.*1537 and conceived as a response to Tudor legislation for the establishment of parochial schools from 1537 onward.

There was a marked increase in the activity of the law schools at Ballyorley, Cahermacnaghten, and Park in the second half of the sixteenth century (6.1.2), which has been attributed to Ó Duibhdábhoireann and Ó Deóradháin lawyers facilitating crown demands for administrative reforms within the lordships during the 1560s and 1570s.[14] A response to new political conditions of that period required acumen on the part of brehon lawyers to negotiate the survival of their profession and to support lordships through change.[15] What this tells us is that narratives of atavism and loss, which tend to dominate views of the fate of literati in the Tudor period, are contradicted by

[11] Orme, *Medieval schools*, 136–7.   [12] Willemsen, *Back to the schoolyard*, 263.

[13] S.J. Connolly 1998 *The Oxford companion to Irish history*, 150. Oxford University Press.

[14] Patterson, Gaelic law, 194–5.   [15] Patterson, Brehon law, 60.

the actions of Gaelic lawyers in old borderlands. This cultural resilience through careful accommodation of change is likely to have extended to the construction of new buildings (*Teach Breac*) and modifications to existing structures (*An Ghráinseach*) to facilitate legal work adapting Gaelic law to the contemporary process of reforming local government alongside traditional scholarship. Negotiating change while attending to tradition is a theme that has emerged at other sites explored in this study. The continuity of control over St Breacán's Chapel at Toomullin, as a focus for the Mac Fhlannchadha and Ó Duibhdábhoireann legal kindreds after it had become a center of the Protestant faith *c.*1615, demonstrates cooperation between resilient literati in finding a place for themselves in the new order (5.2.3). The Park fireplace keystone, with its Irish-language inscription in Gaelic hand, twinned with Counter-Reformation symbolism, reflects the optimism of the lawyer Cormac Mac Aodhagáin in 1627 despite the reduced circumstances of his family (4.5).

The buildings of poets are a particular case (6.3). Arguably, the dark huts used for poetic composition (*botha*), cited as such by poets writing in the fourteenth and sixteenth centuries, were temporary structures that could be conveniently erected and just as easily dismantled when schools broke up. But the remains of a late medieval building attributed to the Ó Dálaigh poets at Dromnea on the Sheepshead Peninsula (6.3.1) suggests that more permanent structures were built too, perhaps for communal activities of poets, such as recitation. The landscape analysis of the setting of the Dromnea building has shown the potential of that approach to allow us into the environment of a kindred of poets. This, and the interpretation of the position of *Teach Breac* in the karst landscape of Cahermacnaghten, has highlighted how literati used the landscape totemically, to communicate the specialized roles of their settlements as places of learning.

Some buildings on the estates of literati remain problematic in terms of their identity. St Mac Creiche's at Ballynoe, and "Ballydaly Church" at the foot of the hill of Claragh, currently hover somewhere between being churches and secular buildings. Others, such as Templenaraha in Edmund Butler's caput of Pottlerath (4.1), and Templemacateer in the western borderscape of the overlordship of Cineál bhFiachach (2.2), have come into view, momentarily, as sites of professional learned activity in the fifteenth and sixteenth centuries. The locus of the law school of the Mac Aodhagáin legal kindred, in the northern bounds of Urumhain, has been proposed as a building in Church Park, Portland, southwest of the kindred's core lands at Ballymacegan and Redwood. Furthermore, it has been suggested that its original identity is *Cluain Lethan*, the early fifteenth-century "capital of Brehon law of Ireland."[16] The genesis of the Church Park building remains ambiguous, with possible origins as a grange chapel of the Augustinian priory of Lorrha, or a purpose-built school of a legal kindred modeled on a church building.

In aspiring to find and place literati in the lordships of Ireland, an archaeology and topography of the borderscapes to which they belonged has been brought back into view, and a more diverse and richly textured picture of historical landscape and built heritage, 1300–1600, has begun to emerge.

---

[16] RIA MS 23 P 16, 206.

A FUTURE FOR LANDSCAPES OF LITERATI

The idea that the landscapes in which autochthonous literati lived and worked were integral to their intellectual and political cultures is a new perspective. The findings of this book are exceeded by the volume of questions that the approach has yielded, leaving much more to be done. The concept of "borderscape," as the domain of the learned, needs to be developed further as the indispensable container of their practices. Archaeological investigations of buildings securely identified with literati on their estates, and repurposed monuments that had specialized functions for them, require archaeological investigation while maintaining dialogue with other disciplines in this field.

FIG. 7.1. Two of three former standing stones (foreground and background) constituting a stone row, at the foot of the ridge known as *An Carnan* ("heap of stones"), on the estate of the Mac Bethadh physicians, Ballinaby, Islay (SC 2254342 © HES.).

Finally, there is potential for some of the approach taken in this study to be applied to known landholdings and buildings of literati in Scotland and Wales. Bannerman's authoritative identification of the estates of the medical kindreds of Mac Bethadh and Ó Conchubhair in west highland Scotland means that there is a magisterial resource in place for fieldwork (Fig. 7.1). Equally, the publication of several volumes of late medieval Welsh poetry by the Poets of the Nobility project, at the University of Wales, is an impressive platform for investigation of the landscapes associated with poets in north Wales.

APPENDIX

Concordance list of townland locations of estates of literati and centers of learned activity consulted for this study (use in conjunction with Fig. 1.2). Alternative names are cited in italics.

	Estate Name	County	Learned Kindred	Art	Territory
1	Ballygalley	Antrim	Ó Gnímh Ó Dálaigh?	poetry	Clann Aodha Buidhe
2	Artigoran	Antrim	Ó Siadhail	medicine	An Rúta
3	Toberdornan	Antrim	Ó Duibhgeannáin	history poetry	An Rúta
4	Evishagaran *Baile Uí Ghéaráin*	Derry	Ó Géaráin	poetry	Ciannacht
5	Barons Court *Fearann an Reacaire*	Tyrone	Mac Con Midhe	poetry	Tír Eoghain
6	Carn *Templecarn*	Donegal	Mac Craith	poetry	Fir Mhanach
7	Kilbarron	Donegal	Ó Cléirigh	history poetry	Tír Conaill
8	Ballymacaward	Donegal	Mac an Bhaird	poetry	Tír Conaill
9	Ballymunterhiggin	Donegal	Ó hUiginn	poetry	Tír Conaill
10	Farrancassidy *Fearann Muintir Uí Chaiside*	Fermanagh	Ó Caiside	medicine	Fir Mhanach
11	Ballyhose	Fermanagh	Ó hEódhasa	poetry	Fir Mhanach
12	Ballycassidy	Fermanagh	Ó Caiside	medicine	Fir Mhanach
13	Boho *Botha Muintire Fialáin*	Fermanagh	Ó Fialáin	poetry	Fir Mhanach

(*continued*)

	Estate Name	County	Learned Kindred	Art	Territory
14	Derryvullan	Fermanagh	Ó Luinín	history poetry	Fir Mhanach
15	Cleenish *Fearann Muintire Cianáin*	Fermanagh	Ó Cianáin	history	Fir Mhanach
16	Derrybrusk	Fermanagh	Ó Fiaich	unknown	Fir Mhanach
17	Arda *Fearann na bArda Muintire Luinín*	Fermanagh	Ó Luinín	history poetry	Fir Mhanach
18	Ballymacmanus *Seanadh Mhic Mhaghnusa*	Fermanagh	Mac Maghnuis	history	Fir Mhanach
19	Ballysheil	Down	Ó Siadhail	medicine	Uí Eachach Cobha
20	Ballyroney	Down	Ó Ruanadha	poetry	Uí Eachach Cobha
21	Ballyward	Down	Mac an Bhaird	poetry	Uí Eachach Cobha
22	Tullycarnan *Lios Toighe Uí Ghnímh*	Down	Ó Gnímh	poetry	Leath Cathail
23	Lackan	Sligo	Mac Fhirbhisigh	history	Tír Fiachrach
24	Ballydoogan	Sligo	Ó Dubhagáin	history poetry	Cairbre
25	Inishmore *Church Island*	Sligo	Ó Cuirnín	poetry	Cairbre
26	Kilboglashy *Ballysadare*	Sligo	Mac an Bhreitheamhan Ua Dúilendáin	law	Luighne
27	Killerry	Sligo	Mac an Óglaigh	law	West Bréifne
28	Ballyvicmaha *Baile Mhic Mhatha*	Mayo	Ó Ceandamháin	medicine	Tír Amhalgaidh
29	Kilmacteige *Oughaval*	Sligo	Ó hUiginn	poetry	Luighne
30	Churchacres *Kilronan*	Roscommon	Ó Duibhgeannáin	history	Magh Luirg

	Place	Family	County	Profession	Region
31	Templeport *Inis Breacmhaigh*	unknown	Cavan	medicine?	Teallach nEachach
32	Derrycassan	Mac Parthaláin	Cavan	medicine	Teallach nEachach
33	Mullynagolman *Tonrregan* *Túaim Drecain*	unknown	Cavan	law poetry	East Bréifne
34	Smarmore *Smirammair* *Imorach Smiromrach*	unknown	Louth	medicine music	Louth
35	Churchfield *Oughaval*	Ó Fearghusa	Mayo	medicine	Umhaill
36	Ballynabrehon	Mac an Bhreitheamhan	Mayo	law	Clann Mhuiris
37	Cloonfinlough	Ó Donnabhair Ó Maoilchonaire	Roscommon	poetry poetry history	Machaire Chonnacht
38	Grange Beg *Grange O'Mulchonry*	Ó Maoilchonaire	Roscommon	poetry	Magh Luirg
39	Kilcloony	Ó hUiginn	Galway	poetry	Conmhaicne Mac Fheóruis
40	Park	Mac Aodhagáin	Galway	law	Uí Mhaine/ Clann Conmhaigh
41	Ballaghdacker	Ó Cuindlis	Galway	history	Uí Mhaine
42	Carrickbeg *Ballymackeagan*	Mac Aodhagáin	Longford	law	Anghal
43	Ballydoogan	Ó Dubhagáin	Galway	history poetry	Uí Mhaine
44	Ballynabanaba	Ó Longargain	Galway	music	Uí Mhaine
45	Ballinkeeny *Mosstown*	Ó Cobhthaigh	Westmeath	poetry	Rathconrath

(continued)

	Estate Name	County	Learned Kindred	Art	Territory
46	Dysart / *Díseart Maoile Tuile*	Westmeath	Ó Cobhthaigh	poetry	Fir Tulach
47	Kilbeg	Westmeath	Ó hUiginn	poetry	Cineál bhFiachach
48	Pallas	Westmeath	Ó Dálaigh	poetry	Cineál bhFiachach
49	Syonan / *Suidhe Adhamhnáin*	Westmeath	Mac Aodhagáin	law	Cineál bhFiachach
50	Maumeen / *Ballynakill*	Galway	Mac an Leagha	medicine	Iarchonnacht
51	Drumacoo	Galway	Ó hAllgaith	medicine	Aidhne
52	Ballysheil	Offaly	Ó Siadhail	medicine	Dealbhna Eathra
53	Lynally	Offaly	Ó Siadhail	medicine	Fir Cheall
54	Ballymacrossan	Laois	Mac an Chrosáin	poetry	Clann Mhaoilughra
55	Finavarra	Clare	Ó Dálaigh	poetry	Boireann
56	Kilweelran	Clare	Ó Callanáin	medicine	Boireann
57	Kilmoon	Clare	Ó Beacáin	history	Boireann
58	Ballyvoe / *Knockfin/Tulach Fionn*	Clare	Mac Fhlannchadha	law	Corca Modhruadh
59	Toomullin	Clare	Mac Fhlannchadha	law poetry	Corca Modhruadh
60	Ballyconnoe	Clare	Ó Connmhaigh	music	Boireann
61	Cahermacnaghten / *Kilbrack*	Clare	Ó Duibhdábhoireann	law	Boireann
62	Coskeam	Clare	Mac an Ghabhann	history	Boireann
63	Noughaval	Clare	Ó Duibhdábhoireann	law	Boireann
64	Duniry	Galway	Mac Aodhagáin	law	Clann Uilliam Uachtair

	Placename	County	Surname	Subject	Territory
65	Ballymacegan	Tipperary	Mac Aodhagáin	law	Urumhain
66	Erry	Offaly	Mac Aodhagáin	law	Muintir Thadhgáin
67	Killcollin	Offaly	Ó Cionga	poetry	Muintir Thadhgáin
68	Knockbarron *Drumcullen*	Offaly	unknown	law?	Fir Cheall
69	Clonaddadoran	Laois	Ó Deóradháin	law	Laoighis
70	Carricksallagh *Onghaval*	Laois	unknown	history?	Laoighis
71	Caherclanchy	Clare	Mac Fhlannchadha	law	Tuadhmhumhain
72	Cloonyconry Beg/More *Cluana uí Chonaire*	Clare	Ó Maoilchonaire	poetry history	West Clann Chuileáin
73	Lettermoylan-Formoyle	Clare	Mac Bruaideadha	poetry	Cineál bhFearmaic
74	Ballyhickey	Clare	Ó hÍceadha	medicine	West Clann Chuileáin
75	Urlan More	Clare	Mac Fhlannchadha	law	West Clann Chuileáin
76	Ardkyle	Clare	Ó Maoilchonaire	history poetry	West Clann Chuileáin
77	Ballybeg *Littleton*	Tipperary	Ó Troightigh	medicine	Éile Uí Fhogartaigh Earldom of Ormond
78	Ballygown	Tipperary	Mac an Ghabhann	history	Urumhain
79	Aghmacart	Laois	Ó Conchubhair	medicine	Osraighe
80	Kyle *Ballyduff Kyleballyduff*	Laois	Mac Caisín	medicine	Osraighe
81	Pallis	Wexford	Mac Eochadha	poetry	Uí Cheinnsealaigh
82	Garrison	Limerick	Mac Craith	poetry	Cuanach
83	Meallaghmore Lower/Upper	Kilkenny	Mac Craith	poetry	Earldom of Ormond

(continued)

	Estate Name	County	Learned Kindred	Art	Territory
84	Pottlerath *Teampall na Rátha* *Ráth of Óengus mac Nad Froích*	Kilkenny	Mac Aodhagáin and Ó Cléirigh scribes visiting	various	Earldom of Ormond
85	Ballyorley *Baile Uí Dheóradháin* *An Ghráinseach*	Wexford	Ó Deóradháin	law	Uí Cheinnsealaigh
86	Ballyegan *Nohaval*	Kerry	Mac Aodhagáin	law	Conallaigh
87	Nohavaldaly	Kerry	Ó Dálaigh	poetry	Iar Mhumhain
88	Inchidaly	Cork	Ó Dálaigh	poetry	Pobul Uí Cheallacháin
89	Pallis *Pailís Még Cárrbaigh*	Kerry	Mac Aodhagáin Mac Dháibhí Dhuibh	law poetry	Iar Mhumhain
90	Ballydaly	Cork	Ó Dálaigh	poetry	Iar Mhumhain
91	Ahalisky	Cork	Ó Fithcheallaigh? Mac an Leagha physician visiting	medicine	Cairbre
92	Curravordy	Cork	Ó Cáinte	poetry	Cairbre
93	Grange Beg/More *Gráinseach Muintire* *Fithcheallaigh*	Cork	Ó Fithcheallaigh	medicine	Uí Bhána
94	Dromnea	Cork	Ó Dálaigh	poetry	Fonn Iartharach

BIBLIOGRAPHY

MANUSCRIPT SOURCES

BL Egerton MS 88, 1564–70, Irish legal and grammatical miscellany compiled by Domhnall Ó Duibhdábhoirenn. London. British Library.

BL Cotton MS Augustus I.ii.40, *c.*1565, A colored map of Offalia, now forming King's and Queen's Counties. London. British Library.

Carew MS 625, 1597, The Clancarthy Survey from the Carew Collection. Lambeth Palace Library.

MPF 1/36, 1602–3, A map of the southern part of Ulster, Ireland, by Richard Bartlett. Kew. National Archives.

MS Laud Misc. 610, The book of the White Earl. Oxford. Bodleian Library.

MS Rawl. B. 486, part iv: miscellany, including historical narratives, genealogies of saints and others, lists of kings, etc. Oxford. Bodleian Library.

NA MPF/1/73, 1572, "A single draght of Mounster" by Robert Lythe. Kew. National Archives.

NKS MS 261 b 4°, Law text. Copenhagen. Royal Library.

NLI Map 34 M, 1734, A map of part of the estate of Robert Dillon Esq. lying in the Barony of Kilconnell and County of Galway, by Thomas Cuttle. National Library of Ireland.

NLI PD 2040 TX, 1868, Sketchbook of antiquities, mainly from Co. Clare by Sir Samuel Ferguson. Dublin. National Library of Ireland.

NLI P4769, Petworth Collection, C 27/A/34, 1626, An abstract of such rents and revenues as do belonge to the right Hon:ble Earle of Thomond together with a rehearsal of the castles and landes out of which ye said rents are due. Dublin. National Library of Ireland.

Ordnance Survey memorandums for Co. Cork, ii. Dublin. Ordnance Survey Ireland.

PRONI D2977/5/1/2/2, Grant by the earl of Antrim of an annuity of £20 to Donell O'Shyell 1637. Public Record Office of Northern Ireland.

RIA MS D v 2, Dublin. Royal Irish Academy.

RIA 14 B 23, Letters containing information relative to the antiquities of the county of Clare, collected during the progress of the Ordnance Survey in 1839, by J. O'Donovan and Eugene O'Curry, i. Dublin. Royal Irish Academy.

RIA 14 C 13, Letters containing information relative to the antiquities of the county of Down, collected during the progress of the Ordnance Survey in 1834, by J. O'Donovan. Dublin. Royal Irish Academy.

RIA 14 C 20, Letters containing information relative to the antiquities of the county of Galway, collected during the progress of the Ordnance Survey in 1838, by J. O'Donovan and T. O'Conor. Dublin. Royal Irish Academy.

RIA 14 D 23, Letters containing information relative to the antiquities of the county of Louth, collected during the progress of the Ordnance Survey in 1835–6, by J. O'Donovan, T. O'Conor, and P. O'Keeffe. Dublin. Royal Irish Academy.

RIA 14 F 9, Letters containing information relative to the antiquities of the county of Roscommon, collected during the progress of the Ordnance Survey in 1837–8, by J. O'Donovan and George Petrie, ii. Dublin. Royal Irish Academy.

RIA 14 G 14, Letters containing information relative to the antiquities of the county of Westmeath, collected during the progress of the Ordnance Survey in 1837–8, by J. O'Donovan and T. O'Conor, ii. Dublin. Royal Irish Academy.

RIA MS 23 P 12, The book of Ballymote, fo. 170r. Dublin. Royal Irish Academy.

RIA MS 23 P 16, 1408–11, Leabhar breac: the Speckled book. Dublin. Royal Irish Academy.

RIA MS 23 Q 6, Law text. Dublin. Royal Irish Academy.

RIA MS 24 B 3, Medical treatises. Dublin. Royal Irish Academy.

TCD MS 1209, 36, 83, 1589, A map of the province of Munster, by Francis Jobson for Lord Burleigh. Trinity College Dublin.

TCD H.3.18, MS 1337/3 Miscellanea, p. 450. Trinity College Dublin.

REPORTS

Cox, P. and McCarthy, M. L. 2009 Cabhail Tighe Breac, Burren, Co. Clare: mortar analysis. Dublin. Carrig.

Fenwick, J. 2008 A preliminary report on the magnetic susceptibility survey of the cashel of Cahermacnaghten (08R179). National University of Ireland Galway.

Fenwick, J. and FitzPatrick, E. 2010 A report on the geophysical survey at the possible site of the Uí Chonchubhair medical school at Aghmacart, Cullahill, Co. Laois. Consent no. 10R44. School of Geography and Archaeology, National University of Ireland Galway.

FitzPatrick, E. 2014 The cultural landscape of the Mac Aodhagáin brehons of Ballymacegan and Redwood, Lower Ormond, Co. Tipperary. Report for Clann Mac Aodhagáin.

FitzPatrick, E. 2007 Archaeological excavation of a building at Cahermacnaghten, Burren, Co. Clare (07E0395). Report to the Department of Environment, Heritage and Local Government.

FitzPatrick, E. 2006 Report to the Department of Environment, Heritage and Local Government in the aftermath of topsoil removal at Cahermacnaghten, Co. Clare.

FitzPatrick, E. and McCarthy, N. 2019 Kilcloony: a settlement of the Uí hUiginn poets and its landscape setting, Kilcloony, County Galway. Cill Chluaine, Conmhaicne Mac Fheóruis. Report for the Milltown Heritage Group. Milltown.

Nicholls, J. 2008 Geophysical survey report: Ballyorley Upper, County Wexford, license 08R103. Target Archaeological Geophysics, for the O'Doran Law School Research Committee.

Tierney, J. 2016 Dromnea bardic school, Kilcrohane, Sheep's Head Peninsula, Co. Cork: conservation and tourism development. Kinsale.

ONLINE SOURCES

Database of Irish Excavation Reports. <https://excavations.ie/>.
Dictionary of Irish Biography. Royal Irish Academy. <https://www.dib.ie/>.
Down Survey of Ireland. Trinity College Dublin. <http://downsurvey.tcd.ie>.
Geological Survey Ireland Spatial Resources. Geological Survey Ireland. <https://www.gsi.ie>.
National Folklore Collection. University College Dublin. <https://www.duchas.ie/en>.
Northern Ireland Place-Name Project. <http://www.placenamesni.org>.
Placenames Database of Ireland. <https://www.logainm.ie>.
Royal Irish Academy Library. <https://www.ria.ie/library/>.

SECONDARY WORKS

Aalen, F. H. A. 1964 Clochans as transhumance dwellings in the Dingle Peninsula, Co. Kerry. *JRSAI* 94 (1), 39–45.

Airs, M. 1989 Architecture. In B. Ford (ed.), *The Cambridge cultural history of Britain, iii: sixteenth-century Britain*, 47–97. Cambridge University Press.

Allingham, H. 1879 *Ballyshannon: its history and antiquities, with some account of the surrounding neighbourhood*. Londonderry. James Montgomery.

Anderson, A. and Anderson, M. O. (eds and trs) 1961 *Adomnán's life of Columba*. London. Nelson.

Andrews, J. H. 2001 The mapping of Ireland's cultural landscape, 1550–1630. In P. J. Duffy, D. Edwards, and E. FitzPatrick (eds), *Gaelic Ireland c.1250– c.1650: land, lordship and settlement*, 153–80. Dublin. Four Courts Press.

An Roinn Oideachais 1981 *Gearrfhoclóir Gaeilge–Béarla*. Dublin. Oifig an tSoláthair.

Bagwell, R. 1890 *Ireland under the Tudors: with a succinct account of the earlier history*, iii. London and New York. Longmans, Green, and Co.

Bannerman, J. 1998 *The Beatons: a medical kindred in the classical Gaelic tradition*. Edinburgh. Birlinn.

Bannerman, J. 1996 The residence of the king's poet. *Scottish Gaelic Studies* 17, 24–35.

Barnwell, P. S. and Mostert, M. (eds) 2003 *Political assemblies in the earlier Middle Ages*. Studies in the Early Middle Ages. Turnhout. Brepols.

Barrowman, C. S. 2015 *The archaeology of Ness: results of the Ness Archaeological Landscape Survey*. Stornoway. Acair.

Barrowman, R. C. 2015 *Dùn Èistean, Ness: the excavation of a clan stronghold*. Stornoway. Acair.

Baug, I. 2006 The quarries in Hyllestad: production of quern stones and millstones in western Norway. In A. Belmont and F. Mangartz (eds), *Millstone quarries: research, protection and valorization of an European industrial heritage*, 55–9. Mainz. Verlag des Römisch-Germanisches Zentralmuseum.

Beaufort, D. A. 1792 *Memoir of a map of Ireland*. Dublin and London.

Beglane, F. 2018 Forests and chases in medieval Ireland, 1169–c.1399. *Journal of Historical Geography* 59, 90–9.

Beglane, F. 2015 *Anglo-Norman parks in medieval Ireland*. Dublin. Four Courts Press.

Bergin, O. (ed. and tr.) 1970 *Irish bardic poetry*. Dublin. Institute for Advanced Studies.

Bergin, O. (ed.) 1923 Unpublished Irish poems xxi: the poet insists on his rights. *Studies: An Irish Quarterly Review* 12 (45), 80–2.

Bergin, O. and MacNeill, J. (eds) 1901 *Eachtra Lomnochtáin [an tSléibhe Riffe]*. Dublin. Gaelic League.

Bermingham, H. 2006 Priests' residences in later medieval Ireland. In E. FitzPatrick and R. Gillespie (eds), *The parish in medieval and early modern Ireland: community, territory and building*, 168–85. Dublin. Four Courts Press.

Best, R. I., Bergin, O., and O'Brien, M. A. 1954 *Book of Leinster, formerly Lebar na Núachongbála*, i, Dublin. Dublin Institute for Advanced Studies.

Bhabha, H. K. 1994 *The location of culture*. London. Routledge.

Bigger, F. J. 1907 Inishmore, Church Island, Lough Gill. *Ulster Journal of Archaeology* 13 (3), 143.

Bisagni, J. (ed.) 2019 *Amrae Coluimb Chille: a critical edition*. Early Irish texts series: 1. Dublin Institute for Advanced Studies.

Blake, H., Egan, G., Hurst, J., and New, E. 2003 From popular devotion to resistance and revival in England: the cult of the Holy Name of Jesus and the Reformation. In D. Gaimster and R. Gilchrist (eds), *The archaeology of Reformation 1480–1580*, 175–203. Society for Post-Medieval Archaeology monograph: 1. Leeds. Maney.

Bliss, A. J. 1967 An inscribed slate from Smarmore. *Notes and Queries* 14 (3), 85.

Bliss, A. J. 1965 The inscribed slates at Smarmore. *PRIA* 64C, 33–60.

Bliss, A. J. 1961 Smarmore inscribed slates. *Journal of the County Louth Archaeological and Historical Society* 15 (1), 21–2.

Bliss, W. H. and Twemlow, J. A. (eds) 1904 *Calendar of papal registers relating to Great Britain and Ireland, v, AD 1396–1404*. London. HMSO.

Bolger, T., Moloney, C., and Troy, C. 2012 Archaeological excavations at Lorrha, Co. Tipperary. *The Journal of Irish Archaeology* 21, 113–37.

Booker, S. 2018 *Cultural exchange and identity in late medieval Ireland: the English and Irish of the four obedient shires*. Cambridge University Press.

Bondarenko, G. 2014 *Studies in Irish mythology*. Berlin. Curach Bhán.

Borlase, W. C. 1897 *The dolmens of Ireland*, i. London. Chapman and Hall.

Bradley, J. 1989 The Chantry College, Ardee. *Journal of the County Louth Archaeological and Historical Society* 22 (1), 6–19.

Breatnach, L. (ed.) 2005 *A companion to the Corpus iuris Hibernici*. Dublin Institute for Advanced Studies.

Breatnach, P. A. 1983 The chief's poet. *PRIA* 83C, 37–79.

Breen, C. 2005 *The Gaelic lordship of the O'Sullivan Beare: a landscape cultural history*. Dublin. Four Courts Press.

Breen, M. 1995 A 1570 list of castles in County Clare. *North Munster Antiquarian Journal* 36, 130–8.

Bremmer, J. N. 2012 Greek demons of the wilderness: the case of the centaurs. In L. Feldt (ed.), *Wilderness in mythology and religion: approaching religious spatialities, cosmologies, and ideas of wild nature*, 25–53. Boston and Berlin. De Gruyter.

Brewer, J. S. and Bullen, W. (eds) 1867 *Calendar of the Carew manuscripts 1515–1574*, i, London. Longmans, Green and Co.

Brewer, J. S. and Bullen, W. (eds) 1869 *Calendar of the Carew manuscripts 1589–1600*, ii. London. Longmans, Green and Co.

Britton, D. and Fletcher, A. J. 1990 Medieval Hiberno-English inscriptions on the inscribed slates of Smarmore: some reconsiderations and additions. *Irish University Review* 20 (1), 55–72.

Brown, A. C. L. 1901 Barintus. *Revue Celtique* 22, 339–44.

Buckley, A. 1978 What was the tiompán? A problem in ethnohistorical organology: evidence in Irish literature. In J. Kuckertz (ed.) *Jahrbuch für Musikalische volks und völkerkunde* 9, 53–88. Cologne. Musikverlage Hans Gerig.

Buckley, V. M. and Sweetman, P. D. 1991 *Archaeological survey of County Louth*. Dublin. The Stationery Office.

Burton, J. and Kerr, J. 2011 *The Cistercians in the Middle Ages*. Woodbridge. Boydell Press.

Byrne, F. J. 1987 The trembling sod: Ireland in 1169. In A. Cosgrove (ed.), *A new history of Ireland, ii: medieval Ireland 1169–1534*, 36–7. Oxford University Press.

Byrne, F. J. 1979 *A thousand years of Irish script: an exhibition of Irish manuscripts in Oxford libraries*. Oxford. Bodleian Library.

Byrne, F. J. 1973 *Irish kings and high-kings*. London. Batsford.

Byrne, M. 1991 A report on the excavation of a cashel at Ballyegan, near Castleisland, Co. Kerry. *Journal of the Kerry Archaeological and Historical Society* 24, 5–31.

Byrne, P. 2014 The northern boundary of Múscraige Tíre. *Ériu* 64, 107–21.

Caball, M. 2012 Culture, continuity and change in early seventeenth-century south-west Munster. *Studia Hibernica* 38, 37–56.

Campbell, E. 2017 Pobul Uí Cheallacháin: landscape and power in an early modern Gaelic lordship. *Landscapes* 18 (1), 19–36.

Campbell, E. 2013 Exploring the medieval and early modern settlement of Noughaval in the Burren. *The Other Clare* 37, 12–17.

Campbell, E. FitzPatrick, E., and Horning, A. (eds) 2018 *Becoming and belonging in Ireland, AD c. 1200–1600: essays in identity and cultural practice*. Cork University Press.

Campion, E. 1571 (reprint 1809) *A historie of Irland, written in the yeare* 1571. Dublin. Hibernia Press.

Carey, J. 1989 Otherworlds and verbal worlds in Middle Irish narrative. In W. Mahon (ed.), *Proceedings of the Harvard Celtic Colloquium* 9, 31–42. Cambridge, Mass. Harvard University Press.

Carney, J. 1975 Eochaidh Ó hEoghusa, poet to the Maguires of Fermanagh. *Clogher Record* 3, 187–211.

Carney, J. (ed.) 1943 *Topographical poems by Seaán Mór Ó Dubhagáin and Giolla-na-Naomh Ó hUidhrín*. Dublin Institute for Advanced Studies.

Carrigan, W. 1905 *The history and antiquities of the diocese of Ossory*, 2 vols, ii. Dublin. Sealy, Bryers and Walker.

Carver, M. and Spall, C. 2004 Excavating a *parchmenerie*: archaeological correlates of making parchment at the Pictish monastery at Portmahomack, Easter Ross. *Proceedings of the Society of Antiquaries of Scotland* 134, 183–200.

Charles-Edwards, T. M. 2000 *Early Christian Ireland*. Cambridge University Press.

Charles-Edwards, T. M. 1976 Boundaries in Irish law. In P. H. Sawyer (ed.), *Medieval settlement: continuity and change*, 83–7. London. Edward Arnold.

Claughton, P. and Rondelez, P. 2013 Early silver mining in western Europe: an Irish perspective. *Journal of the Mining Heritage Trust of Ireland* 13, 1–8.

Cody, E. 2002 *Survey of the megalithic tombs of Ireland, vi, County Donegal*. Dublin. The Stationery Office.

Cole, G. A. J. 1922 *Memoir and map of localities of minerals of economic importance and metalliferous mines in Ireland*. Memoirs of the Geological Survey of Ireland. Dublin. The Stationery Office.

Collins, A. E. P. 1978 Excavations on Ballygalley Hill, County Antrim. *Ulster Journal of Archaeology* 41 (Third Series), 15–32.

Comber, M. 2016 The Irish cashel: enclosed settlement, fortified settlement or settled fortification? With evidence from ongoing excavations at Caherconnell, Co. Clare, western Ireland. In N. Christie and H. Hajnalka (eds), *Fortified settlements in early medieval Europe: defended communities of the 8th–10th centuries*. Oxford. Oxbow.

Comyn, D. (ed.) 1902 *Foras feasa ar Éirinn: the history of Ireland by Geoffrey Keating*, i. London. Irish Texts Society.

Connellan, M. J. 1951 Killery: an artificial adjunct of Tirerrill. *Journal of Ardagh and Clonmacnoise Antiquarian Society* 2 (12), 28–31.

Connolly, S. J. 1998 *The Oxford companion to Irish history*. Oxford University Press.

Connon, A. 2016 Territoriality and the cult of Saint Ciarán of Saigir. In T. Ó Carragáin and S. Turner (eds), *Making Christian landscapes in Atlantic Europe: conversion and consolidation in the Early Middle Ages*, 110–58. Cork University Press.

Cooke, T. L. 1869 On ancient bells. *JRSAI* 1, 47–63.

Cooper, G. J. and Shannon, W. D. 2017 The control of salters (deer-leaps) in private deer-parks associated with forests: a case study using a 1608 map of Leagram Park in the Forest of Bowland, Lancashire. *Landscape History* 38 (1), 43–66.

Costello, T. B. 1940 The ancient law school of Park, Co. Galway. *Journal of the Galway Archaeological and Historical Society* 19 (1–2), 89–100.

Costello, M. A. 1909 *De annatis Hiberniae: a calendar of the first fruits' fees levied on papal appointments to benefices in Ireland AD 1400 to 1535, i: Ulster*. Dundalk. Tempest.

Cotter, C. 2012 *The western stone forts project, volume 2: excavations at Dún Aonghasa and Dún Eoghanachta*. Dublin. Wordwell.

Coxon, C. E. and Coxon, P. 1994 Carbonate deposition in turloughs (seasonal lakes) on the western limestone lowlands of Ireland. *Irish Geography* 27, 28–35.

Crawford, H. S. 1913 Notes on stones used as a cure at Killerry, near Dromahair, and on certain bullauns. *JRSAI* 3 (3), 267–9.

Cronin, P. J. 2001 Mid 20th century mines in the Doolin area, Co. Clare, Ireland. *Proceedings of the University of Bristol Spelaeological Society* 22 (2), 225–33.

Crushell, P. and Foss, P. 2008 *The County Clare wetland survey*. Ennis. Clare County Council.

Cunningham, B. 2009 *The annals of the Four Masters: Irish history, kingship and society in the early seventeenth century*. Dublin. Four Courts Press.

Cunningham, B. 2000 *The world of Geoffrey Keating: history, myth and religion in seventeenth century Ireland*. Dublin. Four Courts Press.

Cunningham, B. and Fitzpatrick, S. (eds) 2013 *Aon amharc ar Éirinn: Gaelic families and their manuscripts*. Dublin. Royal Irish Academy.

Curley, D. 2021 Uilliam Buide Ó Cellaig and the late medieval renaissance of the Uí Maine lordship. In L. McInerney and K. Simms (eds), *Gaelic Ireland (c 600-c.1700): lordship, saints and learning*, 32–45. Dublin. Wordwell.

Curta, F. (ed.) 2005 *Borders, barriers, and ethnogenesis: frontiers in late antiquity and the Middle Ages*. Studies in the Early Middle Ages (SEM 12). Turnhout. Brepols.

Curtis, E. (ed. and tr.) 1941 *Calendar of Ormond Deeds*, v, 1547–1584. Dublin. The Stationery Office.

Curtis, E. (ed. and tr.) 1937 *Calendar of Ormond Deeds*, iv, 1509–1547. Dublin. The Stationery Office.

Curtis, E. (ed. and tr.) 1932 *Calendar of Ormond Deeds*, i, 1172–1350. Dublin. The Stationery Office.

Dalton, J. P. 1921–4 Cromm Cruaich of Magh Sleacht. *PRIA* 36C, 23–67.

Daniel, G. E. 1952 The Prehistoric Society: a report of the meeting held in Dublin. *Archaeology News Letter* 4 (5), 71–5.

Darcy, E. 2021 'The footsteps of that custom . . . still remaining': medieval memory culture and Thomas O'Sullevane's portrayal of the Irish bardic tradition. *PRIA* 122C, 1–24.

Davies, O. 1948 The churches of County Cavan. *JRSAI* 78, 73–118.

Davies, W. 2014 Monastic landscapes and society. In J. H. Arnold (ed.) *The Oxford handbook of medieval Christianity*, 132–47. Oxford University Press.

de hÓir, S. 1983 The Mount Callan ogham stone and its context. *North Munster Antiquarian Journal* 25, 43–57.

Dillon, M. (ed. and tr.) 1966 Ceart Uí Néill. *Studia Celtica* 1, 1–18.

Dillon, M. 1961 The inauguration of O'Conor. In J. A. Watt, F. X. Martin, and J. B. Morrall (eds) *Medieval studies presented to Aubrey Gwynn*, 186–202. Dublin. Colm Ó Lochlainn.

Dinneen, P. S. (ed. and tr.) 1914 *Foras feasa ar Éirinn: the history of Ireland by Geoffrey Keating*, iii. London. Irish Texts Society.

Dinneen, P. S. (ed. and tr.) 1908 *Foras feasa ar Éirinn: the history of Ireland by Geoffrey Keating*, ii. London. Irish Texts Society.

Doan, J. E. 1985 The Ó Dálaigh family of bardic poets, 1139–1691. *Éire–Ireland* 20 (2), 19–31.

Dodgshon, R. A. 1998 *From chiefs to landlords: social and economic change in the western highlands and islands, c.1493–1820*. Edinburgh University Press.

Dodgshon, R. A. 1978 Land improvement in Scottish farming: marl and lime in Roxburghshire and Berwickshire in the eighteenth century. *The Agricultural History Review* 26, 1–14.

Duffy, P. J. 2001 Social and spatial order in the MacMahon lordship of Airghialla in the late sixteenth century. In P. J. Duffy, D. Edwards, and E. FitzPatrick (eds), *Gaelic Ireland c.1250– c.1650: land, lordship and settlement*, 115–37. Dublin. Four Courts Press.

Duffy, P. J., Edwards, D., and FitzPatrick, E. (eds) 2001 *Gaelic Ireland c.1250–c.1650: land, lordship and settlement*. Dublin. Four Courts Press.

Dwyer, P. 1878 *The diocese of Killaloe from the Reformation to the close of the eighteenth century, with an appendix*. Dublin. Hodges, Foster, and Figgis.

Elden, S. 2013 *The birth of territory*. University of Chicago Press.

Ellis, S. G. and Murray, J. (eds) 2017 *Calendar of state papers, Ireland, Tudor period 1509–1547*. Dublin. Irish Manuscripts Commission.

Escolar, M. 2003 Exploration, cartography and the modernisation of state power. In N. Brenner, B. Jessop, M. Jones, and G. MacLeod (eds), *State/space: a reader*, 29–52. Oxford. Blackwell.

Evans, E. E. 1942 *Irish heritage: the landscape, the people and their work*. Dundalk. Dundalgan Press.

Farrell, R. 1991 The Crannog Archaeology Project (CAP): archaeological field research in the lakes of the west midlands of Ireland. In C. Karkov and R. T. Farrell (eds), *Studies in insular art and archaeology*, 99–110. Oxford, Oh. American Early Medieval Studies and the Miami University School of Fine Arts.

Fennell, W. J. 1904 Church Island or Inishmore, Lough Gill. *Ulster Journal of Archaeology* 10 (4), 166–9.

Ferguson, K. 2001 Castles and the Pallas placename: a German insight. *The Irish Sword* 22 (89), 241–8.

Ferguson, S. 1887 *Ogham inscriptions in Ireland, Wales, and Scotland*. Edinburgh. David Douglas.

Ferguson, S. 1879a On the ogham-inscribed stone on Callan Mountain, Co. Clare. *PRIA* 1, 160–71.

Ferguson, S. 1879b On the evidences bearing on sun-worship at Mount Callan, Co. Clare. *PRIA* 1, 265–72.

Ferguson, S. 1879c On the alleged literary forgery respecting sun-worship on Mount Callan. *PRIA* 1, 315–22.

Finan, T. and O'Conor, K. 2002 The moated site at Cloonfree, Co. Roscommon. *Journal of the Galway Archaeological and Historical Society* 54, 72–87.

FitzPatrick, E. 2022 Gaelic political assemblies and power-display in borderlands of Westmeath lordships. In S. O'Brien (ed), *Westmeath: history and society*, 57–79. Dublin. Geography Publications.

FitzPatrick, E. 2021 A learned identity: monuments to Thomas Coffy, at Lynally, Co. Offaly. In T. Dooley, M. A. Lyons, and S. Ryan (eds), *The historian as detective: uncovering Irish pasts*, 141–3. Dublin. Four Courts Press.

FitzPatrick, E. 2019 Finn's wilderness and boundary landforms in medieval Ireland. In M. Egeler (ed.), *Landscape and myth in northwestern Europe*, 113–46. Borders, boundaries, landscapes: 2. Turnhout. Brepols.

FitzPatrick, E. 2018 Gaelic service families and the landscape of *lucht tighe*. In Campbell, FitzPatrick, and Horning (eds), *Becoming and belonging in Ireland*, 167–88.

FitzPatrick, E. 2017 Finn's seat: topographies of power and royal marchlands of Gaelic polities in medieval Ireland. *Landscape History* 38 (2), 29–62.

FitzPatrick, E. 2016 The last kings of Ireland: material expressions of Gaelic lordship *c.* 1300–1400 AD. In K. Buchanan and L. H. S. Dean, with M. Penman (eds), *Medieval and early modern representations of authority in Scotland and the British Isles*, 197–213. London and New York. Taylor and Francis.

FitzPatrick, E. 2015a Assembly places and elite collective identities in medieval Ireland. *Journal of the North Atlantic, Special Volume 8: Debating the Thing in the North II: Selected Papers from Workshops Organized by the Assembly Project*, 52–68.

FitzPatrick, E. 2015b *Ollamh, biatach, comharba*: lifeways of Gaelic learned families in medieval and early modern Ireland. In L. Breathnach, R. Ó hUiginn, D. McManus and K. Simms (eds),

Proceedings of the XIV International Congress of Celtic Studies, Maynooth 2011, 165–89. Dublin Institute for Advanced Studies.

FitzPatrick, E. 2013a *Formaoil na Fiann*: hunting preserves and assembly places in Gaelic Ireland. In D. Furchtgott, G. Henley and M. Holmberg (eds), *Proceedings of the Harvard Celtic Colloquium* 32, 2012, 95–118. Cambridge, Mass. Harvard University Press.

FitzPatrick, E. 2013b The landscape and settlements of the Uí Dhálaigh poets of Muinter Bháire. In S. Duffy (ed.), *Princes, prelates and poets in medieval Ireland: essays in honour of Katharine Simms*, 460–80. Dublin. Four Courts Press.

FitzPatrick, E. 2011 Cahermacnaghten: late medieval/early post-medieval building (08E435). In I. Bennett (ed.), *Excavations 2008: summary accounts of excavations in Ireland*, 41–3. Dublin. Wordwell.

FitzPatrick, E. 2009 Native enclosed settlement and the problem of the 'Irish ring-fort'. *Medieval Archaeology* 53, 290–3.

FitzPatrick, E. 2008 Antiquarian scholarship and the archaeology of Cahermacnaghten, Burren, Co. Clare. *The Other Clare* 32, 58–66.

FitzPatrick, E. 2005 Promontory forts. In S. Duffy (ed.), *Medieval Ireland: an encyclopedia*, 389–91. New York and London. Routledge.

FitzPatrick, E. 2004 *Royal inauguration in Gaelic Ireland c.1100–1600: a cultural landscape study*. Studies in Celtic history: 22. Woodbridge. Boydell Press.

FitzPatrick, E. 2001 The gathering place of Tír Fhiachrach? Archaeological and folkloric investigations at Aughris, Co. Sligo, *Proceedings of the Royal Irish Academy* 101C, 67–105.

FitzPatrick, E. 1998 The early church in Offaly. In W. Nolan and T. P. O'Neill (eds), *Offaly: history and society*, 93–129. Dublin. Geography Publications.

FitzPatrick E. 2003 On the trail of an ancient highway: rediscovering Dála's road. In J. Fenwick (ed.), *Lost and found: discovering Ireland's past*, 165-71. Bray. Wordwell.

FitzPatrick, E. and Clutterbuck R. 2013a Cabhail Tighe Breac Cahermacnaghten: late medieval/early post-medieval Gaelic schoolhouse (10E0147). In I. Bennett (ed.) *Excavations 2010: summary accounts of archaeological excavations in Ireland*, 26–7. Dublin. Wordwell.

FitzPatrick, E. and Clutterbuck, R. 2013b Cahermacnaghten: post-medieval dwelling (10E146). In I. Bennett (ed.) *Excavations 2010: summary accounts of archaeological excavations in Ireland*, 24–5. Dublin. Wordwell.

FitzPatrick, E., Murphy, E., McHugh, R., Donnelly, C. and Foley, C. 2011 Evoking the white mare: the cult landscape of Sgiath Gabhra and its medieval perception in Gaelic Fir Mhanach. In R. Schot, C. Newman, and E. Bhreathnach (eds), *Landscapes of cult and kingship*, 163–91. Dublin. Four Courts Press.

FitzPatrick, E. and O'Brien, C. 1998 *The medieval churches of County Offaly*. Dublin. Government of Ireland.

FitzPatrick, E. and Ó Drisceoil, C. 2016 The landscape and law school settlement of the O'Doran brehons, Ballyorley, Co. Wexford. In I. W. Doyle and B. Browne (eds), *Medieval Wexford: essays in memory of Billy Colfer*, 383–415. Dublin. Four Courts Press.

Flanagan, D. and Flanagan, L. 1994 *Irish place names*. Dublin. Gill and Macmillan.

Flower, R. 1947 *The Irish tradition*. Oxford. Clarendon Press.

Flower, R. 1926 *Catalogue of manuscripts in the British Museum*, ii. London. British Museum.

Foley, C. and Donnelly, C. 2012 *Parke's Castle, Co. Leitrim: archaeology, history and architecture*. Archaeological monograph series: 7. Dublin. The Stationery Office.

Foley, C. and McHugh, R. 2014 *An archaeological survey of County Fermanagh, i, part 1: the prehistoric period; part 2: the early Christian and medieval periods.* Newtownards. Northern Ireland Environment Agency.

Follett, W. 2013–14 Religious texts in the Mac Aodhagáin library of Lower Ormond. *Peritia* 24–5, 213–29.

Forsyth, K. and Tedeschi, C. 2008 Text-inscribed slates. In C. Lowe (ed.), *Inchmarnock: an early historic island monastery and its archaeological landscape*, 128–51. Edinburgh. Society of Antiquaries of Scotland.

Frazer, W. 1896 On 'holed' and perforated stones in Ireland. *JRSAI* 6 (2), 158–69.

Freeman, A. M. (ed. and tr.) 1944 *Annála Connacht: the annals of Connacht (A.D. 1244–1544).* Dublin Institute for Advanced Studies.

Freeman, A. M. (ed.) 1936 *The compossicion booke of Conought.* Dublin. The Stationery Office.

Frost, J. 1893 *The history and topography of the county of Clare: from the earliest times to the beginning of the 18th century.* Dublin. Sealy, Briars and Walker.

Fuller, A. P. (ed.) 1994 *Calendar of entries in the papal registers relating to Great Britain and Ireland, xvii, part 1, 1492–1503.* Dublin. Irish Manuscripts Commission.

Fulton, H. 2019 The Red Book and the White: gentry libraries in medieval Wales. In A. Byrne and V. Flood (eds), *Crossing borders in the insular Middle Ages*, 23–43. Medieval texts and cultures in northern Europe series: 30. Turnhout. Brepols.

Gardiner, M. 2018 Landscape and farming in the north of Ireland in the late Middle Ages and early modern period: the evidence from the uplands. *The Journal of Irish Archaeology* 27, 117–33.

Gillespie, R. 2014 Scribes and manuscripts in Gaelic Ireland, 1400–1700. *Studia Hibernica* 40, 9–34.

Gleeson, D. F. 1962 *A history of the diocese of Killaloe.* Dublin. M. H. Gill.

Gleeson, D. F. 1951 Churches in the deanery of Ormond: Aradh and Ormond Lower. *North Munster Antiquarian Journal* 6 (3), 96–107.

Gleeson, D. F. 1936 Drawing of a hunting scene, Urlan Castle, Co. Clare. *JRSAI* 6, 193.

Gleeson, D. F. 1935 Find of harp peg at Toomullin, Co. Clare. *JRSAI* 5 (1), 148.

Gleeson, P. 2015 Kingdoms, communities, and *óenaig. Journal of the North Atlantic, Special Volume 8: Debating the Thing in the North II: Selected Papers from Workshops Organized by the Assembly Project*, 33–51.

Gosling, P. 2015 Placing names in *Táin Bó Cúailnge*: 'Findabair Chúailnge' and 'Findabair Sléibe'. *Journal of the County Louth Archaeological and Historical Society*, 28 (3), 309–25.

Griffin, K. M., Griffin, K. A., and Griffin, B. J. 2020 *Doolin: history and memories.* Technological University Dublin.

Griffith, M. C. 1991 *Calendar of inquisitions formerly in the office of the chief remembrancer of the exchequer prepared from the MSS of the Irish Record Commission.* Dublin. The Stationery Office.

Griffith, M. C. (ed.) 1966 *Irish patent rolls of James I: facsimile of the Irish Record Commission's calendar.* Dublin. Irish Manuscripts Commission.

Grogan, E. 2005 *The North Munster Project, i: the later prehistoric landscape of south-east Clare.* Discovery Programme monograph: 6. Dublin. Wordwell.

Grose, F. 1791 *The antiquities of Ireland*, i. London. S. Hooper.

Gwynn, A. and Hadcock, R. N. 1970 *Medieval religious houses: Ireland: with an appendix to early sites.* London. Longmans.

Gwynn, E. (ed. and tr.) 1905–35 *The metrical Dindshenchas*, 5 vols. Todd lecture series: 9–12. Dublin. Royal Irish Academy.

Gwynn, L. (ed. and tr.) 1911 The life of St Lasair. *Ériu* 5, 73–109.

Hamilton, H. C. 1885 *Calendar of the state papers relating to Ireland, of the reign of Elizabeth, 1588, August–1592, September*, iv. London. HMSO.

Hardiman, J. 1831 *Irish minstrelsy or bardic remains of Ireland: with English poetical translations*, 2 vols. London. Joseph Robins.

Hardiman, J. (ed.) 1828 Ancient Irish deeds and writings chiefly relating to landed property from the twelfth to seventeenth century: with translation, notes and a preliminary essay. *Transactions of the Royal Irish Academy* 15, 3–95.

Hardiman, J. (ed.) 1826 *Inquisitionum in officio rotulorum cancellariae Hiberniae*, i. Dublin. Grierson and Keene.

Hardiman, J. 1825 A catalogue of maps, charts, and plans, relating to Ireland preserved amongst the manuscripts in the library of Trinity College, Dublin. *Transactions of the Royal Irish Academy* 14, 57–77.

Harmanşah, Ö. (ed.) 2014 *Of rocks and water: towards an archaeology of place*. Joukowsky Institute publication: 5. Oxford and Philadelphia. Oxbow Books.

Harrel, D. (ed.) 1897 *The twenty-ninth report of the deputy keeper of the public records and keeper of state papers in Ireland*. Dublin. HMSO.

Harris, W. (ed.) 1739 and 1745 *The whole works of Sir James Ware concerning Ireland, revised and improved*, 2 vols. Dublin. E. Jones.

Hayden, D. 2019 Attribution and authority in an Irish medical manuscript. *Studia Hibernica* 45, 19–51.

Healy, J. N. 1988 *The castles of County Cork*. Cork. Mercier Press.

Hemp, W. J. 1931 Leac Con Mic Ruis. *Antiquity* 5 (17), 98–101.

Hennessy, W. M. 1871 *The annals of Loch Cé: a chronicle of Irish affairs from ad 1014 to A.D. 1590*, 2 vols. London. Longman.

Hennessy, W. M. and McCarthy, B. (ed. and tr.) 1887–1901 *Annála Uladh: the annals of Ulster, otherwise Annála Senait: the annals of Senat: a chronicle of Irish affairs from ad 431 to A.D. 1540*, 4 vols. Dublin. HMSO.

Herbert, M. 2009 Medieval collections of ecclesiastical and devotional materials: Leabhar breac, Liber Flavus Fergusiorum and the Book of Fenagh. In B. Cunningham, S. FitzPatrick, and P. Schnabel (eds), *Treasures of the Royal Irish Academy Library*, 33–43. Dublin. Royal Irish Academy.

Herren, M. W. 1973 The authorship, date of composition and provenance of the so-called Lorica Gildae. *Ériu* 24, 35–51.

Herren, M. W. 1974–87 The *Hisperica famina*, 2 vols. Toronto. Pontifical Institute Mediaeval Studies.

Herries Davies, G. L. 2011 The chalk outlier at Ballydeenlea, Co. Kerry: a story of discovery. *Irish Journal of Earth Sciences* 29, 27–38.

Hill, G. 1877 *An historical account of the plantation of Ulster at the commencement of the seventeenth century, 1608–1620*. Belfast. McGaw, Stevenson, and Orr.

Historical Manuscripts Commission 1897 *The manuscripts of Charles Haliday: acts of the Privy Council in Ireland, 1556–1571*. London. HMSO.

Hogan, E. 1910 *Onomasticon Goedelicum*. Dublin: Hodges, Figgis and Co.

Hourihan, K. 1991 Rural settlement and change near Bantry 1600–1845. *Bantry Historical and Archaeological Society* 1, 44–53.

Hourihane, C. 2003 *Gothic art in Ireland, 1169–1550: enduring vitality.* New Haven and London. Yale University Press.

Hoyne, M. (ed.) 2018 *Fuidheall Áir: bardic poems on the Meic Dhiarmada of Magh Luirg c.1377–c.1637.* Dublin Institute for Advanced Studies.

Hughes, A. J. 1994–5 Land acquisitions by Gaelic bardic poets: insights from place-names and other sources. *Ainm: Bulletin of the Ulster Place-Name Society* 6, 74–102.

Hunt, J. 1950 Rory O'Tunney and the Ossory tomb sculptures. *JRSAI* 80 (1), 22–8.

Hyde, D. 1899 *A literary history of Ireland: from earliest times to the present day.* London. Fisher Unwin.

Iremonger, S. F. and Kelly, D. L. 1988 The responses of four Irish wetland tree species to raised soil water levels. *New Phytologist* 109 (4), 491–7.

Jarman, A. O. H. and Hughes, G. R. (eds) 1991 *A guide to Welsh literature ii: 1282– c.1550,* revised by D. Johnston (second ed., 1998). Cardiff. University of Wales Press.

Jeffries, H. A. 2010 *The Irish Church and the Tudor reformations.* Dublin. Four Courts Press.

Jeffries, H. A. 2006 Parishes and pastoral care in Ireland in the early Tudor era. In E. FitzPatrick and R. Gillespie (eds), *The parish in medieval and early modern Ireland: community, territory and building,* 211–27. Dublin. Four Courts Press.

Johnston, E. 2013 *Literacy and identity in early medieval Ireland.* Woodbridge. Boydell Press.

Jones, C. 2016 Dating ancient field walls in karst landscapes using differential bedrock lowering. *Geoarchaeology* 31 (2), 1–24.

Kalkreuter, B. 2001 *Boyle Abbey and the School of the West.* Bray. Wordwell.

Kane, R. 1844 *The industrial resources of Ireland.* Dublin. Hodges and Smith.

Keaveney A. and Madden, J. A. (eds) 1992 *Sir William Herbert: croftus sive de Hibernia liber.* Dublin. Irish Manuscripts Commission.

Kelly, E. P. 1991 Observations on Irish lakes. In C. Karkov and R. T. Farrell (eds), *Studies in insular art and archaeology,* 81–97. Oxford, Oh. American Early Medieval Studies and the Miami University School of Fine Arts.

Kelly, F. 2000 *Early Irish farming.* Dublin Institute for Advanced Studies.

Kelly, F. 1988 *A guide to early Irish law.* Dublin Institute for Advanced Studies.

Kelly, J. 2007 A history of Zn-Pb-Ag mining at Abbeytown, Co. Sligo. *Journal of the Mining Heritage Trust of Ireland* 7, 9–18.

Kew, G. (ed.) 1998 The Irish sections of Fynes Moryson's unpublished itinerary. Dublin. Irish Manuscripts Commission.

Kilroe, J. R. 1885 *Explanatory memoir to accompany sheet 55 of the maps of the Geological Survey of Ireland comprising portions of the counties of Sligo and Leitrim,* 8. Dublin. HMSO.

Kinahan, G. H. 1879–88 Sepulchral and other prehistoric relics, counties Wexford and Wicklow. *PRIA* 2, 152–60.

Knott, E. 1957 (reprint 1981) *An introduction to Irish syllabic poetry of the period 1200–1600.* Dublin Institute for Advanced Studies.

Knott, E. (ed. and tr.) 1926 *The bardic poems of Tadhg Dall Ó Huiginn (1550–1591): translation, notes, etc.,* ii. London. Irish Texts Society.

Knott, E. (ed. and tr.) 1922 *A bhfuil aguinn dár chum Tadhg Dall O'Huiginn (1550–1591),* i. London. Irish Texts Society.

Knott, E. 1911 Filidh Éreann go haointeach. *Ériu* 5, 50–69.

Lacey, B. 2006 *Cenél Conaill and the Donegal kingdoms AD 500–800*. Dublin. Four Courts Press.

Lacey, B. 1983 *Archaeological survey of County Donegal: a description of the field antiquities of the County from Mesolithic period to the 17th century AD*. Lifford. Donegal County Council.

Lawlor, H. C. 1925 *The monastery of Saint Mochaoi of Nendrum*. Belfast. Natural History and Philosophical Society.

Leask, H. G. 1960 *Irish churches and monastic buildings, iii: medieval Gothic, the last phases*. Dundalk. Dundalgan Press.

Ledwich, E. 1804 *Antiquities of Ireland: the second edition, with additions and corrections, to which is added, a collection of miscellaneous antiquities*. Dublin. Grueber.

Leerssen, J. 1994 *The contention of the bards (Iomarbhágh na bhfileadh) and its place in Irish political and literary history*. Irish Texts Society subsidiary series: 2. London. Irish Texts Society.

Lennon, C. 2008 The parish fraternities of County Meath in the late Middle Ages. *Ríocht na Midhe* 19, 85–101.

Lennon, C. 2007 Pedagogy as reform: the influence of Peter White on Irish education in the Renaissance. In T. Herron and M. Potterton (eds), *Ireland in the Renaissance, c.1540–1660*, 43–51. Dublin. Four Courts Press.

Lockwood, F. W. 1903 Kilbarron Castle and Church, Co. Donegal. *Ulster Journal of Archaeology* 9 (3), 111–16.

Lockwood, F. W. 1901 Some notes on the old Irish "sweat-houses" at Assaroe, Ballyshannon and Kinlough, Co. Leitrim, and on several rude stone monuments near Bundoran and Ballyshannon. *Ulster Journal of Archaeology* 7 (2), 82–92.

Lloyd, S. 1780 *A short tour and impartial and accurate description of the county of Clare*. Ennis.

Long, C. B., McConnell, B. J., Alsop, G. I., O'Connor, P. I., Claringbold, K., and Cronin, C. 1999 *Geology of south Donegal: a geological description of south Donegal, to accompany the bedrock geology 1:100,000 scale map series, sheet 3/4, south Donegal*. Dublin. Geological Survey of Ireland.

Lowe, C. (ed.) 2008 *Inchmarnock: an early historic island monastery and its archaeological landscape*. Edinburgh. Society of Antiquaries of Scotland.

Lucas, A. T. 1963 National Museum of Ireland archaeological acquisitions in the year 1961. *JRSAI* 93 (2), 115–33.

Mac Airt, S. (ed.) 1944 *Leabhar Branach: the book of the O'Byrnes*. Dublin Institute for Advanced Studies.

Mac Airt, S. and Ó Fiaich, T. (eds) 1956 A thirteenth century poem on Armagh cathedral by Giolla Brighde Mac Con Midhe. *Seanchas Ardmhacha: Journal of the Armagh Diocesan Historical Society* 2 (1), 145–62.

Macalister, R. A. S. 1937–8 On an excavation conducted on Cro-Inis, Loch Ennell. *PRIA* 44C, 248–52.

Mac Cana, P. 1974 The rise of the later schools of *filidheacht*. *Ériu* 25, 126–46.

McCarthy, A. 2001 *Under the shadow of Suífinn: perspectives of Kilcrohane through the years*. Kilcrohane.

McClatchie, M., McCormick, F., Kerr, T. R. and O'Sullivan, A. 2015 Early medieval farming and food production: a review of the archaeobotanical evidence from archaeological excavations in Ireland. *Vegetation History and Archaeobotany* 24, 179–86.

MacCoinnich, A. 2015 Dùn Èistean and the "Morisons" of Ness in the lordship of Lewis: the historical background, *c.1493–c.1700*. In R. C. Barrowman (ed.), *Dùn Èistean, Ness: the excavation of a clan stronghold*, 41–68. Stornoway. Acair.

McCormick, F. 2014 Agriculture, settlement and society in early medieval Ireland. *Quaternary International* 346, 119–30.

McCormick, F., Kerr, T.R., McClatchie, M. and O'Sullivan, A. 2014 *Early medieval agriculture, livestock and cereal production in Ireland, AD 400–1100*. BAR International Series 2647. Oxford. BAR Publishing.

MacCotter, P. 2019 The origins of the parish in Ireland. *PRIA* 119C, 37–76.

MacCotter, P. 2008 *Medieval Ireland: territorial, political, and economic divisions*. Dublin. Four Courts Press.

MacDonald, C. 1845 *The new statistical account of Scotland, xiv: Inverness—Ross and Cromarty*. Edinburgh and London. William Blackwood.

McDonald, K. 2009 The lost tombs of Finner Camp, Co. Donegal. *Defence Forces Review 2009*, 1–9.

McErlean, T. 1983 The Irish townland system of landscape organisation. In T. Reeves-Smyth and F. Hamond (eds), *Landscape archaeology in Ireland*. BAR British series: 116. Oxford: BAR.

McErlean, T. and Crothers, N. 2007 *Harnessing the tides: the early medieval tide mills at Nendrum Monastery, Strangford Lough*. Belfast. Environment and Heritage Service.

Mac Giolla Easpaig, D. 2009 Ireland's heritage of geographical names. *Wiener Schriften zur Geographie und Kartographie* 18, 79–85. Vienna.

McGrath, C. 1957 Í Eódhosa. *Clogher Record* 2 (1), 1–19.

Mac Hale, C. 1990 *Annals of the Clan Egan*. Enniscrone. Conor Mac Hale.

McInerney, L. 2014 *Clerical and learned lineages of medieval Co. Clare: a survey of the fifteenth-century papal registers*. Dublin. Four Courts Press.

McInerney, L. 2012 Lettermoylan of Clann Bhruaideadha: a *résumé* of their landholding, topography and history. *North Munster Antiquarian Journal* 52, 81–113.

McInerney, L. 2008 The West Clann Chuiléin lordship in 1586: evidence from a forgotten inquisition. *North Munster Antiquarian Journal* 48, 33–62.

McInerney, L. and Simms, K. 2021 *Gaelic Ireland (c. 600-c.1700): lordships, saints and learning: essays for the Irish chief's and clans' prize in history*. Dublin. Wordwell.

Mac Iomhair, D. 1965 Townlands of County Louth in AD 1301. *Journal of the County Louth Archaeological and Historical Society* 16 (1), 42–9.

Mac Iomhair, D. 1962 The boundaries of Fir Rois. *Journal of the County Louth Archaeological and Historical Society* 15 (2), 144–79.

McKenna, L. (ed.) 1947a *The Book of Magauran: Leabhar Méig Shamhradháin*. Dublin Institute for Advanced Studies.

McKenna, L. 1947b A poem by Gofraidh Fionn Ó Dálaigh. In S. Pender (ed.), *Féilsgríbhinn Torna*, 66–76. Cork University Press.

McKenna, L. 1940 *Aithdioghluim dána: a miscellany of Irish bardic poetry*, ii. London. Irish Texts Society.

McKenna, L. 1929a A partition of Ireland, part 1. *The Irish Monthly* 57 (672), 330–3.

McKenna, L. 1929b A partition of Ireland, part 2. *The Irish Monthly* 57 (673), 368–72.

McKenna, L. (ed. and tr.) 1923 Poem to Cloonfree Castle. *Irish Monthly* 51 (606), 639–45.

McKenna, L. (ed. and tr.) 1919 Historical poems of Gofraidh Fionn Ó Dálaigh. *Irish Monthly* 47 (547), 166–70.

McKenzie, C. J. and Murphy, E. M. 2018 *Life and death in medieval Gaelic Ireland: the skeletons from Ballyhanna, Co. Donegal*. Dublin. Four Courts Press.

MacKinnon, D. 1912 *A descriptive catalogue of Gaelic manuscripts in the Advocates Library Edinburgh and elsewhere in Scotland*. Edinburgh. William Brown.

Mackley, J. S. 2008 *The legend of St Brendan: a comparative study of the Latin and Anglo-Norman versions*. Leiden and Boston. Brill.

McLeod, N. 2005 Brehon law. In S. Duffy (ed.), *Medieval Ireland: an encyclopedia*, 42–5. New York and London. Routledge.

McLeod, W. 2004 *Divided Gaels: Gaelic cultural identities in Scotland and Ireland* c. *1200–* c. *1650*. Oxford University Press.

McManus, D. 2004 The bardic poet as teacher, student and critic: a context for the grammatical tracts. In C. G. Ó Háinle and D. E. Meek (eds), *Unity in diversity: studies in Irish and Scottish Gaelic language, literature and history*, 121. Trinity College Dublin.

MacNamara, G. U. 1912–13 The O'Davorens of Cahermacnaughten, Burren, Co. Clare. *North Munster Archaeological Society Journal* 2, 63–212.

Mcnamara, M. E. and Hennessy, R. W. 2010 *The geology of the Burren region, Co. Clare, Ireland*. Ennistymon. The Burren Connect Project.

Macnamara, N. C. 1896 *The story of an Irish sept, their character and struggles to maintain their lands in Clare*. London. J. M. Dent.

Mac Neill, E. and Hogan, J. (eds) 1931 A booke of the kings lands founde upon the last generall survey within the province of Ulster, anno le: 1608. MS. Rawlinson A. 237. The Bodleian Library, Oxford. *Analecta Hibernica* 3, 151–218.

Mac Neill, E. and Murphy, G. (ed. and tr.) 1908–53 *Duanaire Finn: the book of the lays of Fionn*, 3 vols. London. Irish Texts Society.

MacNeill, M. 1962 *The festival of Lughnasa: a study of the survival of the Celtic festival of the beginning of harvest*. Oxford University Press.

McNeill, P. and Nicholson, R. (eds) 1975 *An historical atlas of Scotland, c.400–c.1600*. St Andrews. Atlas Committee of the Conference of Scottish Medievalists.

Mac Niocaill, G. (ed.) 1964 *The Red Book of the earls of Kildare*. Dublin. Irish Manuscripts Commission.

Macphail, J. R. N. (ed.) 1910–11 *Highland papers, i.* Scottish History Society, second series: 5. Edinburgh. Constable.

McSparron, C. 2001 The medieval coarse pottery of Ulster. *The Journal of Irish Archaeology* 20, 101–21.

Martin, M. 1703 *A description of the Western Islands of Scotland*. London. Andrew Bell.

Martinón-Torres, M. and Rehren, T. 2005 Alchemy, chemistry and metallurgy in Renaissance Europe: a wider context for fire-assay remains. *Historical Metallurgy* 39 (1), 14–28.

Meid, W. (ed.) 1974 *Táin bó Fraích*. Dublin Institute for Advanced Studies.

Mews, C. J. and Crossley, J. N. (eds) 2011 *Communities of learning: networks and the shaping of intellectual identity in Europe, 1100–1500*. Turnhout. Brepols.

Meyer, K. (ed. and tr.) 1906 *The triads of Ireland*. Dublin. Hodges Figgis.

Miller, D. A. 2000 *The epic hero*. Baltimore and London. Johns Hopkins University Press.

Miller, L. and Power, E. (eds) 1979 *Holinshed's Irish chronicle: the historie of Irelande from the first inhabitation thereof, unto the yeare 1509, collected by Raphaell Holinshed, and continued till the yeare 1547 by Richarde Stanyhurst*. Dublin. The Dolmen Press.

Mitchell, W. J. T. (ed.) 2002 *Landscape and power*. The University of Chicago Press.

Monk, M. A., Tierney, J., and Hannon, M. 1998 Archaeobotanical studies and early medieval Munster. In M.A. Monk and J. Sheehan (eds), *Early medieval Munster: archaeology, history and society*, 65-86. Cork University Press.

Moore, M. J. 1996 *Archaeological inventory of County Wexford*. Dublin. The Stationery Office.

Moreton, S., Lawson, J., and Lawson, R. 2009 Abbeytown mine and quarry, Ballysadare, Co. Sligo. *UK Journal of Mines and Minerals* 30, 34–42.

Morgan, H. 1993–5 'Lawes of Irelande': a tract by Sir John Davies. *Irish Jurist* 28–30, 307–13.

Morley, H. (ed.) 1890 *Ireland under Elizabeth and James the First*. London. Routledge.

Morrin, J. (ed.) 1862 *Calendar of the patent and close rolls of chancery in Ireland from the 18th to the 45th of Queen Elizabeth*, ii. Dublin. HMSO.

Morris, R. K. 1992 An English glossary of medieval mouldings: with an introduction to mouldings *c*.1040–1240. *Architectural History* 35, 1–17.

Morton, K. and Oldenbourg, C. 2005 Catalogue of the wall paintings. In C. Manning, P. Gosling, and J. Waddell (eds), *New survey of Clare Island, v: the abbey*. Dublin. Royal Irish Academy.

Moss, R. (ed.) 2014 *Art and architecture of Ireland: i, medieval, c.400–c.1600*. Dublin. Royal Irish Academy.

Moss, R. 2010 Romanesque sculpture in north Roscommon. In T. Finan (ed.), *Medieval Lough Cé: history, archaeology and landscape*, 119–44. Dublin. Four Courts Press.

Muhr, K. 2014 The place-names of County Fermanagh. In C. Foley and R. McHugh, *An archaeological survey of County Fermanagh I, part 1: the prehistoric period*, 17–54. Newtownards. The Northern Ireland Environmental Agency.

Muhr, K. 1996 *Place-names of Northern Ireland, vi: County Down IV. North-West Down/ Iveagh*. Belfast. Institute of Irish Studies.

Muhr, K. and Ó hAisibéil, L. 2021 *The Oxford dictionary of family names in Ireland*. Oxford University Press.

Mulchrone, K. 1939 (ed. and tr.) *Bethu Phátraic: the tripartite life of Patrick, i, text and sources*. Dublin and London. Royal Irish Academy.

Mulligan, P. 1954 Notes on the topography of Fermanagh. *Clogher Record* 1 (2), 24–34.

Mullin, D. 2011 *Places in between: the archaeology of social, cultural and geographical borders and borderlands*. Oxford. Oxbow Books.

Murphy, D. (ed.) 1896 *The annals of Clonmacnoise: being the annals of Ireland from the earliest period to ad 1408. Translated into English ad 1627 by Conell Mageoghegan*. Dublin. Royal Society of Antiquaries of Ireland.

Murphy, E. 2011 Children's burial grounds in Ireland (*cillíní*) and parental emotions toward infant death. *International Journal of Historical Archaeology* 15 (3), 409–28.

Murray, K. 2012 Interpreting the evidence: problems with dating the early *fíanaigecht* corpus. In S. J. Arbuthnot and G. Parsons (eds), *The Gaelic Finn tradition*, i, 31–49. Dublin. Four Courts Press.

Murray, K. 2005 Fenian cycle. In S. Duffy (ed.), *Medieval Ireland: an encyclopedia*, 166–7. New York and London. Routledge.

Murray, L. P. 1936 The will of James Hussey of Smarmore, Co. Louth, 'priest' (AD 1635). *Journal of the County Louth Archaeological and Historical Society* 8 (4), 303–21.

Mytum, H. 1982 The location of early churches in northern County Clare. In S. M. Pearce (ed.), *The early Church in western Britain and Ireland: Studies presented to C. A. Ralegh Radford*, 351–61. British Archaeological Report. British Series 102. Oxford.

Nagy, J. F. 1985 *The wisdom of the outlaw: the boyhood deeds of Finn in Gaelic narrative tradition*. Berkeley. University of California Press.

National Parks and Wildlife Service 2018 *Conservation objectives: Farranamanagh Lough (SAC 002189)*. Dublin. Department of Culture, Heritage and the Gaeltacht.

Naum, M. 2012 Difficult middles, hybridity and ambivalence of a medieval frontier: the cultural landscape of Lolland and Falster (Denmark). *Journal of Medieval History* 38 (1), 56–75.

Naum, M. 2010 Re-emerging frontiers: postcolonial theory and historical archaeology of borderlands. *Journal of Archaeological Method and Theory* 17 (2), 101–31.

Newton, A. 2000 Ocean-transported pumice in the north Atlantic. PhD diss., University of Edinburgh.

Nic Dhonnchadha, A. 2006 The medical school of Aghmacart, Queen's County. *Ossory, Laois and Leinster* 2, 11–43.

Nicholls, K. W. (ed.) 1994 *The Irish fiants of the Tudor sovereigns: during the reigns of Henry VIII, Edward VI, Philip and Mary, and Elizabeth I*, 4 vols. Dublin. Edmund Burke.

Nicholls, K. W. 1987 Gaelic society and economy in the high Middle Ages. In A. Cosgrove (ed.), *A new history of Ireland ii: medieval Ireland 1168–1534*, 397–438. Oxford University Press.

Nicholls, K. W. 1976 Lordships, *c.*1534. In T. W. Moody, F. X. Martin, and F. J. Byrne (eds), *A new history of Ireland, iii: early modern Ireland 1534–1691*. Oxford University Press.

Nicholls, K. W. 1972 (2nd ed. 2003) *Gaelic and gaelicised Ireland in the Middle Ages*. Dublin. Gill and Macmillan.

Nicholls, K. W. 1970 Some documents on Irish law and custom in the sixteenth century. *Analecta Hibernica* 26, 105–29.

Ní Dhonnchadha, M. 2002 Courts and coteries I, *c.*900–1600. In A. Bourke *et al.* (eds), *The Field Day anthology of Irish writing, iv: Irish women's writing and traditions*, 293–332. New York University Press.

Ní Ghabhláin, S. 1996 The origin of medieval parishes in Gaelic Ireland: the evidence from Kilfenora. *JRSAI* 126, 37–61.

Ní Ghabhláin, S. 1995 Church and community in medieval Ireland: the diocese of Kilfenora. *JRSAI* 125, 61–84.

Ní Mharcaigh, M. 1997 The medieval parish churches of south-west County Dublin. *PRIA* 97C, 245–96.

Nolan, J. P. 1901 Galway castles and owners in 1574. *Journal of the Galway Archaeological and Historical Society* 1 (2), 109–23.

Nugent, P. 2007 *The Gaelic clans of Co. Clare and their territories, 1100–1700 AD*. Dublin. Geography Publications.

O'Brien, D. 2014 *The houses and landed families of Westmeath*. Athlone.

O'Brien, E. 2020 *Mapping death: burial in late Iron Age and early medieval Ireland*. Dublin. Four Courts Press.

O'Brien, E. 1999 Excavation of a multi-period burial site at Ballymacaward, Ballyshannon, Co. Donegal. *Donegal Annual* 51, 56–61.

O'Brien, E. and Bhreathnach, E. 2011 Irish boundary *ferta*, their physical manifestation and historical context. In F. Edmonds and P. Russell (eds), *Tome: studies in medieval Celtic history and law in honour of Thomas Charles-Edwards*, 53–64. Studies in Celtic history: 31. Woodbridge. Boydell Press.

O'Brien, M. A. (ed. and tr.) 1962 *Corpus genealogiarum Hiberniae*, i. Dublin Institute for Advanced Studies.

O'Brien, W. and O'Driscoll, J. 2017 *Hillforts, warfare, and society in Bronze Age Ireland*, Oxford. Archaeopress.

Ó Carragáin, T. 2021 *Churches in the Irish landscape AD 400–1100*. Cork University Press.

Ó Carragáin, T. 2010 *Churches in early medieval Ireland: architecture, ritual and memory*. London and New Haven. Yale University Press.

Ó Cathasaigh, T. 1977–8 The semantics of síd. *Éigse* 17, 137–55.

Ó Clabaigh, C. 2012 *The friars in Ireland 1224–1540*. Dublin. Four Courts Press.

Ó Concheanainn, T. 1973 The scribe of the "Leabhar breac." *Ériu* 24, 64–79.

O'Connell, J. and Costello, M. A. 1958 Obligationes pro annatis diocesis Ardfertensis. *Archivium Hibernicum* 21, 1–51.

O'Conor, C. 1818 *Bibliotheca MS. Stowensis. A descriptive catalogue of the manuscripts in the Stowe Library…*, i. Buckingham. J. Seeley.

O'Conor, K. D. 1998 *The archaeology of medieval rural settlement in Ireland*. Discovery Programme monograph: 3, Dublin. Royal Irish Academy.

O'Conor, K. D. 2000 The ethnicity of Irish moated sites. *Ruralia* 3, 92–102.

O'Connor, P. J. 2001 *Atlas of Irish place*-names. Newcastle West. Oireacht na Mumhan.

Ó Corráin, D. 1993 Corcu Loígde: land and families. In P. O'Flanagan and C. Buttimer (eds), *Cork: history and society*, 63–81. Dublin. Geography Publications.

Ó Corráin, D. 1978 Nationality and kingship in pre-Norman Ireland. In T. W. Moody, *Nationality and the pursuit of national independence: papers read before the conference held at Trinity College, Dublin, 26–31 May 1975*, 1–35. Belfast. Appletree Press.

Ó Corráin, D. 1973 Aspects of early history. In B. G. Scott (ed.), *Perspectives in Irish archaeology*, 64–75. Belfast. Association of Young Irish Archaeologists.

Ó Corráin, D. 1972 *Ireland before the Normans*. Dublin. Gill and Macmillan.

Ó Cuiv, B. 2001 *Catalogue of Irish language manuscripts in the Bodleian Library at Oxford and Oxford College Libraries*: part 1, descriptions. Dublin. Dublin Institute for Advanced Studies.

Ó Cuiv, B. 1984 The family of Ó Gnímh in Ireland and Scotland: a look at the sources. *Nomina* 8, 57–71.

Ó Dálaigh, B. 2008 The Uí Mhaoilchonaire of Thomond. *Studia Hibernica* 35, 35–68.

Ó Danachair, C. 1959 The quarter days in Irish tradition. *Arv: Journal of Scandinavian Folklore* 15, 47–55.

Ó Doibhlin, E. 1970 Ceart Uí Néill: a discussion and translation of the document. *Seanchas Ardmhacha: Journal of the Armagh Diocesan Historical Society* 5 (2), 324–58.

O'Donoghue, B. 1986 *Parish histories and place names of west Cork*. Cork. B. O'Donoghue.

O'Donovan, J. (ed. and tr.) 1860 *Annals of Ireland: three fragments, copied from ancient sources by Dubhaltach MacFirbisigh*. Dublin. Irish Archaeological and Celtic Society.

O'Donovan, J. (ed. and tr.) 1856 *Annála ríoghachta Éireann: annals of the kingdom of Ireland by the Four Masters, from the earliest period to the year 1616*, 7 vols. Dublin. Hodges and Smith.

O'Donovan, J. (ed. and tr.) 1852 *The tribes of Ireland: a satire by Aenghus O'Daly*. Dublin, John O'Daly.

O'Donovan, J. (ed.) 1849b *Miscellany of the Celtic Society*, i, Dublin. The Celtic Society.

O'Donovan, J. 1846a The covenant between Mageoghegan and the Fox, with brief historical notices of the two families. *The Miscellany of the Irish Archaeological Society*, i, 179–97. Dublin. Irish Archaeological Society.

O'Donovan, J. (ed.) 1846b The annals of Ireland, from the year 1443 to 1468, translated from the Irish by Dudley Firbisse or, as he is more usually called, Duald Mac Firbis, for Sir James Ware, in the year 1666. *The Miscellany of the Irish Archaeological Society*, i, 198–302. Dublin. Irish Archaeological Society.

O'Donovan, J. (ed. and tr.) 1844 *The genealogies, tribes and customs of Hy-Fiachrach, commonly called O'Dowda's country*. Dublin. Irish Archaeological Society.

O'Donovan, J. (ed. and tr.) 1843 *The tribes and customs of Hy-Many, commonly called O'Kelly's country*. Dublin. Irish Archaeological Society.

O'Donovan, J. (ed. and tr.) 1842 *The banquet of Dun na n-Gedh and the battle of Magh Rath*. Dublin. Irish Archaeological Society.

O'Flanagan, T. 1826 On the ogham inscription stated to have been discovered some years since on the mountain of Callan in the county of Clare. *Dublin Philosophical Journal and Scientific Review* 2 (4), 133–49.

O'Flanagan, T. 1787 An account of an antient inscription in ogam character on the sepulchral monument of an Irish chief, discovered by Theophilus O'Flanagan, student of T.C.D. *Transactions of the Royal Irish Academy* 1, 3–16.

Ó Gallachair, P. 1975 The parish of Carn. *Clogher Record* 8 (3), 301–80.

O'Grady, S. H. (ed. and tr.) 1929 *Caithréim Thoirdhealbhaigh: the triumphs of Turlough*, 2 vols. London. Irish Texts Society.

O'Grady, S. H. 1926 (reprint 1992) *Catalogue of Irish manuscripts in the British Library*, i. Dublin Institute for Advanced Studies.

O'Grady, S. H. (ed.) 1896 *Pacata Hibernia or, a history of the wars in Ireland during the reign of Queen Elizabeth, especially within the province of Munster under the government of Sir George Carew*, 2 vols. London. Downey.

O'Grady, S. H. (ed. and tr.) 1892–1935 *Silva Gadelica: a collection of tales in Irish*, 2 vols. London. Williams and Norgate.

Ó hInnse, S. (ed. and tr.) 1947 *Miscellaneous Irish annals, A.D. 1114–1437*. Dublin Institute for Advanced Studies.

Ohlmeyer, J. H. 1993 *Civil war and restoration in the three Stuart kingdoms: the career of Randal MacDonnell, marquis of Antrim, 1609–1683*. Cambridge University Press.

O'Kearney, N. 1853 The battle of Gabhra: Garristown in the county of Dublin fought AD 283. *Transactions of the Ossianic Society* 1. Dublin, John O'Daly.

O'Keeffe, T. 2006 The built environment of local community worship between the late eleventh and early thirteenth centuries. In E. FitzPatrick and R. Gillespie (eds), *The parish in medieval and early modern Ireland: community, territory and building*, 124–46. Dublin. Four Courts Press.

O'Keeffe, T. 2003 *Romanesque Ireland: architecture and ideology in the twelfth century*. Dublin. Four Courts Press.

O'Keeffe, T. 2000 *Medieval Ireland: an archaeology*. Stroud. Tempus.

O'Keeffe, T. 1992 Medieval frontiers and fortification: the Pale and its evolution. In F. H. A. Aalen and K. Whelan (eds), *Dublin city and county, from prehistory to present: studies in honour of J. H. Andrews*, 57–78. Dublin. Geography Publications.

O'Kelleher, A. and Schoepperle, G. (ed. and tr.) 1918 *Betha Colaim Chille: life of Columcille compiled by Manus O'Donnell in 1532*. Dublin Institute for Advanced Studies.

Ó Lochlainn, C. 1940 Roadways in ancient Ireland. In J. Ryan (ed.), *Féil-sgríbhinn Eóin MacNeill: essays and studies presented to Professor Eoin MacNeill*, 465–74. Dublin. Three Candles.

Ó Longáin, J. and Gilbert, J. J. (eds) 1872 and 1876 *Leabhar breac, the speckled book*, 2 vols. Dublin. Royal Irish Academy.

O'Mahony, C. 1913 *History of the O'Mahony septs of Kinelmeky and Ivagha*. Cork. Guy and Co.

O'Meadhra, U. 1987 *Early Christian, Viking and Romanesque art: motif-pieces from Ireland*. Theses and papers in North-European archaeology: 17. Stockholm. Almqvist and Wiksell International.

Ó Muraíle, N. 2016 The hereditary medical families of Gaelic Ireland. In L. P. Ó Murchú (ed.), *Rosa Anglica: reassessments*, 85–113. Irish Texts Society subsidiary series: 28. London. Irish Texts Society.

Ó Muraíle, N. 2005a Dinnshenchas. In S. Duffy (ed.), *Medieval Ireland: an encyclopedia*, 132–3. New York and London. Routledge.

Ó Muraíle, N. 2005 Book of Lecan. In S. Duffy (ed.), *Medieval Ireland: an encyclopedia*, 269–70. New York and London. Routledge.

Ó Muraíle, N. (ed.) 2003 *Leabhar mór na ngenealach: the Great book of Irish genealogies, compiled (1645–66) by Dubhaltach Mac Fhirbhisigh*, 5 vols. Dublin. De Búrca.

Ó Murchadha, D. 1982 Is the O'Neill–MacCarthy letter of 1317 a forgery? *Irish Historical Studies* 23 (89), 61–7.

Ó Murchú, L. P. (ed.) 2016 *Rosa Anglica: reassessments*. Irish Texts Society subsidiary series: 28. London. Irish Texts Society.

Ó Nualláin, S. 1989 *Survey of the megalithic tombs of Ireland, v, County Sligo*. Dublin. The Stationery Office.

O'Rahilly, C. (ed. and tr.) 1970 *Táin bo Cúalnge: from the Book of Leinster*. Dublin Institute for Advanced Studies.

O'Rahilly, T. F. 1922 Irish poets, historians, and judges in English documents, 1538–1615. *PRIA* 36C, 86–120.

Ó Riain, P. 2011 *A dictionary of Irish saints*. Dublin. Four Courts Press.

Ó Riain, P. (ed.) 1994 *Beatha Bharra: Saint Finbarr of Cork, the complete life*. Dublin. Irish Texts Society.

Ó Riain, P. 1972 Boundary association in early Irish society. *Studia Celtica* 7, 12–29.

Ó Riordáin, S. P. 1953 (3rd ed.) *Antiquities of the Irish countryside*. London. Methuen.

O'Rorke, T. 1890 *History of Sligo town and county*, 2 vols. Dublin. James Duffy and Co.

O'Rorke, T. 1878 *History, antiquities, and present state of the parishes of Ballysadare and Kilvarnet, in the County of Sligo*. Dublin. J. Duffy and Co.

Orme, N. 2015 Education in medieval Wales. *Welsh History Review/Cylchgrawn Hanes Cymru* 27 (4), 607–44.

Orme, N. 2006 *Medieval schools: from Roman Britain to Renaissance England*. New Haven and London. Yale University Press.

Ó Scea, C. 2012 Erenachs, erenachships and church landholding in Gaelic Fermanagh, 1270–1609. *PRIA 112C*, 271–300.

Ó Súilleabháin, M., Downey, L., and Downey, D. 2017 *Antiquities of rural Ireland*. Dublin. Wordwell.

O'Sullevane, T. 1722 Dissertation. In U. de Burgh, *Memoirs of the Right Honourable the Marquis of Clanricarde, Lord Deputy General of Ireland*, i–clxxxiv. London. James Woodman.

O'Sullivan, A. 2012 The archaeology of early medieval settlement and landscape in Westmeath. In P. Stevens and J. Channing (eds), *Settlement and community in the Fir Tulach kingdom: archaeological excavation on the M6 and N52 road schemes*, 13–24. Dublin. National Roads Authority.

O'Sullivan, A. 2004 The social and ideological role of crannogs in early medieval Ireland, 2 vols. PhD diss. National University of Ireland Maynooth.

O'Sullivan, A. 1998 *The archaeology of lake settlement in Ireland*. Discovery Programme monograph 4. Dublin. Royal Irish Academy.

O'Sullivan, A. 1971–2 Tadhg O'Daly and Sir George Carew. *Éigse* 14, 27–38.

O'Sullivan, A. and Nicholl, T. 2011 Early medieval settlement enclosures in Ireland: dwellings, daily life and social identity. *PRIA* 111C, 59–90.

O'Sullivan, C. M. 2003 *Hospitality in medieval Ireland 900–1500*. Dublin. Four Courts Press.

O'Sullivan, J. and Ó Carragáin, T. 2008 *Inishmurray: monks and pilgrims in an Atlantic landscape, i, archaeological survey and excavations 1997–2000*. Cork. Collins Press.

O'Sullivan, W. 1999 The book of Domhnall Ó Duibhdábhoireann, provenance and codicology. *Celtica* 23, 276–99.

Oxford University Press 2000 *Oxford English dictionary*. Oxford University Press.

Palmer, P. 2001 *Language and conquest in early modern Ireland: English Renaissance literature and Elizabethan imperial expansion*. Cambridge University Press.

Patterson, N. 1989 Brehon law in late medieval Ireland: 'antiquarian and obsolete' or 'traditional and functional'? *Cambridge Medieval Celtic Studies* 17, 43–64.

Patterson, N. 1991 Gaelic law and the Tudor conquest of Ireland: the social background of the sixteenth-century recensions to the pseudo-historical prologues to the *Senchas már*. *Irish Historical Studies* 27 (107), 193–215.

Pelham, H. 1787 *The county of Clare in the province of Munster and Kingdom of Ireland: surveyed and drawn by order of the Grand Jury of the county*. London. Henry Pelham.

Pender, S. 1951 The O Clery book of genealogies: 23 D 17 (RIA). *Analecta Hibernica* 18, 1–198.

Pennant, T. 1776 *A Tour in Scotland MDCCLXXII*, ii. 2nd edition. London. Benjamin White.

Plummer, C. (ed.) 1925 *Miscellanea hagiographica Hibernica: vitae adhuc ineditae sanctorum Mac Creiche, Naile, Cranat*. Subsidia Hagiographica 15. Brussels. Société des Bollandistes.

Plunkett-Dillon, E. 1985 The field boundaries of the Burren, Co. Clare. PhD diss. Trinity College Dublin.

Power, D. 1997 *Archaeological inventory of County Cork, volume 3: Mid Cork*. Dublin. Government of Ireland.

Pracht, M. and Sleeman, A. G. 2002 *Geology of west Cork: a geological description of west Cork and adjacent parts of Kerry to accompany the bedrock geology 1:100, 000 scale map series, sheet 24, west Cork*. Dublin. Geological Survey of Ireland.

Pryce, H. 2000 Lawbooks and literacy in medieval Wales. *Speculum* 75 (1), 29–67.

Qiu, F. 2021 Law, law-books and tradition in early medieval Ireland. In T. Gobbitt (ed.), *Law/ book/culture in the Middle Ages*, 126–46. Explorations in medieval culture: 14. Leiden and Boston. Brill.

Quiggin, E. C. (ed. and tr.) 1913 O'Conor's house at Cloonfree. In E. C Quiggin (ed.), *Essays and studies presented to William Ridgeway on his sixtieth birthday, 6 August 1913*, 333–52. Cambridge University Press.

Quin, E. G. (ed.) 1990 *Dictionary of the Irish language: compact edition*. Dublin. Royal Irish Academy.

Rackham, O. 1976 *Trees and woodland in the British landscape*. London. J. M. Dent.

Rae, E. C. 1971 Irish sepulchral monuments of the later Middle Ages: part II, the O'Tunney atelier. *JRSAI* 101 (1), 1–39.

Raftery, J. 1941 A bronze zoomorphic brooch and other objects from Toomullin, Co. Clare. *JRSAI* 11 (2), 56–60.

Ralph, K. 2014 Medieval antiquarianism: the Butlers and artistic patronage in fifteenth-century Ireland. *Eolas: The Journal of the American Society of Irish Medieval Studies* 7, 2–27.

Reeves-Smyth, T. 2011 Demesnes. In F. H. A. Aalen, K. Whelan, and M. Stout (eds), *Atlas of the Irish rural landscape*, 278–86. Cork University Press.

Rippon, S. 2018 *Kingdom, civitas and county: the evolution of territorial identity in the English landscape*. Oxford University Press.

Roberts, R. 2014 *GGAT 129: Cistercian granges in Glamorgan and Gwent*, 18. Swansea. Glamorgan-Gwent Archaeological Trust.

Rollason, D. 2016 *The power of place: rulers and their palaces, landscapes, cities, and holy places*. Princeton University Press.

Ronan, M. V. 1937 Some mediaeval documents. *JRSAI* 7 (2), 229–41.

Royal Commission on the Ancient and Historical Monuments of Scotland 1984 *Argyll: an inventory of the monuments volume 5: Islay, Jura, Colonsay and Oronsay*. Edinburgh.

Royal Commission on the Ancient and Historical Monuments of Scotland 1980 *Argyll: an inventory of the monuments volume 3: Mull, Tiree, Coll and northern Argyll*. Edinburgh.

Royal Irish Academy 1948 *Catalogue of Irish manuscripts in the Royal Irish Academy*. Dublin. Royal Irish Academy.

Rynne, C. 2019 Milling of cereals in Gaelic and Anglo-Norman Ireland *c.*1200–1500: technology and cultural choice. In Campbell, FitzPatrick, and Horning (eds), *Becoming and belonging in Ireland*, 45–68. Cork University Press.

Salonen, K. 2019 Reformation and the medieval roots of the Finnish education. In K. Sinnemäki, A. Portman, J. Tilli and R.H. Nelson (eds), *On the legacy of Lutheranism in Finland: societal perspectives*, 101–12. *Studia Fennica Historica* 25. Helsinki. Finnish Literature Society.

Seymour, J. D. 1918 *St Patrick's Purgatory: a medieval pilgrimage in Ireland*. Dundalk. Tempest.

Shanahan, B. 2008 Ardakillin royal centre: a report on recent fieldwork carried out by the Discovery Programme at the royal centre of Ardakillin Co. Roscommon. *Group for the Study of Irish Historic Settlement Newsletter* 13, 7–13.

Sheehan, A. 2019 Locating the Gaelic medical families in Elizabethan Ireland. In J. Cunningham (ed.), *Early modern Ireland and the world of medicine: practitioners, collectors and contexts*, 20–38. Manchester University Press.

Sheehan, J. 1982 The early historic church-sites of north Clare. *North Munster Antiquarian Journal* 24, 29–47.

Sherlock, R. 2011 The evolution of the Irish tower-house as a domestic space. *PRIA* 111C, 115–40.

Shirley, E. P., O'Brien, R., and Graves, J. 1867 Extracts from the journal of Thomas Dineley, Esquire, giving some account of his visit to Ireland in the reign of Charles II. *Journal of the Kilkenny and South-East of Ireland Archaeological Society* 6 (1), 73–91, 176–204.

Simington, R. C. (ed.) 1967 *Books of survey and distribution, iv, county of Clare.* Dublin. The Stationery Office for the Irish Manuscripts Commission.

Simington, R. C. (ed.) 1953 *The civil survey AD 1654–56, county of Wexford.* Dublin. The Stationery Office.

Simington, R. C. (ed.) 1938 *The civil survey AD 1654–56, county of Limerick*, iv. Dublin. The Stationery Office.

Simington, R. C. (ed.) 1934 *The civil survey AD 1654–56, county of Tipperary, ii: western and northern baronies.* Dublin. The Stationery Office.

Simington, R. C. (ed.) 1931–61 *The civil survey AD 1654–56, counties of Donegal, Londonderry and Tyrone*, iii. Dublin. The Stationery Office.

Simms, K. 2020 *Gaelic Ulster in the Middle Ages: history, culture and society.* Trinity Medieval Ireland Series: 4. Dublin. Four Courts Press.

Simms, K. 2009 *Medieval Gaelic sources.* Maynooth research guides for Irish local history: 14. Dublin. Four Courts Press.

Simms, K. 2007 The poetic brehon lawyers of early sixteenth-century Ireland. *Ériu* 57, 121–32.

Simms, K. 2005 Bardic schools, learned families. In S. Duffy (ed.), *Medieval Ireland: an encyclopedia.* New York and London. Routledge.

Simms, K. 2004 Medieval Fermanagh. In E. Murphy and W. J. Roulston (eds), *Fermanagh: history and society*, 77–103. Dublin. Geography Publications.

Simms, K. 2001 Native sources for Gaelic settlement: the house poems. In P. J. Duffy, D. Edwards, and E. FitzPatrick (eds), *Gaelic Ireland c.1250– c.1650: land, lordship and settlement*, 246–67. Dublin. Four Courts Press.

Simms, K. 1990 The brehons of later medieval Ireland. In D. Hogan and W. N. Osborough (eds), *Brehons, serjeants and attorneys: studies in the history of the Irish legal profession*, 51–76. Dublin. Irish Academic Press.

Simms, K. 1987 *From kings to warlords: the changing political structure of Gaelic Ireland in the later Middle Ages.* Woodbridge. Boydell Press.

Simms, K. 1983 Propaganda use of the *Táin* in the later Middle Ages. *Celtica* 15, 142–9.

Simms, K. 1978 Guesting and feasting in Gaelic Ireland. *JRSAI* 108, 67–100.

Simms, K. 1977 The medieval kingdom of Lough Erne. *Clogher Record* 9 (2), 126–41.

Simms, K. 1974 The archbishops of Armagh and the O'Neills 1347–1471. *Irish Historical Studies* 19 (73), 38–55.

Sims-Williams, P. 2006 *Ancient Celtic place-names in Europe and Asia Minor.* Publications of the Philological Society: 39. Oxford and Boston. Blackwell.

Sims-Williams P. 1990 Some Celtic Otherworld terms. In A. T. E. Matonis and D. F. Melia (eds), *Celtic language, Celtic literature*, 57–81. Van Nuys. Ford and Bailie.

Smith, B. 2013 *Crisis and survival in late medieval Ireland: the English of Louth and their neighbours, 1330–1450.* Oxford University Press.

Smith, B. (ed.) 1996 *The register of Milo Sweetman, archbishop of Armagh 1361–1380.* Dublin. Irish Manuscripts Commission.

Smyth, W. J. 2006 *Map-making, landscapes and memory: a geography of colonial and early modern Ireland, c.1530–1750.* Cork University Press.

Soja, E. W. 1996 *Thirdspace: journeys to Los Angeles and other real-and-imagined places.* Malden. Blackwell.

Speed, J. 1611/1612 *The theatre of the empire of Great Britaine: presenting an exact geography of the kingdoms of England, Scotland, Ireland.* London.

Stafford, T. 1633 (reprint 1810) *Pacata Hibernia or a history of the wars in Ireland during the reign of Queen Elizabeth: taken from the original chronicles,* 2 vols. Dublin. Hibernia Press.

Stokes, W. 1902 On the deaths of some Irish heroes. *Revue Celtique* 23, 303–48.

Stokes, W. (ed. and [partial] tr.) 1900 Acallamh na senórach. In W. H. Stokes and E. Windisch (eds), *Irische Texte mit Übersetzungen und Wörterbuch,* iv, 1, 1–224. Leipzig, Verlag von S. Hirzel.

Stokes, W. (ed.) 1895–7 (reprint 1993) *The Annals of Tigernach,* 2 vols. Felinfach. Llanerch.

Stout, G. 2015 The Cistercian grange: a medieval farming system. In M. Murphy and M. Stout (eds), *Agriculture and settlement in Ireland,* 26–68. Dublin. Four Courts Press.

Stout, G. and Stout, M. 2016 *The Bective Abbey project, Co. Meath: excavations 2009–12.* Dublin. Wordwell.

Strachan, J. and O'Keeffe, J. G. (eds) 1912 *The Táin bó Cúailnge, from the Yellow Book of Lecan: with variant readings from the Lebor na huidre.* Dublin. Royal Irish Academy.

Sweetman, D., Alcock, O., and Moran, B. 1995 *Archaeological inventory of County Laois,* Dublin. The Stationery Office.

Sweetman, H. S. and Handcock, G. F. (eds) 1886 *Calendar of documents relating to Ireland 1302–1307.* London. Longman.

Swift C. 1996 Pagan monuments and Christian legal centres in early Meath. *Ríocht na Midhe* 9 (2) 1–26.

Thomson, D. S. 1968 Gaelic learned orders and literati in medieval Scotland. *Scottish Studies* 12, 57–78.

Tierney, A. 2013 Tower houses and power: social and familial hierarchies in east County Clare *c.*1350–*c.*1600. *North Munster Antiquarian Journal* 53, 207–25.

Tierney, A. 2005 Pedigrees in stone? Castles, colonialism and Gaelic-Irish identity from the Middle Ages to the Celtic revival. PhD diss. University College Dublin.

Tierney, J. 2016 *Dromnea bardic school, Kilcrohane, Sheep's Head Peninsula, Co. Cork: conservation and tourism development.* Kinsale.

Toner, G. 2004 *Baile*: settlement and landholding in medieval Ireland. *Éigse* 34, 25–43.

Twemlow, J. A. (ed.) 1960 *Calendar of papal registers relating to Great Britain and Ireland, xiv, 1484–92.* London. HMSO.

Twemlow, J. A. (ed.) 1955 *Calendar of papal registers relating to Great Britain and Ireland, xiii, 1471–1484.* London. HMSO.

Twemlow, J. A. (ed.) 1933 *Calendar of papal registers relating to Great Britain and Ireland, xii, 1458–1471.* London. HMSO.

Twemlow, J. A. (ed.) 1921 *Calendar of papal registers relating to Great Britain and Ireland, xi, 1455–1464.* London. HMSO.

Twemlow, J. A. (ed.) 1912 *Calendar of papal registers relating to Great Britain and Ireland, ix, 1431–47.* London. HMSO.

Twemlow, J. A. (ed.) 1909 *Calendar of papal registers relating to Great Britain and Ireland, viii, 1427–47.* London. HMSO.

Twemlow, J. A. (ed.) 1906 *Calendar of papal registers relating to Great Britain and Ireland, vii, 1417–1431*. London. HMSO.

Twigge, R. W. 1909–11 Edward White's description of Thomond in 1574. *Journal of the North Munster Archaeological Society* 1, 75–85.

Ua Cróinín, R. and Breen, M. 1986 Daingean Uí Bhígin Castle, Quin, Co. Clare. *The Other Clare* 10, 52–3.

Vallancey, C. 1786 *Collectanea de rebus Hibernicis*, 4. Dublin. R. Marchbank.

Vallancey, C. 1785 Observations on the alphabet of the pagan Irish and the age in which Finn and Ossian lived. *Archaeologia* 7, 276–85.

Waddell, J. 2014 *Archaeology and Celtic myth*. Dublin. Four Courts Press.

Waddell, J. 1985 *The Bronze Age burials of Ireland*. Galway University Press.

Wakeman, W. F. 1896 Lough Erne and Ballyshannon excursion. *JRSAI* 26, 279–300.

Wakeman, W. 1885 Inis Muiredaich, now Inismurray, and its antiquities. *Journal of the Royal Historical and Archaeological Association of Ireland* 7 (64), 175–332.

Walsh, P. (ed. N. Ó Muraíle) 2003 *Irish leaders and learning through the ages*. Dublin. Four Courts Press.

Walsh, P. 1957 *The place-names of Westmeath*. Dublin Institute for Advanced Studies.

Walsh, P. 1947 *Irish men of learning: studies*. Dublin. Three Candles.

Walsh, P. 1939 *The Mageoghegans*. Mullingar. Westmeath Examiner.

Walsh, P. 1938 *The Ó Cléirigh family of Tír Conaill: an essay*. Dublin. Three Candles.

Walsh, P. 1935 Cnoc Aiste. *Catholic Bulletin* 25, 393–7.

Walsh, P. 1932 Note on two Mageoghegans. *Irish Book Lover* 20, 75–81.

Walsh, P. 1920 *Leabhar Chlainne Suibhne: an account of the MacSweeney families in Ireland, with pedigrees*. Dublin. Dollard.

Warner, R. 1994 On crannogs and kings, part 1. *Ulster Journal of Archaeology* 57, 61–9.

Westropp, T. J. 1916 Notes on certain primitive remains (forts and dolmens) in Inagh and Killeimer, Co. Clare: part xiv (continued). *JRSAI* 6 (2), 97–120.

Westropp, T. J. 1911 Prehistoric remains (forts and dolmens) in the Burren, Co. Clare. *JRSAI* 1 (4), 343–67.

Westropp, T. J. 1906 The ancient castles of the county of Limerick (north-eastern baronies). *PRIA* 26C, 55–108.

Westropp, T. J. 1906–7 Ancient remains near Lisdoonvarna. *Journal of the Limerick Field Club* 3, 52–159.

Westropp, T. J. 1904 Antiquities near Miltown Malbay, County Clare. *Journal of the Limerick Field Club* 2 (8), 250–54.

Westropp, T. J. 1900–2 The churches of County Clare and the origin of the ecclesiastical divisions in that county. *PRIA* 6C, 100–80.

Westropp, T. J. 1897 Prehistoric stone forts of northern Clare (continued). *JRSAI* 7 (2), 116–27.

Westropp, T. J. 1887 The rude stone monuments of Ireland. *JRSAI* 8, 118–59.

White, N. B. (ed.) 1943 *Extents of Irish monastic possessions, 1540–41*. Dublin. The Stationery Office.

White Marshall, J. and Walsh, C. 2005 *Illaunloughan Island: an early medieval monastery in County Kerry*. Bray. Wordwell.

Williams, B. (ed. and tr.) 2007 *The annals of Ireland by Friar John Clyn*. Dublin. Four Courts Press.

Williams, N. J. A. (ed. and tr.) 1980 *The poems of Giolla Brighde Mac Con Midhe*. Dublin. Irish Texts Society.

Williams, B. and Gormley, S. 2002 *Archaeological objects from County Fermanagh*. Northern Ireland archaeological monographs: 5. Belfast. Blackstaff Press.

Willemsen, A. 2008 *Back to the schoolyard: the daily practice of medieval and Renaissance education*. Studies in Urban History 1100–1800: 15. Turnhout. Brepols.

Williamson, T. 2013 *Environment, landscape and society in early medieval England: time and topography*. Woodbridge. Boydell.

Woulfe, P. 1923 (reprint 1993) *Sloinnte Gaedheal is Gall: Irish names and surnames*. Baltimore. Genealogical Publishing.

Ylimaunu, T., Lakomäki, S., Kallio-Seppä, T., Mullins, P. R., Nurmi, R., and Kuorilehto, M. 2014 Borderlands as spaces: creating third spaces and fractured landscapes in medieval Northern Finland. *Journal of Social Archaeology* 14 (2), 244–67.

INDEX OF SUBJECTS

Note: Figures and tables are indicated by an italic "*f*", "*t*", respectively, and notes are indicated by "n" following the page numbers.

For the benefit of digital users, indexed terms that span two pages (e.g., 52–53) may, on occasion, appear on only one of those pages.

INDEX OF PEOPLE

Note: Figures and tables are indicated by an italic "*f*", "*t*", respectively, and notes are indicated by "n" following the page numbers.

The Anglicized forms of Irish family names are cited from K. Muhr and L. Ó hAisibéil 2021 *The Oxford dictionary of family names in Ireland*. Oxford University Press.

For the benefit of digital users, indexed terms that span two pages (e.g., 52–53) may, on occasion, appear on only one of those pages.

INDEX OF PLACES

Note: Figures and tables are indicated by an italic "*f*", "*t*", respectively, and notes are indicated by "n" following the page numbers.

For the benefit of digital users, indexed terms that span two pages (e.g., 52–53) may, on occasion, appear on only one of those pages.